Spectrum Guide to
ETHIOPIA

MPC

Spectrum Guide to Ethiopia

First published 1995 by
Moorland Publishing Company Co. Ltd.,
Moor Farm Road,
Airfield Estate,
Ashbourne,
Derbyshire DE6 1HD,
England

© 1995 Camerapix

ISBN 0 86190 535 0

This book was designed and produced by
Camerapix Publishers International,
P.O. Box 45048,
Nairobi, Kenya

The **Spectrum Guides** series provides a comprehensive and detailed description of each country it covers, together with all the essential data that tourists, business visitors, or potential investors are likely to require.

Spectrum Guides in print:
African Wildlife Safaris
Jordan
Kenya
Maldives
Mauritius
Namibia
Pakistan
Seychelles
South Africa
Tanzania
Uganda
Zimbabwe

01335

3+4+86

Publisher and Chief Executive:
Mohamed Amin
Picture Editor: Duncan Willetts
Editorial Director: Barbara Lawrence
Balletto
Project Director: Debbie Gaiger
Editors: Helen van Houten, Sue Edwards,
Dennis Kiley and Bob Smith
Editorial Assistants: Solomon Tilahun,
Mary-Anne Muiruri and Sophie Brown
Picture Research: Abdul Rehman and
Storm Stanley

Printed and bound in Hong Kong.

4

Editorial Board

Spectrum Guide to Ethiopia is another important addition to the popular series of high-quality and colourfully illustrated *Spectrum Guides* to exciting countries, cultures, flora, and fauna.

A country with one of the richest histories on the African continent, Ethiopia has a wealth of castles, palaces, and ancient churches and monasteries — as well as unique wildlife, bird life, and breathtaking vistas. Yet until this book — the product of months of work by a dedicated team of writers and researchers in the *Spectrum Guides* editorial office and in the field in Ethiopia — there were few, if any, comprehensive guides to its many attractions.

The spectacular photographs are the incomparable work of **Mohamed Amin**, *Spectrum Guides* Publisher and Chief Executive, who has travelled throughout Ethiopia since 1960, and colleague **Duncan Willetts**, whose Ethiopian photographic exploits included scaling cliffs and climbing mountains to capture the rarely seen images in this book.

The logistics co-ordinator was the *Spectrum Guides* International Projects Director **Debbie Gaiger,** who in addition handled the design and layout for the guide.

American **Barbara Lawrence Balletto**, editorial director of *Spectrum Guide to Ethiopia*, worked long and hard to produce an in-depth text, and made significant contributions to the 'Places and Travel' section. A writer and editor living in Kenya, her fascination with Ethiopia stems from numerous trips made to the country since 1986.

The team of editors was led by **Helen van Houten**, who additionally provided general information and made authoritative editorial contributions. Helen, who lived and worked for many years in Ethiopia, was also responsible for maintaining *Spectrum Guides'* in-house style.

Dr Richard Pankhurst, for many years Director of the Institute of Ethiopian Studies of Addis Ababa University, has lived in Ethiopia most of his life and contributed all historical sections of the text. Details of Ethiopia's national parks and sanctuaries, as well as the country's wildlife, bird life, and fauna were written by **Dr Jesse** and **Sheila Hillman**, who both worked for many years as advisers to the Ethiopian Wildlife Conservation Organization. They are now working with the Ministry of Marine Resources in Eritrea.

Conrad Hirsh contributed to the Places and Travel section as well as several of the specialist sections, including those on rafting, camping, trekking, and sports. Conrad has worked in Ethiopia since 1964 and has led river trips and mountain treks since 1979.

Jill Last provided detailed information about the people of Ethiopia and also compiled the specialist sections on traditional dress and arts and crafts. Jill, an artist and writer, was a long-time resident of Ethiopia and now lives in England.

A team of experts spent long hours checking the manuscript and updating information. They included **Sue Edwards**, a botanist/field biologist and science editor, and her husband **Tewolde Berhan Gebre Eqziabher**, the first Ethiopian ecologist who was recently named director of Ethiopia's National Conservation Strategy. The couple are based at the National Herbarium of Addis Ababa University.

Other key members of the editorial team were London-based editor **Bob Smith**, Ethiopians **Solomon Tilahun** and **Worku Sharew**, and Canadian **Susan Stockwell**. **Dr Brigitta Benzing**, a professor in the Department of Sociology at Addis Ababa University and an expert on Ethiopian crosses; numismatist **Dennis Gill**; and angler extraordinaire **Colin Church** all contributed specialist sections.

Spectrum Guide to Ethiopia owes much to the hard work and cooperation of the Ethiopian Tourism Commission, particularly the commissioner, **Ato Rezene Araya**, as well as **Solomon Asfaow** of the Arts and Publications Department and **Fekerte Bekele** of the Tourism Promotion Department, who painstakingly checked the manuscript.

TABLE OF CONTENTS

IN BRIEF

LISTINGS

MAPS

Above: One of Ethiopia's many beautiful birds.

Half-title: Giant lobelia stands sentinel over the beautiful Bale countryside; Title: Flamingos on one of Ethiopia's enchanting Rift Valley Lakes; Pages 6-7: Lalibela priests celebrate the annual *Timkat* ceremony. Overleaf: The unforgettable magnificence of the Simien Mountains. Pages 10-11: Sunrise over the Ethiopian capital of Addis Ababa. Pages 14-15: Elegant lines of the National Palace in Addis Ababa.

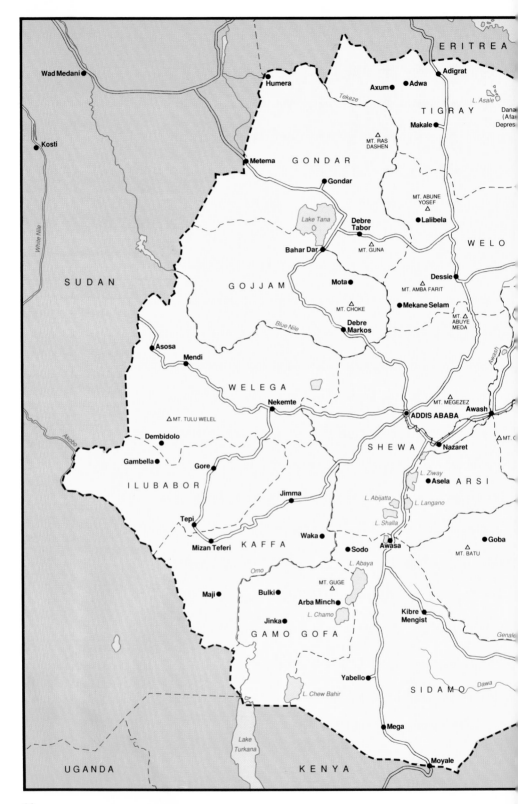

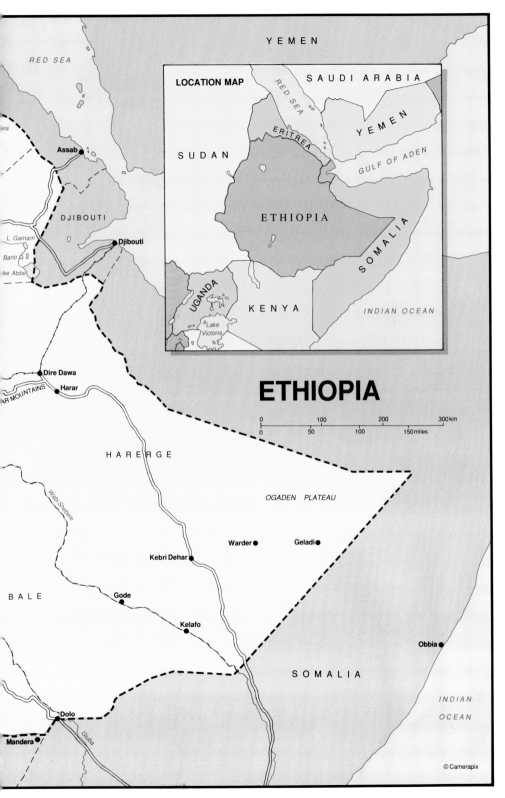

RED SEA

Assab

DJIBOUTI

L. Gamarri

Bario

ke Abbe

Djibouti

SAUDI ARABIA

RED SEA

ERITREA

YEMEN

GULF OF ADEN

SUDAN

ETHIOPIA

SOMALIA

UGANDA

Lake
Victoria

KENYA

INDIAN OCEAN

YEMEN

Dire Dawa

Harar

AR MOUNTAINS

HARERGE

Wabi Shebele

ETHIOPIA

0	100	200	300 km
0	50	100	150 miles

OGADEN   PLATEAU

Warder ●   Geladi ●

Kebri Dehar ●

BALE

Gode

Kelafo

Obbia ●

SOMALIA

INDIAN

OCEAN

Dolo

Mandera

Giuba

© Camerapix

17

The Ethiopian Experience

Ethiopia is old; old beyond all imaginings. As Abyssinia, its culture and traditions date back over 3,000 years. And far earlier than that lived 'Lucy' or *Dinkenesh*, meaning 'thou art wonderful', as she is known to the Ethiopians — the oldest hominid, whose remains were found in a corner of this country of mystery and contrasts.

For Ethiopia is a land of extremes, a land of remote and wild places. Some of the highest, most rugged and inaccessible places on the African continent are found here, such as the jaggedly carved Simien Mountains, offering landscapes reminiscent of America's Grand Canyon — and some of the lowest, such as the forbidding but fascinating Danakil Depression.

Ethiopia is a land of big skies and broad landscapes. In the highlands, the plateau reaches endlessly to a horizon that blends into blue sky speckled with white cumulus clouds, a sky that is an integral part of the landscape. The whole expansive view breathes of the freedom and joy that goes along with open spaces.

However, it is the people of Ethiopia who truly round out the character of this intriguing land. They are intrinsically religious and, as you travel the countryside, you may spy a distant octagonal church topped with an Ethiopian cross and perched on a hill, surrounded by trees. It is certain to be packed on Sundays and on many other occasions, for Ethiopians celebrate some 150 saints days a year. One vivid impression of the capital, Addis Ababa, is people, dressed in traditional white, homespun cotton, seemingly floating in the early morning mists as they make their way down the streets and into the churches.

Church ceremonies are a major feature of Ethiopian life. The events are impressive and unique. The Ethiopian Orthodox Church has its own head, follows its own customs, and is extremely proud of its fourth century origins, which means Ethiopia was Christian long before Europe.

The celebration of *Timkat*, or Epiphany, on 19 January of the Western Gregorian calendar is probably the biggest festival of the year. With great ceremony the sacred *tabot* — a tablet of wood or stone representative of those contained in the Ark of the Covenant — is taken from each church and held overhead by a priest throughout the night. Then with even more ceremony, it is returned to its consecrated resting place. During these colourful occasions priests are bedecked in dazzling brocade robes, carry ornate hand crosses, and move under decorated brocade umbrellas. They chant to the accompaniment of solemn drums and the rhythmic clink of sistrums.

In Addis Ababa, many churches are involved. The day before *Timkat* a whole field is taken over by the ceremony. Tourists are welcome and patient clergy actually help them choose choice observation points for photographing events as the procession leaves the field and slowly parades down the street. In Lalibela, chanting priests form a dramatic silhouette atop the rock from which the famous churches below were hewn. In Gondar, pre-sunrise rituals are performed around the pool surrounding Fasilidas's Bath.

Ethiopia's Islamic tradition is also strong and offers colourful contrast, particularly in the eastern and south-eastern parts of the country. In fact, there were Ethiopian Muslims during the lifetime of the Prophet Mohammed. This rich religious history is brought to life in the romantic walled city of Harar, considered by many Muslims to be a 'holy city' of Islam and an important centre of the Islamic faith on the African continent

---

Opposite (clockwise from top left): Debre Zeit boy radiates the exuberance of youth; Colourfully dressed woman of Bale; Venerable elder near Mount Zuqualla; Young Afar woman from the Asaita area.

Above: Overlooking the still waters of Fasilidas's Bath at Gondar where the faithful take part in *Timkat* (Epiphany), Ethiopia's most important religious festival.

since the tenth or eleventh century AD. Within the walls that have encircled the city for well over 300 years, modern citizens of Harar have their own language, customs, and crafts. The whole city, with its ancient winding streets and tall balconied houses, provides a fascinating insight into Ethiopia's centuries-old Islamic roots.

Even Ethiopian markets have a flavour of their own. Again, 'white' is the overall impression as people, especially the women, are often dressed in traditional clothing. They come to buy and to sell in a confusing but delightful cacophony of constant chatter and bargaining — and a baffling babble of languages. People crowd together, spreading their wares on the ground or in little booths and stalls. Coffee, grain, spices, butter, cloth, jewellery, chickens, cows, goats, camels: all can be found at one market or other.

Coffee originated in Ethiopia and is very important in the way of life. There is no better coffee in the world. The beverage is honoured with its own ceremony, often performed with gentle grace and charm in a home after a delicious Ethiopian meal.

Indeed, it is the charm of Ethiopia that is most infectious. Everyone who spends time here absorbing the 'feel' of the country and its people wants to return. No other place on earth is quite like it.

Welcome to Ethiopia.

Overleaf: The mosque at Nagash near Wukro. This mosque is considered to be Ethiopia's earliest and most holy Muslim Centre.

Travel Brief and Social Advisory

Some do's and don'ts to make your visit more enjoyable.

Ancient wilderness

One of the larger countries in sub-Saharan Africa, covering 1.112 million square kilometres and occupying a large part of the Horn of Africa, Ethiopia is rare in that it has enough unusual wildlife, breathtaking scenery and intriguing historical sites to please even the most seasoned traveller.

Since the government changeover in 1991, the country's eight beautiful national parks and three game sanctuaries — which shelter a wealth of wildlife, including the endemic Walia ibex, gelada baboon, Simien fox and mountain nyala — have become more accessible than ever. And, without masses of tourists having left their mark, they are virtually unspoilt in their splendour: a taste of true Africa.

Ethiopia's intriguing historical and religious sites — including the 'eighth wonder of the world', the ancient rock-hewn churches of Lalibela — are also easy to visit, not only due to the large network of roads (which vary in quality), but mostly because the country's excellent national carrier, Ethiopian Airlines, flies to all major towns on the fabled 'Historic Route' daily.

Accommodation — outside of capital of Addis Ababa — isn't always up to the standards of more well-trodden tourist routes in Africa, but to many, this only adds to the charm of the country: as will the hospitality and friendliness of the Ethiopian people (numbering an estimated fifty-five million), who are proud to show you their country.

Getting There

Ethiopian Airlines is rated one of the best in Africa because aircraft are well maintained, flights are generally punctual, and the airline serves many destinations. Its wide-ranging network operates in all directions out of Addis Ababa. Weekly schedules connect to Europe, other African countries, the Middle East, and the Far East.

The airline flies direct from Frankfurt three times a week; from Jeddah four times a week; from London, Rome, Bombay, and Dubai three times a week; from Athens and Karachi twice a week; and from Aden, Bangkok, Beijing, Muscat, Riyadh, and Sanaa once a week.

Ethiopian Airlines also flies direct from Nairobi and Abidjan six times a week; from Lagos four times a week; from Cairo and Kampala three times a week; from Accra, Bamako, Bujumbura, Dakar, Dar es Salaam, Djibouti, Harare, Johannesburg, Kinshasa, Khartoum, Kigali, and Lilongwe twice a week; and from Brazzaville, Luanda, and Niamey once a week.

Other airlines flying in and out of Addis Ababa include Lufthansa three times a week; Aeroflot and Kenya Airways twice a week; Puntavia (Djiboutian), Saudia, Sudan Airways, and Yemenia once a week.

Landlocked Ethiopia can also be reached on all sides by road, and from Djibouti by rail. There are border posts at Humera, Metema, Moyale, and Dewele.

Visas are required for all visitors to Ethiopia, with the exception of nationals of Djibouti, Eritrea, Kenya, and Sudan. Visitors must obtain visas in advance of their visit from Ethiopian diplomatic missions abroad, where they are readily available.

On arrival, you will be asked to declare your video camera, laptop computer, and any other pieces of sophisticated electronic equipment. These are usually entered in your passport to ensure that you take them with you when you go and do not sell them while in the country. You do not need to declare still cameras, small shortwave radios, calculators, and similar small electronic devices. Professional journalists and photographers must report to the Ministry of Information to get a permit. This can be done through a sponsoring organization. The ministry will

provide you with a 'minder' or staff member to accompany you, if you wish, but it is optional and no longer a government requirement.

There is a small duty-free shop as you enter Addis Ababa airport where incoming passengers can buy consumer goods such as alcoholic beverages, cigarettes, and perfume. You may be subjected to a comprehensive customs check as you enter the country.

When you leave the country, your bags are inspected by X-ray. A word here about what you can take with you: in Ethiopia, it is possible and legal to buy ivory, game skins, and similar items. However, they are not exportable and are subject to being seized at the airport — not just in Addis Ababa but also on arrival at a European or North American airport. It is also highly likely that 'legal' ivory or game skins were improperly obtained. It is best not to buy them in the first place.

Authorities are likely to question possession of antiquities such as church icons and relics, silver and gold jewellery. This includes even the smallest silver cross. If you buy such items, it's wise to take them to the National Museum, where they will be inspected, wrapped, sealed, and stamped to indicate official approval.

Getting Around

Due to difficulty in translating the languages and dialects of Ethiopia into Roman lettering, spellings of names, places and objects will vary. You are sure to come across Mekelle, Makele, Makalle, for example, and everything in between. Be indulgent toward all variations and use your imagination.

By road

A fairly good tourist map, detailing the major roads, points of interest, and distances between major centres is produced by the Ethiopian Tourism Commission (ETC). Roads range from good to pothole-poor — and you should check locally before embarking on trips. Many vehicles are old, barely hanging together, sometimes without lights and often with feeble brakes. Import restrictions on cars have eased in the last few years, so standards are improving. There are some advantages to these ancient vehicles — most drivers move slowly. Even so, the accident rate is relatively high. There are few enforced laws and no maximum speed limits on the open road.

The main streets of Addis Ababa are wide, usually with ample parking. Back streets are narrow and swarm with pedestrians, who assume right of way and can pose a real hazard to unwary motorists. Since the 1991 government changeover many tour agencies and car rental services have opened up. Rental cars are available, both with drivers and without. A driving licence from your own country is valid if your stay is three months or less. If you want to travel out of Addis Ababa, a four-wheel-drive vehicle is a must. You may not need to drive with all wheels engaged, but you will want the sturdy suspension and the high clearance to travel over roads in poor condition.

Taxis are readily available in cities and major towns. These blue-and-white vehicles can be minivans, pickups with a closed canopy and benches at the back, or saloon cars. The larger ones have standard routes on which they pick up and let off passengers, operating like mini buses. Prices are low, they never overload, do not speed, and are good value for money. Once you get the hang of where to catch them and what the routes are, they are a good way of getting around. You can also negotiate with a driver for specific trips, in or out of town, for a short run or by the day. There are no meters; there are standardized prices for the fixed routes, and all prices for special hire should be negotiated in advance to avoid later misunderstandings.

Opposite: Afar man leads his son on a camel, the most reliable means of transport in the desert-like conditions of the dry and dusty Afar (Danakil) region of the country.

Previous pages: Ornate royal crowns on display at the National Palace in Addis Ababa.

Above: Ethiopia's lakes in the Rift Valley offer some spectacular scenery and bird life for travellers throughout the country.

In Addis Ababa, there are also Mercedes Benz taxis operated by the National Tour Operation (NTO), which can be booked at any of the major hotels. Trips are paid for in advance according to destination; again, the taxis are not metered. These taxis are about ten times more expensive, on average, than the little blue taxis hailed on the street.

Slow, very overcrowded city buses ply the streets of Addis Ababa, but — although the most inexpensive form of public transport — they are not advisable for tourists. There are also 'country buses', which are a safe, inexpensive, and convenient way to visit outlying areas. The main bus station in the city is in the Mercato area just north of the new market building. Travellers wanting to take a bus to other towns in Ethiopia should go to the bus station before their trip to learn the day and time of departure, as well as the best time to buy a ticket. It helps if you take along an Ethiopian friend to 'show you the ropes' and guide you through the crowds. When travelling by bus, it is best to arrive half an hour to an hour before departure time. Fares vary according to destination.

All these forms of public transport are quite safe, although as in any crowded situation, you should be alert for pickpockets. You are not expected to tip a taxi driver on a standard route, just as you would not tip a bus driver. But you can tip the driver of a negotiated trip if the service has been good. A tip of ten per cent is considered generous. Most drivers will speak basic English, enough to understand roughly where you want to go, to negotiate and agree a price, but not usually enough to go into detail about your directions or to engage in amiable conversation.

By air

Ethiopian Airlines has an excellent network of scheduled flights serving the entire country. Chartered flights are available through Ethiopian Airlines and

Overleaf: Centuries-old illuminated manuscripts can be found in churches throughout Ethiopia.

Above: Ethiopian Airlines' extensive domestic network takes passengers to all corners of the country and provides a bird's-eye view of the breathtaking countryside.

Relief and Rehabilitation Committee (RRC) Air, with planes that can carry from two to nineteen passengers. It may also be possible to rent a non-governmental organization (NGO) plane — check directly with the NGO for details. It is anticipated that private charter companies will start up in the future, but as of early 1994, only the above actually had a licence for general aviation.

Helicopters, available for hire only from the air force, can carry up to twenty-three passengers.

By train

The Franco-Ethiopian Railway runs from Addis Ababa to Djibouti by way of Nazaret, Awash Station, and Dire Dawa. Although the original steam engines have long since been replaced by diesel, the trains running from Addis to Dire Dawa still have a wild, pioneering atmosphere. The hot, slow journey as the railway descends from the western hills, crosses the floor of the Rift Valley, and ascends again into the eastern escarpment is a unique travel experience, imbued with historical associations. It also affords an opportunity to meet and mingle with ordinary Ethiopians in a way that most other forms of transport deny.

There are both night and day trains between the capital and Dire Dawa, and the trip takes approximately ten hours. There are first, second, and third classes. The Ethiopian Tourism Commission (ETC) or a travel agent can assist you with schedules and reservations, or you can go directly to the station, which is located at the lower end of Churchill Road.

By foot

Several of Ethiopia's more remote areas are excellent for walking safaris, which are offered by a few good tour operators in the country. Walking tours are naturally best planned for the dry seasons, as the mud during the heavy rains can be overwhelming. (See 'Trekking in Ethiopia', Part Four.)

Above: For centuries, the horse has been an important means of transport for Ethiopians, particularly in the highlands of Bale.

When just trekking around Addis, or exploring the historical sites and ruins throughout the country, a normal, sturdy pair of walking shoes or trainers should suffice. Comfortable long trousers are often best for walking. Shorts, in addition to offending cultural mores if worn by women, offer little protection against sandflies, stinging nettles, and other pests.

By horse

Ethiopians have been riding for centuries; farmers, both men and women, ride to and from markets and meetings. It is possible to hire horses in Addis Ababa for guided rides on the outskirts of the city. In the country, if you are adept at sign language and bargaining, you can negotiate with local people for a ride. Treks into such places as the Simien Mountains in northern Ethiopia are generally by mule and horse. Local tour operators can arrange trips such as these, as can agencies which operate out of Addis Ababa.

The people

Ethiopians are proud of their culture and civilization, which pre-date those of Europe. They do not expect or warrant condescending behaviour. For the most part, they are friendly toward visitors. In the cities, you will often find young men — or rather, they will find you — who will offer to guide you about. Unemployment is high, and they will probably be out of work and hoping for a tip and a chance to learn something about your part of the world.

Begging is endemic and an accepted way of life for thousands of poor Ethiopians. You will find beggars at most of the main intersections in Addis Ababa. Even in the rural areas, you will come across the old or the blind standing by the side of the road asking for help in the name of God. While this tends to be disconcerting for Westerners, it is much more accepted in both the Muslim and the Ethiopian Orthodox way of life.

In Addis Ababa, Hope Enterprises on

Above: Ethiopians are friendly and photogenic, such as these charming Afar children near Asaita.

Churchill Avenue runs a low-cost meal service for the needy, and from them you can buy very economical tickets to give to beggars, entitling the bearer to a meal. Many Westerners find that handing out a coupon to help the child on the street is much more acceptable than handing out money.

Traffic police abound, and there is one, often two or three, at every major intersection in Addis Ababa. Bribery and corruption exist, but on a much lower scale than in many other countries in Africa and elsewhere in the world.

You may take photographs of most things and scenes you see. Some people will resent having their picture taken, and it is a courtesy to ask, even if by sign language (such as bowing before taking a photo).

Government installations such as the palaces used by the president and military establishments are off limits, and there are signs saying so — although they are often only in Amharic. Zealous policemen or soldiers may not know the rules and may forbid you to photograph scenes that are offically okay. It is best not to argue with them. Some religious leaders, too, are offended by photos taken on holy ground without prior permission.

People in service industries that you will meet — such as those working in hotels, tour agencies, car hires, and restaurants — are friendly and helpful. Tips of up to ten per cent are an accepted practice and appreciated. At night it is diplomatic to tip the guard who watches your car outside a restaurant. One birr is standard. During the day, street parking boys will want a tip for watching your car while you shop. You are not required to tip them for their unsolicited services.

Safety

Street crime exists mostly in the form of pickpocketing or the snatching of handbags, gold neck chains and earrings. Addis Ababa is overcrowded with migrants coming in to the city from rural areas, especially after the 1991 change of government, which resulted in many displaced and

34

homeless people. You can walk the streets safely in the daytime, although you should be aware of incidents in which people unnecessarily jostle you — a technique pickpockets often use. At night it is wiser to take a taxi to your destination.

In a country where there is extensive poverty it is unwise to display the trappings of a more affluent society. Don't wear gold jewellery on the streets and leave valuables with hotel security. Vehicles are normally safe if locked and valuables are not on display. Be careful, take precautions, but don't let unnecessary fear spoil your enjoyment of a country that has so much to offer.

Weather

Much of Ethiopia is rugged highlands: Addis Ababa stands at an altitude of about

Opposite: Ethiopia's many colourful markets each have a flavour of their own.
Above: Enthusiastic Amhara dancer.
Right: Beautiful girl from the Debre Zeit region.

2,400 metres (7,900 feet). So temperatures are temperate, moderate, even cool — certainly not tropical. Highest daytime temperatures rarely exceed 21 or 22°C (70 or 71°F) and for much of the year seldom rise above 16 or 18°C (61 or 64°F). But temperatures can change by 15°C or more in as many minutes, and a difference of up to 30°C between day and night is possible. Temperatures at night frequently drop to a chilly 10°C (50°F) or less. Most places are also swept by winds that can be strong and dust-laden in dry areas.

Rainfall varies depending on area. In the highlands that occupy about half of the country and include Addis Ababa, the year's rainfall amounts to about 1,000 to 1,500 mm (39 to 59 inches). Despite Ethiopia's famous slogan, 'Thirteen Months of Sunshine' — referring to the thirteen months of the Julian calendar — there are two rainy seasons a year in this area: the irregular short rains, from late January to early March, and the long rains that stretch from June until mid-September.

The rain can be brief and torrential or it can be steady but light, lasting nearly the entire day. The long rains can seem endless, and many expatriate Europeans head for the sun of European summer at that time of year. Some Ethiopians head for the Rift Valley, which may still be wet, but warmer. But when the rains cease the air becomes very dry almost overnight. As Ethiopia lies north of the equator the longest days are in June and July, when there are about forty-five minutes more daylight than in December and January. But long days do not mean 'summer' in Ethiopia. Ethiopians refer to the long rains as 'winter'. Ethiopian New Year, or 'spring', festivities come in September when the long rains stop. May is the warmest month and is usually a time of bright sunny days and strong winds. Daytime temperatures in January run just as high, but the nights are much chillier.

June, July, and August are grey, wet, and cool.

Clothing

Many tourists are surprised at how cool it can be in the Ethiopian highlands. Be prepared for sudden cold weather and mountain storms. During the day in the dry season, lightweight clothing is suitable, but it is advisable to carry a lightweight sweater. A sweater or jacket is useful for evenings. For chilly days in the 'winter' rainy season from June to September, light woollen clothing is comfortable.

As you descend from the highlands the temperature increases dramatically, and you realize that you are truly in the tropics, after all. In the lowlands, light clothing is a must. Canvas or leather walking shoes are practical. A hat is a wise precaution for days in the sun. Even if the weather is not hot, the sun can be intense, and sunglasses are desirable. Sunscreen lotion is also a wise precaution. T-shirts, even tank tops, and knee-length walking shorts are acceptable anywhere outside of the streets of Addis Ababa — although long trousers offer more protection. Swimming costumes are fine at any of the lakesides, but in the cities and towns, short shorts and halter tops are considered improper. It is best to cover up out of courtesy.

What to take

Consumer goods are becoming available but still quite limited by Western standards. Bring with you all the photographic equipment you want. In Addis Ababa, you can buy colour print film in a limited line of brands and film speeds; in smaller towns even that can be problematic. Do not count on buying colour slide film anywhere in the country, even in Addis Ababa.

If you wear glasses, it is wise to carry a spare pair. Bring your own contact lens solutions and sunglasses. Chemists are

Opposite: Giant stelae at Axum are towering reminders of an ancient and powerful kingdom.

Overleaf: Sunset over the Rift Valley's serene Lake Langano.

plentiful, but medications are extremely limited — especially outside Addis Ababa. Keep a supply of items you need, such as anti-diarrhoetics and anti-malarials, sun creams, and mosquito repellents.

Health

A yellow fever vacinnation is necessary only if you are coming from an endemic yellow fever area. Vaccination against cholera is also required for any person who has visited or transited a cholera-infected area within six days prior to arrival in Ethiopia. No other jabs are required. Do, however, check with your doctor, who may recommend gamma globulin shots or refresher vaccines of typhoid and polio before you go. Hepatitis, typhoid, meningitis, and other communicable diseases do exist in the country, but most tourists will run little risk of coming in contact with them.

However, malaria does pose a risk for the traveller. Generally occurring at low altitudes, malaria is now present at altitudes as high at 2,000 metres (6,560 feet). Consult with your doctor about prophylaxis. The general advice is to begin with a chloroquine-based medicine two weeks before you enter a malarial area and continue the weekly medication for a month after you leave. In addition, medication for chloroquine-resistant malaria is a wise precaution, especially when you are actually in the malarial area.

Tsetse flies are also found in Ethiopia, particularly in the Omo Valley and Gambella area, and can be annoying. To date, however, cases of disease attributable to tsetse have been extremely rare.

As in other parts of Africa, some waters do contain bilharzia parasites, so take care where you swim. Lakes Langano and Shalla are bilharzia free.

Poisonous snakes include cobras and puff adders but are very rare. Normal precautions should be observed in such environments as the hot lowland areas.

Raw meat is an Ethiopian delicacy, served either minced with spiced butter or in big hunks, off which bite-size chunks can be carved and dipped in red pepper. Eating raw beef does entail a certain risk of tapeworm, so you may choose to forgo this treat.

Fruits and vegetables can be eaten, with care. Anything that is peeled is all right. Exercise caution with salads and other raw vegetables, considering where they are grown, where they are prepared, and where you are eating them. You shouldn't have to think twice about the food eaten in the better restaurants and hotels in Addis Ababa.

Tap water in the capital is safe to drink, but the more cautious traveller will find local mineral water readily available, along with soft drinks and fruit juices.

Medical facilities are limited, of generally poor standard, and inevitably overstretched. Tourists are advised to use private hospitals and clinics, but even there facilities can be often inadequate. Contact your embassy for referral to a recommended doctor. If you fall seriously ill or someone in your party is badly injured, you may want to consider evacuation to nearby Nairobi or to Europe. Air rescue services are available, and you may wish to make arrangements with one before your trip.

Some tourists take a while to acclimatize to Ethiopia's altitude when they arrive. It is better to take such pursuits as jogging and tennis in small and easy doses until the body becomes used to operating on less oxygen. Those with heart problems should check with their physician before making the journey.

Photography

The scenery in Ethiopia is spectacular and dramatic. The people and cultures are distinctive and photogenic. The country offers the photographer a wide, exciting range of subjects. Outside of the usual prohibition against taking pictures of military sites and presidential palaces, few rules exist beyond those of courtesy. People usually do not mind a photo taken, although in rural areas frequented by tourists, it is customary to pay for these 'photo opportunities'. It is best to negotiate such arrangements before you click the shutter. If you inadvertently break the rules and offend someone, simply but

Above: The beautiful mountain nyala is one of Ethiopia's many endemic wildlife species.

earnestly apologize. Nothing else.

It is wise to bring a good supply of film, although you can buy colour print film in Addis Ababa and in most towns. Colour slide film is hard to come by, although you can sometimes find Ektachrome in Addis Ababa. One-hour colour print processing is available at a number of locations in Addis Ababa and some larger towns. Slides can be processed only in Addis Ababa and the quality is variable.

Communications

The postal system is erratic and slow. Letters within the country, or even within the capital itself, may take days. It can often take two or more weeks for letters to or from North America and most European countries — but can take as little as six days. There is no house delivery service; all mail goes to box numbers.

Parcels to Addis Ababa addresses must be picked up from the main post office on Churchill Road and undergo customs inspection. The process of retrieving a parcel can be exasperating as neither staff nor system is reliable.

Most towns have post offices and all the major hotels sell stamps and will post letters for their clients. Major hotels also offer fax and long-distance telephone services for their guests, although the latter can be expensive.

The government has offices that offer telephone and fax facilities without the surcharges hotels add. One of these is located in the Telecommunication head office on Churchill Road in downtown Addis Ababa, another at the Economic Commission for Africa (ECA) head-quarters. Overseas telephone rates in general in Ethiopia are reasonable, particularly when compared with other African countries. In 1994, it cost approximately ten birr (two US dollars) a minute to call the United States. Local rates are also good. There are red or yellow public phone boxes for local calls, although they are often hard to find. Happily, many kiosks and small shops have phones available to the public at fifty Ethiopian cents (or centimes) a call. Don't rely on the telephone directory, which is often out of date. It is best to call '97' and

Above: Gondar and its castles are one of the many attractions on Ethiopia's famous 'Historic Route'.

ask the operator for a number you do not know. An even better plan is to find the numbers you need by asking others and then keeping your own mini-directory.

When to go

Tourists generally avoid the heavy, long rains, June to mid-September, although this is when the Blue Nile Falls (or *Tis Isat*) are at their most spectacular. But they are still impressive at any other time of year, which is good touring time for all other attractions in the country. Especially interesting are times of religious festivities. After the rains stop, beginning around Ethiopian New Year on 11 September, yellow '*meskal*' daisies carpet almost any open space, the world turns bright and sunny after the long rains, and 'spring' festivals abound. An important celebration is *Meskal*, or the Finding of the True Cross, which is celebrated on 26 September.

January is the most important month from the point of view of religious festivities. First is Christmas, celebrated on 7 January. Then comes the most colourful ceremony of the year, *Timkat* or Epiphany,

on 19 January. Timing your visit for this celebration is worthwhile, and an experience to be remembered.

For birds and other wildlife, it is more a matter of 'where' rather than 'when'. (See 'Bird Life: An Ornithological Paradise' and 'Wildlife: Uniquely Ethiopian', Part Four.)

Where to stay

Tourism in Ethiopia is just beginning to burgeon after decades of problems. You no longer need permits to travel, and restrictions on where tourists can stay have been lifted. Nevertheless, tourists are generally encouraged to keep to hotels that are government owned and run.

In Addis Ababa, the Sheraton and the Hilton are the top standard. Just below it are a number of two- or three-star government and private hotels, all adequate but not luxurious. Outside the capital standards vary.

In many of the major towns south of

Overleaf: The stunning Blue Nile Gorge, Ethiopia's version of the Grand Canyon.

Above: Hora Lake, one of Ethiopia's beautiful Rift Valley lakes.

Addis Ababa, a private chain runs hotels that were once quite good but that now seem to be declining in standards of facilities and services.

In the main tourist towns, new government hotels are struggling under adverse conditions. The buildings, rooms, and furnishings are relatively new, good, beautifully sited, artistically decorated and turned out. But there may be no hot water, or the water may be on for only an hour or two each day (if you are lucky). Electricity cannot be relied on. Conditions are somewhere between spartan and four-star luxury, and the visitor must be prepared to do without what many would consider basic amenities.

At the other extreme when travelling in rural Ethiopia, you can find generally clean and well-kept little local hotels, with no bath or toilet but a chamberpot under the bed and a pitcher of water beside it. These will cost from three to ten birr — approximately one or two dollars for a night's stay.

Camping is another option; some hotels allow camping on their grounds for a modest fee. National parks have campsites, and camping is generally safe. In a beautiful site, with a campfire, it is a

Above: *Meskal* daisies, unofficially Ethiopia's 'national flower', appear in vast fields each September after the rains.

marvellous way to spend the night. (See 'Camping in Ethiopia', Part Four, and Listings.)

National flag

Three wide horizontal stripes of green, yellow, and red. Green symbolizes the fertility of the country, yellow the religious freedom found there, and red the lives sacrificed in the protection of national integrity.

National flower

Although a declared 'national flower' does not exist, the *meskal* daisy is considered to be one by most Ethiopians. A yellow daisy-like flower, it blooms in profusion in September and is a sure sign of Ethiopian 'spring'. Whole fields turn gold and people pick large bouquets. The flower is a happy symbol of a happy time of year.

Above: Flying high, the Ethiopian flag remains a proud symbol of a proud nation.

Overleaf: Fascinating murals adorn the walls and ceilings of Ethiopia's churches and monasteries, such as these at the Church of Saint Mary of Zion in Axum and (on page 47) Petros and Paulos (top) and Chelekot Selassie in the Tigray region.

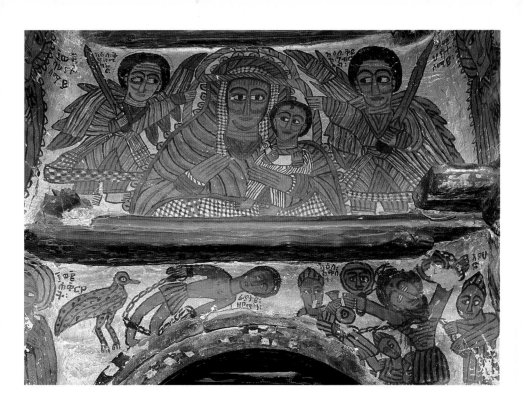

PART ONE: GEOGRAPHY, AND PEOPLE

Above: Lake Hayq, near Dessie, capital of the Wollo region.

Opposite: Villagers steer their cattle along the road encircling Lake Bishoftu.

Land of Kings and Legends

From television images of the country's serious droughts in the early 1980s, many foreigners think of Ethiopia as a dry and barren place, devoid of beauty and greenery. This could hardly be further from the truth.

It is undoubtedly a land of contrasts — there are hot, dry, and barren places, as well as rolling hills, fertile highlands, savannah, and mountainous regions that often see frost and sometimes even snow. There are deserts, canyons, gorges, and a wealth of beautiful waterfalls, lakes, and rivers. It all combines to make Ethiopia a country of breathtaking scenery that changes constantly from one region to another, a microcosm of an entire continent in a nation the size of France and Spain combined.

This contrasting countryside is largely due to the tumultuous volcanic activity that shaped the area some forty million years ago, when the Ethiopian landmass — part of ancient Gondwanaland — was shaken by a massive upheaval of the earth, which opened deep faults in the crystalline bedrock and its overlying sedimentary layers. Through these faults oozed a bubbling brew of white-hot basaltic lava that slowly spread and cooled over a large expanse of the land. At the epicentre of this activity, in the north of the country, the lava reached a thickness of about 3,000 metres (9,840 feet). Subsequent erosion produced many of the dramatic physical features that still entrance travellers today. Nowhere are these precipices, gorges, and jagged pinnacles of rock more prominent — or more stunningly beautiful — than in the northern Simien region, at the edge of one of Africa's major mountain massifs.

That same outpouring of lava also contributed to another major feature of the Ethiopian landscape — a giant tear across the surface of the earth that can even be seen from space: the Great Rift Valley. Extending nearly 6,000 kilometres (3,720 miles) from Syria, through the Red Sea, Ethiopia, and down to Mozambique, this spectacular and abrupt cutting away of the land never fails to strike a traveller with surprise and awe. The Rift Valley is also home to seven large and beautiful lakes in the heart of the country, caused by the millennia of heavy rainfall that deluged Africa at the same time northern Europe was going through its 'Ice Age'.

This varied geological past has made Ethiopia a vast and bountifully endowed natural haven for many kinds of wildlife. More than 800 species of birds are found in Ethiopia, of which twenty-eight are found exclusively in the country. There are also 103 separate mammal species, seven of which are endemic.

Colourful cultures

The people of Ethiopia are as diverse and contrasting as the country itself. Although nearly half of the population adheres to the deeply rooted Christian faith of the Ethiopian Orthodox Church, a large percentage is Muslim, and there are some who practise ancient forms of Judaism. People's livelihoods vary from hunter-gatherers, nomads, and agriculturalists to factory workers and professors. They speak an astonishing eighty-three languages with 200 dialects, of which Amharic is the *lingua franca* of the country. Each group has some slight cultural difference even from its nearest neighbours.

Aware and proud of these differences, Ethiopia's people have worked together and prevailed over periodic famine, war and disease for centuries, and continue to do so as the country goes through even more changes in the closing stage of the twentieth century.

Perhaps the people of Ethiopia owe this seemingly inborn sense of survival to their earliest ancestors, who walked this land millions of years before them. For the north-east was the birthplace of 'Lucy', or *Dinkenesh*, meaning 'thou art wonderful'. The world's earliest known hominid, *Dinkenesh* lived more than three million years ago and her bones now lie at rest in the Ethiopian National Museum. This

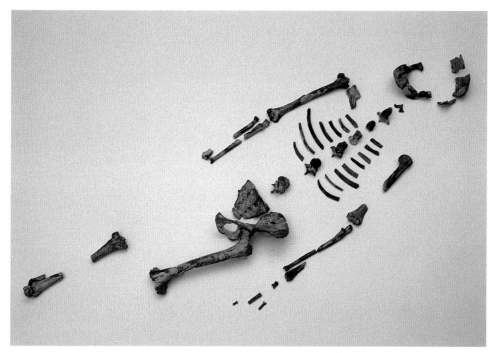

Above: The famous skeleton known popularly as 'Lucy' is just one of the discoveries made by researchers in the Afar region of Ethiopia.

important archaeological find, combined with many other prehistoric discoveries — including Stone Age tools up to 1.7 million years old and vibrant cave paintings — bears testimony to the region's remarkable antiquity.

Recorded history for the Ethiopian region also began at an early period. Three thousand years before the birth of Christ the ancient Egyptians sent expeditions down the Red Sea in quest of gold, ivory, incense, and slaves. They called this territory the 'Land of Punt'. Although this term was used for both sides of the Red Sea, most of the goods seem to have come from the Ethiopian area.

The country's rich tapestry of history is woven with fascinating facts and legends: the often-told tale of King Solomon and the Queen of Sheba; the journey of the Ark of the Covenant, which is now said to rest in Axum; the growth of the ancient Axumite kingdom and the birth of Christianity; the later rise of Islam; the story of King Lalibela, who is reputed to have founded eleven rock-hewn churches, still in existence to this day and considered among the Wonders of the World; the fabled castles of Gondar.

This ancient history melds with the modern to make Ethiopian the unique and unforgettable country it is today.

Overleaf: Ancient stone carvings, like these near Dillo (top) and at Tiya, testify to Ethiopia's remarkable antiquities.

Page 53: Solemn and serene, a priest emerges from one of Lalibela's spectacular rock-hewn churches.

52

The Land: Canyons and Valleys, Mountains and Lakes

Ethiopia, which covers an area as large as France and Spain combined, is situated in the north-eastern Horn of Africa, equidistant between the equator and the Tropic of Capricorn. It is a country of immense geographical contrasts. High mountains, which in the Simien and Bale ranges tower well over 4,000 metres (13,120 feet) above sea level, give way to flat lowlands, sinking below sea level in the Danakil Depression. Temperatures range from the icy cold of the high mountains, with frost and in places even snow; through the temperate highlands, the site of most of the country's historic settlements and agriculture; to the torrid lowlands, one of the hottest places in the world.

Differences in rainfall are equally dramatic, the torrential downpours of the highlands contrasting with minimal precipitation in the parched, almost waterless lowlands. Vegetation is just as varied, with tropical rainforest, mostly in the west; deserts and semi-desert scrublands, mainly in the east and south; and fertile but largely deforested regions in many areas of medium to high elevation.

Though there are many variations in altitude, temperature, rainfall, and vegetation, three main regions may be discerned:

• The High Plateau, which comprises most of the north, central, and part of the south of the country;
• The Great Rift Valley, which bisects the plateau in a north-easterly to south-westerly direction and is the site of numerous lakes, many of them of tourist interest; and
• The Lowlands, mainly situated to the north, east, and south-east of the country, as well as on the Sudanese and Kenyan frontiers.

The geology of Ethiopia is based on an old crystalline block, which once also covered an immense area from the Brazil plateau to Decaan in India. Formed early in the earth's history, this block later cracked and its three component parts — America, Africa, and Asia — drifted apart. The country's bedrock belongs to the earth's first continent — a continent known by geologists as Gondwanaland, of which Africa forms the largest intact remnant.

The hard crystalline rocks of the African block consist of granites and gneiss and contain many valuable mineral deposits. Parts of the Ethiopian area were once under the sea, so that there are also many sedimentary rocks, mainly limestones and sandstones, in addition to later volcanic materials found in layers above the old crystalline rocks.

The Simiens

In some places the more recent rocks have been eroded by rain, with the result that the original rocks have been exposed. Nowhere is this more prominent — or stunning — than in Ethiopia's northern Simien region. This was the epicentre of much volcanic activity about forty million years ago, and the resulting outpouring of a boiling mass of white-hot basaltic lava reached a thickness of some 3,000 metres (9,840 feet) in this area before it stopped. Subsequent erosion of this volcanic sheet has produced the dramatic highs and lows of the Simiens: deep precipices and gorges, tall pinnacles of jagged rock, and weird, broken landscapes.

The plateau basalts produced by this vast spreading thickness of lava have been responsible for the building up of great tablelands in the centre and north-west of the country and in the eastern highlands between Harar and Sidamo, which are now considerably eroded.

Opposite: Fisherman tries his luck as the sun sets over Lake Awasa.
Overleaf: Captivating sunset over the Adwa mountains in northern Ethiopia.

Above and opposite: The Danakil Depression in north-east Ethiopia drops to more than 100 metres (328 feet) below sea level. It is an area of continuing seismic activity, with earth tremors frequently felt amidst the hot yellow sulphur fields and several still-active volcanoes.

Overleaf: Lake Shalla is the deepest Ethiopian Rift Valley lake at 260 metres.

One of the most important features of this region of Africa resulted from faulting and cracking on its eastern side. This has caused the Great Rift Valley, which extends from the Middle East to Mozambique, passing in a north-south direction right through Ethiopia. This shearing of the earth's surface occurred at the same time that the Arabian Peninsula, geologically a part of Africa, was sundered from the rest of the continent.

Volcanic activity, which has continued until today, finds expression in volcanoes in Ethiopia's Danakil Depression, as well as in the hot springs in many parts of the country. Earth tremors are often felt, and exposed cones of old volcanic plugs are seen throughout the plateau.

After the Rift opened, much of this area was flooded by the inrushing waters of the Red Sea, a flood that was subsequently stemmed by fresh volcanic activity that raised barriers of basaltic lava. Behind these barriers the trapped inland sea that

had formed began to evaporate under the fierce heat of the tropical sun — a process that is almost complete today. Only a few scattered, highly saline lakes — Gamarri, Affambo, Bario, and Abbe — remain. Elsewhere, there are huge beds of natural salt — which, at points, are calculated to be several thousands of metres thick.

Land of lakes

Another striking feature of Ethiopia is the large number of lakes, almost all of them in the Rift. They include Ziway, Langano, Abijatta, Shalla, Awasa, Abaya, and Chamo, which are situated in their own local systems of 'inland drainage'. These lakes were formed by the millennia of heavy rainfall that hit Africa during the same period the 'Ice Age' was affecting northern Europe. Although they are slowly evaporating — 'small puddles compared to their former size', says one geographer — their shrinkage has exposed huge areas of alluvial soil that allow prosperous and

Above: The beautiful and serene crater lake on Mount Wonchi gives little hint of its volcanic past.
Opposite: The country's many agriculturalists have come to terms with their various environments.
Overleaf: A camel train carrying salt bars from the Danakil Depression — a sight unchanged for centuries.

productive agriculture and created a rich environment for wildlife and birds.

Ethiopia's largest lake, Tana, on the other hand, is the result of the damming of natural drainage from the area on the western plateau now covered by the lake. The Blue Nile Falls (*Tis Isat*) are at the point where the overflow from the lake drops over the edge of a lava flow.

The country also possesses a number of beautiful lakes formed out of extinct volcanoes, such as that on Mount Zuqualla, or interconnected volcanoes like that on Mount Wonchi. Both are within easy access of Addis Ababa.

The Great Rift Valley

The traveller to Ethiopia will be amazed by the sudden and surprising changes in both landscape and climate. If you are journeying eastwards through the Ethiopian highlands, you will quite suddenly find yourself confronted by the Great Rift Valley: an abrupt falling away of the land through diminished landscapes to the valley floor, often more than 2,000 metres (6,560 feet) below. Following precipitous winding roads downwards, you will become acutely aware of the tremendous impact that altitude has on the climate and culture of this country. Starting from the plateau, in the space of less than an hour's drive the clear invigorating air of the mountains gives way to the desiccating heat of the savannah and then desert; tidy, regular agricultural fields give way to the harsher realities of pastoral nomadism; Afro-alpine flora and fauna are replaced by scattered herds of plains game, stunted shrubs, and gracefully spreading acacia trees.

The world's principal types of economic activity are all represented. Thus, there are agriculturalists, many of them practising plough agriculture, in the plateau's extensive highlands; pastoralists in the more widespread lowlands, some of them situated in the Great Rift Valley; and a remnant of hunters and gatherers in the vicinity of many rivers, lakes, and forests

The People: An Ancient Heritage

in the south-west and west — as well as factory workers in and around some of the principal towns, most notably Addis Ababa, Dire Dawa, and Bahar Dar.

Ethiopia, like most countries in Africa, is a multi-ethnic state. Although the original physical differences between the major ethnic groups have been blurred by centuries, if not millennia, of inter-marriage, there remain many who are distinct and unique.

Ethnic differences may also be observed from the great variety of languages spoken in the country, of which there are an astonishing eighty-three, with 200 dialects. These can be broken into four main groups: Semitic, Cushitic, Omotic, and Nilo-Saharan.

The Semitic languages of Ethiopia are related to both Hebrew and Arabic. The Ethiopian languages of this family are derived from Ge'ez, the language of the ancient Axumite kingdom, which was also the language of of the country's literature prior to the mid-nineteenth century, as well as parts of most present-day church services.

Ethiopia's Semitic languages are today spoken mainly in the north and centre of the country. The most important of them in the north is Tigrinya, which is used throughout the Tigray region.

The principal Semitic language of the north-western and centre of the country is Amharic, which is the language of Gondar and Gojjam, as well as much of Wollo and Shewa. Moreover, Amharic is also the official language of the modern state, the language of administration, and the language of much modern Ethiopian literature.

Two other Semitic languages are spoken to the south and east of Addis Ababa: Guraginya, used by the Gurage in a cluster of areas to the south of the capital, and Adarinya, a tongue current only within the old walled city of Harar and used by the Adare, also known as Harari, people.

The Cushitic languages, which are less closely related than the Semitic, are found mainly in the south of the country. The most important tongue in this group is Afan Oromo. It is used in a wide stretch of country, including Welega and parts of Ilubabor in the west, Wollo in the north, Shewa and Arsi in the centre, Bale and Sidamo in the south, and Harerge in the east.

Other Cushitic languages in the area comprise Somalinya, which is spoken by the Somali in the Ogaden region to the east as well as in the neighbouring Somali Republic and part of Djibouti, and the Sidaminya language, used in part of the Sidama region. Cushitic languages, however, are also used in the north of the country, namely Afarinya, spoken by the Afar of eastern Wollo and the northern half of the Djibouti Republic; Saho, in parts of Tigray; and Agawinya, in small pockets in different parts of western Ethiopia.

The Omotic group of languages, which comprise considerably fewer speakers than either the Semitic or the Cushitic, are spoken in the south-west of the country, mainly in the Gamo Gofa region. They have been given the name in recent years because they are spoken in the general area of the Omo River.

The Nilo-Saharan languages, largely peripheral to Ethiopian civilization, are spoken in a wide arc of the country towards the Sudan frontier. They include, from north to south, Gumuz in Gondar and Gojjam, Berta in Welega, and Anuak in Ilubabor.

Unique and diverse

The various ethnic groups also have some special characteristics. The Tigrinya- and Amharic-speaking people, who live mainly in the north and centre of the country, are generally agriculturalists, tilling the soil with ox-drawn ploughs and growing *teff* (a

Opposite (clockwise from top left): Addis Ababa schoolgirl; Amhara man in the Simien Mountains; Harari youngster at the walled city's busy market; Young Oromo shepherd.

Overleaf: The Wollo regional capital of Dessie is spread over a small valley at the foot of Mount Tossa.

local millet), wheat, barley, maize, and sorghum.

Both groups share the legacy of ancient Axum and are mainly Ethiopian Orthodox, or Monophysite Christians. They share a long tradition of independence, have long, valued military prowess and skill in imperial government, and tend to look down on manual labour other than agriculture. Essentially religious, their churches and monasteries are highly respected and constitute storehouses of religious and historical treasures.

The Tigrinya speakers, by their language and history, identify themselves intimately with the old Axumite tradition. Living in the north of the country, they have in many cases close family and other ties with the people of Eritrea but tend to be more isolated than the Amharic speakers from the non-Semitic peoples of the south.

The Amharic speakers have long felt themselves closely associated with the post-Axumite imperial government. For many centuries they played a uniquely important role in the empire's administration. This brought them into close contact with the people of the south, with whom there was much intermarriage.

The Gurage, the most southerly of the Semitic speakers, are said to be the descendants of military colonists from the north. They are therefore reputed to have a mixed Semitic-Cushitic heritage.

Enset

Most of the population practises farming and herding, but there are also many craftsmen. Most Gurage, like their Cushitic neighbours, subsist largely on *enset* or 'false banana', but also cultivate other crops. Although physically somewhat resembling the banana tree, *enset* produces a thicker stem and more erect leaves. Its root, stem, and leaf stalks provide a carbohydrate, which, after laborious and lengthy processing, can be cooked as porridge or made into sticky, unleavened bread.

Some Gurage adhere to the Ethiopian Orthodox faith; others are Muslims. Still others subscribe to the local, traditional animist faith, which also to some extent influences members of the other religions.

The Gurage society is one in which there is little specialization by class or sex in the performance of everyday tasks, and no stigma is attached to any kind of work. The hunters and artisans, however, belong to a separate group, generally known as Watta or by the Gurage themselves as Fuga. These people have adopted the Gurage language and customs, not only as go-betweens to the spiritual world, but as technicians and house builders.

Many Gurage travel to Addis Ababa and other regional centres seasonally as labourers and engage in occupations traditionally looked down upon by the peoples of the north. They have long been recognized for their manual skills, their gift for organization, and their adaptability.

By far the most numerous of the Cushitic speakers are the Oromo. Once a nomadic people of pastoralists, the majority of them are now largely sedentary, engaged in agriculture, though the inhabitants of the more arid areas are cattle breeders.

Most Oromo living in the centre of the country have adopted Christianity, while those towards the periphery to the south, west, and east have embraced Islam. Their own traditional animist religion is also prevalent in many areas.

Though several 'Oromo monarchies' emerged in the nineteenth century, Oromo society was, and still is, traditionally based on the *gada* or age-group system, in which a man's life is divided into age-sets of eight years, sons normally following two sets behind their fathers. The group is governed by men in the fourth set, between the ages of twenty-four and thirty-two, who hand over power after eight years. Many commentators argue that Oromo tradition therefore tends to be more egalitarian and 'democratic' than that of their northern neighbours.

The Oromo vary quite a lot in physical type and skin colour and generally they are tall, handsome people.

The Somali are very largely pastoral nomads or semi-nomads living in hot and arid bush country. Almost entirely Muslims, their social organization is based on clans, and it is to these relatively small

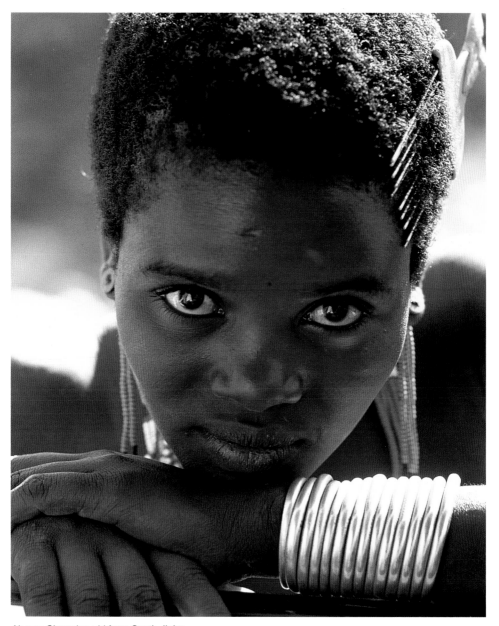

Above: Charming girl from South Jinka.

units of social organization that they are primarily loyal. Clan quarrels over access to water and grazing rights are frequent.

The Sidama speakers, who may be subdivided into several smaller groups, the Alaba, Derasa, Hadiya, Kambata, and the Sidama proper, are mainly agriculturalists. Some use ox-drawn ploughs, others iron-pointed digging sticks. Like the farmers of

Overleaf: Afar man near Asaita in Ethiopia's north-eastern region.

Above: Farmer near Addis Alem threshing *teff*, a local grain from which *injera*, the national bread, is made.

the north, they cultivate grain, coffee, and tobacco. They also grow *enset*, which gives a higher, more dependable yield than any other crop and is drought resistant. The people who cultivate it have developed a character for meticulousness, hard work, and cooperation. The men build the huts and grow vegetables with the wives' help, while the women also do the trading, cleaning, and cooking.

Pythons

The Sidama are a fascinating people, with most of the population adhering to the local animist faith, but others professing Christianity or Islam. Some of the old pagan practices linger on, such as a belief in the 'Eye' and 'sacred trees'. Pythons are believed to be a reincarnation and are kept in houses and fed on meat. Not surprisingly, their reputation as house guards is quite considerable.

The Sidama have traditional local rulers, whose position is strengthened by age-group organization similar to that of the Oromo *gada* system.

The Afar, most of whom occupy one of the most inhospitable desert or semi-desert areas in the world, have long been regarded as a fierce and warlike people. They are certainly proud and individualistic, and somehow manage to eke a living out of the challenging wilderness in which many of them live.

The majority of the Afar are semi-nomadic pastoralists, but a minority have settled, notably those in the Aussa oasis. Almost all are Muslims, and are organized into confederacies, tribes, and clans. The nomads live in small, isolated groups with the camel as their beast of burden, and keep sheep, goats, and cattle.

A forty-centimetre (28-inch) curved knife is the characteristic weapon or tool carried by the Afar men, but they are often well provided with rifles. They are known for the back-breaking work they do hacking out salt blocks from the desert floor for doing trade in the highlands.

The Omotic speakers were traditionally organized into small kingdoms, notably those of Kaffa and Janjero. Mainly agriculturalists, they in general still adhere to a traditional animist faith.

Above: Colourfully dressed women take a break from their bartering at the busy Bati market.
Opposite: Each of Ethiopia's many ethnic groups has its own unique style of homes. One of the most striking and unusual is that of the Dorze people in the vicinity of Arba Minch.

The Nilo-Saharans are to an extent agriculturalists, though others are hunters, or herdsmen. Generally organized into family-based units, most are animists.

Traditional dress

The people of Ethiopia wear many different types of clothing. The traditional dress of the Christian highland peasantry was made almost entirely out of white cotton cloth.

Since the time of Tewodros men have worn long, in many cases jodhpur-like, trousers, a tightly fitting shirt, and a *shamma* or loose wrap, often with coloured stripes at either end; women wear a full skirt surmounted by a *shamma*.

Noblemen and women used to wear silk cloaks, which in the case of people of the highest status were decorated with silver or even gold, while warriors would sport short lion-skin capes. In cold mountainous areas men and women might wear a *burnous* or black woollen cape, and shepherd boys a woven woollen cap.

The Muslims of Harar by contrast wore much more colourful dress. The men were often dressed in shortish trousers covered with a coloured wrap; the women clad in fine dresses usually of red, purple, or black.

The lowland Somali and Afar wore long, often brightly coloured cotton wraps, while some of the cattle-herders in the lake district had clothing made of skins.

Traditional dress may still be seen throughout much of the countryside, especially in areas far removed from towns, but it is steadily being supplanted by modern or 'European' clothing, which is now predominant in most urban areas. National dress is, however, widely worn for festivals, particularly by women.

PART TWO: PLACES AND TRAVEL

Above: Unique circular mural of apostles in Tigray's Abune Yemata church.

Opposite: Although sometimes difficult to reach, like the incredible Abune Yemata church, Tigray's fascinating rock-hewn churches are definitely worth the effort, for they are often adorned with centuries-old murals and are repositories for many priceless religious artefacts.

The Historic Route: Mountains and Gorges, Mystery and Grandeur

The well-trodden path through Ethiopia's famous and fascinating historic places — which shelter priceless relics from a powerful and religious ancient civilization — also leads one through some of the most breathtaking scenery. The country changes from farm and moorland plateau north of Addis Ababa to culminate, much farther north, in the highest point in Ethiopia, Ras Dashen, which, at 4,543 metres (14,901 feet) is the fourth highest mountain in Africa.

That peak stands in the spectacular Simien Mountains, a region that includes many lofty summits, which rise out of a craggy countryside that resulted from the erosion of basalt lavas calculated to be nearly 3,000 metres (10,000 feet) thick. Along this 'Historic Route' you will also find the *lowest* point in Ethiopia: the Danakil Depression, dipping to more than 100 metres (328 feet) below sea level.

The whole area was — and still is — shaken by massive seismic movements and volcanic activity. The result: chasms and canyons that stretch as far as the eye can see.

The first such evidence of this geological wonder is the Blue Nile Gorge, which rivals America's Grand Canyon. Equally impressive are the beautiful Blue Nile Falls (*Tis Isat*), which lie near the place that adventurers and explorers of decades gone by sought with such fervour: the source of the Blue Nile, Ethiopia's Lake Tana.

One of the conveniences of Ethiopia's 'official' Historic Route is that you can fly much of it, hopping from the major points of Bahar Dar to Gondar to Axum to Lalibela, travelling by scheduled Ethiopian Airlines flights, with stopovers of a day or two in each place. But if you have time and don't mind some stretches of rough road, tracing the route on the ground reveals scenery you would miss by air and gives you a much better feeling for this ruggedly beautiful area.

Whether by land or by air, a good first stop on this route is the town of Bahar Dar, situated on the edge of the fabled Lake Tana.

Getting there

Bahar Dar, 578 kilometres (358 miles) from Addis Ababa, 183 kilometres (113 miles) from Gondar and 554 kilometres (343 miles) from Axum, is served by road and air, with daily Ethiopian Airlines flights.

When to go

Visit at any time of the year, but the falls are at their best towards the end of Ethiopia's great rainy season (which runs from June to September) and in the month or so following, from late September to mid-October. For most of the year the falls are white, but during the rainy season they carry down so much mud that they become a rich reddish-brown.

Where to stay

In Bahar Dar, Bahar Dar Ghion Hotel, Tana Hotel. In Dejen, Tizale Dejen Hotel. In Debre Markos, Tourist Hotel. See Listings. Throughout Ethiopia, along most roads, are a variety of local 'no-star' hotels, with rooms consisting chiefly of bed and bedding, a basin, and a chamber pot. These vary considerably in degrees of cleanliness but are quite cheap and may be just the ticket for the more adventurous visitor. Keep in mind that the drive from Addis Ababa to Bahar Dar can take a full day. A picnic lunch and drinking water are advisable.

Sightseeing

Heading **north-west** out of Addis Ababa on the good asphalt **Dejazmach Belay Zeleke Street** (also called the Gojjam Road), the road winds its way up the side of **Mount Entoto**, which offers a superb view of the sprawling capital below. A **lookout point** at the top marks the spot where the road begins its descent to the plateau, which extends all the way to the

Above: The church of Debre Libanos stands on an ancient monastic site overlooking part of the Blue Nile.

Blue Nile Gorge. To the left, one can glimpse the peak of **Mount Sululta**; to the right, the **Gorfu Mountains**.

Eighty-two kilometres (51 miles) from the city is the beginning of the **Blue Nile Gorge**, where a sheer cliff drops more than 1,000 metres (3,000 feet) into a spectacular gorge formed by the **Zega Wodel River**, one of the Blue Nile tributaries. At this point, a **marker** indicates the turn **right** to the **Debre Libanos monastery**, which is approximately five kilometres (three miles) from the turnoff along an asphalt road.

The monastery, perched beneath a cliff on the edge of a gorge, overlooks a tributary of the Blue Nile. The original monastic buildings of Debre Libanos have long since disappeared, having been destroyed, it is said, during the wars of Ahmed Gragn. They were replaced by a succession of structures, the latest of which is a spectacular **modern church** erected after World War II on Emperor Haile Selassie's orders. Note the **mosaic figures** on the façade. The church also has beautiful **stained glass windows** and contains some interesting **mural paintings**

by the well-known Ethiopian artist Afewerk Tekle. To the **left** of the church is the **nuns' residence**, built in the 1920s, and to the **right** behind the church is a **cave** containing holy water. Nearby are the huge **monks' kitchens**, dating from the early 20th century. Although women are not allowed to enter the monastery, they can visit other areas of the compound.

The monastic establishment was founded in the thirteenth century by Tekle Haymanot, one of the Ethiopian Orthodox church's most renowned saints. Legend claims that Tekle Haymanot played an important role in the transactions that led to the end of the Zagwe dynasty, when the last of its rulers, Na'akuto La'ab, it is said, abdicated in 1270 in favour of Emperor Yekuno Amlak, the first monarch of the Solomonic line. As a reward for Tekle Haymanot's services Debre Libanos was made the senior monastery of Shewa region.

In the early seventeenth century the monks of Debre Libanos, because of the Oromo advance, migrated to Azzezo, north of Lake Tana. They were neverthe-

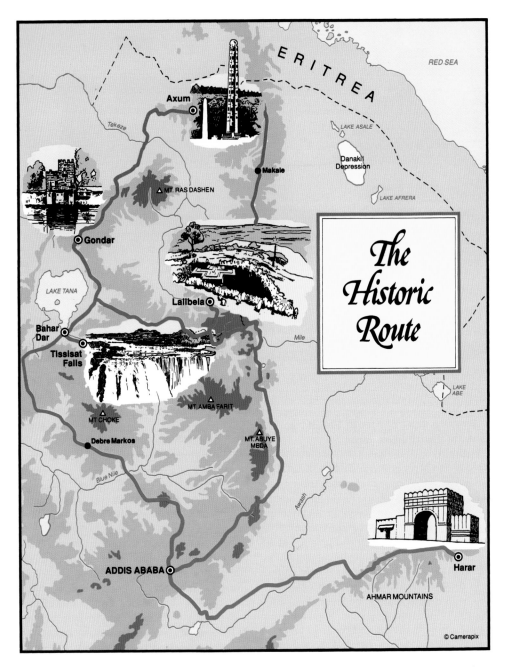

The Historic Route

less still regarded as one of the pillars of the Orthodox Christian faith and played an important role in the politics of the then capital Gondar, where they were much involved in a theological controversy on the nature of the Trinity.

The monastery was, however, later reconstituted in Shewa and was particularly important during the reign of Emperor Menelik, who travelled there during his last fatal illness to sample its reputedly curative holy waters. Many noblemen and others also used to go there on pilgrimage, and many important figures were buried within the monastic precincts. Later, in 1937, during the Italian occupation of Ethiopia, the Debre Libanos monks incurred the wrath of the Fascist viceroy Graziani, who ordered their execution 'all without distinction'; 297 monks were accordingly shot, after which he proudly reported, 'of Debre Libanos there remains no more trace'. The **bones** of the martyred monks can be seen at the monastery to this day.

Visit the **House of the Cross**, which is decorated internally with interesting **paintings** and said to house a **cross** that belonged to Tekle Haymanot.

A hundred metres beyond the monastery's turnoff, a five-minute walk to the **right**, towards the gorge, is a **bridge** from which there is a fine view of the countryside far below. This bridge is popularly described as sixteenth-century Portuguese but was in fact built in the late nineteenth century by an Ethiopian nobleman, Emperor Menelik's uncle, Ras Darge. It is possible to climb down below the bridge to where some **waterfalls** start their 600-metre (2,000-foot) plunge to the valley below, or walk along the cliff edge to look back at the falls and the bridge.

Continuing on from the Debre Libanos turnoff, the main road travels **west** along the edge of the plateau, passing through the small towns of Fiche, Gebre Guracha, and Goha Tsiyon. It is here that the long, winding descent — more than 1,000 metres (3,000 feet) into the main body of the gorge — begins, taking about forty-five minutes to reach the reddish-brown waters of the **Blue Nile**. For centuries the river formed a natural barrier between Shewa and Gojjam regions, but now a modern **bridge** spans the turbulent water. There are guards on the bridge and photography — as well as stopping — are prohibited, although there is no warning sign saying so. A good point to take a break is in the shade of some trees just past the bridge, where a waterfall tumbles over a cleft in the cliff.

Remember that temperatures are hot at the bottom of the gorge — rising to 39°C (102°F) at midday — and visitors must bring along their own 'shade' and refreshments.

Past the bridge, the road continues into Gojjam region and up the escarpment to the plateau on the other side, where lies the town of **Dejen**. If Bahar Dar — some 350 kilometres (217 miles) away at this stage — seems to be a bit of a push, you may want to rest the night at the small Tizale Dejen **hotel** here, which is perched on the edge of the gorge.

You may choose at this point to take the **turnoff** to the **north-east** just past Dejen. Leading through the village of **Mota**, it is much less scenic than the western route to Bahar Dar but is of better condition and is slightly shorter. The historic **monastery** of **Murtule Maryam** can be reached along this alternative route by turning **right** at the village of **Gunde Woin** and driving for another thirty kilometres (19 miles).

If you opt to stay on the **western Gojjam road**, you will also find some small private hotels in **Debre Markos**, seventy-one kilometres (44 miles) further along, which is also served by Ethiopian Airlines three times a week. Originally known as Mankorar (meaning 'Cold Place' in Ge'ez), Debre Markos is the capital of Gojjam, the region almost surrounded by the Blue Nile.

The town was the seat of government in the 1880s of a local Gojjam chief, Ras Adal, who later assumed the name and title of *Negus* (King) Tekle Haymanot. He subsequently founded the fine church of Markos (Saint Mark), after which the settlement soon came to be known as Debre Markos, literally meaning 'Place of Mark'.

King Tekle Haymanot's **church of Markos** is the town's principal church, and is well worth a visit. It contains pale but beautiful **paintings**, some of them depicting the king himself, as well as many illustrating scenes of biblical and other religious history.

Several small villages and 250 kilometres (155 miles) later — the last forty of which are through some spectacular countryside — the road once again meets up with the mighty Blue Nile at the town of Bahar Dar, on the border of Gojjam and Gondar regions, at the edge of Lake Tana.

Overleaf: The misty deluge of the spectacular Blue Nile Falls produces rainbows that shimmer across the gorge.

Bahar Dar first rose to importance in the late sixteenth or early seventeenth century, when the capital of Ethiopia was located in the vicinity of the lake. During the reign of the Emperor Susneyos (1606-1632) Bahar Dar attracted the interest of the Jesuits, who erected a tall (for that time) two-storey building in the compound of Saint George's church. This place of worship was renowned far and wide, so much so that the settlement was often spoken of as Bahar Dar Giyorgis.

Bahar Dar: Lakeside Town

Bahar Dar for centuries has been a place of commercial importance. It was and still is visited by *tankwas* (papyrus canoes) made by a lakeside people called the Woyto, who ply these craft across the waters of the lake. Open at the back end, the boats appear dangerously fragile as they slide over the surface, but they continue to carry passengers and goods to and from the many islands in the lake as they have done for centuries. These reed boats were, and still are, constructed at Bahar Dar and in the nearby Fogerra area.

Sightseeing

Bahar Dar, situated as it is on the southern extremity of Lake Tana, provides access to both the lake and its many islands, and to the Blue Nile Falls (*Tis Isat*). The visitor to Bahar Dar will no doubt see *tankwas* on the lake shore and may at times catch glimpses of their construction. Still standing is the **building** erected by the Jesuit Pero Paes, which can be seen in the compound of **Saint George's church**.

The town today, with its wide, palm-lined avenues and gardens overflowing with tropical vegetation, is a place of con-siderable economic and commercial impor-tance, with a cotton factory, a polytechnic, and a teacher training institute, as well as a growing number of modern shops, offices, hotels, and restaurants. Bahar Dar's two **markets** are both worth a visit: the general market, displaying colourful woven cloth and a wide range of supplies (including coffee); and the roadside market, specializ-ing in baskets. There are also a variety of **handicraft and weaving centres**.

It is only a five-minute drive from the town, across the **Blue Nile bridge**, to the spot where the famous river flows out of Lake Tana. Take the **second turning** to the **left** after the bridge, where a **signpost** directs visitors to the **Blue Nile Children's Home and Training Centre,** and continue to the lake's edge. The area by the lake is remarkably rich in bird life.

Emperor Haile Selassie's modest **palace** is on a small **hill** to the **right** of the road about two kilometres (one and a half miles) along the main road after the bridge. A **signpost** marks the **turnoff** to the **asphalt road** leading to the palace, which overlooks the river at a spot where **hippopotamus** are sometimes seen and offers a chance to inspect part of the monarch's private **library**, **reception room**, **bedroom**, and **bar**. Tours can be arranged through tour agents in Addis Ababa.

Bahar Dar, though bustling and pretty, is often looked at as just a base from which to visit the area's two main attractions: the **Blue Nile Falls** and **Lake Tana**.

Smoke of Fire

Known locally as *Tis Isat* — 'Smoke of Fire' — the Blue Nile Falls is the most dramatic spectacle on either the White or the Blue Nile rivers. Four hundred metres (1,312 feet) wide when in flood, and dropping over a sheer chasm more than forty-five metres (150 feet) deep, the falls throw up a continuous spray of water, which drenches onlookers up to a kilometre away. This misty deluge produces rainbows, shim-mering across the gorge, and a small per-ennial rainforest of lush green vegetation, to the delight of the many monkeys and multicoloured birds that inhabit the area.

To reach the **falls**, which are about thirty-five kilometres (22 miles) away, drive **south** from the town for about half an hour, and stop at **Tis Isat village**. Here travellers will quickly find themselves surrounded by a retinue of sometimes overzealous youthful guides who, for a small fee, will show the way and point out several places of historic interest *en route*.

After leaving the village the footpath

meanders first beside open and fertile fields, then drops into a deep rift that is spanned by an ancient, fortified **stone bridge** built in the seventeenth century by Portuguese adventurers and still in use. After a thirty-minute walk, a stiff climb up a grassy hillside is rewarded by a magnificent view of the falls, breaking the smooth edge of the rolling river into a thundering cataract of foaming water.

A rewarding but longer trek is to walk along the east bank all the way to the back of the falls; crossing the river by *tankwa*.

The site overlooking the waterfall has had many notable visitors over the years, including the late eighteenth-century traveller James Bruce, and, in more recent times, Queen Elizabeth II of Britain.

Lake Tana: Source of the Blue Nile

Rivalling the attraction of the Blue Nile Falls are the thirty-seven islands scattered about on the 3,000-square-kilometre (1,860-square-mile) surface of Ethiopia's largest body of water, Lake Tana. Some twenty of these islands shelter **churches** and **monasteries** of significant historical and cultural interest. They are decorated with beautiful **paintings** and are the repository of innumerable treasures.

The islands and peninsulas of Lake Tana can most conveniently be approached by boat from the port of Bahar Dar, on the southern side of the lake, though boats crossing the lake can also be obtained at the port of Gorgora on the northern shore. You can hire a boat from the Maritime Transport Authority, based in Bahar Dar. There is a minimum charge of 150 birr per hour, and as the nearest monastery — Kebran Gabriel — is about a two-hour return trip, expect to spend a minimum of 300 birr. It is more economical to team up with other travellers for lake crossings.

Sightseeing

Interesting and historic churches and monasteries on or around the lake can be found on the islands of **Birgida Maryam, Dega Estefanos, Dek, Narga, Tana Cherkos, Mitsele Fasilidas, Kebran** and **Debre Maryam**, as well as the peninsulas of **Gorgora, Mandaba,** and **Zeghe**, which has long been renowned for its coffee.

These places all have excellent **churches**. Though founded much earlier, most of the buildings date from the late sixteenth or early seventeenth century. Many have beautiful **mural paintings** and **church crosses**, and house **crowns** and **clothes** of former kings.

Access for the most part is closed to women, who are allowed to land on the banks of the islands but not permitted to proceed any further. The clergy, who are usually very good humoured, can sometimes be prevailed upon to bring some of their treasures to the water's edge.

Women are, however, permitted to visit churches on the Zeghe peninsula and the nearby church of **Ura Kidane Mehret**, as well as **Narga Selassie**.

Kebran Gabriel, the nearest monastery to Bahar Dar, is a principal tourist attraction for male visitors only, as this is one of the places where women are forbidden. Originally established in the fourteenth century and rebuilt during the reign of Emperor Iyasu I (1682-1706), it is an unassuming but impressive building with a distinct cathedral atmosphere.

Ura Kidane Mehret is another popular attraction that is open to women. Located on the Zeghe peninsula, the design of the monastery dates from the same period as that of the one at Kebran Gabriel but is a more decorative building, arched over with a huge conical thatched roof and painted inside and out with colourful **frescoes** depicting scenes from biblical lore and from the history of the Ethiopian Orthodox Church.

Overleaf: Many of Lake Tana's islands and peninsulas shelter churches and monasteries of historical and cultural interest.

The third principal attraction amongst the islands of Lake Tana is **Dega Estefanos**, which, like Kebran Gabriel, is closed to women. Although farther away from Bahar Dar (allow a day to get there and back and about 1,000 birr for the boat journey), it is well worth visiting. A steep trek up a winding path leads towards the **monastery** on the summit. Some ninety metres (300 feet) above the surface of the lake are the low, round, thatched-roof buildings that house the monks, and nearby an arch set into a high stone wall leads to a grassy clearing, at the centre of which stands the **church of Saint Stephanos**. Despite the fact that it houses a Madonna painted during the reign of Emperor Zara Yaqob (1434-1468), it is a relatively new building, erected about a century ago after the original structure had burned down in a grass fire.

The real historic interest in Dega Estefanos, however, lies in its **treasury**, secreted away under a massive antique lock, which is opened with a huge iron key. Here, together with numerous piles of brightly coloured ceremonial robes, are the glass-sided coffins containing the **mummified remains** of several of the former emperors of Ethiopia: Yekuno Amlak, who restored the Solomonic dynasty to the throne in 1270; Dawit, late fourteenth century; Zara Yaqob, fifteenth century; Za Dengel, early seventeenth century; and Fasilidas, also seventeenth century.

Also of interest is the sixteenth-century **Susneyos Palace** near Gorgora, which served as a 'blueprint' for the famous Gondar palaces. It was built for Emperor Susneyos, founder of the Gondar dynasties, by Catholic missionaries.

Bird lovers should make a point of visiting **Fasilidas Island**, near the eastern side of the lake, which is the breeding base for a number of wetland species.

Fifty-five kilometres (34 miles) north of Bahar Dar is the roadside town of **Werota**, where history buffs would be wise to take a deviation off the main road to Gondar. A turn to the **right** at this junction will — fifty-seven kilometres (35 miles) further on — bring one to **Debre Tabor**. (The town can also be reached by road from the east from Weldiya, on the Addis Ababa–Makale highway.)

Debre Tabor

An historic settlement dating back to the early eighteenth century, Debre Tabor is situated in the spectacular mountainous country that lies east of Lake Tana.

In the eighteenth and early nineteenth centuries the town was an important Ethiopian capital. Founded by Ras Gugsa Mersa, the Oromo ruler of Begemder region, it was successively the seat of government of three of his sons and later of his famous grandson Ali Alula, often termed Ali the Great, who was known to several early nineteenth-century European travellers.

The town in later years became the capital of the renowned Emperor Tewodros II, who in the 1860s came into conflict with the British Government and committed suicide at nearby Mekdela. His successor, Emperor Yohannes IV (1872-1889), also resided for a time at Debre Tabor before making his capital at Makale.

Places to see in and around the town include the **ruins** of the old **palace**; the old **church of Debre Tabor**, which gave its name to the settlement; in addition, the fine, late nineteenth-century **church of Heruy Giyorgis**, which was founded by Emperor Yohannes and contains **drums**, **crosses**, and other **artefacts** dating from his time.

You now need to retrace your steps to Werota, where a turn **north** puts you back on the main road to Gondar. Approximately 130 kilometres (80 miles) further north, it is a must on Ethiopia's Historic Route.

Opposite: Ornate murals adorn the walls and ceilings of many of Lake Tana's ancient churches and monasteries.

Gondar: The Camelot of Africa

You have only to stroll through the banqueting halls and gaze down from the balconies of the many castles and palaces here to imagine the intrigue and pageantry that took place back in the seventeenth and eighteenth centuries, when Gondar, then the Ethiopian capital, was home to a number of emperors and warlords, courtiers and kings.

Gondar became the capital of Ethiopia during the reign of Emperor Fasilidas (1632–1667), who was responsible for the building of the first of a number of castle-like palaces to be found here. He established a tradition that was followed by most of his successors, whose buildings greatly enhanced the grandeur of the city.

Gondar rose to prominence after Ethiopia went through a long period without a fixed capital and emerged in the seventeenth century as the largest settlement in the country. It was an important administrative, commercial, religious, and cultural centre and was noted for the skill of its many craftsmen.

The city retained its pre-eminence until the middle of the nineteenth century, when Emperor Tewodros II moved his seat of government to Debre Tabor and later to Mekdela. As a result, Gondar declined in importance and was subsequently looted in the 1880s by the Sudanese Dervishes. By the early nineteenth century the city was a mere shadow of its former self. More recently, several historic buildings were damaged by British bombing during the Ethiopian liberation campaign of 1941. Most of Gondar's famous castles and other imperial buildings nevertheless have survived the ravages of time and together constitute one of Ethiopia's most fascinating antiquities.

Getting there

Gondar, 748 kilometres (464 miles) from Addis Ababa, 183 kilometres (113 miles) from Bahar Dar, and 360 kilometres (223 miles) from Axum, can be reached by a good road, which skirts the eastern side of Lake Tana before crossing the fertile district of Dembeya. The town has its own airport, some ten kilometres (six miles) away in the Azzezo area, and can therefore also be reached by air. Ethiopian Airlines has daily flights in and out of the town.

When to go

Gondar, like all Ethiopia's historic sites, can be visited at any time of the year. The city is, however, a particularly good place to witness Genna, Ethiopian Christmas, on 7 January, and especially Timkat (Epiphany) celebrations on 19 January.

Where to stay

The town has one excellent modern government hotel, the Goha, which has a breathtaking view of the city. There are also several other good hotels, including Terara Hotel, Quarra Hotel, and Fogerra Hotel. See Listings. Be warned, however, that all the hotels in town are hampered by the fact that water is available for only a half hour in the morning and another half hour in the evening.

Sightseeing

The oldest and the most impressive of Gondar's imperial structures is the two-storeyed **palace of Emperor Fasilidas**, which is built of roughly hewn brown basalt stones held together with mortar. Said to have been the work of an Indian architect, the building has a flat roof, a rectangular tower in the south-west corner — which affords a view of Lake Tana in the distance — four smaller domed towers and a battlemented parapet.

Other buildings in the 'imperial quarter' of Gondar include the **library** of Fasilidas's son **Emperor Yohannes I** (1667–1682); a nearby **chancellery**; the saddle-shaped castle of Yohannes's son, **Emperor Iyasu I** (1682-1706); the large hall or 'house of song' of **Emperor Dawit III** (1716-1721), in which many ceremonies took place in former days; the long V-shaped reception and banqueting hall of **Emperor Bakaffa** (1722-1730); and the two-storeyed palace of the latter's redoubtable consort, **Empress Mentewab**. The palace compound is also

Above: Still-standing castles and palaces hint at the grandeur of days gone by in the former capital of Gondar.
Overleaf: Spellbinding mural adorns the ceiling of Debre Birhan Selassie church at Gondar.

the site of the **grave** of one the most remarkable nineteenth-century foreign travellers to Ethiopia: Emperor Tewodros's close friend **Walter Plowden**, a sometime British consul.

In addition to the fine structures in the imperial compound, visitors should be sure to see the **palace of Ras Mika'el Se'ul**, and the **house of the** *Echege*. The former, a small structure modelled on the Fasilidas castle, owes its name to its most important occupant, who became Gondar's dictator during the decline of the monarchy in the eighteenth century. The latter building is a round structure once inhabited by the *Echege*, the second most important official of the Ethiopian church. This little-known building is located in one of the humbler parts of the town and to many is known only by its urban registration

number: House No. 1, in Kebele 11. It can be reached by a short but interesting walk through the town.

Several notable Gondarine structures are to be seen outside the town. The most impressive, located in the Kaha River valley south of Gondar, is a well-preserved **'bathing palace'** variously attributed to Fasilidas or Iyasu I. It stands in a rectangular, neatly walled depression, which is filled with water once a year for the *Timkat* (Epiphany) celebrations, and, though popularly referred to as a 'bathing palace', was in fact probably constructed for such celebrations. Not far away stand the ruins of a small **pavilion** said to have been the mausoleum of a horse named Zobel belonging to Fasilidas, Iyasu, or some other Gondarine monarch of former times.

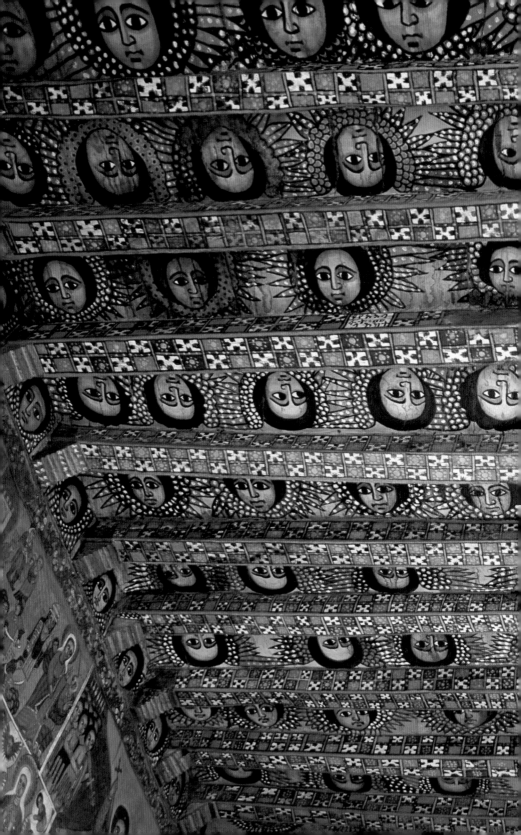

Rulers of this era also developed the area in the hills north-west of the town — called Kweskwam after the home of the Virgin Mary — as a kind of 'Capitol Hill' for government buildings. Most are now ruins, including the largest — a square, three-storeyed castle with flat parapet roof and battlemented walls, embellished with a series of bas-reliefs of various Ethiopian animals. Visitors to the **church** here can, on request, see many fine old **Gondarine manuscripts** and enter a **crypt** containing the skeletal remains of the famous eighteenth-century Empress Mentewab, her son Emperor Iyasu II, and grandson Emperor Iyo'as.

Gondar was the site of numerous fine **churches**, a number of which have survived to this day. One of the most impressive is that of **Medhane Alem**, a round structure built during the reign of Emperor Fasilidas. Standing in the middle of the town, its walls are decorated with numerous Biblical paintings. Three other churches, **Gemjabet Maryam**, **Atatami Mika'el,** and **Ilfign Giyorgis**, all of which have some **paintings**, are situated within the palace compound. Other churches, among them that of **Tekle Haymanot**, lie in its immediate vicinity.

Perhaps the finest of the **Gondarine churches** is that of **Debre Birhan Selassie** or 'Trinity at the Mount of Light', which stands on raised ground about a half an hour's walk to the north-east of the town. An imposing, though small, rectangular structure, its ceilings are decorated with beautiful winged angels, and its walls with impressive scenes depicting biblical events, including the life of Christ, Mary, and the saints and martyrs. There is also a **painting** of the church's founder, Emperor Iyasu I.

Historical buildings and palaces aside, a trip to the Gondar market is also worthwhile, providing many colourful scenes for the avid photographer, as well as a few bargains.

The Falashas

About one kilometre (half a mile) **north** of the Gondar limits (where there is a barrier), just off the main road, lies the tiny village of **Wolleka**, which was formerly inhabited by Falashas, or Judaic Ethiopians.

The Falashas call themselves Bete Isra'el and practise Judaism, which was the dominant religion of north-western Ethiopia for millenia. After the coming of Christianity and its adoption as the state religion, leaders from the north-east gradually penetrated and converted most of the Bete Isra'el. The penalty for not accepting conversion was loss of land. The remaining Bete Isra'el communities had to subsist on marginal land, and pottery, blacksmithing, and weaving became important parts of their economy. Recent research has shown that it was probably Bete Isra'el artisans who physically built the Gondar castles and provided many of the other artefacts that supported the Gondarine culture.

After a mass evacuation to Israel in 1991, only a few individuals still live in Ethiopia. Examples of their curious artefacts, earthenware pots, and figurines, made by their Christian neighbours who have remained behind, may, however, be purchased at the village, as well as in Gondar itself. The Falasha figurines, made of black or red pottery, are unique and in great demand. Visitors can also see the old synagogue and former Bete Isra'el homes.

Your journey now takes you along the main northern all-weather road, through some spectacular scenery, until you reach a point 101 kilometres (63 miles) north of Gondar, where the town of Debark is the base from which to visit — as Homer once said — the place where Greek gods vacationed and played chess on the peaks: the unforgettable Simien Mountains.

Simien Mountains National Park

The ancient game of chess also came to the mind of Rosita Forbes when, in 1925, she penned *From Red Sea to Blue Nile — A Thousand Miles of Ethiopia*:

'The most marvelous of all Abyssinian landscapes opened before us, as we looked across a gorge that was clouded amethyst to the peaks of Simien. A thousand

thousand years ago, when the old gods reigned in Ethiopia, they must have played chess with those stupendous crags, for we saw bishops' miters cut in lapis lazuli, castles with the ruby of approaching sunset on their turrets, an emerald knight where the forest crept up on to the rock, and, far away, a king, crowned with sapphire, and guarded by a row of pawns. When the gods exchanged their games for shield and buckler to fight the new men clamoring at their gates, they turned the pieces of their chessboard into mountains. In Simien they stand enchanted, till once again the world is pagan and the titans and the earth gods lean down from the monstrous cloud banks to wager a star or two on their sport.'

These gigantic 'chesspieces' are actually hard cores of volcanic outlets from which the surrounding material has eroded away over the centuries — one of the most distinctive characteristics of these highlands, which constitute one of the major mountain massifs in Africa. The region includes many summits above 4,000 metres (13,000 feet), and culminates in the highest point in Ethiopia, Ras Dashen, which, at 4,543 metres (14,901 feet), is also the fourth highest mountain in Africa. It is not a difficult mountain to climb and can be reached by travelling through the park.

The park is 179 square kilometres (111 square miles) in area and lies between 1,900 and 4,430 metres (6,200 and 14,530 feet). It is in the Afro-alpine zone and the temperature regularly falls below freezing at night. Daytime temperatures range from 11.5° to 18°C (53° to 64°F). The rainfall averages 1,550 mm (60 inches) a year.

Getting there

Debark, the base from which to explore Simien Mountains National Park, is 850 kilometres (527 miles) from Addis Ababa, 101 kilometres (63 miles) from Gondar, and 256 kilometres (159 miles) from Axum and can be reached by road through Bahar Dar and Gondar. Visitors can also fly to Gondar on one of Ethiopian Airlines' daily flights and arrange transport from there to Debark, either privately or by bus or taxi.

When to go

The best time to visit is the dry season, from December to March. Travel is difficult during the long rainy season between June and September, when several rivers may be flooded and difficult to cross, trails are slippery, and fog frequently obscures the view throughout the day. October, November, and December are the coldest months.

Where to stay

The nearest hotel accommodation is in Gondar, as hotels in Debark are not geared to foreign tourists, with the possible exception of the Simien Hotel. A small, local hotel, it has a very amiable and cooperative management, excellent food, delicious coffee, cold beers, and is bug free. Within the park, facilities were limited in 1994 to camping, and all equipment must be brought in. Tourist rest houses, once available in the park, were unfortunately destroyed in the fighting that occurred in the early '90s, but it is hoped that in the near future these facilities will be restored.

Sightseeing

Although the dry-weather road up to Sankaber Camp and Ambaras was rehabilitated in 1994, transport of the four-legged variety is by far the more reliable means of getting around for a more serious exploration of the park. If you have driven your own vehicle to Debark, leave it at the local police station (or at the Simien Hotel) for safe keeping while you take your tour of Simien. Then set about the business of renting pack and riding animals and hiring guides for the six-hour trip into the park. Make sure to examine each animal carefully before selecting it, and clarify the terms of your rental of animals and equipment before you depart. (See 'Trekking in Ethiopia: Trails of Adventure', Part Four.)

Although it helps to enquire in Addis Ababa before you leave for Debark about recommended dealers and current prices,

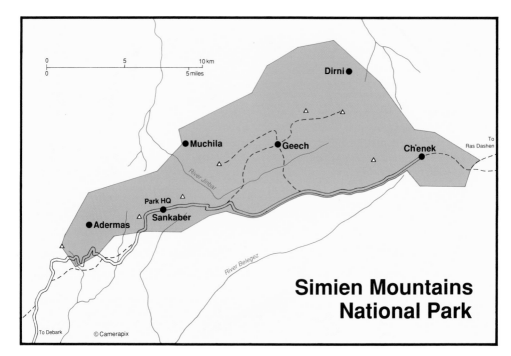

Simien Mountains National Park

©Camerapix

hiring guides, mules, and muleteers is done through the national park headquarters in an efficient and honest manner, alleviating stress-producing haggling.

Suitable clothing for extreme temperatures of hot and cold are needed as the diurnal swing is considerable. Waterproof clothing is also necessary, as are a hat and sunscreen lotion: the sun at these altitudes can burn fiercely. Water is available from the various streams, but should be treated. It is wise to remember that the main luggage is loaded on the pack animals for the day, so requirements during the day should be carried in a separate pack. The nearest medical help is in Debark.

There are various campsites and tracks to follow and it is best to take the advice of the guides. The topography of this small park is breathtaking. Climbing up from Debark on mules, through extensive farmland, the visitor is unaware of the dramatic scenery about to unfold. The land forms various small plateau areas, and the edges of these plunge dramatically to the lowlands to the north and east. The edges of these gorges form the perfect habitat for the animal that this park was set up to protect — the **Walia ibex**.

Generally the first stop is **Sankaber Camp**, a trek that leads mainly through cultivated areas to the 3,230-metre (10,600-foot) campsite. From this point, you can walk to the edge of the **abyss**, where you get your first glimpse of the spectacular scenery. Much of the vegetation has been altered by humans over the years and few trees will be seen in the area except the introduced eucalyptus. But in inaccessible areas, such as the escarpment, natural habitats are preserved and plants such as *Hypericum revolutum* (**St. John's wort**) and **heather** (*Erica arborea*) will be seen as small trees or bushes, and many smaller herbs form carpets of colour. Among these are many species of *Alchemilla*, the tall spikes of various *Kniphofia* species or '**red-hot pokers**', and carpets of small blue **lobelia** flowers.

Probably the easiest animal to see in this area is the **gelada baboon**, which is endemic to Ethiopia. These baboons are grass eaters and will be seen in family units in many areas, one male guarding his harem of females and young ones. They are also known as the 'bleeding heart baboons' as there are red areas on the chest that show the sexual state of the animal.

Above: Simien Mountains National Park is home to the endemic gelada baboon.

The **klipspringer** may be spotted on rocky areas, its hooves specially adapted to the terrain. The small **grey duiker** is present in any area where there is enough cover to protect it from its enemies.

Though it is named after this area, the **Simien fox**, which is also referred to as the Simien jackal or Ethiopian wolf, is very rarely seen here now. It is more common in Bale Mountains National Park in the south of the country. Its high-pitched call may be heard at night, and its bright red coat is distinctive during the day. It feeds on the many species of rodents found here.

The animal most visitors wish to see is the **Walia ibex**. The male of this member of the wild goat family has magnificent heavily ridged horns sweeping back over its shoulders. The Walia live on the crags of the steep escarpment, their hooves clinging to the smallest ledge.

Birds of the area often provide spectacular aerobatic displays off the sheer cliffs, using the air currents peculiar to the terrain. **Lammergeyers** and **choughs** are present, as well as endemics such as the **thick-billed raven**, **black-headed siskin**, **white-collared pigeon**, **wattled ibis**, **white-billed starling**, **spot-breasted plover**, and **white-backed black tit**.

From Sankaber, the track leads through meadows, forests and some cultivated areas to **Geech**, a trip of about three to three-and-a-half hours by mule. Geech, at 3,660 metres (11,800 feet), is worth a stay of at least two days: there are several good lookout spots where one may see Walia, gelada, and klipspringer, and breathtaking views from nearby **Gidgergot**, **K'adadit**, **Saha**, and **Emietgogo**. Just east of K'adadit you have a chance to see the striking black-and-white **colobus monkeys** in the lowland forests if you have *very* good binoculars.

From Geech to the next stopping-off point, **Ch'enek**, the trek takes two-and-a-half to four hours, and you may have to dismount and walk part of the way where the climb is steep. The Ch'enek campsite offers superb views, and there are many places for seeing Walia ibex. There are also **caves** to be explored, and this is the only place in the park where — if you are extremely lucky — you can see **rock hyrax**,

Above: The spirit of teamwork prevails with the hardy Amhara people of the highlands.

the small mammal that looks like an overgrown guinea pig but is distantly related to the elephant.

After a stop at Ch'enek, the traveller usually returns to Sankaber (three to four hours) and from there to Debark (five to six hours). But if arranged in advance, more extensive trips can be made to **Buahit**, at 4,437 metres (14,550 feet), which is outside the national park; **Ras Dashen**, Ethiopia's highest peak; and the lowlands. Three game scout camps exist in the lowlands at **Dirni**, **Muchila**, and **Adermas**, but a trip here is a real expedition and recommended only for more hardy travellers able to walk under tough conditions and cope with rock climbing. A trip from Ch'enek along the foot of the escarpment to the **Wolkafit Pass** and Debark lasts about five to seven days.

The Amhara

The people of this area are the Amhara, speaking Ethiopia's official tongue, Amharic. Most belong to the Ethiopian Orthodox Church, but several Muslim settlements were established in the Simien in the

sixteenth century, so the region today contains members of both religious groups.

Most people in this area are farmers, with the Muslims sometimes supplementing their income by trading. Barley and oats are the crops grown in the higher altitudes, with *teff* a little lower down. Life is hard and their inefficient farming methods have caused them to move higher and higher up the mountain slopes into areas less suited for cultivation. But still they retain a distinct pride and independence. They are suspicious of strangers, especially those who dispense largesse and condescension. Yet they will respond to overtures of genuine friendliness and respect with a hospitality that knows no bounds.

The staple item in the Simien Amhara diet is barley, from which they make *injera*, the flat, spongy, sourdough pancake that is the basis of most Ethiopian meals. They also make an unleavened bread (*dabbo*) from barley, they eat roasted barley (*kolo*) for snacks, and the Christians even drink barley in the form of *tella* and *korefi*, mildly alcoholic beverages. Meat is generally eaten only on holidays, of which there are many throughout the year, but pork is forbidden to both Christians and Muslims. Sheep, goats, eggs, and chickens are the usual sources of animal protein.

The Amhara house consists of a circular wall of thin poles stuck into the ground, with cross withies laced to them that are then plastered with a mixture of mud, dung, and *teff* straw, which is applied in layers. When it hardens, it provides a weatherproof barrier, which lasts for many years. However, many houses, especially in the mountains, are stone built. The conical thatched roof is supported by one central pole. There are small storage areas for cooking utensils, and the main area serves as sleeping and living quarters. There are no windows or chimneys — the smoke escapes through the thatch. Although it is quite small, the Amhara house still manages to accommodate the farmer, his wife, and unmarried children — and for a short time even married children, until they have their own house. As the farmer becomes wealthier, this *sar bet*, as it is called, gives way to a rectangular *korkoro bet* with tin roof.

There is no marketplace in the Simiens, but items like sheep, chickens and eggs, local bread, and various grains are available for sale. The price is negotiable and you are expected to bargain. You can also buy hats, baskets, and items of jewellery typical of the area. *Shammas* and *gabbis*, the homespun cotton shawls worn by both men and women, are usually available only on special order.

Join the main road back at Debark and your journey again heads **north-east** into Ethiopia's northernmost region of Tigray.

The Tigray

The Tigray people who inhabit this region speak a Semitic language called Tigrinya, a descendant of Ge'ez, the ancient tongue of Ethiopia. Though they have experienced frequent and severe famine conditions, they remain hardy and resilient farmers — wherever soil conditions permit. *Teff*, wheat, and barley (where *teff* won't grow) are the main crops, together with beans, lentils, onions, and potatoes. Irrigation and terrace farming are used on the steep slopes, but because firewood is scarce dung is burned for cooking rather than put on their fields. Large numbers of cattle, sheep, and goats are also kept, their hides and wool going into leather products and warm blankets and cloaks. Livestock, which is kept safe at night in a separate courtyard with a high stone wall, grazes the pasturelands by day — causing serious overgrazing in an almost barren land.

The Tigray houses are usually square and stone built, though some are round, with flat roofs of wood covered with sod and wide overhanging eaves. Outside, stone steps lead to the roof where the family goats are kept at night. Sometimes there are added towers and grain stores. The interior is simply a large single room with a central post and a fireplace hollowed from the earth floor — the smoke escapes from a broken water pot that serves as a chimney. More 'modern' homes have tin roofs with gable ends.

From Debark, it is 256 kilometres (159 miles) along the main road into Tigray to one of the star attractions on Ethiopia's Historic Route: **Axum**. A small and lowly town surrounded by dry hills, modern Axum does not easily yield evidence of the splendours and pageantry of its glorious past, but take a closer look: half-buried remnants of temples, fortresses, and rich palaces make this Ethiopia's most historic site, and a place that for over a millenium has been the principal centre of Ethiopian Christianity.

Axum: Mysterious Monoliths

Although its very early history is still unknown, Ethiopian legends first recorded in the fourteenth-century *Kebre Nagast* (Book of Kings) make Axum the capital of the Queen of Sheba in the tenth century BC, It does seem certain that a high civilization was established here in Axum by immigrants from southern Arabia in the centuries before the Christian era, and by the first century AD — the time of the earliest historical records — Axum was well known to Greek traders as a fine city and also as the centre of a considerable empire.

Rising to importance around the time of the birth of Christ, Axum was the capital of the far-reaching Axumite kingdom, which dominated the vital crossroads of Africa and Asia for almost a thousand years. Its principal ecclesiastical building, the **Church of St Mary of Zion**, is where, according to Ethiopian legend, the Ark of the Covenant resides, within a special sanctuary chapel. The Axumites introduced a universal written language, Ge'ez, and created a new imperial power and political cohesion in this part of Africa. They also gave Ethiopia its first organized religion — Christianity — in the fourth century AD.

The spectacular rise of Islam in the seventh century was the main cause of the decline of Axum. Although there was no direct aggression, Arab influence in the Red Sea cut off trade and cultural relations and Ethiopia found itself isolated from the rest of the world. Axum's dramatic end was caused by the rebellion against the Axumite kingdom and Christianity led by Queen Yodit or Gudit, who destroyed much of the ancient city, overthrew its last king, and killed the royal princes — thus

Above: Carving on fallen stela in Axum is said by some to symbolize the Ark of the Covenant.

interrupting the Solomonic line. In folklore, Queen Yodit is remembered as a monster and a destroyer of churches.

However, after the decline of the Axumite realm the city remained Ethiopia's religious capital, as well as the place where several medieval emperors made their way to celebrate their coronation rites. The town abounds in archaeological remains, including the graves of kings, the foundations of a palace, inscribed tablets, and great carved obelisks.

Getting there

Axum, 1,005 kilometres (623 miles) from Addis Ababa, 360 kilometres (223 miles) from Gondar, 220 kilometres (136 miles) from Makale, and 529 kilometres (328 miles) from Lalibela, can be reached by road or by air on one of Ethiopian Airlines' daily flights to the town.

When to go

Although Axum is worthy of a visit at any time, the town is particularly interesting during the time of church festivals, notably Christmas (7 January) and Epiphany (19 January), as well as at the end of November, the festival of Maryam Zion, to whom the great Church of Saint Mary is dedicated.

Where to stay

The Ezana Hotel, the Kaleb Hotel, the Axum Ghion Hotel, and the recently built Yoha Hotel. See Listings.

Sightseeing

Just **north** of the town square stand a number of famous **obelisks**, or **monolithic stelae**, with which Axum is widely identified. In ancient times there were seven of these monoliths of granite standing together, but the biggest, which was the largest monolith in the world — measuring over thirty-three metres (108 feet) and weighing about 500 tonnes — fell at some remote period in the past, and now lies in broken segments on the ground to the right of the standing stelae. The second largest stela, about twenty-four metres (79 feet) high, had also fallen and was stolen during the Italian Fascist

Above: The sanctuary chapel at Axum is said to be the last resting place of the long-sought-after Ark of the Covenant.

occupation on the personal orders of the Italian dictator Mussolini. It was taken to Rome in 1937. Though eligible for return in accordance with the Italian Peace Treaty of 1947, it has thus far not been repatriated, although Ethiopian scholars and patriots are now campaigning for its return. The third largest stela, which is slightly smaller, measuring twenty-three metres (75 feet), still stands in Axum.

All seven giant stelae are made of single pieces of granite and have identical decoration. Each was erected in the centre of a step platform of stone on a terrace of polished limestone. At the base of each standing stela is a stone **altar** containing several bowl-shaped cavities, which it is thought served as receptacles for sacrificial offerings to the dead. Each stela resembles a tall, slender, multi-storeyed house in the architectural style of the Axumite houses and palaces, which had walls displaying an alternate recession and projection and were made of alternating horizontal layers of stone and timber, with projecting ends of timber-beams, technically called 'mon-

key heads', and a flat roof surrounded by a parapet.

The stelae are even decorated with representations of doors, windows, and, in some cases, door handles. Riveted to the top at the front and back were inscribed **metal ornaments** in the form of the pagan crescent and disc, symbols of the moon, with an arc at the top of the stela representing the cosmic universe.

In addition to these obelisks there are a number of others of various degrees of excellence, including many roughly hewn, undecorated, slabs of stone.

To the **left** of the principal obelisks, in the Park of the Stelae, one can enter the newly excavated **tomb of Ramha**, a former king of Axum.

Also of great interest is Axum's **Church of Saint Mary of Zion**. There are in fact two such churches, one old and one new, both located in a spacious walled compound directly opposite the Park of the Stelae. The older, a rectangular battlemented building, was put up in the early seventeenth century by Emperor Fasilidas,

the founder of Gondar; the much more modern structure was erected nearby by Emperor Haile Selassie, who opened it in the company of Queen Elizabeth II of Great Britain in 1965. The older structure, by far the more interesting of the two, is the guardian of many **crowns** of former Ethiopian rulers and other valuables, which have been put in a small museum-like building in the compound. Unfortunately, the latter two are closed to women, who are, however, allowed to inspect some of these treasures, which are carried to the edge of the restricted areas for this purpose.

The church **courtyard** also contains many **antiquities**. These include **sculpted stones**, which formed part of the old demolished church. Visitors may also see the **stone thrones** on which the monarchs of the past were crowned.

Nearby is a small **national museum**, open to visitors on payment of an entry fee, which houses a remarkable collection of antiquities. There are several stones bearing Sabaean and Ge'ez inscriptions, as well as many other artefacts, including clay figurines that reveal the hair style current in ancient Axum.

From the museum it is a walk of less than half a minute to the **ruins** of the original **Church of Saint Mary of Zion** which, according to tradition, was erected soon after the advent of Christianity as the state religion in the early fourth century. This, or a later edifice in its place, was described twelve centuries later by a visiting Portuguese priest, Francisco Alvares, but was destroyed shortly afterwards by the Muslim conqueror Ahmed Gragn.

Also of immense historical importance in Axum is a trilingual **inscription** erected by the early fourth-century King Ezana to record his victories. It is written in three scripts, Sabaean, Ge'ez, and Greek, and is housed in a specially constructed park in the centre of the town. Of archaeological interest near the park is a **tomb** believed to be that of King Bazen, who is said to have reigned at Axum at the time of the birth of Christ.

Perhaps the greatest mystery about this strange and ancient city is the claim that it is the last resting place of the Ark of the Covenant — a claim connected in Ethiopian tradition to legends of the Queen of Sheba and King Solomon, whose son Menelik is said to have brought the Ark to Axum some 3,000 years ago and founded the Solomonic dynasty of which Haile Selassie was the last reigning emperor. The well-guarded **sanctuary chapel** of the Ark

of the Covenant stands in the town, which the visitor may approach but never hope to enter.

There are a number of sites associated by local folk with the Queen of Sheba herself. Amongst these the most notable is a huge water reservoir, hewn out of solid rock, known as the **Queen of Sheba's Bath**, which forms the focal point of the annual ceremony of *Timkat* (Epiphany) in which, each January, a replica of the Ark is carried out in procession.

Almost equally impressive are the ruins of the so-called **Queen of Sheba's Palace** or **Taakha Maryam**, which stands on the outskirts of town on the Gondar road. Of particular interest here are a still-intact **flagstone floor**, thought to have been a **throne room**, and a number of **stairwells**, which hint at the existence of at least one upper storey. There are also private **bathing areas** of sophisticated design and a well-preserved **kitchen** dominated by two brick ovens.

Across the road, in a field facing the palace, visitors may also inspect a number of

Above: The old church of Saint Mary of Zion at Axum houses many beautiful, ornate crowns of several former Ethiopian Emperors.

rough-hewn **granite stelae**, some standing more than four metres (13 feet) high, some fallen and broken. Most are undecorated but one, the largest, is carved with four horizontal bands, each topped by a row of circles in relief. This crude obelisk, much older than those in the Park of the Stelae, is thought by the townspeople to mark the **grave** of the Queen of Sheba. No excavation work has been carried out beneath it, however, and the field in which it stands is now entirely given over to farmers, who grow crops and graze their cattle there.

Another **monument** of great importance, about three kilometres (two miles) away overlooking the dramatic **Adwa Mountains**— near which Emperor Menelik defeated the Italians in 1896—is square in plan and measures about sixty metres (197 feet) on each side. The walls, which have long since crumbled, show signs of having originally been projected at the corners to form four towers — possibly the very towers which, in the sixth century, the monk Kosmos described as being adorned with brass unicorns.

Beneath the fortress, steep stone **stairways** lead down into a number of underground **galleries** and **chambers**, which are roofed and walled with massive dressed granite blocks that fit precisely against one another without any mortar in the joints. Local tradition says this cool, dark warren was once the **treasury** used by Emperor Kaleb (514–542 AD) and also by his son Gebre-Meskal. It is now known as the **tomb** of Gebre-Meskal. With a torch, it is possible to see several empty **stone coffers,** which still lie within — coffers believed to have once contained great riches in gold and pearls. Further rooms, as yet unexcavated, extend into the hillside blocked off behind thick granite walls.

Visitors with sufficient time to travel outside the town should not miss the **Lioness of Gobedra**, a drawing of a lioness cut in relief on a large piece of stone at a village of that name. This is located in an area around which the Axumites once quarried their stone. At one place on the track to the Lioness one can clearly see a row of small holes made by the quarry workers in an attempt to disengage a large block of granite. To reach the Lioness, you retrace your track four kilometres (2.5 miles) towards Gondar and clamber up the rough terrain; about a half-hour's walk.

On towards Makale

Ethiopia's earliest known capital, **Yeha**, is less than two hours' drive from Axum through some dramatic highland scenery. As the birthplace of the country's earliest high civilization, it is well worth visiting. To get there, head **east** for twenty kilometres (12 miles) to **Adwa**. Continue along the main road towards Adigrat for another twenty-four kilometres (15 miles) and then turn north on to a short **dirt track**, where you will see the imposing ruins of Yeha's **Temple of the Moon** about four kilometres (2.5 miles) to the right of the track.

The ruins of this large, pre-Christian temple, erected around the fifth century BC, consist of a single roofless oblong chamber twenty metres (66 feet) long by fifteen metres (50 feet) wide. The windowless ten-metre-high (33-foot-high) walls are built of smoothly polished stones, some of them more than three metres (ten feet) long, carefully placed one atop the other without the use of mortar.

Immediately beside the temple is a **modern church** dedicated to **Abune Aftse,** one of the Nine Saints from Syria who founded many important monasteries in northern Ethiopia in the fifth and sixth centuries. The building's front façade has been fitted with **stones** from the original temple, which are decorated with **reliefs** of ibex with lowered horns. The church contains many **crosses**, old **manuscripts** and **stones** bearing ancient **Sabaean inscriptions**, which can be seen on request.

Archaeological research at Yeha has unearthed many historical treasures, including a number of Sabaean inscriptions and a variety of animal figurines. Several of these antiquities are on display in the National Museum in Addis Ababa.

Debre Damo

Forty-eight kilometres (30 miles) from Axum along the main road to Adigrat will bring you to the village of **Inticho**, and twenty-five kilometres (15.5 miles) beyond the village, the flat-topped mountain of **Debre Damo** will come into view on the **left**. A few kilometres later a **signpost** indicates the turn to Debre Damo, some twenty-four kilometres (15 miles) away on a rough, four-wheel-drive-only **track**. After the track ends, it is a two-hour stiff uphill walk to a cliff, at the top of which is the ancient **monastery** of Debre Damo.

The monastery, which dates back to early Axumite times, is said to possess the oldest existing intact **church** in Ethiopia. Legend has it that Abune Aregawi, one of the Nine Saints who came from Syria in the sixth century, while wandering at the foot of the cliff, judged that the plateau land above him was a suitable place on which to live a solitary life. God, hearing his wish, commanded a snake living on the mountain-top to stretch down and lift up the holy man, who made Debre Damo his abode.

The mountain, because of its virtual inaccessibility, was later made a place of detention for male members of the Axumite royal dynasty, to prevent them from conspiring against the ruling monarch. Subsequently, during the wars of Ahmed Gragn, Emperor Lebna Dengel and his consort, Queen Seble Wengel, by then fugitives, sought refuge on Debre Damo, and it was there that the unfortunate monarch died in 1540.

The visitor, lacking the kind snake that helped the monastery's founder to ascend the mountain, will have to go up with the help of a **rope** lowered by the friendly monks, who will not, however, allow women to enter. The summit, when eventually reached some twenty-four metres (78 feet) later, offers panoramic views over the surrounding countryside and complete seclusion and peace for the 100 or so monks and deacons who live there. Though local people give food and supplies, the monastic community is virtually self-sufficient, growing selected crops and rearing male sheep and goats. The monastery also has its own reservoirs — spectacular caverns hewn deep beneath the surface of the cliff-top centuries ago —

Opposite and above: Access to the Debre Damo monastery, which dates back to early Axumite times, is only by rope, but the treasures within are worth the arduous ascent.

which provide the monks with water throughout the year.

Debre Damo church, which is called after Abune Aregawi, is built in Axumite style. The beams and ceiling of the ancient church, around which the monastery is built, are beautifully decorated with **carved wooden panels** depicting lion, elephant, rhinoceros, snakes, gazelle, antelope, giraffe, and camels. Although there are no murals as such, a large number of **paintings** are preserved there, including several that depict the legend of the foundation of Debre Damo by Abune Aregawi.

The treasures secreted within, kept intact through the country's 1,400 tumultuous years of history because of that arduous, dangerous ascent, include an extensive collection of **illuminated manuscripts**, among them the oldest surviving fragments of texts anywhere in Ethiopia. The church now houses about fifty manuscripts, although the monks claim that they formerly possessed no less than a thousand.

Some twenty-five kilometres (15.5

miles) east of Debre Damo, the road you've been following from Gondar leads to the town of **Adigrat**, where it joins up with the main Addis Ababa road. To the south lies **Makale**, capital of Tigray, and one of Ethiopia's most interesting regional seats.

Makale: Castles and Caravans

Makale is a town situated on an almost treeless plain, bounded on the west by the **Geba River**, one of the tributaries of the Takazze, and on the north and east by a low range of mountains. It owes its importance to **Emperor Yohannes IV** (1871–1889), who had a special liking for the place, for it was there that he was reputedly conceived. He also made it his capital during his reign.

Getting there

Makale, 777 kilometres (482 miles) from Addis Ababa, 260 kilometres (161 miles) from Axum, and 279 kilometres (173 miles) from Lalibela, is served by road and air via daily flights on Ethiopian Airlines.

When to go

Makale can be visited at any time of the year, but if used as a base for visiting the hotter-than-hot Danakil Depression, is best during the cool months between December and February.

Where to stay

Green Hotel, Harambee Hotel, Adulis Hotel, Ambassador Hotel, and the unique Castle Abraha, which was once the palace of Dejazmach Abraha Aura. See Listings.

Sightseeing

Turning **south** at Adigrat, travel for another sixty-nine kilometres (43 miles) to the small town of **Wukro**. Just past the town is one of Ethiopia's many **rock-hewn churches**, Cherkos, which, unlike some of the others, is easy to visit as it is just off the main road. Ten kilometres (six miles) to the north is **Nagash**, the site of a mosque and the country's first Islamic settlement.

Fifty-six kilometres (35 miles) past Wukro, the main road takes a sharp turn to the west and leads into Makale. The principal point of interest here is Emperor Yohannes's **palace**, which has been turned into an interesting **museum** housing manuscripts, books, and furniture from the emperor's time, including a large and ornately carved wooden **throne**. Monday is **market day** in Makale. In addition to being the largest market for rock salt in the country, it offers visitors a colourful view of the local community and a good opportunity for photographs.

Tours can be arranged from the town to visit several nearby **rock-hewn churches** — of which there are no less than two hundred in the region. Often perched on cliffs or carved into rock crevices, these fascinating churches are beautifully decorated and some house important religious artefacts.

The Danakil Depression

Makale is also a good vantage point from which to witness the **camel caravans** climbing up from the forbidding **Danakil Depression**, carrying tablets of salt. The Depression is one of the hottest and most inhospitable places on earth, with many points more than 100 metres (328 feet) below sea level and noontime temperatures soaring above 50°C (122°F). It is the site of the famous dry **salt lake** from which Ethiopians since time immemorial have obtained their *amoles* (bars of salt) used both for consumption and as 'money'. Mined by the Afar people, the salt is loaded on camels and taken up into the highlands, where it is in considerable demand and fetches a good price.

Makale can be used as a base for trips to

the **Afar (Danakil) area**, the vast region to the east where the Danakil Depression is located. For obvious reasons, excursions should be made in the cool months from December to February. Anyone wanting to make this trip must be prepared for a long, rough, extremely hot journey and be able to carry a minimum of ten litres of drinking water per person per day. The **track** down the escarpment starts from **Agula**, about twenty kilometres (12 miles) **north** of Makale. It is best to consult a local tour operator about how, when, and if it is possible to make the trip.

The landscape here seems carved from the infernos of hell and is a reminder of the past and present furies that have ravaged this region, with volcanic cones rising above the scabs of black lava. It is possible to visit the **salt flats** where the salt is mined and, amazingly, there is also wildlife to be seen here, particularly **zebra** and **wild ass**.

Although this place may seem un-inhabitable, it is nevertheless home to a hundred thousand or so **Afar nomads**, who somehow manage to wrest a living — thanks to the salt — from this challenging and inhospitable wilderness, using the camel as their beast of burden. (See 'The North-East: A River to the Beginnings of Mankind', Part Two.)

After the decline of the Axumite empire, lamenting their lost grandeur, Ethiopia's rulers retreated with their Christian subjects to the central plateau, protected by the immense eastern escarpment and deep river valleys. This is where the journey on the country's Historic Route really comes to a climax, on a natural 2,600-metre

Above: The devoted must also be brave to transverse the narrow ledge, which overhangs a precipice, leading to the small, two-room rock-hewn church of Abba Daniel in the Dugum area.

(8,500-foot) rock terrace surrounded on all sides by rugged and forbidding mountains in the northern extreme of the modern region of Wollo: the marvellous monastic settlement of Lalibela.

Lalibela: Eighth Wonder of the World

Once the thriving and populous capital city of a medieval dynasty, **Lalibela** is now not much more than a village. It is scarcely visible against a horizon dominated by the 4,200-metre (13,776-foot) peak of **Mount Abune Yosef**. But this anonymity is a deceiving camouflage, for in this remote highland settlement some 800 years ago,

safe from the prying eyes and plundering hands of hostile interlopers, a noble king fashioned a secret marvel.

Formerly known as Roha, it now bears the name of King Lalibela (1181–1221), a member of the Zagwe dynasty. Shortly after his birth at Roha, the future king's mystical life began to unfold. Legend has it that one day his mother saw him lying happily in his cradle surrounded by a dense swarm of bees. Recalling an old Ethiopian belief that the animal world could foretell the advent of important personages, the second sight came upon her and she cried out: 'The bees know that this child will become King.' Accordingly she called her son 'Lalibela', which means 'the bee recognizes his sovereignty'.

Lalibela's older brother, Harbay, the

Opposite top: A unique ceremonial fan, thought to date from the fifteenth century, is housed in the Debre Tsion church near Dugum.
Opposite: The beautiful Enda Medhane Alem rock-hewn church features many bas-reliefs and carvings.

Above: *Timkat* (Epiphany) celebrations at the famous rock-hewn Bet Giyorgis.

incumbent monarch, was naturally disturbed to hear this news and became jealous. As the years passed, he began to fear for the safety of his throne, decided to eliminate his rival, and unsuccessfully tried to have his brother murdered. Persecutions of one kind or another continued for several years, culminating in a deadly potion that left the young prince in mortal sleep. During the three-day stupor, Lalibela was transported by angels to the first, second, and third heavens, where God ordered him to return to Roha and build churches, the like of which the world had never seen before. The Almighty, it is said, further told the prince how to design those churches, where to build them, and how to decorate them.

After Lalibela returned to mortal existence, Harbay, acting on instructions from the Lord, went to pay homage to him and beg his forgiveness. The two brothers then rode together on the same mule to Roha, and Harbay abdicated in favour of his younger brother. When Lalibela was crowned, he gathered masons, carpenters, tools, set down a scale of wages, and

purchased the land needed for the building. The churches were built with great speed, because the angels continued the work at night.

Those who scoff at such whimsical folklore are soon silenced when they glimpse the famous **Lalibela churches**. Physically prised from the rock in which they stand, these towering edifices seem to be of superhuman creation in scale, workmanship and concept. Some lie almost completely hidden in deep trenches, while others stand in open quarried caves. A complex and bewildering labyrinth of tunnels and narrow passageways with offset crypts, grottos, and galleries connects them all. Throughout this mysterious and wonderful settlement, priests and deacons go about their timeless business, scarcely seeming aware that they are living in what has become known as the Eighth Wonder of the World.

Getting there

Lalibela, 642 kilometres (398 miles) from Addis Ababa, 279 kilometres (173 miles) from Makale, and 241 kilometres (149

Above: Elaborate frescoes adorn the interior of the Bet Maryam church in Lalibela.

miles) from the Wollo regional capital of Dessie, is served by road and by air on daily flights of Ethiopian Airlines — except in the rainy season, when the airstrip has to be closed.

When to go

Always a place of unparalleled fascination, Lalibela is particularly interesting during religious celebrations, notably those of Ethiopia's Christmas (7 January), *Timkat* (19 January), and Easter, when Christians pour into the area from far and near.

Where to stay

Lalibela has two good modern government hotels, the Seven Olives and the more recently built Roha, as well as several small, satisfactory private ones. See Listings.

Sightseeing

There are two ways to get to Lalibela. The shorter route from Makale is to travel about 189 kilometres (117 miles) **south** to **Kobo**, where a 78-kilometre (48-mile) stretch of rough road leads **westwards** to Lalibela. The preferred route — because of better road conditions — is to continue along the main road past Kobo for another forty-five kilometres (28 miles) and turn **west** at **Weldiya**. Forty-three kilometres (27 miles) later, turn **north** at the village of **Dilb**. Thirty kilometres (19 miles) later you'll join up with the main road to Lalibela at the village of **Kulmesk**, where you turn **left**.

Seeing all the **Lalibela churches**, which are cut out of soft red volcanic tuff, takes a long time, but it is well worth it. Although the ten main churches are within a very short distance of the town centre, there are others some distance away. Visiting any church entails a lot of walking, much of it over steep gradients.

Despite cooling breezes, the heat of the sun here in the Ethiopian highlands is intense and it is gentle relief, after a stiff climb through the town, to plunge into the dark, almost air-conditioned, chill of a doorway carved deep into rock. Most of the churches are unlit, so remember to take a good torch.

The churches can actually be divided

Above: Oblivious to visitors, a devoted Lalibela monk continues with his daily prayers.

into two main groups — one to the **south** and the other to the **north** of a **stream** known locally as the **Jordan River**.

The first group of churches lie in their rock cradles one behind the other north of the river. They are six in number: **Bet Golgotha**, **Bet Mika'el** (also known as Bet Debre Sina), **Bet Maryam**, **Bet Meskel**, **Bet Danaghel**, and **Bet Medhane Alem**.

The first church most travellers visit is Bet Medhane Alem, the largest of all the Lalibela churches. Taking the form of a Greek temple, it is unusual in being entirely surrounded by **square-shaped columns**, with a further forest of twenty-eight massive rectangular columns supporting the roof inside. In a corner of the church, one can see three empty **graves** said to have been symbolically dug for the biblical personages of Abraham, Isaac, and Jacob. A theory put forward by various scholars is that Bet Medhane Alem is a copy in rock of the original Church of Saint Mary of Zion at Axum.

A few minutes' walk from Bet Medhane Alem is Bet Maryam, which stands in a spacious **courtyard**. It is the most beloved

— not only of the Lalibela clergy, but also of the many pilgrims streaming into its courtyard on holy days. Legend says that King Lalibela also favoured this church above all, and attended mass there daily. A **'box' of the royal family** of Lalibela is still shown on the **western wall** of the courtyard opposite the main entrance.

A deep square **pool** in the courtyard is said to have miraculous properties, and infertile women dip themselves in the algae-covered waters at certain times of the year, particularly at Christmas.

Dedicated to Mary, the mother of Christ, this church is alone amongst the Lalibela monoliths in that it has a **projecting porch**. The remains of early unusual **frescoes** can be seen on the ceiling and upper walls, and there are many **elaborately carved details** on the piers, capitals, and arches.

In the **northern wall** of the Bet Maryam courtyard is the excavated **chapel** of Bet Meskel. It is a broad gallery, with a row of four pillars dividing the space into two aisles spanned by arcades. One spandrel between two arches contains a **relief cross** beneath stylized foliage, a decorative motif often found in Lalibela. Bet Meskel also contains several large **caves**, some of them inhabited by hermits.

Jutting out at the south of the Bet Maryam courtyard is the little **chapel** of Bet Danaghel, which is connected with one of the most fascinating legends of Lalibela. Priests will tell you that the chapel was constructed in honour of maidens martyred under Julian the Apostate, who ruled Rome in the mid-fourth century, the time when Christianity was first brought to Axum. It is said that fifty young maidens, nuns, and novices, who lived a pious life under the supervision of their abbess Sofia in Edessa (present-day Turkey), were ordered to be killed by Julian when he passed through the town and learned of the nunnery. The abbess and her young maidens were beheaded. This tiny chapel in the mountains of Ethiopia helps keep alive the memory of their modest contemplative life and their last moment of bravery in professing their Christian faith.

A **tunnel** at the southern end of the Bet Maryam courtyard leads to the interconnected churches of Bet Golgotha and Bet Mika'el, which, together with the **Selassie Chapel** and the **Tomb of Adam**, form the most mysterious complex in Lalibela. Its holiest shrine, the Selassie Chapel, is housed here, and — according to the whispers of the priests — perhaps even the **tomb** of King Lalibela himself. It is likely that some of the most beautiful **processional crosses** of Lalibela will be shown to you here. One, a very rich and elaborate metal cross, black with age and decorated with inlaid circles, is said to have belonged to King Lalibela. His **rod** and **stool**, also said to have been his **throne**, may also be shown to you.

While the ancient entrance to this group was probably from the west, passing the hollowed block of the Tomb of Adam, the courtyard is now entered from the **south**, being connected by the trench leading off the Bet Maryam church. A **side door** leads to the first church, Bet Mika'el, which is considered a twin church of the more northern Bet Golgotha. Two **windows** in the southern wall of Bet Golgotha give

Above: Priest emerges from the silent sanctuary of Lalibela's Bet Abba Libanos.

light to two **shrines** — the **right-hand** one to the Selassie Chapel and the one on the **left** to the **'Iyesus Cell'** (Cell of Jesus), located at the **east** end of the **right-hand nave** of the church proper. Not far from the **'tomb of Christ'** — an arched recess in the **north-east corner** of the church — is a movable **slab** set into the floor, said to cover the most secret place of the holy city: the **tomb** or **crypt** of King Lalibela.

Bet Golgotha, although simple in its architecture, houses some of the most remarkable pieces of **early Christian Ethiopian art: figurative reliefs**, rare elsewhere in the country. The 'tomb of Christ' displays a recumbent figure in high relief with an angel in low relief above its head. The figures of seven saints, mostly larger than life, decorate arched niches in the walls.

A doorway at the **east** end of the **right-hand nave** of Bet Golgotha opens on to the Selassie Chapel, a place of greatest sanctity that is rarely open even to the priests, and very few visitors have been permitted to enter it. The **shrine** is completely impri-

Above: Not far from Lalibela is Na'akuto La'ab, a veritable jewel of a church built in a cave.

soned in the rock and features three **monolithic altars**. The **central altar** displays a **relief** decoration of four winged creatures with hands raised in prayer, thought to be representations of the Four Evangelists.

The simple but impressive Tomb of Adam is a huge square block of stone, which stands in a deep trench in front of the **western** face of Bet Golgotha. The **ground floor** of this hollowed-out block serves as the **western** entrance to the first group of churches, and the **upper floor** houses a **hermit's cell**. A **cross** is the only decoration of the 'tomb'.

The group south of the Jordan River comprises four churches: **Bet Amanuel**, **Bet Merkorios**, **Bet Abba Libanos**, and **Bet Gabriel-Rufa'el**.

Bet Amanuel is perhaps the finest of the group, its elaborate **exterior** much praised by art historians. Its **walls** imitate the alternate projecting and recessing walls of an Axumite building. The structure contains a large **hall** with four **pillars**, and its **windows**, which are irregularly placed, are also Axumite in style. A **spiral staircase**

leads up to an **upper storey**. The most striking interior feature is the **double frieze** of **blind windows** in the vaulted nave, the lower frieze being purely ornamental and the upper one consisting of windows alternating with decorated areas. In the **rock floor** of the **southern aisle** a hole opens into a long, subterranean **tunnel** leading to neighbouring Bet Merkorios.

Chambers and **cavities** for sacred **bees** in the outer wall of the courtyard are a reminder of the bees that prophesied kingship to Lalibela. Some of the chambers, however, are the **graves** of monks and pilgrims who wanted to be buried in this 'holy city'. In this outer wall two further **underground passages** have been discovered leading to Bet Merkorios.

Bet Merkorios, partially collapsed and recently restored, is thought to have originally served a secular purpose — perhaps that of a house of justice, as amongst the secular objects found in recently excavated trenches were shackles for the ankles of prisoners. The Lalibela clergy only much later turned it into a shrine for worship, and the part serving today as a church occupies the **eastern** end of a **subterranean hall** that opens to a **courtyard**. The naked walls of Bet Merkorios were once covered with rich **paintings** on cotton fabrics, which were attached to the walls by a thick layer of clay, ox blood, and straw. For their better preservation they were removed and can now be seen in the National Museum in Addis Ababa. They were most likely painted in Gondar, and it is thought they originate from the early seventeenth or eighteenth century.

Bet Abba Libanos, which is separated from the surrounding land on only three sides, is a structure of great charm, and a good example of a **cave church**. It resembles Bet Amanuel in that its walls are chiselled in Axumite style.

It is suspected that Bet Gabriel-Rufa'el was also not originally intended to serve as a church, largely because of its disorientation and unusual plan. The labyrinthine floor plan features three angular **halls** with pillars and pilasters that are squeezed between two **courtyards**. The most impressive part of the church is the monumental **façade**. Although usually entered from the top of the rock near Bet Amanuel in the **east** by a small **bridge** of logs leading over the central trench, you may also approach from the **east** by a series of small **tunnels**, a gallery-like **passage** and another log **bridge** ten metres (33 feet) above the courtyard. From the **north** a **path** leads from the outer trench to a narrow chiselled-out ridge of rock called the 'path to heaven'. This in turn leads up steeply to the roof of the church, although there is no entrance from this point.

Also to the **north** of the Jordan, but much further to the **west**, and somewhat isolated from the others, is the remarkable church of **Bet Giyorgis**, possibly the most elegant of all the Lalibela structures. It is located in the **south-west** of the village on a sloping rock terrace. In a deep pit with perpendicular walls, it can only be reached through a **tunnel**, which is entered from some distance away through a **trench**.

Legend says that when King Lalibela had almost completed his churches, he was severely reproached by Saint George — who in full armour rode up to him on his white horse — for not having constructed a house for him. Lalibela thereupon promised the saint the most beautiful church, and Saint George apparently supervised the execution of the works in person, as attested by the fact that the monks today still show the **hoof marks** of his horse to visitors.

Standing on a three-tiered plinth, Bet Giyorgis is shaped in the form of a Greek cross, and has **walls** reminiscent of Axumite architecture. The church also has an elaborately shaped **doorway**.

There are several other **rock churches** within a day's journey of Lalibela. Keep in mind that access to them often requires long walks and stiff climbs or rides by mule. They include **Yemrehanna Krestos**, six hours by foot and mule to the northeast of Lalibela, a remarkably beautiful structure built (not excavated) in typical Axumite style within a **cave**; **Arbatu Entzessa**, southwest of Yemrehanna Krestos and detached from the rock on only two sides; **Bilbila Giyorgis**, west of Arbatu Entzessa, only the façade of which is visible; and **Sarsana Mika'el**, which is detached on three sides. Also of interest is the church of **Ashetan Maryam**, located in the mountain high above the town, with an impressive view of the surrounding countryside; **Na'akuto La'ab**, a veritable jewel of a church built in a **cave**, accessible via a motorable road; and **Ukre Mestale Christos** near Sekota, where the mummified remains of several *wag-shums* — former rulers of Wollo — are to be found. Mules and guides are easily obtained for visits to these more out-of-reach churches.

Leaving Lalibela and its wonders behind, you retrace your steps back to Kobo, where you once again join the main road **south**, on the final leg of your journey back to Ethiopia's capital city. After forty-five kilometres (28 miles), you'll come to the town of **Weldiya**, where a road branches off west to Lake Tana. But you'll continue **south** for another 125 kilometres (78 miles) to Wollo's regional capital of **Dessie**, spread over a small valley at the foot of **Mount Tossa**.

Above: Priest at Lalibela's holiest shrine, the Selassie Chapel, brings what is said to have been the processional cross and walking stick of King Lalibela into the light.

A year after people in the town had seen the Great Comet of 1882, Emperor Yohannes IV christened the place 'Dessie' — which means 'my joy' in Amharic. At the time of the Italian Fascist invasion of 1935-1936, Emperor Haile Selassie moved his headquarters for a time to Dessie.

The town's important position between the lowlands and the plateau — and between Addis Ababa and Asmara — has contributed to its growth as an important commercial centre, and it is served by daily Ethiopian Airlines flights. The major hotel is the Ambasel, which has a restaurant. Although not a tourist centre, the local market with its bustling crowds is interesting to see.

From Dessie to **Kombolcha**, the next town along on the way, is only twenty-three kilometres (14 miles), but the road has some sharp curves as it winds its way down the face of the escarpment. The route is quite a scenic one, lined with clumps of **eucalyptus trees**, cactus (the exotic *Opuntia* spp.), and the rehabilitated hillside of olive forest. Watch your step for the next 113 kilo-

metres (70 miles) to the town of **Senbete** — mist often collects in the small valleys along the route in the early morning, caused by the steam rising from hot springs in the area, and during the rainy season some portions of this road may become inundated.

With the **escarpment** — its top often veiled with clouds — to the **west** and the **Tarmaber Pass** to the **south-west**, the scenery along this route is quite pleasant, and the small village of Senbete makes a nice stopover, particularly on a Sunday for the large **market** held there. Hundreds of people from many different ethnic groups converge to buy and sell cattle and camels, as well as a variety of other items that include high-quality cloth, jewellery, spices, chickens, and chewing tobacco.

If you miss that market, try the town of **Robit** forty-one kilometres (25 miles) further **south**, which has an equally colourful — if not quite as large — **market** every Wednesday. Many picturesque people come from as far away as fifty kilometres (31 miles) to sell tanned and coloured hides, honey, sandals, and agricultural produce.

Passing over the **Robit River**, the road gradually ascends from the Rift Valley floor, through cultivated areas where sorghum, maize, cotton, and tobacco are grown, to the village of **Debre Sina**, located on a hill at the base of the Tarmaber Pass, and continues upwards along the face of the **escarpment** until it cuts through the 3,250-metre-high (10,660-foot-high) mountain via a 587-metre-long (1,925-foot-long) **tunnel**. The stretch of road here again is a most scenic one, affording good views of the **Rift Valley** at several points along the way. After you go through the **Tarmaber Pass** tunnel, look out for a turning on the **left**. It leads up and over one of the tunnels on the main road. From there along the edge you overlook what must be some of the most spectacular scenery in the world. Even on the main road the views from the various vantage points are awe inspiring. Troops of **gelada baboons** can often be seen in this area.

Fifty-seven kilometres (35 miles) further along the main road from Robit there is a rough **track** to the **south** of the road which, after fifteen kilometres (nine miles) of winding round the side of the mountains, brings you to the brink of the **escarpment** above the **Wufwasha forest**. **Gelada baboon**, **rock hyrax**, and some spectacular **birds of prey** can be seen here. Below is one of the few unspoilt **juniper forests**, with giant trees up to sixty metres (197 feet) tall.

Back on the main road, it is thirty-five kilometres (57 miles) to **Debre Birhan**, the last important settlement on the southward journey.

Debre Birhan

Debre Birhan has a remarkable early history. The settlement was founded by one of Ethiopia's most important early rulers, Emperor Zara Yaqob (1434-1468), when at night his compatriots saw a heavenly light over the area. This vision, which was vividly described by old Ethiopian authors, was almost certainly Haley's Comet, which appeared in 1456, in the latter part of Zara Yaqob's reign.

Zara Yaqob, according to his chronicle, thereupon decided to make the place his permanent residence and named it Debre Birhan, meaning 'Place of Light'. He accordingly ordered his chiefs and nobles to collect wild olive trees and other wood for the construction of a palace and a stout surrounding wall, the likes of which no previous ruler had ever erected. The monarch spent much of his time in this palace, and it was there that he must have carried out many of the governmental and religious reforms for which he is remembered. In the vicinity of his palace he also built a fine church, which was fitted, the chronicle proudly claims, with a 'strong lock' — perhaps an innovation of the time.

After Zara Yaqob had lived at Debre Birhan for 'a long time' a major epidemic broke out, killing many people in the capital. The emperor, remembering a divine promise that disease would not come near a place of worship, thereupon erected a new church, called Bet Kirkos, whereupon the epidemic was checked and failed to approach the palace.

Though beloved by Zara Yaqob, the town was abandoned by the monarch's son and successor, Be'ide Maryam, who chose another capital, after which his father's palace and other buildings at Debre Birhan soon fell to ruin. The settlement was not heard of for over two centuries, until a successful Shewan chief called Nagasi made it his residence. Debre Birhan was, however, later used by several of his successors, notably by King Sahle Selassie (1813-1847), who had a fine palace there in which he spent several months a year.

The town was subsequently almost destroyed when the reforming Emperor Tewodros advanced into Shewa in 1855. On that occasion Sahle Selassie's son and successor, King Haile Melekot, ordered that his father's palace should be burnt to the ground.

Menelik, the founder of modern Ethiopia, later resided at Debre Birhan on several occasions. He was so pleased with the area that he ordered the construction in

1865 of a new capital at a nearby place called Liche, five kilometres (three miles) to the north-east, but, under pressure from the then emperor, Yohannes IV, soon abandoned it in favour of Debre Birhan. For several years Menelik considered the latter town his capital but later moved to nearby Ankober. Liche, though abandoned almost immediately after its establishment, is still the site of many stately **ruins** about ten minutes' drive from the road.

Because of its location on the main trade route to the north, Debre Birhan has remained a roadside town of considerable importance. It is the site of a modern **woollen goods factory**, which is on the right side of the road at the beginning of the town. Here are woven the thick **blankets** for the Addis Ababa market. Traditional woollen goods are also in abundance, especially the little **hats** made and worn by shepherd boys and the famous black, white, and brown Debre Birhan **carpets** in traditional designs of lions and birds. You may be able to pick up some good bargains on market day, which is Saturday.

Also of particular interest is the **Selassie,** or **Trinity, Church**, which was rebuilt by Menelik in 1906 and contains many interesting **mural paintings**.

Debre Birhan, with its several hotels and restaurants, is also a convenient base for sightseeing to Ankober and other parts of northern Shewa.

Ankober

Although not on the direct road back to Addis Ababa, it is worth the short detour on a mountainous and beautiful forty-one-kilometre (25-mile) road leading **eastwards** from Debre Birhan to visit the town of **Ankober** — if for the view alone, for it is built on the lip of the great **escarpment**. When driving in areas of high altitude like this, travellers should look out for two interesting and unusual trees: the giant **lobelia** with its tall seed stem, and the beautiful *kosso* (*Hagenia abyssinica*) **tree**, whose rich cascades of red flowers have been used in Ethiopia since time immemorial for the treatment of tapeworm.

An old capital of Shewa region,

Ankober was founded by King Amha Iyesus and was strategically well placed, for it stood on a height commanding the only route leading from the eastern lowlands to the Shewan plateau. The town in the early nineteenth century was one of the principal places of residence of King Sahle Selassie, the founder of the Shewan state, and had a population estimated at between ten and fifteen thousand. The settlement was visited by all the European travellers who made their way to his court. They report that the town was dominated by the king's palace. Most of the buildings in the royal compound were traditional Ethiopian round houses, but a few built by two Greek craftsmen, Demetrios and Yohannes, were of European design. These artisans also erected a **palace**, the remains of which can still be seen, at **Angolela**, situated to the **west** of the present **main road**.

As a capital and the residence of a succession of kings, Ankober was unusual in having had no less than five churches. The oldest, dedicated to Saint George, was built by King Amha Iyesus, the founder of the town, and was surrounded by a beautiful grove of wild fig and euphorbia trees. The next oldest, that of Saint Mary, was erected by Amha Iyesus's son, Asfa Wossen. It was surmounted by a large bronze cross which could be seen from a great distance away, above the dark foliage of the surrounding juniper trees. The three other churches were founded by King Sahle Selassie.

Ankober was partially destroyed at the time of its occupation by Emperor Tewodros in the 1850s but was subsequently rebuilt by Sahle Selassie's famous grandson, King Menelik. The latter made it his capital until he and his court abandoned it in 1878 to move south to Entoto and later to Addis Ababa.

The shift of royal residence resulted almost inevitably in the decline of Ankober, which rapidly shrank in population, though it remained until the end of the century a fairly significant settlement on the trade route to the coast. The lion's share of the country's import-export trade was, however, later taken over by the Ad-

Above: Ruggedly beautiful countryside near Ankober.
Overleaf: The Church of Saint Michael commands an impressive view of the surrounding countryside from its position at the tip of the 'natural cross' on a mountaintop near Gishen north of Dessie.

dis Ababa–Djibouti railway, after which Ankober lost most of its *raison d'etre*. The population then dwindled greatly, the palace and many other buildings of the town were abandoned, and before long they fell into ruin.

Though much of old Ankober has disappeared, the **palace ruins** can still be seen, and the two old round **churches** of **Maryam** and **Medhane Alem**, some of the finest examples of early nineteenth-century Ethiopian architecture, remain well-frequented places of worship. If you park your vehicle in the village, a guide will show the way to these landmarks.

Below Ankober, among the hills, is the village of **Aliyu Amba** — the site of a century-old market and mosque — which can be reached by way of an incredibly steep but well-surfaced fifteen-kilometre (nine-mile) road through some spectacular countryside.

Back at your Debre Birhan base, you may want to ask a knowledgeable local guide to take you to two rather unusual places of interest. **Arubarya Medhane Alem**, **north-west** of Debre Birhan, is one of several places in the country where you'll find **caves** with **mummified corpses** in them. Equally as interesting are communities like **Adjana Mika'el west** of Debre Birhan, where a whole church community lives in **caves** that have been partitioned into dwellings. The **church** itself is also in a cave.

From Debre Birhan it is another 130 kilometres (81 miles) back to **Addis Ababa** — although you may wish to make a small side trip some twenty kilometres (12 miles) before you get to the city, where a turn to the **left** will take you down a long **gravel road** to the **dam** on the **Legedadi River**. The dam, which supplies Addis Ababa with most of its water, was completed in 1970, and the **lake** formed by it is home to a myriad of **water birds**. A small **bar** serves refreshments and, by special arrangement with the Water Resources Development, rooms may be booked at the **guest house** for overnight stays.

The North-East: A River to the Beginnings of Mankind

A journey into Ethiopia's north-east winds its way along with one of the country's major rivers, the Awash, through a landscape that reveals much about millennia of volcanic activity. Rolling hills are interspersed with gorges, craters, and hot springs. Many of the smaller 'crater lakes' and dams are within easy reach of Addis Ababa.

The route passes through two of Ethiopia's nine national parks: Awash and Yangudi-Rassa. Although each is bordered on one side by the Awash River, these are mainly dry country parks, and the wildlife here reflects that. Beisa oryx, greater and lesser kudu, gerenuk, Grevy's zebra, and two species of baboon can be seen in this area, as well as the rare predecessor to the domestic donkey, the wild ass.

At Hadar, on the boulder-strewn volcanic floor of the Great Rift Valley, a breathtaking archaeological discovery was made in 1974: an almost complete hominid skeleton at least 3.5 million years old — humankind's oldest known ancestor.

The northern portion of the route leads into still drier country, the fascinating but forbidding Danakil Depression, where the land has dropped — in places to more than 100 metres (328 feet) below sea level.

A few scattered, highly saline lakes nearby complete the geological picture of this region — lakes that are the only reminders of the time when the inrushing waters of the Red Sea flooded the area following the subsidence of the Rift.

But to begin your journey to the north-east, you must first travel south-east from Addis, on the Debre Zeit (Bishoftu) Road, to the town of the same name.

Getting there

Debre Zeit, fifty kilometres (31 miles) from Addis Ababa, is served by a good tarmac road, as are most of the towns *en route* to Awash National Park, which is on the main Addis-Assab highway.

When to go

This part of the country is good to see at any time of the year, but is particularly worth visiting if you wish to escape Addis Ababa during the 'big rains' between June and September.

Where to stay

In Debre Zeit, the Hora Ras Hotel, and the Bekele Mola Hotel. New hotels are also appearing rapidly with the opening up of the economy. In Mojo, the Total Motel and Bekele Mola Hotel. In Nazaret, the Bekele Mola Hotel, the Adama Ras Hotel, which has a swimming pool, and the new Plaza Hotel. See Listings.

Sightseeing

As you head out **south** of Addis Ababa on the **Debre Zeit road** (where Dejazmach Beyene Merid Street and Beyene Aba Sebsib Avenue merge), it is worth visiting the beautiful **Bihere-Tsige Flower Garden**, which is located about ten kilometres (six miles) from the Piazza. To get there, turn **right** at the **sign** opposite the **Saint Joseph cemetery** and follow the road down over the **railway**, veer **right** and you will find the entrance to the garden on your **left**. This 400,000-square-metre (478,000-square-yard) horticultural wonder features more than 6,000 varieties flowers, shrubs, and trees. The **Akaki River** flows through the grounds. With its small restaurant, the garden makes a delightful stopping-off point and is a popular venue for wedding parties.

Mount Zuqualla

Back on the main road to Debre Zeit and thirty-five kilometres (22 miles) from Addis Ababa is the village of **Dukem**, which marks the turn-off for another enjoyable detour: the volcanic cone of Mount Zuqualla, which towers some 600 metres (2,000 feet) over the surrounding

Above: A spectacular view and a beautiful crater lake reward those who venture to the top of Mount Zuqualla, just south of Addis Ababa.

countryside. After passing a **fruit stand** (which sells grapes from the nearby vineyards) on the **right** and the **bridge** before the Dukem, begin to look for an obscure **dirt track** on the **right** in the middle of the village. Turn **right** onto this track, which takes you past some **stables** on the **left**. Nearby, at an **intersection**, bear to the **right**, taking the route passing between two houses. This will lead to another small village, **Wember Maryam**, at the base of Mount Zuqualla. An **alternative route** is to take a **secondary** road that starts in the middle of Debre Zeit town and turns **right**, leading to the **south-west** and Zuqualla.

The winding, steep **road** that goes to the summit is very rough and suitable for strong four-wheel-drive vehicles only, so you may opt to go by foot. If that is the case, park your vehicle at Wember Maryam and hire a watchman (*zebenya*) to guard it. Hire another villager as a guide, who will point out the shortcuts to the top. But be warned: the climb is strenuous and takes about three hours up and two-and-a-

half hours down. It is well worth the effort, however, when you see the **panoramic view** down the **Rift Valley** to the **east**, the **lakes** to the **south**, and **Mount Entoto** and **Addis Ababa** far to the **north**.

Two kilometres (1.2 miles) across and sixty metres (197 feet) deep, the **crater** is occupied by a shallow **lake**, well known as a holy lake. For many centuries there has been a **monastery** at the top of the mountain. Ahmed Gragn destroyed one of the buildings, but the octagonal church of **Gebre Menfes Kidus** was rebuilt in 1912 and is still in use today. Twice a year, in March and October, the *tabot* comes out of the church and is carried processionally around the lake before it is carried back into the church. Many pilgrims come for the festivities, which are quite colourful and interesting to see — similar to the *Timkat* celebrations.

The inside rim of the crater is covered with juniper and eucalyptus forest, as well as a heavy growth of trailing lichens. You can climb down the 800 metres (250 feet) or so to the edge of the crater lake if you

Above: Boating, water-skiing, and bird-watching are popular activities at Hora Lake, by Debre Zeit.

wish, but swimming is prohibited by the local clergy. Don't forget to bring your binoculars: **bird life** abounds, and the beautiful black-and-white **colobus monkey** can sometimes be seen.

Debre Zeit

From Dukem, it is only about ten kilometres (six miles) to the thriving town of **Debre Zeit**, which is also known by the Oromo name of Bishoftu, and is the site of the **air force base** and the **veterinary institute**. At an altitude of 1,900 metres (6,200 feet), it enjoys a warmer climate than the capital city. This, together with the fact that the town lies within a circle of **five crater lakes**, makes it a popular weekend resort for Addis Ababa residents. Just before entering Debre Zeit on the **right** side of the road there is a **fruit juice cafe** where refreshing drinks and various other foodstuffs are on sale. The terrace of this little bar overlooks shallow **Lake Chalaklaka**, which is the periodic feeding ground for thousands of **flamingos**.

The town itself is resplendent with pepper trees, bougainvillea, flame trees,

and frangipani. Its main **hotel**, the Hora Ras, is situated off to the **left** of the main highway on the rim of the largest **crater**, **Hora Lake**, where **boating** and **water-skiing** are popular and there are many species of **birds** to be seen, including **cormorants**, **pelicans**, **grebes**, **shovellers**, **storks**, and a myriad of brightly coloured **passerines**. You can enjoy a good meal or just sip a cool drink from the terrace of the hotel, which affords a splendid view of the lake below.

There are also **camping facilities** by the lake. Swimming is not recommended. At the end of the rainy season — usually around the beginning of October, a big, colourful **festival** to celebrate the beginning of the spring planting season is held under huge fig trees at the lake shore across from the hotel.

Continuing down the same road, you drive past the **Veterinary Training Centre** on your **right** before coming to two more **lakes**: **Babogay** on your **left** and **Kuruftu** further down the road on your **right**. Other lakes in the area worth a visit are **Green Lake** — famous for its

Above: Small but cheerfully painted local hotel at Debre Zeit.

bird life — and the deep **Lake Bishoftu**.

Twenty-six kilometres (16 miles) on from Debre Zeit is the town of **Mojo**, where two main roads — one leading south to the Rift Valley lakes and Kenya; the other east to Nazaret, Awash, and Harar — intersect. There are one or two small **restaurants** here, which cater essentially to the in-transit motorist, and two small **hotels** provide basic accommodation.

Hippo pools

Keeping straight on towards Nazaret, an interesting side trip can be made to the **Koka Dam** and a nearby **hippo pool** on the **Awash River**, about ten kilometres (six miles) off the main road. This side road, however, is hard to locate. Between Mojo and Nazaret, look on the **right** for a small section of **tarmac road**, which becomes a good **gravel road**. This is the road that leads to the dam, built with funds given to Ethiopia as part of Italy's war reparation.

To get to the hippo pool, a local guide is essential. The correct track leads to a simple **gate** where a small **entrance fee** is collected by the owners of the track — be sure to keep the ticket to give back on the way out. Past the gate, you'll continue on a rough narrow route following the river. Watch for **hippo** and **crocodile**, and listen to the sounds of the many **birds**. At the main **viewing point**, you can park your vehicle and walk along the river a short distance to see the surfacing hippo — or even try your hand at **fishing**, if time permits.

You can continue on this **track** through the **Wonji Sugar Estate**, which will put you back on the **main road** just inside **Nazaret**.

Named after the biblical settlement of Nazareth, this fast-growing agricultural and commercial centre is one of the biggest cattle collecting points in the country, and — because it is surrounded by **papaya and citrus plantations** — is known to be a place from which to buy excellent fruit. Again, graceful pepper trees, colourful bougainvillea, flame trees, and frangipani abound in the town's streets, and a pleasant stay can be had at the Adama Ras Hotel, built around its central swimming pool. Several other hotels also provide reasonable accommodation.

From Nazaret, the main road now turns to the **north-east** and heads for Dire Dawa, following the sole **railway line** in the country. After about twenty-four kilometres (15 miles) you will come to the small village of **Wolencheti**, and some twenty kilometres (12 miles) past that the road enters a tortured landscape with volcanic features. This rugged terrain contains many **lesser kudu**, often considered the most beautiful of the antelope. Other wildlife that may be seen along the road here are the **greater kudu**, **klipspringer**, the tiny **dik-dik,** and oryx.

It is all really a lead-up to the 'main event' on this journey: one of the country's most popular national parks.

Awash National Park: Craters and Kudus

Awash National Park is situated in the lowlands to the east of Addis Ababa, on the main **Addis-Assab highway**, which bisects the park. Its southern boundary is, in part, the **Awash River**, one of the major rivers of Ethiopia, which swings north soon after leaving the park and eventually disappears into the wastes of the Afar (Danakil) region.

The park covers an area of 827 square kilometres (319 square miles), most of which lies at an altitude of around 900 metres (2,950 feet). In the middle of the park is the dormant volcano of Fantale, reaching a height of 2,007 metres (6,583 feet) on its rim. Temperatures in the park are hot and can reach as high as 42°C (107°F). Nights are cooler, with temperatures between 10° and 22°C (50° and 72°F). Rain mainly falls between February and April, and June to August, and averages 619 mm (24 inches).

Getting there

Awash National Park is 211 kilometres (131 miles) from Addis Ababa, 95 kilometres (59 miles) from Nazaret, 146 kilometres (90 miles) from Debre Zeit, 273 kilometres (169 miles) from Dire Dawa and 277 kilometres (172 miles) from Harar. It is easily reached in about a three-and-a-half hour's drive along the main Addis-Assab Highway, a good tarmac road.

When to go

All times of year are suitable for a visit, but the flush of green growth after the start of the rains (February and June) marks a particularly good time.

Where to stay

In Awash National Park, accommodation is provided by a **caravan lodge**, called Kereyu Lodge, on the edge of the gorge. The caravans are very basic — no running water, just a bucket — but there is a **restaurant** and the view is outstanding. Other than this view, the site is hot and unscenic. The lodge does have a small **swimming pool** but more than likely it will not be filled with water, which is scarce in this area. Beware of the over-bold **baboons** and definitely do not feed them. Reservations for the lodge can be made in advance through tour agents in Addis Ababa. See Listings.

The far better alternative is camping at sites situated on the edge of the river, above the falls. Large spreading trees provide ample shade and shelter a wonderful collection of birds. All equipment will need to be brought, and food must be carefully guarded against the bold **grivet monkeys**. One tap provides river water, which is not suitable for drinking. All drinking water will need to be brought into the park. Malaria can be a serious problem, and visitors must take precautions. The nearest medical help is in Metahara.

In Awash town, the Buffet de la Gare (also known as the Buffet d'Aouache) provides accommodation and good food at reasonable rates.

Sightseeing

Ninety-one kilometres (56 miles) past the village of Wolencheti, the road crosses the **railroad track** and **Lake Basaka** is visible to the **right**. This lake is a **bird sanctuary,** which supports **cormorants**, **herons**, and

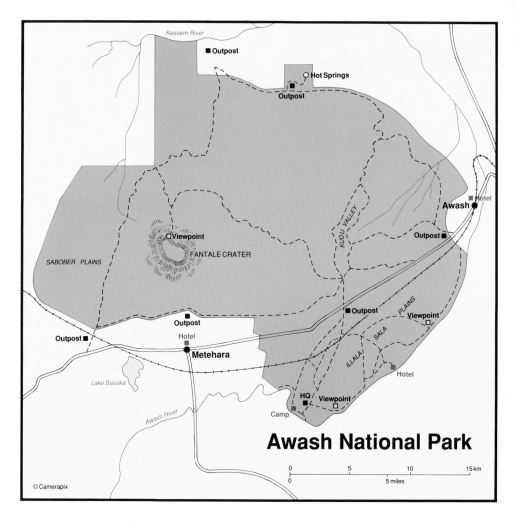

Awash National Park

Kessem River

■ Outpost

○ Hot Springs

■ Outpost

Hotel

Awash ●

■ Viewpoint

Outpost ■

FANTALE CRATER

SABOBER PLAINS

KUDU VALLEY

PLAINS

■ Outpost

Viewpoint □

■ Outpost

Outpost ■

Hotel

SALA

● Metehara

ILLALA

Hotel

Outpost ■

Lake Basaka

HQ Viewpoint □

Awash River

Camp

```
0        5        10        15 km
0              5 miles
```

© Camerapix

other water birds and is visited by **pelicans** and **flamingos** from other areas of Ethiopia.

Just across the railroad track is a **road** to the **left**, which runs behind Fantale to the **Aware Melke Plantation**. It is possible to take this road and drive to the top of Fantale and then down and on to the main park entrance, but this should only be attempted with a guide and a 4WD vehicle.

It is probably wiser to pass through the town of **Metahara**, about ten kilometres (six miles) after which you'll find the **main entrance** to the park on your **right**. This will allow you to travel comfortably down towards the **Awash River**, which constitutes the southern boundary of the park. The road leads to the **park headquarters**

and the **campsites**, which are situated near the dramatic **Awash Falls** where the river enters its gigantic gorge. A small **museum** is also located here, which houses various stuffed birds, mammals, and reptiles, as well as some educational and interpretative materials on the area's flora, fauna, geology, and peoples. From the campsites, you can take a short drive west, following the river, or drive a few hundred metres to the Awash Falls viewpoint, where concrete stairs lead down to the river below the falls.

The park is traversed by a series of well-maintained tracks, which take in the most spectacular of the many scenic attractions. For a small fee, it is possible and advisable to hire a park guide at the headquarters.

Above: The Awash forms the southern boundary of the Awash National Park.
Overleaf: The park headquarters and campsite are situated near the dramatic Awash Falls, where the river enters its gigantic gorge.

Sometimes you are allowed in the main park, on the left of the road, only with an armed guide/guard — especially if the local people have been fighting among themselves.

Vegetation here is typical of a hot, dry area. The plains are covered by grass species and scattered small trees. Areas of shallow soil over rock are covered in dense thickets of acacia species. The rocky valleys to the north of the park are heavily bushed. Along the river is a thin belt of dense riverine forest, including large fig trees.

One of the main features of the park is the **Fantale volcano**, on the southern flank of which can be seen the dark scar of the latest **lava flow** of 1820. The slopes of the mountain hold evidence of former sixteenth-century dwellings, seen as remains of walls and settlements of considerable proportion. The interior of the mountain-top crater — where the wispy white breath of steam vents can be seen — is still used by the local people, the Kereyu, for grazing their livestock on a seasonal basis.

In fact, the Kereyu and their cattle are often spied inside the park, especially in times of drought. In 1993, they had even built villages directly below Kereyu Lodge. Under pressure from the government, they reluctantly moved out in early 1994, but the issue of land rights and Kereyu involvement in the park is far from resolved.

Hot springs

Another feature of the park is the **hot springs** or *Filwoha* (meaning 'hot water'), situated in the extreme north of the park. These can be reached by either one of two **scenic tracks**, which start opposite the **main gate** on the far side of the road and bear **right**, progressing either along the floor of the beautiful lower **Kudu Valley** or along the top of the **ridge**. Ask at the gate about road conditions and take a game scout with you to avoid any problems with the local people.

The water of these springs and rivers is in the region of 36°C (97°F) and is used by

Above: Beisa oryx share a shady spot in Awash National Park with a Swayne's hartebeest, an endemic subspecies.

---

the local people for watering stock. The unbelievably clear blue pools surrounded by doum palms invite the dusty traveller to wash off the dust of the day — but be warned, the water is hot.

The **plains** to the **south** of the main road are excellent for game viewing and are bordered to the south by the spectacular **Awash Gorge**, plunging 250 metres (820 feet) to the river. The western end of the gorge is marked by the Awash Falls, which can vary in intensity from a murky reasonable flow to a raging chocolate-coloured torrent, depending on the rainfall and the activity of the hydroelectric scheme at Koka.

The wildlife of Awash reflects its dry nature. The **Beisa oryx** is seen on many of the more open areas, and **greater** and **lesser kudu** in the bushed areas. **Soemmering's gazelle** have distinctive white rumps and are often seen with the oryx. A small population of the endemic subspecies **Swayne's hartebeest** was translocated here, but only a handful now remain. The tiny **Salt's dik-dik** appears frequently under the dry acacia bushes and **Defassa waterbuck** are seen in the bushed area by the river. There are two species of **baboon** here — the **Anubis** and the **hamadryas**. Though each species has very different social structures, they hybridize in the area near the river. Other **monkeys** seen are **colobus** in the riverine forest and **grivet** in drier areas. Fantale crater provides a different habitat, supporting **mountain reedbuck** and **klipspringer**. **Crocodile** and **hippopotamus** are seen both in the Awash River and in the cooler parts of the hot springs and rivers in the north. **Lion**, **leopard**, **serval**, **caracal**, and **wildcat** are all seen infrequently.

Bird life

The **birds** of Awash are numerous, with more than 300 species on record. A checklist is available at the park headquarters museum. The campsites near the museum, in fact, are an excellent place to sight birds. Here, above the quiet murmur of the river, one can hear the exuberant chatter of **green wood-hoopoes**, the rollicking duet of **red-and-yellow barbets**, or the soft lament of the **emerald-spotted wood dove** — to name only a few. **Carmine bee-eaters** manoeuvre over the water, homing in on their airborne prey.

There are several **bustard** species in the park and **secretary birds** can be seen in the grass plains. The raptors are represented by **fish eagles**, **tawny eagles**, **lanner** and **pygmy falcons**, **black-shouldered kites**, and **dark chanting goshawks**. **Bee-eaters** and **kingfishers** provide splashes of colour, as do the **rollers**. **Ostriches** stalk across the plains and the immense **lammergeyer** soars above Fantale searching for bones to smash.

Bordering the park, a twenty-eight-kilometre (17-mile) stretch of the Awash River offers a superb one- or two-day **rafting trip** — if the water level allows it — featuring lots of spirited rapids, wildlife, and impressive rugged cliffs and side canyons. The trip starts at the Awash

Falls and ends at the beach below the town of Awash Station, with an optional overnight at small hot springs sacred to the Kereyu people. (See 'Shooting the Rapids: White Water Rafting in Ethiopia', Part Four.)

Awash Station

Named after the Awash River, which the road and railway both cross at this point, the town of **Awash Station** adjoins the national park and is near a wide plain that abounds in oryx and gazelle. On Mondays, there is a colourful Afar **market** here, where authentic Afar and Kereyu crafts and decorations can be found. Awash is the midway stop for the train between Dire Dawa and Addis Ababa, and the Buffet de la Gare provides accommodation — as well as cold beers and delicious Greek and Italian cuisine — at reasonable rates and is redolent of a bygone era. The two elevated rooms at the back — known as the Imperial Suites — have large bathrooms (albeit with cold water), but bring a net or coils in case of mosquitos. The Buffet serves as a good stopover for those who prefer to drive shorter distances while en route to Dire Dawa and Harar or points north.

Shortly after Awash Station is the point where the road divides, one route running **northwards** to the Red Sea port of Assab; the other eastwards to Dire Dawa (see 'The East: Railway to the Sea', Part Two). Take the former to venture even further into the north-east of the country. This road is known as the 'Assab Road', for it eventually ends up — 666 kilometres (413 miles) from Awash — at the Eritrean Red Sea port of Assab.

Head **north** from Awash, where the road swings left to follow the Awash River, and after driving 153 kilometres (95 miles), you'll come to the town of **Gewane**. This is true Afar country, and you will undoubtedly see many of these nomadic people in the town.

Hostile and fierce, proud and individualistic, the Afar use the camel as their beast of burden but also keep sheep, goats, and cattle on the edge of the Afar (Danakil) region or in the vicinity of the Awash River, where coarse grass grows. This grass is not only for grazing — it is used for making the woven mats that cover the small round huts in which the women and children sleep.

The Afar women dress in long brown skirts and adorn themselves with gaily beaded necklaces and brass anklets, while the tall, dark, and bearded men wear a cotton cloth like a toga across the shoulder and usually carry a huge forty-centimetre (16-inch) knife — their universal weapon and tool. Men also carry rifles and belts full of bullets.

In the few fertile areas near the Awash River, the Afar are able to grow maize, tobacco, dates, and cotton, as well as support vast herds of livestock. Most of them live on a diet of meat and milk, sharing their food with each other as they share everything else they possess within their clan. However, interclan competition and rivalry is often fierce.

The nomadic hut in which they live is made of an armature of boughs bound with palm fibre and covered with mats, and is owned by the women. This is the only piece of property not held in common. The huts are placed in groups, usually surrounded by a hedge or wall to protect their animals from rival clans and other ethnic groups. When on the move, the hut is loaded on camels by women, who will erect it in a new location later. The women also collect the wood and water, prepare the food, grind the grain (when there is any), weave the mats and milk containers, and look after the herds.

Occasionally one will see a more permanent type of Afar dwelling, called a *dabou*, in areas of sandstone or pumice. Two-and-a-half metres (eight feet) high with thick walls and thorn and rubble roofs, these houses are inhabited by clan elders and others not involved in herding.

Gewane serves as a base from which to visit one of Ethiopia's lesser known — and lesser visited — national parks.

Above: Stark white minaret of the Asaita mosque stands out dramatically against a cloudless blue sky.

Yangudi-Rassa National Park

The little-developed **Yangudi-Rassa National Park** is 4,730 square kilometres (2,933 square miles) in area, with altitudes of 400 to 1,459 metres (1,300 to 4,800 feet). Temperatures are high, as in Awash National Park. Very little rain falls in this semi-desert — hence the vegetation is semi-arid grass and trees with succulent scrub.

Getting there

Yangudi-Rassa is about sixty kilometres (37 miles) from Gewane and is bisected by the main Assab road.

When to go

As temperatures are hot, it is better to visit during the cooler months between December and February.

Where to stay

There are no facilities in the park, but camping is allowed anywhere. Yangudi-Rassa is administered from the town of Gewane and visitors may stay there. Be forewarned: malaria can be severe in the area, and full precautions must be taken. It is advisable to bring your own mosquito net if you plan on staying overnight here.

Sightseeing

Travel **north** from Gewane for about sixty kilometres (37 miles), where the park is situated to the **east** of the **Assab road**. There is no specific entrance point or park headquarters. **Tracks** within the park are passable to certain distances. It is best to enquire at the Wildlife Conservation Office in Addis Ababa before you go as to current conditions.

Yangudi-Rassa was created for the protection of the **wild ass**, an endangered species and ancestor of the domestic donkey. There are also **gerenuk, Soemmering's gazelle, Beisa oryx, Grevy's zebra,** and **hamadryas baboon** here — all indicators of the dry habitat. The park is also considered excellent for its **bird life**.

Crossing the **Awash River** as you head

out of the park, head once again **north** on the main **Assab Road**, where, about eighty kilometres (50 miles) past the town of **Mille** — just past the town of **Semera** — a **dirt track** leads **north** to the famed **archaeological site** of Hadar. It was here that the oldest evidence of human origins yet discovered was unearthed in the form of 'Lucy' or *Dinkenesh* — a fossilized skeleton of a female hominid who walked this part of the earth more than three million years ago. (See 'History: From *Dinkenesh* to Dynasties', Part One.) The area remains an active archaeological site: digs are ongoing and discoveries continue to be made. It is best to arrange your visit beforehand with the Regional Tourism Bureau in Asaita.

Not far past the town of **Semera** there is also a **turning** to the **south**, which, after forty-nine kilometres (30 miles) leads to the town of **Asaita** and — after another thirty kilometres (19 miles) — to the town of **Affambo**. It is from these two places that you can explore the chain of **saline lakes** that mark the end of the Awash River as it comes to rest in the Afar (Danakil) region.

A word of warning, however. While in principle an official permit is not necessary to visit a place like Asaita, its traditional self-view as autonomous makes it the sort of place you would not want to casually roll into, following a map. It is best to clear your visit to this area first with an Asaita regional representative in Addis Ababa or the Regional Tourism Bureau in Asaita. Make thorough enquiries about security in the area.

All the lakes are scenically beautiful, with abundant **bird life**. They are best visited by hiring a knowledgeable villager from one of the nearby towns as a guide, as the tracks leading to the lakes can be difficult to find. **Lake Gamarri** is the first in the chain and can be found by taking a **rough track** from the town of Asaita, while lakes **Affambo** and **Bario** are closer to the town of Affambo. A **dirt track** past Lake Bario follows the Awash River until it comes to the last lake — and the largest — in the chain: **Lake Abbe**, on the Djibouti border. **Zebra** and **wild ass** can often be

seen grazing in the countryside here.

The Assab Road continues on into Eritrea and up to the Red Sea, but this — and any route to the north from here — is only for serious and well-prepared expeditions. It is better to backtrack at least as far as **Mille**, where eight kilometres (five miles) further on, a **road** to the **west** will lead to a change of scenery and a pleasant alternative route back to Addis Ababa.

Bati

Ninety kilometres (56 miles) after the turnoff from the Assab Road is the bustling town of **Bati**. Try to time your visit here for a Monday, as that is **market day**. You'll be joined by as many as 10,000 other people, as Bati has long been the site of Ethiopia's largest cattle and camel market and — with the exception of Addis Ababa's Mercato — the largest market of any kind in the country. The Afar from the eastern lowlands come here, bringing their wares by camel to sell in the highlands. Items of particular interest for sale at this colourful market are *amoles* (salt bars) from the Danakil Depression; coffee and spices; herbs, lentils, and vegetables; and a variety of products that include soap, coffee cups, beads and trinkets, knives, pins and nails, and batteries. Among the many **curios** that can be purchased at the market are jewellery and wooden stools.

If you plan on staying any length of time in this area, it is best to overnight in **Kombolcha** or the Wollo capital of **Dessie**, where there is a choice of reasonable hotel accommodation.

It is at Kombolcha, in fact, where you turn **south** to begin your trip back to **Addis Ababa** — a journey of about 374 kilometres (232 miles) — that leads through some breathtaking **Rift Valley** scenery and **Debre Birhan**, a town of historical interest. (See 'The Historic Route: Mountains and Gorges, Mystery and Grandeur', Part Two.)

The East: Railway to the Sea

Harerge, the easternmost region in Ethiopia, covers a striking variation in land and people. The area is home to some of the best coffee in the world.

In the south of the region, Somali-speaking nomads wander across endless red wastes of savannah, in a landscape dotted with termite mounds, with their herds of camels and cattle, following the sparse rains. Eastwards, dust, wind, and the baking heat of the merciless midday sun create an environment where only the strong and cunning survive.

Although the region is largely desert and low-lying savannah, Harerge's northern reaches are mountainous and fertile, and it is here where the country's only stretch of railway bisects the tip of the region, leading from the nation's capital to the port of Djibouti on the Gulf of Aden.

This railway, which plays an extremely important role in the modern Ethiopian economy, carrying a large share of its imports and exports, was first conceived by the Swiss craftsman Alfred Ilg, who arrived in the country in 1877 to take up the post of technical adviser to Emperor Menelik. It was a mammoth undertaking and fraught with problems.

For every kilometre of line, more than seventy tonnes of rails, sleepers, and telegraph poles had to be transported — not to mention sand, cement, water, and provisions for the workers. The terrain was difficult: two large viaducts and many smaller earthworks had to be built within the first fifty or so kilometres of line, and others further inland. To minimize cost, a narrow gauge of only one metre was adopted, but expensive iron sleepers had to be used in view of the presence of termites, which could be expected to consume anything made of wood.

While costs continued to soar, the French, British, and Italian governments began to haggle over the 'international-ization' of the line. It all came to a head in December 1906, when the three foreign countries, without consulting Menelik, signed a Tripartite Convention 'dividing' Ethiopia among themselves. By this agreement the British and Italians recognized that any railway between the Djibouti border and Addis Ababa should belong to France, while the French government agreed that the line should extend no further than Addis Ababa.

The Tripartite Convention spelled an end to hopes of internationalizing the railway. The French government ordered the railway company to repay its debts to the British and, since this was impossible, it was liquidated in January 1908. A new railway company was established two months later, under the control of a French bank.

The line was eventually extended to Akaki — twenty-three kilometres (14 miles) from Addis Ababa — by 1915, and eventually reached the capital two years later, a full twenty years after the beginning of construction work at Djibouti. The service, which has operated ever since, traverses a line of 785 kilometres (487 miles), has twenty-nine tunnels — one of them nearly 100 metres (328 feet) long — and thirty-four stations.

Although the original agreement specified that the line would run inland by way of Harar, the railway company soon realized that they could save money by avoiding the Harar mountains and instead pass through the nearby lowlands. It was therefore decided that the line should run to a place which Menelik chose to call New Harar — later better known by its local name, Dire Dawa.

Dire Dawa: Railway Town

The town of Dire Dawa, which was almost entirely the creation of the railway, sprang

---

Opposite: Busy Bati has long been the site of Ethiopia's largest cattle and camel market and is second only to Addis Ababa's Mercato as the largest market of any kind in the country.

Above: The town of Dire Dawa was almost entirely the creation of Ethiopia's only railway line, which runs from Addis Ababa to the port of Djibouti.

into existence in 1902 when the railway builders, advancing inland from the coast, reached that point on the line. The railway company then ran into financial and other difficulties, with the result that construction of the line stopped and the town remained the railway's terminal for over a decade.

Getting there

Dire Dawa, 453 kilometres (281 miles) from Addis Ababa, 278 kilometres (172 miles) from Awash Station and fifty-four kilometres (33 miles) from Harar, is served by road, rail, and air, through daily flights of Ethiopian Airlines.

The railway runs overnight and daily services, seven days of the week, between Dire Dawa and Addis Ababa. The journey takes between ten and twelve hours, and there are three classes. Tickets should be purchased twenty-four hours in advance and are very reasonably priced.

When to go

Dire Dawa can be visited at any time of the year.

Where to stay

The good, new Sai Hotel (no alcohol); the Ras Hotel, which has a restaurant and a swimming pool; the reasonable and clean Omedla Hotel, and the old Continental Hotel, near the railway station.

Sightseeing

From **Awash Station**, keep **right** when the road forks, one leading north to Assab and the other heading **east** towards Dire Dawa. The village of **Asebot** is about sixty kilometres (37 miles) further on. Several kilometres off the main road to the north-east is **Asebot Mountain**, at the top of which is one of Ethiopia's most famous monastic enclaves: the **monastery of Asebot**.

Twelve kilometres (seven miles) down the road from Asebot is **Mieso**, which marks a **junction** of two roads, both of which lead to Dire Dawa.

If you have a four-wheel-drive or other sturdy vehicle, you may choose to carry on **straight** on the **old main road**. However, because of security problems and flooded rivers during the rainy season, it is best that you check on the local situation at either Mieso or Dire Dawa before you set out. This route is about 160 kilometres (99 miles), some twenty kilometres (12 miles) shorter than the alternative, which, however, is easier, safer, faster, and much more scenic.

Haven for mountain nyala

For the latter route, turn **right** at **Mieso** and pass through the town of **Asbe Teferi**. If you turn **right** in the town on an all-weather dirt road, eighteen kilometres (11 miles) later you'll come to the **Kuni-Muktar Mountain Nyala Sanctuary**, established in 1990 to provide a second conservation area for the endemic **mountain nyala** (the first is Bale Mountains National Park). It comprises two small hills, with areas of natural forest on the peaks, as well as open grassland and plantation forest. The **World War II battle site** of **Gasera** is reached by travelling through the sanctuary. Again, it is best to check with local authorities before you visit this area, as there are occasional security problems.

Back on the **main road** at Asbe Teferi, head for the town of **Arbereketi**, where you'll turn **left** (**east**) towards Dire Dawa. From here it is a 126-kilometre (78-mile) pleasant drive along a very scenic stretch of road to the town of **Kulubi**, where each year at the end of December, the annual **renewal of the miracle of Saint Gabriel** is held. Tens of thousands of pilgrims converge on the **church** up the hill from the town, usually either in fulfilment of a vow or, in the case of the afflicted, in hope of a miraculous cure. The truly faithful and sturdy actually walk the sixty-some kilometres from Dire Dawa to the church.

About thirty-one kilometres (19 miles) past Kulubi is the **junction** with the main Dire Dawa-Harar road, at Dengego village. A turn **left** will take you into **Dire Dawa**, a town of about 98,000 people. Dire Dawa consists of two distinct settlements, separated by the **Dechatu stream**, which for most of the year is only a dry bed but during the rains flushes into a torrent.

Railway town

To the **north** and **west** of this water course lies 'Kezira'. This is the 'modern' half of the town, which was planned, and at first largely erected, by the railway's engineers. This area consists of the **railway station** and its installations, stores, and workshops, as well as many houses, shops, offices, and other modern buildings.

This part of town differs from most other Ethiopian settlements in that it was constructed in a carefully thought-out manner, with straight, asphalt roads and well-aligned buildings. It is also unusual in having piped water, which comes from two nearby natural **springs**, and a drainage system.

On the other side of the river lies '**Megala**', site of Dire Dawa's very substantial traditional **Kefira market**, which handles an immense variety of goods. A melting pot for the peoples of the surrounding region, this market is surrounded by an agglomeration of local Arab-style houses, which are painted in various hues and are set in a maze of winding, unplanned streets.

With **camel trains** plodding in from the dusty plains and Somali, Afar, and Oromo people hustling about in a variety of different types of traditional dress, this section of town is particularly colourful.

Don't use your vehicle to get around here; it is much more fun to take advantage of the **horse-drawn buggies** (*gharis*), which provide a cheap taxi service.

The town also is home to cement and textile factories, a number of well-stocked shops, two cinemas, two secondary schools, and two hospitals. Ask in Dire Dawa for directions to the nearby **caves** — some featuring **stalactite** and **stalagmite** formations — with **prehistoric paintings**, evidence that humans have inhabited this part of Africa for more than 20,000 years.

The caves and their paintings provide a fitting transition for the startling contrast of your next move into the living past: the walled city of Harar.

Above: The impressive Shewa Gate, one of seven entrances to the walled city of Harar.

Harar: Window on the Past

Harar came into formal existence in 1520 when a local amir, Abu Beker Mohamed, moved his capital there from Dakar, site of an older nearby settlement. His rule, however, was soon cut short, for he was murdered five years later by Ahmed ibn Ibrahim al Ghazi, better known as Ahmed Gragn or Ahmed the Left-Handed. Gragn left his homeland in 1530-1531 to begin a *jehad* or holy war against the Christian Ethiopian empire. He overran much of it, but as a result of Portuguese intervention was defeated and killed in 1543. (See 'History: From *Dinkenesh* to Dynasties', Part One.)

The city, impoverished by war, faced many difficulties. The Oromo advanced into the surrounding countryside, isolating Harar and causing Gragn's nephew and successor, Nur ibn al-Wazir Mujahid, to erect strong encircling walls, which ever since that time have been one of the city's most dominant features.

For the next three centuries Harar remained an independent, inward-looking, and often militantly theocratic city state. However, the town was an important trading centre, issuing its own currency. Its many inhabitants included merchants who travelled far and wide, particularly to Egypt, Arabia, and India. Others were engaged in agriculture and grew excellent coffee as well as the mild stimulant *chat* (*Catha edulis*).

Harar also was, and still is, well known for its handicrafts, including weaving, basketmaking, and bookbinding. The town was also renowned for its Islamic learning and scholarship.

Harar ceased to be an independent city state in 1875 when the Egyptians, then bent on establishing an East African empire, occupied it and killed its ex-ruler, Amir Abd al-Shakur. The Egyptian occupation, however, lasted only a decade, after which another amir, Abdullahi, took over. He was later defeated by King — later Emperor — Menelik in 1887, after which Harar became an integral part of the Ethiopian empire. In the ensuing period many foreigners settled in Harar, among them the famous French poet Arthur Rimbaud, who spent some of his last years in the city.

The first ruler of Harar after Menelik's occupation was his cousin Ras Makonnen, a progressive aristocrat interested in modernization. He was responsible for introducing the country's first hospital and leprosarium. Despite such developments Harar was adversely affected by the construction at the turn of the century of the Djibouti–Addis Ababa railway. The line was originally planned to pass through the city, but for reasons of economy was subsequently diverted to Dire Dawa. Much of Harar's trade in consequence moved to Dire Dawa, with the result that Harar was left a city living largely in the past.

Ras Makonnen is today best remembered as being the father of Emperor Haile Selassie. The latter, who was born in the vicinity of the city, was brought up in Harar and subsequently served as one of its governors. He long afterwards appointed his second son, Prince Makonnen, as governor of Harerge region and created for him the title of Duke of Harar.

Getting there

Harar, which has no airport, is 523 kilometres (324 miles) from Addis Ababa, 332 kilometres (206 miles) from Awash Station and fifty-four kilometres (33 miles) from Dire Dawa. It can be reached by a good, scenic asphalt road.

When to go

Harar can be visited at any time of the year.

Where to stay

The town has an old but satisfactory government hotel (the Ras) and several private ones, but many people prefer to stay at Dire Dawa.

Sightseeing

Head **south-east** out of **Dire Dawa** along the winding, fifty-four-kilometre (33-mile) **asphalt road** between the railway town and **Harar**, said to be one of the most scenic in the world. It follows the edge of a **stream** up

a large **valley** where **camels** are often seen bearing their loads. During the winding ascent to the escarpment, the road — resurfaced in 1994 — climbs almost 800 metres (2,600 feet) in less than twenty-five kilometres (15.5 miles) and, once you reach the top at Dengego, affords a spectacular view of the **Rift Valley** plains below.

Twenty-nine kilometres (18 miles) out of Dire Dawa the road passes by **Lake Adele**, with its numerous **ducks** paddling near the reed-lined shore. After another five kilometres (three miles), you'll see **Lake Alemaya**, near **Alemaya** village, on the **left**. A **road** just past the village leads to the first-rate **Alemaya Agricultural University**, where there is a small **zoo**. But continue on the **main road** for another twenty kilometres (12 miles) or so to reach Harar, the capital of Harerge region, situated just off the southern edge of the **Chercher Mountains** in a semi-arid setting with a view of the hills — where some of Ethiopia's best **coffee** is grown — falling away beyond.

Harar is a fascinating and enjoyable place to visit. It is advisable, however, to obtain the services of a guide when entering the old town. Not only can you easily get lost, but in some quarters there is an element of hostility — especially from children — to foreigners.

On reaching the town and entering its stout old **walls**, the traveller meets the Harari, or Adare, as they are called by the neighbouring Oromo. For the most part, the Harari live in two-storeyed, rectangular flat-roofed brown stone or whitewashed houses set in a labyrinth of narrow winding streets. This style of house — called a *gegar* — is unique in Ethiopia and is reminiscent of the coastal Arab architecture.

The main room has raised platforms of various levels to determine the status of guests and household members. In this area, the inside walls are painted with ochre or red earth and covered with woven cotton cloth or carpets and elaborately decorated with bowls, dishes, basketry, and other hand-crafted items made by the women. Usually eleven niches are set in the wall for displaying cups and pots.

A bright splash of colour is provided by the Harari women strolling through the town, often dressed in red, purple, or black

Above: Harari women add bright splashes of colour to the town with their brilliantly hued clothing.

Opposite: Harari homes are unique and reminiscent of coastal Arab architecture. Bowls, dishes, and basketry are hung in stylized fashion on the wall, but all are functional.

dresses with velvet trousers and bright orange shawls and balancing heavy bundles of cloth or baskets on their heads.

Travelling outside the walls one enters a different and apparently more modern world, with twentieth-century type villas and offices, as well as the **government hotel**. Harari homes on this side of the wall are generally the more traditional 'grass house': a hut with a wattle and daub circular wall and a centre pillar supporting a conical thatched roof.

Harari men build both kinds of houses and make major repairs, but it is the women who do the day-to-day maintenance.

Places of interest inside the city include the impressive centuries-old **walls**, which originally had five **gates** until 1889, when under Menelik's rule, two more were erected. At the centre of the city is a **circular piazza**, and from here there are streets leading to each gate in the city wall.

On the **central square**, facing the main street, is the Ethiopian Orthodox Church of **Medhane Alem** (Redeemer of the World), which was erected by Menelik II towards the end of the nineteenth century. The church contains many traditional **religious works of art**.

In the centre of **Ras Makonnen Square** is an equestrian **statue** of the ras, cast in bronze by well-known Ethiopian artist Afewerk Tekle. Facing the square is part of the **Military Academy**, founded by Emperor Haile Selassie, which is decorated with interesting **stained glass windows** depicting Ethiopian rulers of the past, designed by the same artist.

Also of interest is **Ras Makonnen's palace**, a stately old building, and the **Jami Mosque**, dating back to the seventeenth century. Women are not allowed to enter and photography is not permitted.

Near the mosque is the fine, large **Rimbaud House**, said (incorrectly) to have once been occupied by the famous French poet of that name.

There are two small markets in the walled town. The **Muslim Market** is quite photogenic, with its white buildings and colourfully dressed women selling their fruit, grain, baskets, and other wares. On the north side of the market is a small, white mosque-like structure, which is the **tomb** of Abu Said Ali, an early Muslim religious leader of the town. Beneath his tomb is said to be a **well** that can provide water for the entire town in case of siege.

143

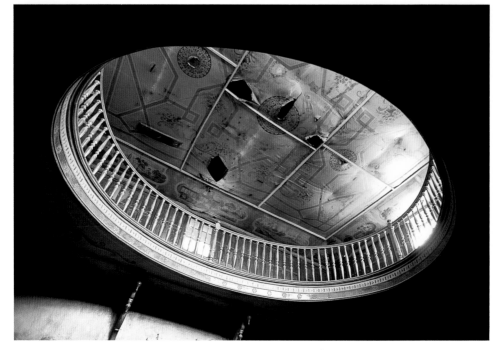

Above: Architecturally interesting interior of the famous Rimbaud House at Harar, said (incorrectly) to have once been occupied by the famous French poet of that name.

The **Christian Market** is separated from the other market due to a custom arising partly from tradition and partly because some products are prepared in a manner that prohibits Muslims from using them.

Hararı women have been known for their **basketwork** for centuries and still weave intricate creations from coloured fibres and grasses. Harar is also famed for the work of its **silversmiths**, who craft beautiful anklets, necklaces, arm bands, silver chains, bangles, and earrings out of the precious metal. Although these items can be purchased at the market, some of the best selections can be found in the homes of the craftsmen and women. These **'shops'** are scattered throughout the town, but local guides will direct a visitor. The **leprosarium** at Bisidimo, on the road to Jijiga, also has an excellent selection of baskets for sale.

There are also two museums in Harar: a **government museum** housing a variety of **antiquities** from Harar and nearby regions, including **memorabilia** of the patriot Dejazmach Tefera. Make sure to visit the roof of this building for a superb view of the city.

A **community museum** attached to the **Cultural Centre**, where the visitor may drink *kuti*, a delicious local brew made from coffee leaves and milk, has a variety of exhibits relating to the Harari culture.

Hyena men

Harar is also famous for its **'Hyena Men'** who, as evening falls, set themselves up at points along the outskirts of the city. These men make their living by laying on a remarkable show, throwing meat, offal, and bones to packs of wild **hyena** that come down from the surrounding hills, apparently answering to names which the Hyena Men chant hypnotically. The few Ethiopian birr that the watchers are expected to pay are well worth the privilege of being party to so bizarre a spectacle.

A day-long excursion (if you start early) is possible from Harar to visit the Valley of Marvels (also called Rock Valley), the Babille Elephant Sanctuary, and the town of Jijiga. It is probably best that you check on the security of this area before you begin your trip.

Above: An incredible feature of Harar is the 'Hyena Men', who bravely feed — by hand and mouth —the unpredictable beasts each evening on the outskirts of the city.

Travelling **east** from Harar on a graded **gravel road** that leads to the Somali border, look back for some attractive **views** of the old walled town before all signs of urban life are left behind. About twenty kilometres (12 miles) from Harar, after passing through the hills east of the city, there is a well-marked track to the right of the main road. Turn here and continue for about five kilometres (three miles) to Bisidimo, one of the first rehabilitation and training centres established for lepers. Here one can find excellent baskets and carpentry items for sale and also learn the history of the settlement.

Back on the main road, after another ten kilometres (six miles) you'll come to the town of **Babille**, the site of **hot thermal springs** used to supply much of eastern Ethiopia with bottled water. Ten kilometres (six miles) beyond these springs the road passes through the fascinating **Valley of Marvels**. Given its name by the Italians, the valley is filled with unusual **volcanic formations** where tall columns of black and red rock, withered and twisted by the elements, stand topped by loose, precariously balanced boulders.

Babille Elephant Sanctuary

South of Babille is the large — 6,982 square kilometres (4,329 square miles) — **Babille Elephant Sanctuary**, which sits at an altitude of 1,000-1,788 metres (3,280-5,865 feet). The sanctuary consists of semi-arid open woodland and contains an unknown number of mammals, including **black-maned lion, kudu,** and **wild ass**. It was created for the protection of the endemic subspecies of **elephant**, *Loxodonta africana orleansi*, but visitors are unlikely to see any as they are few in number and very shy. Eighty kilometres (50 miles) north-east of Babille is **Jijiga**, an important administrative and commercial centre, situated at the bottom of the foothills of the Chercher Mountains and looking on to a vast **plain** that merges into the Ogaden. The daily **market** here is a good place from which to buy such articles as yellow or golden amber necklaces, silver jewellery, and beautifully woven mats.

The South-East: Highland Wilderness

For most visitors to Ethiopia, the south-east can be summed up in two words: Bale Mountains. For it is this mountain range that dominates the landscape, rising from the extensive surrounding farmlands. At its epicentre is the spectacular Bale Mountains National Park, an area of high-altitude plateau that is broken by numerous dramatic volcanic plugs and peaks, beautiful alpine lakes, and rushing mountain streams that descend into deep, rocky gorges on their way to the lowlands below.

As you ascend into the mountains you will experience changes in the vegetation with altitude, from juniper forests to heather moorlands and alpine meadows, which at various times of the year exhibit an abundance of colourful wild flowers.

The national park is the largest area of Afro-alpine habitat in the whole of Africa, giving unlimited opportunities for some fantastic mountain walks, horse trekking, scenic driving, and the chance to view many of Ethiopia's endemic mammals and birds.

The Oromo

As you pass through the small region of Arsi and into Bale, which is largely bordered by the winding Wabi Shebele River, you'll no doubt meet members of the predominant ethnic group in this area: the Arsi Oromo.

The Oromo are divided into six main groups and about 200 subgroups, in each of which you may find slight variations on the dominant cultural structure. The *gada* system — or government by age-groups — is universal throughout the groups. (See 'The People: Proud of Their Ancient Heritage', Part One.)

The people vary considerably in physical type but on the whole tend to be tall and handsome. The men wear the typical Ethiopian white toga, called a *waya*, and, in addition to clothing made of cotton, the women often still wear leather, decorating the skins with embroidered beadwork, and wear lavish bead, copper, and heavy brass jewellery.

The Arsi Oromo are true herdsmen. Their beasts have ritual status and are surrounded by all manner of beliefs and superstitions. On the more practical side, cow dung is used for fuel, milk pots, floors, and walls; diet consists of meat, milk, blood, butter, and cheese as well as barley bread. Ownership of cattle is a status symbol: a man who owns more than a thousand is entitled to wear a crown.

Oromo houses are built by the men, although the women help with the thatching. There are three main types of dwelling (*mana*); the first two are the more usual, circular structure. Their main difference is in the shape of the roof, one being steeply domed, the other much flatter with an overhang. The third type is also domed, but the rafters are planted in the ground and form both the walls and the roof. Other Oromo ridicule this type of hut, saying that the Arsi live in 'birds' nests'; most houses are finished with an ostrich egg or pot at the apex.

The Arsi Oromo are one of the most southern of the Oromo groups, extending east into Harerge and south into Bale on both sides of the Wabi Shebele River.

Getting there

Dinsho, where the headquarters of Bale Mountains National Park is located, is 425 kilometres (263 miles) from Addis Ababa, 176 kilometres (109 miles) from Awasa, 210 kilometres (130 miles) from Asela and forty-six kilometres (28 miles) from Goba. It is served by a good gravel road.

When to go

The best time to visit is late October to December, when the flowers are still in full display but rain is less likely.

Where to stay

In Sodere, Sodere Resort Hotel; also campsites. In Asela, the Ras Hotel and the Ketar Hotel. In Dinsho, a self-help lodge provides rooms and bed as well as a kitchen block incorporating a sauna/

Above: Arsi Oromo women gather outside a typical home, which is often finished off with an ostrich egg or a pot at the apex.

shower unit. Bedding is available for hire, but you may prefer to bring your own. In Robe, the rather dingy Bekele Mola Hotel. In Goba, the Ras Hotel. See Listings.

Camping is possible in Bale (for those who wish to trek into the mountains, with or without horses, this is essential), both within the park and, with permission, at the park headquarters at Dinsho. All equipment, particularly warm sleeping bags, will need to be brought in, including food, although there is a small local market twice a week. The water in the area is safe to drink, being from either rain or stream in origin.

Remember that the sun at these altitudes can burn strongly and sun screen lotions and hats should be used. Rain, which can become icy cold sleet, can fall at most times of year and it is advisable to have warm, waterproof clothing and to pitch camp by early afternoon if travelling at a wet time of year.

The nearest medical help is in Goba.

Sightseeing

There are two routes from Addis. The first, which is more asphalted than the other, travels along the floor of the **Rift Valley**, past the lakes of **Langano, Abijatta**, and **Shalla** to **Shashemene**, where there is a major **left turn** to Goba (See 'The Rift Valley: Land of Lakes and Remote Wilderness', Part Two).

The second route takes you via **Nazaret** and Asela. But before you get on the main road to Asela, you may wish to take a detour to visit the village of **Sodere**, a favourite weekend or day retreat for Addis Ababa residents. To get there, turn **right** at the first main **intersection** in Nazaret and then **left** at the little village of **Melkasa**, home of an agricultural research station, where an **asphalt road** leads to Sodere. The resort itself takes advantage of the volcanic **mineral springs**, which bubble to the surface to fill the hotel's two blue **swimming pools** with clear, hot water; and of the nearby **Awash River**, which lends a

147

part of its riverine forest to provide giant shade trees.

There is **hotel accommodation** (make reservations through the Filwoha Baths in Addis), **camping** possibilities, a **restaurant**, and a new, fully equipped conference hall accommodating 150 people. Walks in the surrounding countryside afford views of **vervet monkey** and **baboon**, as well as **crocodile, hippo,** and a wealth of bird life.

Backtracking slightly to **Melkasa**, turn **left** now and head **south** for some fifty-nine kilometres (37 miles) to **Asela**, the capital of Arsi region. A twentieth-century settlement, Asela has been the site of considerable agricultural development since the end of World War II.

This road takes you **south** along the eastern wall of the **Rift Valley**, below the **Arsi Mountains** to the **east**. Once over the pass between **Mount Kaka** and **Mount Nkolo** you'll drop down to the plateau area around **Dodola** — 123 kilometres (76 miles) from Asela — where you join the route into the mountains from Shashemene. The road climbs then into the **Bale Mountains**, a spectacular ascent up the **Zetegn Melka Valley**.

Twenty-nine kilometres (18 miles) from Dodola, you'll pass through the town of **Adaba**. This charming settlement holds a **market** every Tuesday, where thousands of people flock from the nearby countryside, as well as from the more distant area of Arsi.

The road first meets the park near **Sebsebe Washa**, a rocky outcrop to the **left** of the road, where a notorious bandit is said to have had his hideout. The **main road** crosses the northern end of the park in the **Gaysay Valley**, and the **park head-quarters** is just beyond the small village of **Dinsho**.

Bale Mountains National Park

Bale Mountains National Park is 2,400 square kilometres (1,488 square miles) in area, covering a wide range of habitats and ranging in altitude from 1,500 to 4,377 metres (4,920 to 14,357 feet), the highest point in southern Ethiopia. The area of the park is divided into two major parts by the spectacular **Harenna escarpment** that runs from east to west. North of this escarpment is a high-altitude plateau area, which is formed of ancient volcanic rocks and dissected by many rivers and streams that have cut deep gorges into the edges over the centuries. In some places this has resulted in scenic **waterfalls**.

Temperatures on the plateau range from -7°C to 26°C (19°F to 79°F) depending on the season. The dry season is cold at night and hot during the day, while the wet season has more moderate temperatures. The rainfall is high, averaging 1,150 mm (45 inches), and usually falls between March and October, as well as other months.

The vegetation here is graded according to altitude. Around Dinsho, in the north, there are grass riverine plains, bordered by bands of bushes, particularly *Artemisia afra* (sagebrush) and *Hypericum revolutum* (St. John's wort). Wild flowers such as *Lobelia* spp., *Geranium* spp., *Kniphofia foliosa*, and *Alchemilla* spp. form carpets of colour. Fringing the hills are stands of *Hagenia abyssinica* and *Juniperus procera* and above them are montane grasslands. Higher up the mountains heather (*Erica* spp.) grows, either as small bushes or as mature trees. The high Sanetti Plateau at 4,000 metres (13,120 feet) is characterized by Afro-alpine plants, some coping with the extreme temperatures by becoming small and others by becoming large. The best example of the latter is the giant lobelia (*Lobelia rhynchopetalum*), whose stems stand high against the skyline.

Wild flowers are many and various, but the dominant plants are the *Helichrysum*, or 'everlasting' flowers. The everlastings can be seen in many forms, but the grey bushes of *H. splendidum* are most striking, especially when covered with their yellow flowers. Also attractive are the silver grey-green cushions of *H. citrispinum* — but be warned, these cushions are full of fine spines.

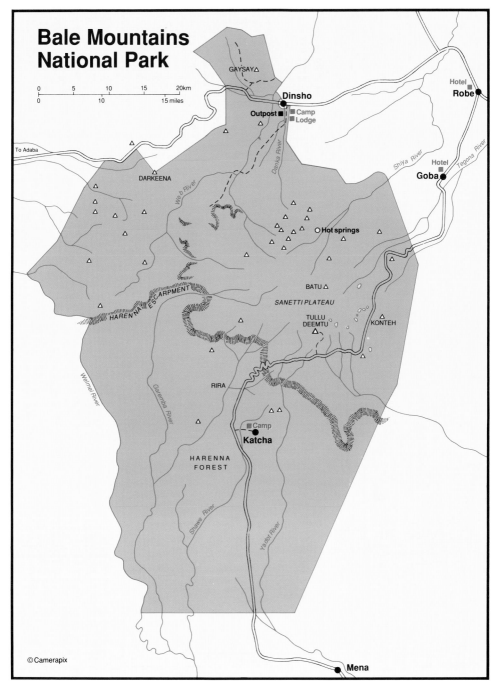

Bale Mountains National Park

0 5 10 15 20km
0 10 15 miles

To Adaba

GAYSAY △

Dinsho

Outpost ■ ■ Camp
■ Lodge

Danka River

Shiya River

Hotel ■
Robe ●

Tegona River

DARKEENA

We'b River

Hotel ■
Goba ●

○ Hot springs

BATU △

SANETTI PLATEAU

HARENNA ESCARPMENT

TULLU
DEEMTU △

KONTEH

Welmel River

Garemba River

RIRA

■ Camp
Katcha ●

HARENNA
FOREST

Shawe River

Yadot River

© Camerapix

● **Mena**

The southern part of the park is heavily forested, after the land falls away from the high plateau in a dense heather belt, draped with many lichens. Below this, the forest is zoned according to altitude and includes genera such as *Podocarpus*, *Hagenia*, *Schefflera*, *Rapanea*, and *Celtis*.

Sightseeing

The park can be divided into three main regions. The north is riverine plains, bushland, and woodland, and there are many animals to be seen here. The centre of the park is a high plateau of 4,000

149

Above: The chestnut-red coat of the endemic Simien fox is in strong contrast to the grey vegetation of the Bale Mountains National Park, where it is most likely to be seen.

metres with many small peaks rising from it, including the highest point in southern Ethiopia, **Tullu Deemtu**. Here, the **Simien fox**, or jackal, is most easily seen. The plateau is crossed by the highest all-weather road in Africa. The southern part of the park is forest.

The wildlife of Bale includes many endemic species. The park was originally established to protect two of these: the mountain nyala and the Simien fox, which, despite its name, is more frequently seen in Bale than in the Simien Mountains National Park. The **mountain nyala** are best seen in the **Gaysay** area of the north where they spread out over the grass plains. Other wildlife here includes **Menelik's bushbuck**, an endemic subspecies in which the males are a very dark colour, numerous **Bohor reedbuck**, **grey duiker**, **warthog**, **serval cat**, **colobus monkey**, and **Anubis baboon**.

The high plateau is particularly noted for the Simien fox, whose chestnut-red coat is in strong contrast to the grey vegetation. It preys on the numerous species of rodent found here, the biggest of which is the **giant molerat**, *Tachyoryctes macrocephalus*. This subterranean animal, endemic to the Bale Mountains, can weigh as much as one kilo (2.2 pounds).

The forest of the south is so thick that animals are difficult to see, but there are three species of pig here — **warthog**, **bushpig**, and **giant forest hog**. There are also **lion**, **leopard**, **spotted hyena**, and rarely, **African hunting dog**, which is normally found in much more open habitat.

The **birds** of Bale include sixteen endemic species, many of which are easily seen. These include **wattled ibis**, **black-winged lovebird**, **blue-winged goose**, **Rouget's rail**, and **thick-billed raven**. **Wattled cranes** are often seen on the high plateau in the wet season, when they breed.

There are three ways to explore Bale Mountains National Park: by four-wheel-drive vehicle, by foot, or by horse.

Driving

Although the park is better suited for

Above: The stately and beautiful mountain nyala, another of Ethiopia's endemic species, is best seen in the Gaysay area in the north of Bale Mountains National Park.

walking or riding, being a mountainous and fragile environment, there are nevertheless a few **roads** and **tracks**, which can be negotiated with a four-wheel-drive vehicle.

A good area to explore first is **Gaysay**, which provides a good morning's or afternoon's wildlife watching and should not be missed by any visitor to the Bale Mountains. The area derives its name from the little Gaysay River that flows into the Web River near Dinsho.

As you drive from the direction of Dodola, the **main road** crosses part of the Gaysay area just before reaching Dinsho. The **park entrance gate** lies just **north** of the main road seven kilometres (4.3 miles) before the village, and a **small track** from the gate leads you across the **Gaysay River** and then divides at the base of the mountain. The **eastern** arm affords good views of the plains west of the **Web River** and goes for four kilometres (2.5 miles) to **northern boundary fence** at the small **Albabo stream. Colobus monkey** are often seen in the *Hagenia* forest before the first

stream crossing. There is a small **photographic hide** about ten minutes' walk up the first stream through lovely *Hagenia* trees.

The **left fork** of the track goes for three kilometres (two miles) to the **northern boundary fence** around the west flank of **Boditi Peak**. There are good views of the **Gaysay Valley** and its associated marshes brimming with **reedbuck**.

The Gaysay area guarantees every visitor views of the endemic **mountain nyala** in considerable numbers — as many as 400 have been seen here in a single afternoon. In addition there are numerous **grey duiker, warthog**, and **Menelik's bushbuck** with beautiful jet-black males. **Colobus** and **baboon** are sometimes seen here and, if you have sharp eyes, the beautiful **serval cat** can be seen hunting in the long grass. On very rare occasions **leopard** are sighted, and sometimes a pair of the endemic **Simien fox. Birds** abound, especially in the forested areas, and are usually heard if not seen.

Another spectacular drive is the one

Above: Delicately leaved thistle in Bale is one of the country's many endemic species of flora.

from **Goba south** to Dolo-Mena, which crosses the eastern part of the national park and the **Sanetti Plateau**. This is the **highest all-weather road** in Africa, and crosses the 4,000-metre (13,120-foot) contour through some of the loveliest mountain scenery on the continent that can be viewed from the comfort of your vehicle. In early 1994, it was even possible to drive on a track off the main road to the top of Tullu Deemtu — Ethiopia's second-highest mountain at 4,377 metres (14,357 feet).

The **road** climbs up from Goba through beautiful juniper and *Hagenia* forest. In the wet season the red-hot poker (*Kniphofia*) blooms beneath the trees, attracting brilliant iridescent **Tacazze** and **malachite sunbirds**. The forest gives way to giant St. John's wort (*Hypericum revolutum*) woods — a narrow zone that is soon succeeded by heather (*Erica*) moorlands. Then you are out of the forest and into the open of the mountains proper. Vistas reach out to the strange pinnacles of **Chorchora Peak** on the **left**, one of the park boundary markers, and across the sheer-sided **Tegona River Gorge** on the **right**.

Another steep zigzag climb across heather and scrub-covered slopes takes you to the **plateau**, through portals of weird five-metre (16-foot) tall columns of giant lobelia. The plateau is studded with numerous shallow **alpine lakes**, with views to the steep-sided volcanic plug of **Konteh Tullu** to the **south** and the long, craggy ridges of **Mount Batu** — 4,203 metres (13,786 feet) — to the **west**.

The **road** continues climbing gently now, past **Crane lakes** at the base on Konteh. This is the centre of the best area for seeing **Simien fox** and, on rare occasions, **mountain nyala**. The spectacular views can be even more awe-inspiring if you take the steep climb to the top of Konteh, or the longer (one-and-a-half hour) climb to the summit of domed **Tullu Deemtu** (meaning 'red mountain' in the Oromo language) to the **west** of the road.

The main road skirts the base of Tullu Deemtu and continues south to the edge of the **Harenna escarpment**, forty kilometres (25 miles) from Goba, before descending through a series of breathtaking hairpin bends. The initial heather scrub gives way after a few kilometres to *Hagenia*, heather, and St. John's wort forest; later merging into lush *Podocarpus* forest: enormous trees covered in mosses, ferns, and 'old man's beard' lichens. This continues down the small **escarpment** of **Rira**, where, looking back, you see the tall **rock towers** of **Gujurule**, their tops often shrouded in cloud and mist. Around their base is glorious mixed forest with bamboo and many clear, sparkling **streams** that are the source of the **Shawe River**, which the road later crosses before it ends, almost 100 kilometres (62 miles) from Goba.

The **park boundary** is shortly before this as you cross the **Shisha** — a small tributary of the **Yadot River**. The forest gives way abruptly to dry, lowland wooded grasslands at about 1,600 metres (5,250 feet), and about ten kilometres (six miles) later the little village of **Dolo-Mena** is reached. Dolo-Mena is 110 kilometres (68 miles) from Goba, but a reasonable undertaking for a day's drive is from Goba to the southern edge of the plateau, with perhaps a descent of the escarpment into the forest below, followed by the return to Goba. A good **campsite** exists at Katcha, after Rira on the **left** of the road, along a track to a **quarry**. This is a good base for walking in the bamboo forest and, for the more energetic, exploring the Gujurule volcanic plugs.

A third, rough, eleven-kilometre (seven-mile) **track** leads **south** from the **park headquarters** compound at Dinsho. This track crosses the interesting **natural bridge** over the **Danka River**, where **hyrax** can be seen. It then runs beneath cliffs through heather to the edge of the **Web River Gorge**. It ends in a broad, flat valley, from where it is an easy forty-minute walk to the beautiful **Finch'Abera waterfall**, where the Web and Wolla rivers join. If you are lucky you may see **Simien fox** in the area at the end of the track.

Walking

Bale Mountains National Park is essentially a walking area, with short walks being easily accomplished in the Dinsho area, or from anywhere along the roads and tracks within the park.

One of the easiest walks begins at **Dinsho headquarters**, where a one-kilometre (half-mile) **nature trail** leads up **Dinsho Hill**. This gives a brief introduction to the plants and animals of the area. There is the added opportunity of seeing **mountain nyala** at close quarters on foot in the fenced **sanctuary** here. From the top of the 3,240-metre (10,630-foot) hill, good views on a clear day in all directions help in understanding the layout of the park.

Walking on **Gaysay Hill** is rewarding in terms of the views and the chances of seeing wildlife at close quarters. The fittest will find the steep climb to the **Boditi** summit — at 3,520 metres (11,545 feet) — worthwhile for a spectacular view of the **Gaysay River** flats and south into the main park areas.

A very enjoyable day-long walk can be had from Dinsho up the **Web Valley** to **Gasuray peak**, at 3,325 metres (10,908 feet). A traverse of the uplands to the north along the connecting spur to the **Adelay ridge** leads you through beautiful heather and grass glades with the strange grey hummocks of *Helichrysum citrispinum*, one of the 'everlasting' flowers. **Mountain nyala**, **klipspringer**, **Menelik's bushbuck**, and **warthog** are commonly encountered here. A steep descent off the north-east corner of Adelay brings you back down to the **main road** and **Dinsho** village.

The **Sanetti Plateau** is crowned by several peaks that add a good walk to the drive over it. Although **Konteh Tullu** looks formidable, only twenty minutes of steep scrambling from its base gives magnificent views from the top in all directions. Starting from the main road at its base, it takes one-and-a-half hours to reach the summit of **Tullu Deemtu**. **Hares** and **rodents** abound up here, despite the sparse vegetation cover. **Mountain nyala** are often seen below the summit to the south.

Mount Batu, a short distance to the north, is a longer walking prospect but can be done in a long day from the plateau road. The mountain is very craggy and more rugged than Tullu Deemtu in appearance, and seemingly more mountainous, although it is a few metres lower. A **leopard** has been sighted near the top, as have klipspringer and **mountain nyala**, while montane **birds** such as the **chough** and **lammergeyer** soar overhead. It is strongly recommended that a guide be taken for the climb up Mount Batu.

Horse trekking

Although short riding trips can be arranged in the Dinsho area, it is far more worthwhile to set aside at least four days to enjoy a horse trip to the full. Arrangements are best made beforehand by letter or phone, but horses can be organized for a morning departure if requested the previous afternoon.

Various routes can be followed, and it is best to take the advice of your local guide from Dinsho. A particularly nice route is to travel up the **Web and Wolla valleys** from Dinsho, where you pass the **Finch'Abera waterfall** before reaching the beautiful **campsite** of **Moraro** at 3,750 metres (12,300 feet). Next day, travel up the **Wasama Valley** beneath the **peaks** of the same name, stopping to see and taste the strange **mineral springs** before making the steep ascent onto the **Sanetti Plateau**. Camp beneath **Mount Batu**'s crags at the head of the **Shiya Valley** before climbing Batu the next day. You can ride across the 'arms' of the Batu horseshoe and camp beside lovely **Gabra Guracha Lake**, set beneath towering cliffs in the head of the **Tegona Valley**. On the last day, ride across the plateau and its lakes to be met by your vehicle at the Goba–Mena road. (The horses return to Dinsho at their own pace.)

An alternative route is to cross from the **Wasama** to the **Worgona Valley**, past the magnificent sheer cliff of **Arch'aah**, or ride down the side of the **Shiya Gorge** from the base of **Batu** into the **Worgona Valley**. From here a steep ascent across one of the **Kara Worgona passes** then leads down into the **Danka Valley**, past **Batu Tiko**'s craggy plug. Camp overnight beneath the strange **'balancing' rocks** and return to Dinsho in an easy stage the next day.

Slightly longer trips can be made ascending the **Web Valley** all the way to its source near **Mora Bowa mountain**, then turning **east** through one of the passage-

ways between the strange **lava flows**, or **Rafu** with its **rock pillars** on the edge of the **Kubachenna Gorge**. These take you onto the **Sanetti Plateau** further south, from where you can return to Dinsho via Wasama, Moraro, and Wolla — alternatively ride on across the plateau and its lakes to Tullu Deemtu or Batu and the road beyond to be collected by your vehicle.

Wildlife densities are not high on any of these trips, but what you do see will be surprising and unusual. Birds abound, especially water birds on the lakes and streams.

Fantastic fishing

The other 'supreme attraction' of Bale is the thirteen **mountain streams** and many ice-cold **tarns** that teem with fat and beautiful **brown and rainbow trout**. Stocked with fry from Kenya in the 1960s, these fish have flourished in the mountain waters and offer a challenge few fly-fishers would wish to resist. The self-help lodge at Dinsho is the headquarters of the **Bale Trout Fishing Club**. (See 'An Angler's Paradise', Part Four.)

Once you have thoroughly explored the fascinating Bale Mountains, a thirty-two-kilometre (20-mile) drive **east** will lead you to what have essentially become the 'twin towns' of **Robe** and **Goba**, although Goba is slightly to the **south** of Robe. Goba, which was founded as a regional capital early in the nineteenth century, lies under a 2,775-metre (9,100-foot) high mountain wall and has its own **airstrip**, as well as a **governor's palace** and administrative buildings. Some kilometres from the town are the remains of an old **rock church**. Although Goba is by far the largest town in this part of the country, Robe is the faster growing and livelier of the two. Goba's market, in the heart of the town, and the sprawling Robe market, on a flat plain adjacent to that town, are well worth a wander, with some very well-made baskets and thick hand-spun woven cotton blankets, *buluko*, on sale, as well as the usual assemblage of extremely photogenic people — but remember to use tact before attempting photography.

Sof Omar: Caves of Mystery

Follow the **road east** from Goba for 120 kilometres (74 miles), through a low valley filled with thorn trees and weird funnels of **termite hills**, and you'll come across one of the most spectacular and extensive underground **caverns** in the world: the **Sof Omar cave system**. Formed by the **Web River** as it changed its course in the distant past and carved a new channel through limestone foothills, the Sof Omar system is an extraordinary natural phenomenon of breathtaking beauty.

Here, the Web River vanishes into this giant underground world with its arched portals, high eroded ceilings, and deep, vaulted echoing chambers. These caves, now an important **Islamic shrine** named after the saintly Sheikh Sof Omar, who took refuge here many centuries ago, have a religious history that predates the arrival of the Muslims in Bale — a history calibrated in thousands, not hundreds, of years.

The first religions of this part of Africa revolved around spirit worship and ghost cults in which the most powerful supernatural beings were believed to attach themselves to trees, rocks, and, most forcefully, to caves, which became places of veneration where prayers were offered up and sacrifices made. Even today, the visitor to Sof Omar will see many signs of the persistence of such pagan beliefs and practices.

The **approach** to the caves is made through the tiny **village** of **Sof Omar**, perched on the cliffs above the Web River. To the rear of the village is a dark, gaping **crevice** down which a precipitous narrow **footpath** winds to the floor of the **first cave**.

You can explore the caves on foot, without special climbing equipment, but you must take proper precautions and not go alone. Torches or other lighting are needed, and another must is the map provided in the official brochure, available from the Ethiopian Tourism Commission as well as at the site. Local guides will also carry a copy of the map.

In this realm of dry, cool caves nature has worked a marvel of architecture — soaring pillars of stone twenty metres (66 feet) high, flying buttresses, fluted archways, and tall airy vaults. Finally, the river itself is reached, a sunless sea flowing through a deep gorge. Standing on a balcony near the roof, one has a spectacular view of the river rushing along its course below.

The large central hall of Sof Omar, the 'Chamber of Columns' — so named after the colossal limestone pillars that are its dominant feature — is one of the highlights of the cave system. At another part of the network there is a small gap in the rocks through which the river passes, about two-and-a-half metres (eight feet) wide, where a **bridge** can be made with driftwood to go across. The most direct route through the caves passes these and many other remarkable sights, and takes about an hour at a good walking pace.

Inside the caves, the only living creatures are **bats** (which do not usually trouble the visitor), **fish**, and **crustaceans**. **Crocodile** are to be found in the river nearby but, perhaps fortunately, seem to shun the caves themselves. The countryside around abounds with wildlife — **dikdik** and **kudu**, **serval cat**, **rock hyrax**, **giant tortoises**, **snakes**, and **lizards** as well as more than fifty species of **birds**.

Shek Husen

Back on the **main road** from Goba, continue heading **east**, where the road takes a **sharp bend** as it crosses the **Web River** and begins to head **north**, where you'll pass through the towns of **Ginir** and **Jara** before coming to Shek Husen, seventy-eight kilometres (48 miles) north of Ginir. The site, Ethiopia's most important place of Muslim pilgrimage, is situated on the borders of Arsi and Bale regions and quite close to the border of Harerge.

Shek Husen is visited twice a year by many thousands of pilgrims from all over eastern Ethiopia, and comprises a large complex of **mosques**, **shrines**, and **tombs** surrounded by a **stout wall**. There are also

Above: The eerie but beautiful Sof Omar cave system is one of the most spectacular and extensive underground cave systems in the world.

a number of man-made **caves** and artificial **ponds** in the area. Holy white chalk from the caves is taken back by the pilgrims to many parts of the country.

Although the map shows a 'dry weather road' leading from Shek Husen to join up with the main Asela–Nazaret road, it is impossible to cross the Wabi Shebele River, which intersects the **road** just **west** of the town, so you have to retrace your steps back through **Goba** for the return journey to Addis Ababa.

The Rift Valley: Land of Lakes and Remote Wildernesses

A journey into the south-western portion of Ethiopia is as much a 'pilgrimage' to naturalists as a trip to the north is to historians. Beautiful scenery, a chain of sparkling lakes, abundant wildlife and bird life, and a kaleidoscope of colourful cultures all combine to make this part of the country unique.

Of course, it is the topography of the remarkable Great Rift Valley itself that adds much to the appeal of this region. Funneled between two dramatic escarpments, this representation of the last great massive movement of the earth is home to a marvellous string of lakes that stretch from Ethiopia south into Kenya, Tanzania, and beyond. Interestingly, each Ethiopian lake has its own character, even those that lie side by side.

In addition to its chain of lakes, the Ethiopian section of the Rift also boasts a 'chain' of fascinating national parks: Abijatta-Shalla, Nechisar, Mago, and Omo — again, each unique in its own way.

This part of the country is also home to many diverse peoples and cultures: the Dorze, famed for their weaving of cotton cloth; the Konso, who for centuries have practised terracing and intensive agriculture in their steep land. Along the Omo River, the Karo, Geleb, Bume, Mursi, Kwegu, Bodi, and others live a life that is still principally nomadic or pastoral, with some hunting and gathering or fishing.

Unaffected by the ways of the modern world — so near and yet so far from them — these people remain as remote and unchanged as the land in which they live.

Getting there

Abijatta-Shalla Lakes National Park, 215 kilometres (133 miles) from Addis Ababa, 145 kilometres (90 miles) from Mojo and fifty-five kilometres (33 miles) from Lake Ziway, can be reached by a good asphalt road.

When to go

The area is pleasant at any time of the year, but the rainy months between March and April and June and September bring a fresh flush of grass and are a good time to visit.

Where to stay

In Debre Zeit, the Hora Ras Hotel and the Bekele Mola Hotel. In Mojo, the Total Motel and Bekele Mola Hotel. In Meki, the Bekele Mola Hotel. In Ziway, the Bekele Mola Hotel. At Lake Langano, the Bekele Mola Hotel, the Wabe Shabelle Hotel; also private chalets and campsites. See Listings.

At Lake Shalla, a small **rest house** on the **southern shore** can be hired, which is reached by travelling through **Shashemene**, turning **west** on the **Sodo road**, and then turning **right** (**north**) in the village of **Aje** and travelling for sixteen kilometres (ten miles) to the shore at **Gike**. Furniture and bedding are provided but all other equipment will need to be carried in, including all drinking water. There are also campsites within the national park, but it is best to check with the Wildlife Conservation Organization headquarters in Addis Ababa before you go as to the security and the possibilities of camping.

Malaria can be a problem around all the lakes in this area and it is advised that precautions be taken. The nearest medical help is at Shashemene.

Sightseeing

Head **south** out of Addis on the **Debre Zeit road** where, after seventy-three kilometres (45 miles), the town of **Mojo** will be on your left and a turning **right** (**south-west**) marks the start of the journey down the **Rift Valley road** to the lake region.

After twenty kilometres (12 miles) or so, you'll cross the **bridge** at the **Awash River** as it enters the man-made **Koka Lake**, where **hippo** loll amidst vast flocks of

Egyptian geese. The lake is a product of the **Koka Dam**, a hydroelectric power project that supplies much of Addis Ababa's electricity. (See 'The North-East: A River to the Beginning of Mankind', Part Two.)

From Koka, the road stretches away through what used to be acacia woodland but is now so denuded by the charcoal industry it can barely be described as acacia scrub. Some forty-one kilometres (25 miles) down the road from Koka is **Meki**, where a Bekele Mola Hotel serves as a good stopping-off point for a cold drink. The road then follows the shore of **Lake Ziway**, which can be glimpsed through the now sparse forest. The town of **Ziway** itself is twenty-nine kilometres (18 miles) past Meki, but there are several obvious turn-offs to the **left** (**south-east**) of the road that lead to the shore of the lake.

Five **islands** dot the surface of Lake Ziway, which, at 400 square metres (1,312 square feet), is the largest in this northern cluster of five Rift Valley lakes. At least three of these islands were the site of medieval churches.

The largest island — once known as Debre Tsion, or Mount of Zion, but now called **Tullu Gudo** — is still the site of a **monastery**, which holds some valuable **illustrated manuscripts**. In fact, the oldest written Ethiopian records about Axum were found here, giving support to the belief that Lake Ziway's islands were settled by Axumites who fled with the Ark of the Covenant at the city's destruction.

The island inhabitants, who for centuries practised terraced agriculture, speak a language of their own, which has close similarities to that of the Gurage to the west and the Harari to the east. Many of the local people have **reed boats** similar to the *tankwas* that ply the waters of Lake Tana. (See 'The Historic Route: Mountains and Gorges, Mystery and Grandeur', Part Two.)

Because of the lake's many **fish**, which include the *Tilapia nilotica*, a **fishing sta**tion was set up in the area a few years ago. This has had the incidental effect of attracting a considerable number of **water birds** — including **knob-billed geese, pelicans,** and an occasional **saddlebill stork** — to the lake's edge, where they can easily be seen and photographed.

The fishery project supplies the several restaurants of nearby Ziway town and Addis Ababa with excellent fresh fish. The town is also home to a model **seminary and training centre** run by the Ethiopian Orthodox Church. Another prominent feature is the **Ziway Horticultural Corporation**, whose gardens can be seen from the road, which exports fruit and vegetables to several European countries, as well as fresh cut flowers to Holland.

Ten kilometres (six miles) past Ziway is **Adami Tulu**, where a **hill** to the **left** of the road, surmounted by the ruins of an old **fortress**, towers over the village, which is the site of an **agricultural research station**. There is a **turning** to the **left** just before the hill where the dusty **track** leads to the **Bulbula River's** exit from Lake Ziway. The lake end is blocked by a barricade of black **lava** over which the river pours. This is a haven for birds; **gulls, herons, hammerkops, ibises,** and **egrets** enjoy fishing in the pool just below the falls.

Before reaching the turnoff to Lake Langano, which is about forty-five kilometres (28 miles) from Adami Tulu on the east side of the road, you will cross over the Bulbula River. Just before the **bridge** and the **village** there is a **track** to the **right** at the top of the slope that leads to the edge of **Lake Abijatta**, situated to the **west** of the road, directly across from Lake Langano. At certain times of the year the greatest congregation of birds on Abijatta can be seen here.

However, before the next bridge over the Horacallo River, which connects lakes Langano and Abijatta, a **turning** to the **right** leads to the more usual area of exceptional **bird viewing**. Here thousands of **flamingos** rim the blue bays of the lake with pink,

Opposite: Sun sets over the waters of Lake Langano, a popular weekend retreat for Addis Ababa residents.

Above: Two hotels on Langano's lakeshore make perfect bases from which to explore the lake and nearby Abijatta-Shalla Lakes National Park.

great white pelicans display their fishing prowess, pied kingfishers hover and dive, the distinctive cry of the African fish eagle fills the air and cormorants and darters form strange silhouettes against the setting sun as they roost on dead acacia trees.

To Lake Langano

At the Horacallo bridge it is possible to turn left along a track that leads to Lake Langano, and there are good camping spots here along the northern shore, although due to uncertain security in this area, using non-established campsites is not recommended. It is better to take the main track to the lake, which is a bit farther on, leading left to first the Wabe Shebelle Hotel and, ten kilometres (six miles) later, to the Bekele Mola Hotel. Both of these hotels offer beaches in addition to camping grounds.

Lake Langano's soft brown waters are set against the blue backdrop of the Arsi Mountains, which soar to 4,000 metres (13,120 feet). A few birds make Langano their home, but this resort is less for the nature lover than the watersports enthusiast and sun-worshipper. Although there are hippo, the crocodile population is fortunately small, and you can waterski, windsurf, sail, swim, or sunbathe on the sloping sandy beaches. Boats and waterskis are sometimes available on an hourly rental basis from both hotels on the lake, whose beaches are popular camping spots.

Langano and Shalla are the only two lakes in the country considered safe — bilharzia free — for swimming. Despite its brown colour, the water in Langano is clean and pleasant.

You will often see local Oromo women in the area, who are prepared to sell jewellery or utensils: copper or brass bracelets, bead necklaces, and milk pots decorated with cowrie shells.

Opposite: Lake Shalla, the deepest Ethiopian Rift Valley lake, is home to the continent's most important breeding colony of great white pelicans, which can often be seen at the water's edge.

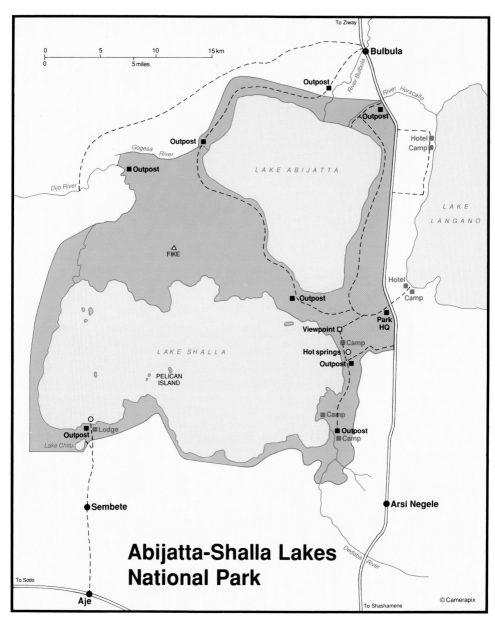

To Ziway
Bulbula
Outpost
River Bulbula
River Horacallo
Outpost
Hotel
Camp
Gogesa River
LAKE ABIJATTA
Dijo River
Outpost
Outpost
LAKE LANGANO
△ FIKE
Hotel
Outpost
Camp
Viewpoint □
Park HQ
Camp
LAKE SHALLA
Hot springs
Outpost
PELICAN ISLAND
Camp
Lodge
Outpost
Camp
Lake Chitu
Outpost
Camp
Sembete
Arsi Negele

Abijatta-Shalla Lakes National Park

Dedaba River
To Sodo
Aje
To Shashamene
© Camerapix

0 5 10 15 km
0 5 miles

Abijatta-Shalla Lakes National Park

Using Lake Langano as your base, it is an easy side trip to visit Abijatta-Shalla Lakes National Park, which is 887 square kilometres (550 square miles) in size, 482 (300) of these being water.

The altitude of the park ranges from

1,540 to 2,075 metres (5,051 to 6,806 feet), the highest peak being **Mount Fike**, situated between the two lakes. The temperatures can be high, reaching 45°C (113°F) at maximum and 5°C (41°F) at minimum. Rain falls between March and April and June and September, averaging 500 mm (19.5 inches).

Lakes Abijatta and Shalla are both terminal lakes but they are very different in nature. The surrounding area is mainly acacia woodland, some of which is very degraded by man. Lake Abijatta is a shallow pan, being only fourteen metres (46 feet) deep, and its level fluctuates periodically, caused by human activity in part but often from natural causes which as yet have not been fully understood. The beaches of both lakes are unstable and saline, and vehicles must not venture too close as there is a very real danger of sinking.

Lake Shalla, by contrast, is the deepest Ethiopian Rift Valley lake at 260 metres (853 feet). It is an exceptionally beautiful and still largely untouched stretch of water, with several hot sulphurous springs that bubble up by the shore and flow into the lake. These are often used by people seeking cures for various ailments.

The sides of the lake are steep and rocky, often right down to the shore. Although swimming is considered safe, it may feel strange: the colour of the water is like cold tea and there is a high concentration of salts, making it feel soapy to the touch. Few fish are found in this lake.

Sightseeing

Abijatta can best be reached by taking the **turnoff** directly across from the **Langano turnoff**, which is described above. The **track** to Lake Shalla is now the **main trail** through the national park. It turns **west** off the **main road** about five kilometres (three miles) **south** of the **Bekele Mola Hotel turnoff** and is clearly marked by a **sign**. Neither the road to Lake Shalla nor the road to Lake Abijatta should be attempted with two-wheel-drive vehicles without reliable information on the current condition of its surface. Do not leave the main track. It is also recommended that vehicles not be left unattended at either Abijatta or Shalla.

Drive in through the **park gate** and follow a reasonably good **track** (in dry weather), which leads first to a spectacular **lookout point** with a view over the countryside and both Abijatta and Shalla. The vegetation has been adversely affected by people in many areas, mainly because of charcoal production and livestock grazing,

particularly along the roads.

Bird life is profuse in this area: the bright **yellow masked weaver**, the **red-rumped buffalo weaver**, **red-billed hornbill**, **African fish eagle**, **Didric's cuckoo**, **Abyssinian roller**, and **superb starling** are all regularly seen.

The **track** emerges at the **lake shore** of Shalla, where again a vast profusion of **ducks**, **geese**, **coots**, **waders** and shore birds of every kind mingle with **flamingo** and **pelican** at the water's edge. A river runs into the south-east corner of the lake, and there is a wonderful camping spot near this point. From the campsite, a twenty-five-minute walk up the river leads to a scenic waterfall.

The park was created for the many species of aquatic birds that use the lakes, particularly **great white pelicans** and **greater** and **lesser flamingo**. Lake Shalla has **islands** in it that are used as **breeding sites** by many birds, and is in fact home to the continent's most important breeding colony of great white pelicans. Because of the lack of fish, the birds fly to Lake Abijatta — which has no islands — to feed. Other birds include **white-necked cormorant**, **African fish eagle**, **Egyptian geese**, various **plover** species, and **herons**.

Mammals seen here are not numerous but include **Grant's gazelle** — the northern limit for this species — **greater kudu**, **oribi**, **warthog**, and **golden jackal**.

If it's wildlife you want to see, continue your journey **south**, where **Nechisar National Park** lies tucked between lakes Abaya and Chamo, and near the Gamo Gofa regional capital of Arba Minch.

Nechisar National Park

Many of Ethiopia's picturesque Amharic place names conjure up instant and colourful images of their locations, and *Nechisar* National Park is no exception. *'Nech'* means white and *'Sar'* means grass — and the combination 'white grass' vividly describes the broad plains area of Nechisar National Park.

The park is 514 square kilometres (319 square miles) in area, 78 (48) of these being

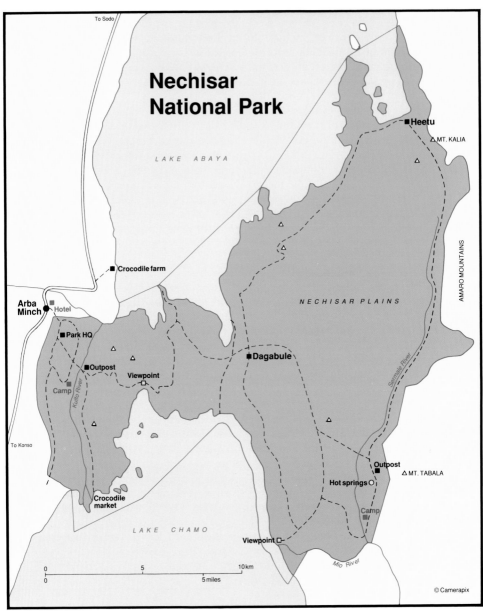

Nechisar National Park

LAKE ABAYA

■ Heetu
△ MT. KALIA
△

■ Crocodile farm

AMARO MOUNTAINS

NECHISAR PLAINS

△
△
△

Arba
Minch ■ Hotel

■ Park HQ
△
△
■ Outpost
Viewpoint
□ ■ Dagabule
Camp
△
Sermale River

To Konso
△

Crocodile
market

Outpost ■
△ MT. TABALA
Hot springs ○
Camp

LAKE CHAMO

Viewpoint □

Mio River

0   5   10 km
0   5 miles

© Camerapix

water. Altitude ranges from 1,108 to 1,650 metres (3,634 to 5,412 feet) and temperatures between 11° and 26° C (52° and 79°F). Rainfall averages 880 mm (34 inches) and mainly falls from March to May and September to November.

Getting there

The nearby town of Arba Minch is 510 kilometres from Addis Ababa, 252 kilometres from Shashemene and 90 kilometres from Konso, at the border of Sidamo region. It is served by an all-weather gravel road and also by air four times a week on Ethiopian Airlines flights. However, getting local transport is a problem unless private arrangements can be made.

When to go

It is best to avoid the rains, as roads can be impassable at this time due to the black cotton soil in many areas.

Above: The Wendo Genet Resort Hotel, near Shashemene, is known for its therapeutic hot springs.

Where to stay

In Wendo Genet, the Wendo Genet Resort Hotel, run by the Wabe Shebelle Hotels Administration. In Awasa, the Wabe Shebelle Hotels, both of which have a swimming pool and one has tennis courts. Both are on the lake, although one is closer to the highway. In Sodo, the Bekele Mola Hotel (also known as the Damte Hotel), which, although once acceptable, has now seriously deteriorated. In Arba Minch, the Bekele Mola Hotel enjoys a spectacular position of the edge of a bluff — looking out to the lakes and the mountains beyond —but suffers from lack of maintenance and negligent management. In Nechisar National Park there is no hotel or lodge accommodation, but camping is permitted.

Sightseeing

From Shalla, it is a short drive through a **farm development project** where sisal, sunflower and groundnuts line the road, to the 'crossroads' town of **Shashemene**. Shops line the busy high street here and most of the town's business appears to

take place in the centre of the road, where horse-drawn vehicles narrowly miss the gesticulating traders and truck drivers. A left turn at the main crossroads at the entrance to the town will take you to Bale, and if you keep straight you will eventually end up at the Kenya frontier — although this is a journey recommended only for the adventurous traveller with a sturdy, preferably four-wheel-drive, vehicle.

It is 800 kilometres (500 miles) from Addis Ababa to the Kenya border, which is about two days' driving time. Note that the road condition on the Ethiopian side of the border is better than on the Kenyan side.

Although our journey should continue to the west, it is only slightly out of the way — and very worth the while — to make a couple of interesting side trips.

Just past Shashemene, if you continue **straight** on, a modern **telecommunications building** stands on the **left** side of the road, where there is a **signpost** indicating the **turn** to the small 'paradise' of **Wendo Genet**. The **road** winds for fifteen kilometres (nine miles) through increasingly

beautiful country until you reach the lovely wooded valley in which the **Wendo Genet Resort Hotel** is situated. Turn **left** in the **village market square** to ascend the **track** to the hotel, where an avenue of cypress trees heralds your arrival, with the **entrance** just a little further along on the **left**. The old but interesting hotel is set in **gardens** of citrus, palm and pine with a magnificent view from the terrace over the Rift Valley. This is a place to enjoy comfortable modern accommodation and excellent food — particularly the Sunday buffet lunch — but it is really known for providing an opportunity to bathe in the natural **hot springs** and small **hot pool** here, which lie only a few metres from a cold, clear rushing **mountain stream**. Walks up the valley or in the surrounding forest give a spectacular view and a chance to observe the abundant **bird life**, as well as black-and-white **colobus monkeys**.

Lake Awasa

Returning to the **main road south** you will come to the Sidamo regional capital of **Awasa**, situated on the shores of beautiful **Lake Awasa**. Enclosed by a gentle chain of mountains, the lake provides an ideal spot for fishing and boating. The lake — twenty-one metres (69 feet) deep, with a circumference of sixty-two kilometres (38 miles) — boasts good **hotels** and **campsites**, as well as an interesting countryside featuring coffee plantations, fruit groves and the Bale Mountains rising away in the east. The town is also the site of an **agricultural research station**.

The lake waters teem with **fish**, including **barbus**, **tilapia,** and **catfish** in great numbers. A fair-sized local fishing community using small boats and simple nets and lures thrives on these stocks, as do many species of birds. A grassy **dike** built to contain the lake's steadily rising water level is convenient for walks, sightseeing, and bird watching — for which the lake is particularly known. The abundant **storks** and **herons** mingle with **kingfishers**, **darters**, **plovers**, **wild ducks**, **Egyptian geese**, **crakes,** and

cormorants, creating a colourful spectacle. In a four-wheel-drive vehicle, it is possible — and pleasant — to drive all the way around the lake, where you will see a myriad of birds as well as picturesque Sidama villages.

The town of Awasa itself is an interesting attraction, with a bustling and attractive outdoor **market** that gives something of the flavour of the life and commerce of the region.

The Sidama

The **Sidama** people who inhabit this region play a major role in Ethiopia's coffee export trade but are especially known for their beautiful beehive-shaped **woven houses**. Bamboo is used for the framework, which is then covered with grass and *enset* leaves as the rainy season approaches. A small front porch shades the entrance. Inside, the family have the right side of the house and the calves the left. Furniture is simple, usually just wooden bedsteads and stools. Near the main hut, a fence of woven bamboo or euphorbia surrounds the vegetable plot. The men build the huts and grow vegetables with their wives' help, and the women go to market, clean, and cook.

Senkele Sanctuary

Backtracking now to **Shashemene**, head **west**. A **turning south** after thirty kilometres (19 miles) leads to the largely undeveloped **Senkele Sanctuary**, fifty-four square kilometres (33 square miles) of savannah and wooded grassland that was established to protect its resident population of **Swayne's hartebeest**, one of Ethiopia's endemic subspecies. The sanctuary is also home to about twelve other species of mammal — including **oribi**, **Bohor reedbuck,** and **greater kudu** — and ninety-one species of birds.

Sixty kilometres **west** of Shashemene is the village of **Alaba Kulito**, where a **turn** to the **left** — or **south-west** — leads to **Sodo**, another seventy kilometres (43 miles) farther on. Often referred to as Wolayta Sodo after the district in which it

Opposite: The waters of beautiful Lake Awasa teem with many varieties of fish. It is also renowned for its abundant bird life.

is situated, the town is the site of a huge and very colourful open-air **market**, which is well worth a visit. Sodo stands on the border between the regions of Gamo Gofa, Sidamo, and Kaffa — one of Ethiopia's main coffee-growing areas. Kaffa is thought to be the original home of the coffee plant. (See 'The West: Fertile and Exotic', Part Two.)

The Wolayta

In this region east of the Omo River, hundreds of stone monoliths bear witness to the long-time habitation of this area by early humans, and the people who live here today are very likely from fairly early stock. Light-complexioned with regular features and short stature, the Wolayta belong to the vast Ometo language group.

These people belong to either the Muslim or the Christian religion, although traces of the old pagan religions still survive in places, together with ancient near-forgotten Christian traditions difficult to distinguish, celebrated in temples hewn from the rock, similar to those found in Tigray.

The Wolayta cultivate most of the cereal crops as well as cotton, *enset*, and tobacco. Their huts are large and beehive-shaped, built in the midst of gardens, with one or more ostrich eggs perched atop the roof as fertility symbols. Viewed from inside, the plaited structure and concentric rings of the roof framework appear wonderfully intricate and neat. These astonishingly roomy houses are divided into several compartments by screens of bamboo. The cattle, sheep, and goats who share the house are not only safe from predators but provide a form of 'central heating' on chillier nights.

Lakes Abaya and Chamo

Turn east at Sodo and travel along a **gravel road** that offers a magnificent view of **Lake Abaya**. The road eventually swings **south**

and runs along the western shore of this lake, the longest and largest — at 1,160 square kilometres (719 square miles) — of all of Ethiopia's Rift Valley lakes. Another marvellous lake, the 551-square-kilometre (342-square-mile) Lake Chamo, lies just to the south; the two lakes are ringed by savannah plains and smoky mountain crests.

The best point from which to explore these two lakes — which many consider to be the most beautiful in the Rift Valley — and the national park, of which part of their surface is an integral part, is from the

regional seat of **Arba Minch**. To get there, continue to head **south** on the **main road**, keeping the shore of Lake Abaya on your **left**. You'll pass through the small village of **Mirab Abaya**, and from that point it is sixty-two kilometres (38 miles) to Arba Minch.

From the town on the ridge of land that divides Abaya and Chamo there are commanding views of the panorama all around, including both **lakes** with **Nech-isar** on the eastern side and, to the west, the **Guge** range of mountains. The out-

standing beauty of the neck of land between the two lakes has earned it the sobriquet of 'Bridge of Heaven'.

The equally poetic Arba Minch — meaning 'forty springs' — takes its name from the bubbling streams that spring up amid the undergrowth of the luxuriant groundwater forest, which covers the flats beneath the town. The beautifully located but scandalously run-down Bekele Mola Hotel in the town offers accommodation and serves as a good base from which to explore this alluring area.

Above: Lake Chamo is particularly known for its large and impressive crocodile population.

The shores and islands of Abaya and Chamo are populated by farming peoples such as the **Ganjule** and the **Guji**, both of whom also have ancient traditions of hippo hunting. The Guji ply the waters of Lake Abaya in the elegantly curved high-prowed *ambatch* boats similar to those depicted on the tombs of the ancient Egyptian pharaohs. Made of extremely light wood, an *ambatch* is capable of transporting several cattle at one time and is sufficiently sturdy to withstand any attack by crocodiles, which are present in large numbers — and large sizes — on both lakes.

Crocodiles

A good place to view **crocodiles** is on the shore of **Lake Chamo**, just **south** of the town, at a place popularly referred to as the *azzo gabaya* or **crocodile market**. This spot offers one of Africa's most impressive displays of big crocs. So great is the crocodile population in the lakes that they are now being hunted commercially, but some of the lake shore is within the park to protect their breeding grounds.

An unusual attraction is the **crocodile farm** close to the Abaya port at the north-east sector of Arba Minch, where visitors can see at close hand these primaeval creatures at various stages of growth.

Much of **Nechisar National Park** can be enjoyed in a full day's drive from the Bekele Mola Hotel, or from your own **campsite** in the fig tree forest near the **park headquarters**. But full exploration of the park needs more time, and probably a second camp near the **hot springs** in the east. In any case, a four-wheel-drive vehicle is a must to cope with the steep rocky inclines and the wet-season mud.

The park's vivid contrasts will linger long in your memory — a swath of white grass against the backdrop of clearly defined, deeply cut hills and mountains. From the **escarpment** on which Arba Minch stands you look down on the clear blue waters of Lake Chamo and the sandy beaches of its northern shores, covered by crocodiles lounging in the sun.

To the north, **Lake Abaya**'s surface is a startling contrast of dark red, a colour caused by the suspended load of ferrous hydroxide in its waters. At the base of the escarpment is a large area of evergreen groundwater forest around the **Kulfo River**, as well as the 'forty springs' after which Arba Minch is named. The western edge of the Rift Valley forms an impressive backdrop to the west.

Within the forest you'll find shy, chestnut-red **bushbuck**, the comical **bushpig**, troops of **Anubis baboons** and **vervet monkeys**. One forest glade, with the Kulfo River flowing nearby, is a perfect **camping site**, but the baboons may make it less peaceful — especially if they choose that day to sleep and live in the same area.

So large are the forest trees of fig and others that other animals and birds are not easily seen. The birds nest high up in the canopy and you need to be an expert in bird calls to identify them. At dusk, you may see a **genet** scuttling through the undergrowth in search of its supper.

The heat and dust of Africa hit you with surprise as you leave the cool haven of the forest and cross the bridge into the white savannah on the other side. The **road** twists and turns through a thick belt of bush, sometimes climbing precipitously above the lakes, at others descending down to their shores. As it swings between both lakes, you get sudden and stunning views of the blue and dull red waters, studded with islands. The clear lake beaches are ideal nesting sites for crocodiles, which lay their eggs deep beneath the warm sand and remain near them until they hatch.

The most commonly seen creatures of Nechisar's bush and savannah are two extremes of antelope: the large **greater kudu**, with its spectacular spiral horns and white-striped flanks, and the minuscule **Guenther's dik-dik**, usually seen in pairs, as dik-dik are monogamous.

At first sight the Nechisar plains, which you encounter when you leave the peninsula between the two lakes, seem surprisingly empty. But dotted among this apparently endless sweep of golden white grass are herds of **Burchell's zebra**, which mingle with **Grant's gazelle** and an occasional **Swayne's hartebeest** — an endemic subspecies. Also seen are **black-backed jackal** and the **African hunting dog**.

Above: Unstable as they may look, the high-prowed *ambatch* boats that ply the waters of Lake Chamo are amazingly sturdy. Larger ones are capable of transporting several cows at a time.

The plains end at the **eastern** edge of the park, at the foot of the hills and mountains of Sidamo region. With their wooded areas, cut through by many small river valleys, these hills provide a stunning contrast to the plains. Though not as spectacular as many in Ethiopia, each of the few **hot springs** at the foot of the hills are carefully tended and 'protected' by a small piece of cloth to appease the spirits that dwell within.

Woodlands fringe the base of the hill, providing a fitting habitat for the shy **colobus monkey**.

Above: Dorze woman hand-spins cotton in front of her unique home.

Birds galore

The birds of the area are many and varied, reflecting the different habitats within the park. Hornbills are particularly striking. Both the **red-billed** and **grey hornbill** are common here, and the **Abyssinian ground hornbill**, with its brilliant blue and red wattles and curious open casque above the beak, is also seen. The **fish eagle** is ever-present with its haunting cry, **kingfishers** are numerous along the Kulfo River, and **rollers** can be seen on the bushes of the isthmus. Various **bustard** species are also found in the park, including the large and impressive **kori**.

As well as their crocodiles and bird life, lakes Abaya and Chamo are famous for their sport fishing, especially for **Nile perch** — often weighing more than 100 kilos (220 pounds) — and for the fighting **tigerfish**. Boats can be hired through the maritime authority in Arba Minch, but fishing gear is not provided — and getting permits from a difficult bureaucracy has frequently proved a frustrating project.

An interesting detour from Nechisar, and well worth the effort, is the twenty-six kilometre (16-mile) drive up into the hills to the **west** of Arba Minch to the old village of **Chencha**. **Picturesque houses**, accompanied by the magnificent backdrop of the lakes in the Rift far below, give glimpses of ancient Ethiopia.

The Dorze

The inhabitants of this village are known as the **Dorze**, one of the many small segments of the great Ometo language group of southern Ethiopia. Once warriors, they have now turned to farming and weaving to earn a living. Their success in the field of weaving has been phenomenal and the Dorze name is synonymous with the best in woven cotton cloth. Chencha, in fact, is famous for the fine cotton *gabbis* or **shawls** that can be bought there.

Each amazing Dorze bamboo house has its own small garden surrounded by *enset*, beds of spices and cabbage, and tobacco (the Dorze are passionate smokers). The main house is a tall — up to twelve metres (39 feet) — bee-hived shaped building with an aristocratic 'nose', which forms a

Above: Eerie line-up of wooden totems, erected by the Konso people over the graves of the dead.

reception room for guests and is usually furnished with two benches. The vaulted ceiling and walls of the spacious and airy houses are covered with an elegant thatch of *enset* to form a smooth and steep unbroken dome.

When a Dorze house starts to rot or gets eaten by termites, the house is dug up. Bamboo is sewn round it to keep it in shape, and everyone rushes to help carry it. With poles poked horizontally through the building, men, women, and children all join in the effort — with a fine complement of singing — to move it to its new site. A house lasts for about forty years and is then abandoned.

Yabello Sanctuary

Ninety kilometres (56 miles) **south** of Arba Minch is the village of **Konso**, which is on the border of Sidamo region. A **turn** to the **west** here will take you, 155 kilometres (96 miles) later, to the town of **Yabello**, where a **turn south** eventually leads to **Moyale** on the **Kenya border**, some 200 kilometres (124 miles) away. Just to the **north** and **east** of the **Yabello junction** is the 2,496-square-kilometre (1,548-square-mile) **Yabello Sanctuary**. Originally established for the protection of **Swayne's hartebeest**, Yabello has now become an important sanctuary for birds and features some 194 species. These include the endemic **Stresemann's bush crow** and **white-tailed swallow**. The sanctuary itself is a dry savannah/acacia bush area with some low hills as well as an area of juniper woodland nearby. In addition to Swayne's hartebeest, its red soils are home to twenty-four other species of mammal, including **greater and lesser kudu, gerenuk,** as well as **Burchell's zebra**.

Although there are no visitor facilities in the sanctuary, visitors can find hotel accommodation in the town of Yabello nearby.

The Konso

The region to the **south** of Konso and Yabello is inhabited by the **Konso** people. Except for trading with the neighbouring Borena for salt or cowrie shells, outside influence had, until recently, virtually passed by the Konso. A pagan society, they erect eerie wooden totems replete with phallic symbols over the graves of the dead and have numerous cults based around the breeding and veneration of serpents. The Konso have adopted a complex age-grading system similar to that of the Oromo. (See 'The People: Proud of Their Ancient Heritage', Part One.) Sacred drums, symbolizing peace and harmony, are circulated from village to village according to a fixed cycle and are beaten in rituals that mark the transition from one age-grade to the next.

The cornerstone of Konso culture, however, is a highly specialized and successful agricultural economy that, through **terracing** buttressed with stone, enables these people to extract a productive living from the none-too-fertile hills and valleys that surround them. The stone shoring employed in these extensive and intricate terraces is echoed in the dry-stone walls that surround most Konso villages and that protect low-lying fields from flash floods and marauding cattle. Stone is also used for grinding grain, sharpening knives and spears, making anvils and constructing dams. It is as much a part of Konso life as soil.

The material is just as evident in the beautiful small stone and wood houses, tightly packed with roofs touching and overlapping in their crowded compounds. The Konso are experts on wood of all kinds and know the durability of the massive timbers that keep a house standing for eighty years or more. Inside each house there is a short wooden entrance tunnel, causing the visitor to enter on hands and knees — and permitting the occupant to decide whether it is friend or foe.

The Konso men build the houses, spin and weave, and carve wood and ivory. The women do the gardening and, surprisingly, stone walling.

Konso industriousness finds its vehicle in a cooperative ethic that enables farmers to enlist the support of communal work parties from their own and surrounding villages to build walls and terraces, and to sow and harvest the principal crops — sorghum, potatoes, and cotton. Konso weaving, also a communal activity, is highly productive and the thick cotton blankets (called *bulukos*) for which this region is famous are much prized throughout Ethiopia.

Not all of Konso life is dominated by hard work. Evening is a particular time of relaxation, when young men and women sing and dance to a hypnotic stamping rhythm, forming fluid circles and squares punctuated with warlike leaps and bounds and much provocative shaking of the hips and breasts.

With the all-weather road — and various missions — passing through Konso, the people are no longer so isolated. One sign of assimilation occasionally seen is Konso ploughing their fields with oxen, as is done in other parts of Ethiopia. The Konso also meet up with the neighbouring **Borena** to trade for salt or cowrie shells.

The Borena

The Borena, probably the most traditional of all Ethiopia's Oromo groups, are semi-nomadic pastoralists whose lives revolve exclusively around the million or so head of cattle they own. They live to the **east** of the Konso on the low hot plains of the southern savannah. They work all day and every day in the long dry season just to keep their vast herds watered every three days, calculating precisely the number of men needed to haul the water and the number of cattle a well will support, which may be as many as 2,500.

The famous wells are an extraordinary feature of the culture. Approached by a long cutting, slanting down to ten metres below the surface of the earth, just wide enough for two columns of beasts to pass each other, is the top of the well and the drinking troughs. Every two metres down there is a stage where the men and women toss the water in giraffe-hide buckets to the person above them. The deepest well recorded has eighteen stages.

The Borena people have semi-permanent villages or family groups of huts that are attached to the same well. The houses they live in, more permanent than the true nomadic hut, are made of grass over a wooden framework, often with the lower part of the walls reinforced with a screen of branches. They remain surprisingly cool in the heat of the day. Around the houses are the cattle enclosures, built as protection against lions.

Tall, thin-lipped, and graceful with elegant manners, the Borena are essentially peaceful people who believe that angry words are dangerous and violence unthinkable.

The Borena and the Konso are just two of the fascinating peoples who live in the wildernesses of southern Ethiopia. For an even more kaleidoscopic sampling of the colourful cultures and people of this area, you must travel back to Konso and head **west**, into the remote **Omo Valley**.

The Omo: Wild and Wonderful Wilderness

Rising in the highlands south-west of the capital of Addis Ababa, the Omo River courses south for almost 1,000 kilometres (620 miles) but never reaches the sea. It is the sole feeder of Lake Turkana, East Africa's fourth largest lake, which the river enters just north of the Kenya border.

As it tumbles off the escarpment, the Omo passes from an Afro-alpine environment and rain forest on into savannah country, and finally into searing desert lands. Through the millenia its flood-swollen waters have cut stupendous gorges. Wild game roam in abundance on both banks, while strange and colourful birds dart in and out of the lush vegetation.

Reckoned by enthusiasts to be one of Africa's premier locations for the sport of white water river rafting, its early fury takes it through gorges hundreds of metres deep and over formidable cataracts before it later snakes more peacefully amidst dense jungles and finally across the colourful desert terrain. Its waters boil with fish and the huge shapes of crocodile and hippo. (See 'Shooting the Rapids: White Water Rafting in Ethiopia', Part Four.)

On the final leg of its journey south to Turkana, the Omo forms the border between Kaffa and Gamo Gofa regions. It's here that Ethiopia's largest nature sanctuary, the Omo National Park, is located. It is one of the richest in spectacle and game and yet one of the least visited areas in east and central Africa. Another sanctuary, Mago National Park, has also been established on the east bank of the river: a land of endless, distant horizons. In the dense acacia scrub of the park, close to the river — and in the broad rolling grasslands and deserts that surround it — the traveller enters a lost world, across which few vehicles have ever travelled and which few foreign eyes have ever seen.

Both parks can offer incredible spectacles of oryx, giraffe, zebra, hartebeest, gerenuk, and gazelle — as well as lion, buffalo, and elephant. Both also have the merit of being far from the beaten track and virtually unexplored, and thus are places in which game can be seen in a truly natural state. Increasing poaching by the local people, however, is beginning to threaten this previously undisturbed habitat.

Along this southern stretch of the Omo, far away from any sort of 'civilization', indigenous peoples such as the Bume and the Karo practise a combination of cattle-keeping and flood-retreat agriculture, which has replaced what was once — as little as several decades ago — pure pastoralism.

Fascinating peoples

The lower Omo is home to a remarkable mix of small, contrasting ethnic groups — not only the Bume and the Karo, but also the Geleb, the Bodi, the Mursi, the Surma, the Arbore, and the Hamer, to name but a few. Lifestyles are as various as the tribes themselves. The Bume and Karo mingle with the pastoral Geleb and the transhumant Hamer. The Mursi and the Surma, meanwhile, mix basic subsistence cultivation with small-scale cattle-herding — lives of harsh simplicity uncluttered by the pressures of the modern world.

Lacking any material culture and artefacts common to more 'civilized' peoples, these tribes find unique ways in which to

Above: 'Lip plates' and ear lobe discs are important distinctions of female beauty in Mursi society.

express their artistic impulses. Both the Surma and the Karo, for example, are experts at body painting, using clays and locally available vegetable pigments to trace fantastic patterns on each other's faces, chests, arms, and legs. These designs have no special symbolic significance but are created purely for fun and aesthetic effect, each artist vying to outdo his fellows.

Scarification, on the other hand, which is also popular amongst most of the peoples of the lower Omo, does contain a number of specific symbolic messages. For example, Mursi warriors carve deep crescent incisions on their arms to represent each enemy that they have killed in battle.

Elaborate hairstyles are another form of personal adornment. Hamer women wear their hair in dense ringlets smeared with mud and clarified butter and topped off with a head-dress featuring oblongs of gleaming aluminium; Geleb and Karo men sculpt and shave their hair into extravagant shapes, with special ochre 'caps' of hair usually containing several ostrich feathers.

Jewellery tends to be simple but striking — colourful necklaces, chunky metal wristlets and armlets, shiny nails appended to skirts, multiple earrings, and so on.

The insertion of wooden and terracotta discs into the ear lobes is a widespread custom, and Mursi and Surma women also progressively split and stretch their lower lips to make room for similar discs there, too. Though these 'lip plates' may appear bizarre to outsiders, the Mursi and Surma regard them as signs of beauty — generally speaking, the larger the lip plate the more desirable the wearer.

At certain seasons, a visitor may be lucky to chance on colourful and dramatic traditional ceremonies. Periodically young men of both the Mursi and the Surma tribes engage in ritual stick fighting. These duels are conducted with the utmost vigour since the winners, and those judged to have shown the greatest bravery, are much admired by nubile girls.

Another important event, seen by few tourists, is the Hamer 'jumping of the bull' ceremony. In this rite of passage, youths are required to jump onto the backs of a

Above: Gleaming aluminium head-dresses decorate the dense ringlets of Hamer women.

line of thirty or forty cattle, run the whole length of this formidable obstacle, jump down onto the other side and then repeat the entire procedure three more times without falling. Finally they walk out of the arena through a special gateway, after which they are judged to have passed from boyhood to manhood.

A trip along the wild and wonderful Omo River offers many opportunities to meet the colourful local people, as well as experience 'getting away from it all' such as you've never known before.

Getting there

Jinka, the nearest town to Omo and Mago national parks, is 809 kilometres (501 miles) from Addis Ababa, 138 kilometres (86 miles) from Konso, and 228 kilometres (141 miles) from Arba Minch. It can be reached by road via two routes. The first goes to Arba Minch and Konso and then on to Jinka via Kakko and Kay Afer. The second goes south-west through the mountains from the Bulki-Sodo road. The latter route, when fully improved, will cut more than 100 kilometres (62 miles) from

the Jinka-Addis Ababa drive and will also avoid the heat of the lowlands.

Jinka is also served by four weekly Ethiopian Airlines flights, although local transport is a problem if you arrive by air. Omo National Park can also be flown into by charter during the dry season.

When to go

All times of the year are suitable for visits as the roads dry out quickly after the rains, although certain sections may be impassable for brief periods. The best time is probably just after the rains have finished, in June/July or December/January, when the grass will be green.

Where to stay

In Jinka, the Orit Hotel or the Omo Hotel. The South Omo Research Centre guest house, still under construction in 1994, will provide welcome accommodation when it opens. There is no accommodation in Mago or Omo national parks, but there are several pleasant campsites (all equipment must be taken). The tented camp of Dimitris Assimacopolous, sixty-five kilo-

Above: Cattle cross the mighty Omo River with the help of two Kwegu men and their sturdy dugout canoe.

metres (40 miles) from Konso on the Weyto River; Roussos's Murle Lodge, on the banks of the Omo River in the Murle Controlled Hunting Area; and a guest house at Omo Rate may all be able to provide accommodation, but it is best to enquire in Addis Ababa about these places before you go. See Listings.

There is no fuel after Jinka, and even there supplies may be scarce — you would be better off fuelling up in Arba Minch.

Tsetse flies in the bushbelt lowlands by the Omo River can make life quite uncomfortable, and precautions must be taken for malaria, which is a severe problem throughout this area. The nearest medical help is at Jinka and there is a hospital at Arba Minch.

Sightseeing

From **Konso** an all-weather **gravel road** heads **west**, winding through hilly country and providing nice views of Konso villages and terracing. The road crosses the **Delbina River**, where there are good **campsites**. If you choose to put up camp here, it is imperative that you make good

arrangements for one or two local watchmen to fend off the sometimes large number of youths who come to spectate and have been known to steal.

Past the Delbina, the country is increasingly wild and dry, with *Commiphora* and *Boswellia* species furnishing a type of **frankincense** sold at the side of the road by Konso and Tsemay boys. Sixty-five kilometres (40 miles) from Konso you'll cross the **steel bridge** that spans the **Weyto River**, where **crocodiles** may be seen sunning themselves on the sand banks. The acacia-forested **east bank** conceals the **tented camp** of Dimitris Assimacopolous, used for hunting before the August 1993 ban and now re-opened for general visitors.

Not far to the **west** there is a **junction** where a **left turn** leads to Arbore, Turmi, and Omo Rate, while continuing **straight** will take you through the villages of **Key Afer** and **Kakko** before reaching **Jinka**, some 138 kilometres (86 miles) from Konso.

An **alternative route**, avoiding Arba Minch and Konso, was being upgraded in

Above: Jinka townspeople await the arrival of an Ethiopian Airlines flight. The town, the nearest to Omo and Mago national parks, is served four times a week by the airline.

1994. Instead of turning off at Sodo to Arba Minch, you would continue **straight**, in a **south-westerly** direction through the mountains on the **Bulki-Sodo road**. A **turnoff** at **Gelta**, 131 kilometres (81 miles) from Sodo, leads to Jinka.

Jinka

Not so long ago Jinka was just a remote rural market village. Now it has become a modern little town serving as administrative centre for the South Omo Zone, which includes the ethnic groups of Ari, Banna, Hamer, Geleb, Bume, Karo, Kwegu, Bodi, Male, Tsemay, and Arbore.

Laid out with wide streets and benefitting from a mild climate — which has encouraged an exuberant growth of mango and other trees — Jinka is one of Ethiopia's most pleasant small towns. Catering to the more modern inhabitants and visitors with an **airstrip**, **petrol station**, **Montessori kindergarten**, and **bank**, it also serves the surrounding countryside with a large and colourful Saturday **market**. This market is well worth a visit, as is

the **South Omo Research Centre** (still under construction in early 1994) with its **museum**. The centre is situated on the **Bulat hill**, overlooking the town with a spectacular view, and will be a resource for anthropologists, tourists, and townspeople.

Although Jinka enjoys four flights a week from Addis Ababa, the usefulness of these flights to the tourist is limited by the lack of any reliable vehicles for hire. It is certainly possible that some tour operator will step in to fill this need, so enquiries in Addis Ababa might be worthwhile.

Jinka's best hotel is the Orit, right next to the airstrip, with self-contained rooms (water is pumped into the holding tank whenever you want a shower) and a **lively bar**. The Omo Hotel across the road is a close second. Good **Ethiopian food** can be found at several establishments near the market, but a walk up the hill from the Orit to the **Selam Snack Bar** can reward the enterprising diner with a memorable fresh and spicy repast, served under a canopy of passion fruit vines — especially if the owner is given some advance

179

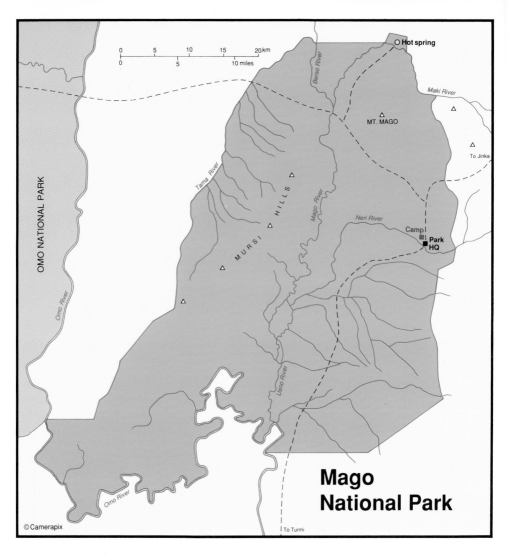

Mago
National Park

©Camerapix

warning. If it's the season for fruit, ask for fresh papaya juice.

The town is the last place from which you can stock up on supplies and outfit yourself for camping in the nearby Mago and Omo national parks.

Mago National Park

On the eastern bank of the Omo River, Mago National Park is 2,162 square kilometres (835 square miles) in area, ranging in altitude from 450 to 2,528 metres (1,476 to 8,292 feet), the latter being the height of Mount Mago situated in the north of the park. Temperatures here

swing between 14° and 41°C (57° and 106°F) and rainfall, which falls from March to May and October to December, is low, being 480 mm (19 inches) on average.

Sightseeing

If you are interested just in seeing Mago National Park, the quickest and most direct route is from Jinka, where there is a small thirty-five-kilometre (22-mile) **track** leading down a very steep **escarpment** to the plains below, where the **park headquarters** and **campsites** are located.

Although there is very little in the way of driving circuits in the park, about five kilometres (three miles) from the headquarters a **turnoff** to the **left** leads to the **Mago River,**

180

where you cross a **bridge** and climb up a short but steep **escarpment** to the grassy **plateau** that is the northern extension of the **Mursi Mountains** (also called the Ngalibong Mountains). The track, which was improved in late 1993 but is vulnerable to rain damage, crosses the plateau and drops into dense bushbelt along the **Omo River**, reaching the river itself at a point called **Omo Mursi**, where a few Mago National Park **rangers** are stationed.

This outpost is opposite a **track** that leads thirty-two kilometres (20 miles) to the **Omo National Park headquarters** at Mui River. Unfortunately, however, the **ferry** constructed by the Wildlife Organization was never successfully put into service and today lies rusting on the steep mud banks. Omo Mursi attracts a small but steady flow of visitors who want to see and photograph the Mursi people, famous for the large clay discs that the women wear in their slit lower lips.

Above: Handsome Tsemay boy near Konso.

Another route into Mago, however, is the preferred one because it offers the opportunity to travel through the varied villages of the colourful and diverse ethnic groups found in the region. It also usually affords better wildlife viewing and still winds up at the Mago park headquarters and the campsites. For this route, backtrack to the **junction** midway between Key Afer and Konso, where you'll turn **right (south-west)** on the road to Arbore, Turmi, and Omo Rate.

The Tsemay

This part of the broad **Weyto Valley** is inhabited by the Tsemay, handsome and photogenic people who, like most of the small ethnic groups of the far south-west, practise a combination of pastoralism and shifting opportunistic rain-fed agriculture.

Continuing **south** down the Weyto Valley, walled on the right by the precipitous rocky mountains of Tsemay and Hamer, a small settlement with a police station appears on the left. This village is known as **Arbore**. The Arbore people are very closely related to the Borena and share their unique adornments, such as aluminium bead necklaces.

Past Arbore, obscure **tracks** lead out onto the surface of **Chew Bahir** (Lake Stefanie), which presents an awesome spectacle of blistering saline lake bed bounded in the distance by jagged mountains. **Oryx** and **gazelle** sometimes frequent the lake bed, which, if dry, offers the temptation of smooth high-speed driving in any direction. But this is no place to break down, so exercise caution and follow the advice of a local guide, whose presence is definitely advisable.

The road leaves the Weyto Valley and makes a dramatic ascent to the Hamer country by following one of the major dry watercourses that spill off the highlands. Just outside **Turmi**, ninety-five kilometres (59 miles) from the **Weyto bridge**, a **well** on the edge of the broad, sandy, and usually dry **Kaske riverbed** is the sole good source of water for miles around and visitors frequently camp nearby.

The Kaske is lined with beautiful acacias and tamarinds, in which **colobus, baboons**, and many **birds** may be seen. An added bonus is the procession of extremely picturesque and striking Hamer girls coming to fetch water or cultivate the adjacent papaya orchard. And the Turmi Monday **market** is not to be missed, with large numbers of Hamer coming to buy, sell, and exchange news.

At Turmi, a **track** leads **north** to **Dimeka** and joins the **Konso-Jinka road** at Key Afer, offering the possibility of a circuit that is shorter and less remote than the one including Omo Rate, Murle, and Mago National Park described next.

Omo Rate

From Turmi, the **main road** goes **south-west**, descending into ever-drier country, eventually reaching the small village of **Omo Rate**, site of a grandiose but now moribund North Korea-planned agricultural project, with an extensive park of rusting clapped-out tractors its main legacy. People go to Omo Rate either to visit the **Geleb village** on the **far bank** of the Omo or to try to cross the Omo on the **ferry**, which may be working or not, available for use or not — in any of the four possible combinations.

If you want to cross to the west bank of the Omo (to drive to Omo National Park, for instance) then enquire in Addis Ababa with the National Tour Operation (NTO) and the Ethiopian Wildlife Conservation Office (EWCO) about the situation. Plan on having some fuel for the outboard engine that powers the ferry. If you wish to spend the night at Omo Rate, you could ask about the **guest house** there, or ask permission to put up a tent in the guest house parking lot.

Visiting the Geleb village entails hiring a local boatman to paddle you across. The village is interesting architecturally and the Geleb people have their own distinctive dress and decoration. As in all villages that are on the 'south-west ethnic circuit', payment is expected for photos — usually one birr per photo.

Backtracking toward Turmi, after fifteen or twenty kilometres (nine or 12 miles) a **track** to the **left** leads to **Murle**, **Karo**, and eventually, Mago National Park. As this track can be a bit obscure — due to alternate routes, turnoffs to villages, and the like — it would be advantageous to have a guide.

On the way to Murle, where Nasos Roussos has built attractive and comfortable **bandas** on the banks of the Omo, the road traverses some beautiful savannah, where large herds of **oryx** and **Grant's gazelle** may be seen. In fact, this area (known as the **Murle Controlled Hunting Area**) is usually far superior for wildlife viewing to Mago itself. Here one can also see **carmine bee-eaters** riding the backs of **kori bustards**, who serve as 'beaters' for their insectivorous riders.

If **Roussos's Murle Lodge** is indeed open for tourists (enquire in Addis Ababa beforehand), it offers an oasis of shade, comfort, and security, as well as an excellent base for wildlife viewing and visits to **Karo villages**. If it is not available, it's best to push on to Mago, ninety kilometres (56 miles) from Murle, as camping in the Karo area has been bedeviled by thefts and harassment. Also, as tribal raids and conflicts are still very much a reality, it is advisable to continually ask the news of the country ahead, even if visitors are excluded from the hostilities.

From Murle the **track** continues **north**, passing near the major Karo village of **Dus**, and then entering the increasingly dense bush of Mago National Park. Although Mago has many species of wildlife, it must be said that the density of the bush — possibly due to widespead poaching and subsequent population decline of the animals that keep the bush down — makes viewing more difficult than farther south in the Murle Controlled Hunting Area. The track was in terrible condition in late 1993 and arrival at the cool, clear **Neri River**, where the **campsites** are located, is much appreciated. The campsites are shady, fire pits and a latrine are there, and a refreshing bath in the Neri is only a three-minute walk away. The nearby **park headquarters** will provide day and night guards for the camp and, if desired, a park ranger to accompany you while driving in the park.

Mago National Park is mainly grass sa-

Opposite: The extravagant *Diaphananthe fragrantissima* orchid cascades from a tree overhanging the Omo River.

vannah, with some forested areas around the rivers. It was set up to conserve the large numbers of plains animals in the area, particularly **buffalo, giraffe,** and **elephant.** Also seen here are **topi** and **lelwel hartebeest,** as well as **lion, leopard, Burchell's zebra, gerenuk,** and **greater** and **lesser kudu.**

The birds are also typical of the dry grassland habitat, featuring **bustards, hornbills, weavers,** and **starlings. Kingfishers** and **herons** can be seen around the Neri River, which provides an alternative habitat.

Omo National Park

On the west bank of the Omo River, Omo National Park is 4,068 square kilometres (1,570 square miles) in area and its highest point is 1,183 metres (3,880 feet). Temperatures are high, ranging from 14° to 41°C (57° to 106°F), and the rainfall averages 500 mm (19.5 inches) a year, falling between March and April and September and October.

Sightseeing

This large and beautiful park has been hardly visited in the last two decades, as getting there has been so difficult (although until the early 1970s, Ethiopian Airlines had twice-weekly scheduled flights to an airstrip in the park, where the long-time Ethiopia resident Carl-Gustav Forsmark had a wonderful tented camp by the Mui River).

The only access to Omo National Park is via **Omo Rate,** by **ferry** to the **west bank** of the **Omo River,** and **north** to the border settlement of **Kibish,** where a seventy-five-kilometre (46-mile) unmaintained **track** leads to the Omo Park **headquarters.** However, in early 1994, a GTZ project was working on the long-neglected route from Mui River up to Maji, which is tenuously linked to Jimma. When this road is passable, a drive from Jimma, besides being extremely interesting in itself, will bestow the reward of visiting this truly wild and untamed area.

Anyone planning to attempt a visit to Omo National Park should first contact EWCO for the latest information on access, road conditions, security, and so on. The European Union has been talking about spending as much as US$20 million on Omo National Park and, if this happens, great changes could occur soon.

In the **central area** of the park is a pleasant **campsite** on the **Mui River,** set amidst large fig trees. Water is present all year, though it may be confined to pools. Park staff will inform visitors which pools are safe to use, as some **crocodiles** are resident here.

Also in the centre of the park on the Mui River, which is a tributary of the Omo, is the **park headquarters** and new **airstrip.** From here one can set out in essentially four different directions to explore the park — **south** toward Kibish, **east** to the point opposite Omo Mursi, **north-west** to Maji, or across the Mui River and **north** into a beautiful area of grassland, scattered thickets, and small hills. Take a ranger.

Vegetation in the park is typical of a hot dry area, with sweeping grasslands, wooded grasslands, and belts of forest along the rivers. The Omo River has along its length a wide belt of acacia thicket. The grass plains are relieved by bands of hills to the north and south of the park headquarters. There are **hot springs** at **Lilibai** and **Kuma.**

Prolific wildlife

The park is an extensive wilderness area and its wildlife can be prolific. This includes large herds of **eland, buffalo,** and **elephant,** as well as **giraffe, cheetah, lion, leopard,** and **Burchell's zebra. Lesser kudu, lelwel hartebeest, topi,** and **oryx** are all found here, as well as **deBrazza's** and **colobus monkeys** and **Anubis baboon.** The 306 **bird** species recorded here include many that will be familiar to East African visitors.

Seeing elephant in Omo is a matter of timing, for much of the year they are from accessible parts of the park, but recent visitors have seen herds of eland numbering as many as 400. Lion are not infrequently found near the Lilibai hot springs, where many animals come to drink in the dry season.

All this area is populated with interesting small tribal groups, such as the Surma, Mursi, and Kwegu.

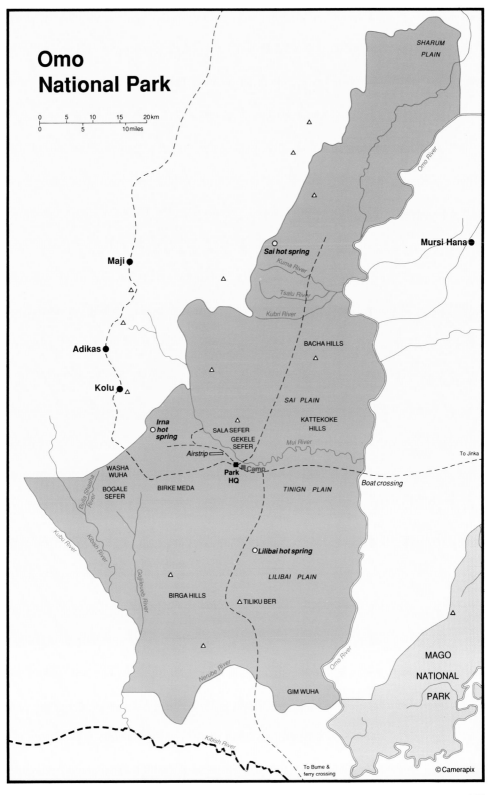

Omo
National Park

Sai hot spring

Mursi Hana

Maji

Adikas

Kolu

Irna hot spring

BACHA HILLS

SAI PLAIN

KATTEKOKE HILLS

SALA SEFER

GEKELE SEFER

Mui River

Airstrip

To Jinka

WASHA WUHA

Park HQ

Camp

Boat crossing

BOGALE SEFER

BIRKE MEDA

TININGN PLAIN

Lilibai hot spring

LILIBAI PLAIN

BIRGA HILLS

TILIKU BER

MAGO

NATIONAL

PARK

GIM WUHA

SHARUM PLAIN

Omo River

Kuma River

Tsalu River

Kubri River

Bulla Shasha River

Kubu River

Kibish River

Gajileueb River

Nerube River

Omo River

Kibish River

To Bume & ferry crossing

©Camerapix

The West: Fertile and Exotic

The traveller who journeys westwards from Addis Ababa can be forgiven for thinking that Ethiopia is entirely a highland country. The vistas of the high plateau, the bracing climate, the chill in the air at night — all these things seem somehow limitless.

On the westward road, this illusion is steadfastly preserved throughout the giant sprawling region of Welega but begins to give way almost as soon as the traveller enters Ilubabor — a region that is as exotic as its name. Tropical forests cover the land and colobus monkeys chatter in the leafy branches and move in troops across the farmers' fields.

After having become familiar with the highlands of Ethiopia, which have been tamed to the plough for millennia, it comes as a startling surprise, here in the west, to find humanity once again in direct competition with the forces of the wilderness — a competition that is not easily won.

Unfortunately, because of the tremendous influx of Sudanese refugees from across the border in recent years, Ilubabor is now only a shadow of its former self, and the once abundant wildlife in the area has reportedly decreased considerably owing to the encroaching human population. It is best to check with the Ethiopian Tourism Commission in Addis Ababa as to current local conditions before making the journey.

Nevertheless, a trip following the Baro, the greatest river of Ilubabor, on its lazy meandering course across the western Ethiopian lowlands to the border of the Sudan — where it eventually empties itself into the broad body of the White Nile above Khartoum — is a fascinating one.

Your best bet is to head for the charming, sleepy town of Gambella, which serves as a good base from which to explore the country's westernmost game preservation area, Gambella National Park.

Gambella: A Link with the Past

Situated on the banks of the Baro River, Gambella has the charming, somewhat run down, slightly passé atmosphere of a once active colonial town. And this is exactly what it is, for at the turn of the century it was a major river port that, through the Sudan, acted as an outlet for a substantial share of Ethiopia's rich coffee trade.

The establishment of a commercial station on the Baro was first envisaged as a step towards the formation of an inland shipping service linking that river with Khartoum, and more generally Ethiopia with Sudan and Egypt. This move made sense to both Britain and Ethiopia. For Britain, then in control of Sudan, the proposed service offered an opportunity of opening up trade with western, and possibly also central, Ethiopia, which was linked by railway with Djibouti and almost entirely dependent on France. The scheme was more attractive because Ethiopia's natural riches were thought to be found primarily in the west.

Emperor Menelik, Ethiopia's ruler at that time, saw the project as an opportunity to develop trade in a hitherto isolated area, as well as a way of asserting his independence of the French colonial government in Djibouti with which he was then at loggerheads.

Menelik therefore agreed to give the British an enclave on the Baro River. The agreement was signed by the emperor and the British representative in Addis Ababa,

Opposite: Sunset on the Baro, the greatest river of the western Ilubabor region.

Captain Harrington, in May 1902. It granted the British government of Sudan an area at Itang on the Baro River not exceeding 400 hectares (988 acres) 'to be administered and occupied as a commercial station' so long as Sudan was under Anglo-Egyptian rule.

Later study, however, showed that a position further upstream from Itang would allow boats to operate for a longer period of the year. An alternative location was therefore agreed upon. It became known as Gambella and was inaugurated as a port and customs station in 1907.

Steamers, which took seven days to sail down to Khartoum and eleven days to return against the current, were soon plying between Gambella and Khartoum, and Gambella soon grew into a major trading centre. It handled Ethiopia's export of coffee, beeswax, and, to a lesser extent, skins, as well as the import of cotton cloth, salt, sacks, various provisions, and liquors.

Unlike most Ethiopian settlements, Gambella was built to a plan with straight roads and strictly aligned buildings. These included the residence and office of the local British commissioner, for many years Captain J.K. Maurice; a sub-office of the Bank of Abyssinia, later the Bank of Ethiopia; and the dwellings of many foreign merchants, mainly Greeks. Beyond the compound there was an Ethiopian settlement clustered around the customs post and telegraph station, and the premises and warehouses of the Ethiopian Motor Transport Company.

The enclave reverted to Ethiopian rule after the independence of Sudan, and the shipping service to Khartoum that had operated for almost half a century ceased in 1955. The Ethiopian government has plans to reactivate and redevelop the facilities at Gambella and it is hoped that the river trade can be resumed, returning to this region much of its lost economic importance.

In the meantime, this sleepy town with its lazy, relaxed lifestyle dominated by the long noontime siesta holds many attractions for the traveller and is a convenient gateway to the broad vistas of the western Ethiopian plains.

Getting there

Gambella, 753 kilometres (467 miles) from Addis Ababa, 72 kilometres (45 miles) from Dembidolo, 394 kilometres (244 miles) from Nekemte, and 171 kilometres (106 miles) from Metu, is served by two major roads from the east. It also has a good airport and is accessible by air, via four weekly Ethiopian Airlines flights.

When to go

The town and region can be visited at any time of the year but, as in other regions of the country, the roads are easier to negotiate in the dry season.

Where to stay

In Ambo, the Ethiopia Hotel, which has a swimming pool. In Dembidolo, several small local hotels. In Gambella, the Gambella Ethiopia Hotel. See Listings.

Sightseeing

Your trip **west** begins by taking **Arbeynoch Street** from Addis, which turns into the **Ambo Road**. Just as you get near the city limits, the road passes through a **potter's village**, where outdoor stalls and small shops display and sell decorative **figurines** and a fascinating variety of traditional **household utensils**.

Eighteen kilometres (eleven miles) from the capital is the **Gefersa reservoir** on the **left**, which supplies Addis Ababa with its water. Fed by the Akaki River and surrounded by small forests of eucalyptus trees, the reservoir is home to **pelicans**, **cormorants**, and **Egyptian geese**. Just before the reservoir, also on the left, is the **Pineta**, an Italian-type restaurant complete with *bocci* **(bowls) pitch**, which is well frequented by Addis Ababa residents on Sundays.

A few kilometres beyond the reservoir to the **north** is the modern **Church of Saint Mary**. Shortly thereafter, the **main road** passes through the village of **Menagesha**, which is in the depression between **Mount Menagesha** and **Mount Sululta**. In the village there is a motorable **dirt track** to the **left** leading to **Maryam Church** at the foot of Mount Menagesha. A small **village**

of potters, whose ancestors settled here in Menelik's time, live a little to the right of the church and can be seen at work using traditional methods. The finished products are for sale.

The shape of an upside-down pudding basin, Mount Menagesha is said to be an ancient coronation place for Ethiopian rulers and is climbable from the Addis Ababa side after an hour's walk from the main road and a hectic scramble up the steep wooded incline. Alternatively, there is a **track** — less than an hour's walk — up the **west** side to the practically deserted **monastery** on top. The long grass and thick bushes provide plenty of cover for wildlife and birds.

Menagesha Forest

Three kilometres (two miles) past the village of Menagesha, a **sign** for **'Spring Farm'** points the way to the base of **Mount Wuchacha** in the **Menagesha Forest**. Turn off on to the **gravel road** and keep going for about fifteen kilometres (nine miles). When you reach **Suba village**, turn **left** immediately after the **bridge** on to the **dirt track** that leads directly up into the forest.

The western slopes of Mount Wuchacha are covered in superb forest, the last of Addis Ababa's indigenous trees: giant junipers and *zigba (Podocarpus gracilor)*. Mingled in with these two forest giants, some of which are more than 400 years old, is a lush undergrowth of giant lobelia and giant groundsel. The **track** winds upwards to a delightful **picnic spot**, a level place between huge juniper trees. Above this the forest gradually thins out to wild roses, *kosso (Hagenia abyssinica)*, and giant heath until it finally emerges at the actual **rim** of the crater valley, which is extensively farmed.

The forest was originally planted by Emperor Zara Yaqob and was reserved as crown land in the old system. It is now a state park and the birds and animals that live here are protected. Among these, the black-and-white **colobus monkey** is probably the most spectacular. **Menelik's bushbuck** and **duiker** are present but often concealed in the thick undergrowth.

The motorable **track** ends just beyond

Above: The spectacular colobus monkey can sometimes be seen leaping from tree to tree in the Menagesha Forest.

the treeline, where there is a little **lodge** that former ruler Mengistu built. In 1994, this lodge was being done up for visitors, who are also welcome at the beautifully refurbished **Forestry Training Centre** below the campsite. The latter has a **guest house** and can be booked through either the Wildlife Conservation Office or the Forestry Department of the Ministry of Natural Resources and Economic Development in Addis Ababa.

From this point hiking is the way to go. A narrow **footpath** leads along above a small valley at the far end. It forks into several directions. The **left-hand track** ascends the **northern** sweep of the **crater rim** and gradually climbs up to the very highest point, the **centre path** leads up through the crater itself to the far rim, and the **right** either to **Mogli summit**, an arduous vertical climb, or round the back of the lower peak immediately on the **right**.

Klipspringer are occasionally seen at these high points, but domestic cattle are regrettably far more frequent.

Above: Addis Alem's richly decorated Church of Saint Mary was intended by Emperor Menelik II to be the southern equivalent of the Church of Saint Mary of Zion at Axum.

Continuing on **west** from Menagesha village, the **Ambo Road** descends to the village of **Holetta** (also known as Genet) — the first place in Ethiopia with a **water mill**, which was built in 1909 on the **Holetta River**, a tributary of the Awash River.

Addis Alem

Past Holetta, the road crosses a series of small valleys formed by the streams that run into the Holetta River. Fifty-five kilometres (34 miles) outside of Addis Ababa is the village of **Addis Alem**, which has a short but interesting history and is a good place to stop and look around.

Emperor Menelik, when confronted by an acute shortage of wood in Addis Ababa at the end of the nineteenth century, conceived the plan of moving his capital to the west, in the vicinity of the forest on Mount Menagesha. For his new settlement he chose the site of present-day Addis Alem, literally meaning 'New World', which was given this name by Menelik's consort, Queen Taytu. He had his

craftsmen begin work on a palace there but soon changed his mind — perhaps because of the shortage of water in the area — and decided to retain Addis Ababa as his capital.

During the short period that Menelik was interested in this village, he built a church and several buildings that were used as his palace. These structures still stand at the top of a small **hill** that commands a view of the surrounding plains and the hills beyond. The **road** to the top of the hill is on the **west** side of the town and is marked by a **sign** on the **left** reading **'Debre Tsion'**. The road is about one kilometre (half a mile) long and goes up into the compound of these interesting buildings.

The **Church of Saint Mary** was intended by Menelik as the southern equivalent of the Church of Saint Mary of Zion at Axum. The church and sanctuary are decorated with an amazing variety of interesting **paintings** depicting wildlife, biblical scenes, and various Ethiopian rulers. Near the church a **museum** contains

Above: Colourful and aromatic piles of exotic spices at the Mercato.

the clothes and decorations of several former Ethiopian rulers and their families, and south of the church compound is the restored part-time **residence** of Menelik. Below this building is the large, elliptical former **dining hall**. The *tukul* west of the compound was once the **kitchen**.

The area between Addis Alem and Ambo, fifty kilometres (31 miles) farther on, is interesting for it contains the intersection of three of Ethiopia's major river basins: those of the Awash, the Omo, and the Guder.

Shepherd boys along this stretch of road occupy their spare time by making hats from grasses, as well as clever models of Ethiopian houses, cars, jets, and even helicopters made from the pith of reeds. These unique items, although somewhat fragile, make good mementos and toys.

Ambo, also known as Hagre Hiwot — meaning 'Land of Life' — sits at an altitude of 2,050 metres (6,724 feet). The town is popular with Addis Ababa residents because it is close enough to drive there, enjoy the sun and **hot mineral water pool**,

and drive back to the capital on the same day. But if you are inclined to stay the night, the Ras Hotel across the road from the pool provides good accommodation.

It is from the nearby springs at Senkele that Ethiopia's principal bottled mineral water, also called Ambo, is drawn. The town also has a colourful **market**, with Saturday being the major market day.

The magnificent **crater lake** of **Wonchi** can be reached from Ambo by four-wheel drive or on horseback by arrangement with the local farmers' association, where a guide can also be hired. The thirty-five-kilometre (22-mile) walk takes about seven hours, which means spending the very cold night camping on the crater rim, where you can expect to be hassled by the local people.

Guder Falls

Twelve kilometres (seven miles) past Ambo on the **main road** are the small but beautiful **Guder River Falls**, which can be seen on the **south** side of the road after passing through the small village of

191

Above: Local villagers use sturdy dugout canoes to traverse the waters of Lake Wonchi.
Previous pages: The breathtakingly beautiful crater lake of Wonchi.

Guder. A popular export-quality red wine has been named after the town, which is the centre of the country's premier wine-growing district. **Vineyards** stretch out across the rolling dun-coloured slopes on both sides of the road, interspersed with picturesque farmhouses and villas.

The border between Shewa region and its western neighbour, Welega, is crossed at the village of **Bako**, where vineyards give way to extensive **coffee plantations** tended by industrious farmers of Oromo stock, who make up the bulk of the population in this region. Welega is also renowned as the region where Ethiopia's famed **frankincense** is collected and where, together with Sidamo, Ethiopia's **gold reserve** comes from. The frankincense produced here is exported to Sudan, Egypt, and the Middle East.

You will cross the **Gibe River** at the town of Bako, site of an agricultural research station, before you come to the regional capital of **Nekemte**, a substantial marketing and coffee-forwarding centre 188 kilometres (117 miles) from Guder.

Also known as Lekemt, the somewhat drab and undistinguished town was founded in the mid-nineteenth century by a local ruler, Bekere Godana. Places to visit include the old local **palace**, the **Museum of Culture**, and several nearby **churches** and **waterfalls** — including the **Bereda** and **Anger Falls** on the Didesa River.

The people who inhabit Welega, Shewa, Bale, Kaffa, and Ilubabor are mostly members of the Mecha Oromo groups, mixed agriculturalist pastoralists.

Those who live in the area between the Gibe and Didesa rivers were once virtually cut off from the central administration by vast gorges and the rushing waters, and only relatively recently have they changed their customs with the advent of a coffee-based economy and the rural feeder roads that go with it finally bringing them out of their cultural isolation.

The scattered homesteads of the farmers dot the landscape here, resembling small villages: the main house is surrounded by other houses of the family and the typical thatched-roofed grain stores called *gotera*.

Above: Just off the main road past the village of Guder, the small Guder River Falls are quite attractive if glimpsed during or just after the rains but are no more than a trickle during the dry season.

The whole compound is surrounded by a thick acacia thorn fence.

Although circular, thatched, and walled with *chika* (mud mixed with straw), the huts are somewhat different from the *tukuls* typical of the northern plateau. One aspect is the stretching of the eaves, which are supported on poles, forming a small verandah where firewood and calves can be kept. The interior is more often partitioned, at least into two rooms. The central part forms the main circular room with fireplace and sleeping platform, also made of *chika*. The second room encircles the main room and is divided and used as a bedroom for husband and wife, for storage, and for the kitchen.

Gold mines

If you keep straight on past **Ghimbi**, 113 kilometres (70 miles) west of Nekemte and the site of an interesting roadside **woodcraft centre**, the road passes through the town of **Nejo** seventy-one kilometres (44 miles) later.

Near the town is said to be the oldest **gold mine** in the world, thought by some to be the source of the legendary 'King Solomon's Mines' featured in the novel of the same name by Rider Haggard. The **road** continues in this **north-westerly** direction, touching the wildlife-rich **Didesa River Valley**, to the border town of **Asosa**, 163 kilometres (101 miles) from Nejo.

Dembidolo

To continue **west** and on to Gambella, however, you need to turn **left** a few kilometres past Ghimbi on the **main road** to **Dembidolo**, 211 kilometres (131 miles) from the turnoff. Also known as Sayo, Dembidolo is a beautiful town that sprang up as a commercial centre in the nineteenth century. Since then it has become a sizeable place, with several small local **hotels**, deep **wells,** and a **goldsmith's shop** where you can see craftsmen at work. The town is also known for its good honey wine, or *tej*.

Although the main road through the town continues west and then bends south and then west again into Gambella, it is shorter and simpler to take the road leading **south-west** out of Dembidolo to the riverside town.

There is an element of nostalgia, as well as unique charm, about **Gambella** today. It is a town living largely in the past, with many curious vestiges of former times: massive old brick **warehouses** and **stores**, now used to service local trade points along the Baro River system inside Ethiopia; thatched colonial-style bungalows surrounded by unkempt hedges; streets laid out on a grid pattern; and magnificent 'flame trees' reminiscent of a European settlement in India. The old **wharves**, solidly built, have been hardly touched by the passing years.

The town and its environs are situated in the low Nilotic plain between the Ethiopian plateau and the Sudan border, in an area of immense warm grasslands interspersed with scrub forests. The **Baro River** is a site of constant activity, with people collecting water, bathing, washing clothes, fishing, travelling in dugout canoes, or merely relaxing along the sandy beach. Fish are plentiful and provide opportunities for excellent meals of **Nile perch**, **carp**, **tigerfish**, or **catfish**.

Although the countryside around the town once teemed with wild animals of all kinds: elephant, buffalo, roan antelope, waterbuck, hartebeest, tiang, white-eared kob, and crocodile, their numbers have been considerably diminished due to the influx of Sudanese refugees from across the nearby border. Bird life, however, remains prolific, and the visitor can expect to see large numbers of **eagles**, **falcons**, **vultures**, **ducks**, **geese**, **cranes**, **herons**, **storks**, and myriads of smaller birds.

Gambella is a good base from which to explore the nearby bush, particularly the Gambella National Park.

Gambella National Park

One of Ethiopia's least developed parks and receiving few visitors, **Gambella National Park** is located on the **Akobo River** system. It was originally created for the protection of an extensive swamp habitat and the wildlife there.

The park is 5,060 square kilometres (1,954 square miles) in area, and its altitude ranges between 400 and 768 metres (1,312 and 2,519 feet). Rainfall is 1,500 mm (58.5 inches) a year, falling between April and October. Temperatures are high. The vegetation here is mainly grassland and *Terminalia/Combretum* wooded grassland, with extensive areas of swamp. Malaria is a problem and precautions must be taken.

Sightseeing

The park contains many species representative of neighbouring Sudan and not found elsewhere in Ethiopia, such as **Nile lechwe** and **white-eared kob**, the latter migrating in large numbers. **Roan antelope**, **topi**, **elephant**, **buffalo**, and **giraffe** are also present. The most important bird species present here is the **whale-headed stork**, an unusual large-billed, tall bird seen standing in the swamps.

There are no facilities within the park, which is administered from the town of Gambella.

A rough **track**, often flooded in the rainy season, follows the **northern bank** of the Baro as it flows out of Gambella towards the Sudanese border, a distance of some 130 kilometres (81 miles). The terrain is flat, marshy in places and generally fertile, although there is little tradition of agriculture.

The Anuak

The indigenous **Anuak** people are mainly fisherfolk in this region, and the crops they do grow — such as sorghum — do not reach their full potential because of the extremely basic methods of cultivation employed.

There are few large villages, as people prefer instead to group together around a

Above: Gambella town was once intended to be a major 'port' on an inland river shipping system that never came to be.

mango grove in an extended family compound of no more than five or six huts. These buildings, used solely as sleeping quarters, have floors of polished, compact mud, extremely low doorways let into walls decorated with engraved patterns depicting animals and magical symbols, and thatched roofs — often of many tiers for better protection against tropical downpours and blazing sun — that sometimes extend down almost to ground level.

During daylight hours the majority of family members stay in the open air, fishing, attending to the chores in the fields, or simply lounging in the shade of the leafy mango trees and smoking long pipes of heady aromatic tobacco.

The women, naked to the waist, wear elaborate bead necklaces and heavy ivory and bone bangles above the elbow, and have their hair closely cropped, sometimes shaven.

Both men and women indulge in a further decorative fancy, common among all the Nilotic peoples of Ethiopia and Sudan, of having the front six teeth of the lower jaw removed at about the age of twelve. This is said to have been originally a precaution against the effects of tetanus, or 'lockjaw'.

As the **track** meanders along the course of the Baro further and further to the **west** of Gambella, the town's modernizing influence fades and you'll find yourself among people who have rarely seen foreigners and whose contacts with the influences of the industrial era are remote in the extreme.

Only since the late 1970s have government-established schools begun to reach the children of this area and, for the majority of the population, the twentieth century still remains just a distant rumour.

The **Baro**, at this point, is a beautiful river, rich in bird life — **geese**, **egrets**, **ibises**, **kingfishers**, and **pelicans** — and decorated with the greens and purples of floating water-hyacinth. Fish stocks are plentiful, both in the river itself and in the pools and lakes that flooding creates in the near reaches of the surrounding countryside.

197

The Nuer

Past the sizeable settlement of **Itang**, the Anuak give way to their cousins, the **Nuer**, who are primarily cattle herders, though they also fish. Nuer are more social in their habits than the Anuak and live together in villages of several hundred at widely spaced intervals along the river banks.

They are comely people, with long, handsome faces and extremely dark, satiny complexions. Both men and women favour a style of decorative scarification, which raises the skin of chest, stomach, and face in remarkable patterns of bumps and cicatrices. Other forms of personal ornamentation include heavy bone bangles, bright bead necklaces, and spikes of ivory or brass thrust through a hole pierced in the lower lip and protruding down over the chin.

Bright-eyed, intelligent, and endlessly curious, the Nuer are very far from meriting that ill-judged epithet 'primitive', but theirs, undoubtedly, is a simple culture, uncomplicated by the need to adapt to rapid changes and uncluttered by the pressures, phobias, and anxieties of the modern world.

In the evenings, these gentle, charming people bring in their scattered herds from grazing grounds on the surrounding plains to camps established on the banks of the Baro River. Nuer love of cattle is legendary, often expressed in poems and songs of great beauty extolling the virtues of favourite beasts.

From Gambella, you begin your return journey east, which dips down into the birthplace of coffee, the Kaffa region and its capital, Jimma.

Opposite top: Young Nuer boy looks after his beast carefully; his people's love of cattle is legendary. Opposite left: Cheerful Anuak woman and child near Gambella. Opposite: Nuer women, as well as men, favour decorative skin scarification, with a spike of ivory or brass thrust through the lower lip.

Jimma: Capital of Coffee Country

The home of Ethiopian coffee and, indeed, the first home of all the coffee in the world (See 'The World's Favourite Drink', Part Four), the fertile Kaffa region has as its capital the town of Jimma, which lies at the southern end of the Ethiopian plateau on the west of the Rift in rolling hilly country where temperatures are never higher than 29°C (85°F). This frost-free environment, which gets a substantial 1600 mm (62 inches) of rain each year, is perfect for growing a huge variety of foodstuffs, including grains, legumes, and root crops.

Jimma owes its origin to the establishment of an early Oromo monarchy. Its rulers had their capital at a place called Jiren and lived in a palace filled with soldiers and servants, eunuchs and concubines, lawyers, writers, and musicians. Markets in the area had to be staggered to avoid conflict; 30,000 people, for example, attended the great Thursday market at nearby Hirmata. Jiren and Hirmata later coalesced to form the present-day town of Jimma.

The great trade routes passed through Jimma because of the ease of travel where no great mountains, deep rivers, or gorges bar the way and cultural influences were absorbed from Gondar, Kaffa, and other surrounding regions.

The old Jimma kingdom, which at its height covered 13,000 square kilometres (8,000 square miles), was sufficiently rich to pay tribute to Menelik when he expanded his sway in the late 1800s. Jimma thus avoided the reprisals visited on its neighbours and gained a reputation for wealth and greatness, with agriculture and a budding coffee industry flourishing.

Getting there

Jimma, 335 kilometres from Addis Ababa, 252 kilometres from Metu and 423 kilometres (262 miles) from Gambella, is served by a good asphalt road as well as by air on daily flights of Ethiopian Airlines.

199

When to go

Jimma can be visited at any time of the year.

Where to stay

In Gore, several small local hotels. In Jimma, the Jimma Ethiopia Hotel, the Gibe Ethiopia Hotel, and several other small, local hotels. In Weliso, the Weliso Ethiopia Hotel. See Listings.

Sightseeing

As you head **east** towards Gore, you'll leave Gambella via an elegant and modern single-span **bridge** — the longest of its kind in Ethiopia — over the **Baro River**. The view from the bridge over the riverside town presents an exotic spectacle of soft orange flamboyants and mauve jacaranda trees amidst villas set back from wide and leafy streets. In the waters below children fish and townspeople come down to bathe, keeping a wary eye out for the numerous small crocodiles that sun themselves upon the sandspits along the river. The local people, in fact, only bathe in areas they know to be safe, and it is best to heed their advice if you get the urge to go for a swim. In 1968, a U.S. Peace Corps volunteer, ignoring the warnings of the locals, was eaten by a crocodile when he went swimming in the Baro at Gambella. The grisly photos taken after the croc was shot and cut open are still hawked in the town.

The **road** from Gambella then enters a series of expansive winding curves that take it a thousand metres up the escarpment, back into considerably cooler highlands. Here, 146 kilometres (91 miles) from Gambella, the people of the nearby town of **Gore** have established a colourful **market** on the very edge of the escarpment, up to which the plain-dwellers below sometimes venture with their trade — strangers in a strange land, speaking languages that are totally unrelated to the Semitic Amharic and Cushitic Oromo tongues that dominate much of the rest of Ethiopia.

Dressed in warm clothing and goatskin caps to fend off the chill of the evening air at 2,000 metres (6,560 feet), the highland peoples are ever reluctant to venture down into the burning deserts that surround them on all sides.

This westernmost highland settlement of Gore, one of the most important towns in western Ethiopia and the capital of Ilubabor, came into existence in the nineteenth century, when it was the headquarters of one of Emperor Menelik's principal commanders, Ras Tessema Nadew. Set in fine mountain scenery, the settlement is renowned for its honey and is the site of the chief's old **palace** and two **churches**, dedicated respectively to the Virgin Mary and Saint George.

Metu

Twenty-five kilometres (15.5 miles) from Gore is the regional capital of **Metu**, surrounded by singing forests filled with brightly plumed birds. The mood here is that of a frontier settlement — the frontier being not a political one but rather the intangible borderline between raw nature and the endeavours of man.

Ethiopia's **Oromo** people, who have committed themselves to pushing this frontier back in their steady westwards expansion, crowd into Metu on holidays and weekends, drinking and listening to music in its many small **bars**, or offering their produce for sale in its open **market** — produce that includes berries and wild honey as well as the more familiar grains and vegetables of established agriculture. At night a small generator chugs and puffs bravely for an hour or two before it is closed down and darkness and silence fall over the town.

A thirteen-kilometre (eight-mile) detour off the main road at Metu leads the traveller to the village of **Bechu**, which occupies an irregular clearing in the midst of a dense thicket of trees. From here, an hour's downhill walk through green glades on a narrow and at times barely discernible **path** is rewarded with a view of one of Ethiopia's many splendid **waterfalls** where the **Sor River** pours over the lip of a broad chasm 100 metres (328 feet) deep. A natural amphitheatre, heavily overgrown with weird tree ferns and tall grasses, this is a delightful spot in which to

Above: Coffee, one of the world's favourite beverages, was 'born' in the Kaffa region of Ethiopia.

savour the primal atmosphere of Ilubabor and to catch a glimpse of nature as it must once have been throughout much of Africa before the coming of humanity.

The road continues through **Bedele**, 115 kilometres (71 miles) east of Metu. A turn left on the road that runs north here will take you back to Nekemte and the main east-west road. Bedele's claim to fame is the newest and largest **beer factory** in Ethiopia, making, of course, 'Bedele' beer.

The **road** to Jimma takes a sharp bend **south** after Bedele, and continues in a southerly direction until it crosses into Kaffa region.

Coffee country

The modern town of **Agaro**, 93 kilometres (58 miles) south of Bedele, is the first town you come to in this region. It is set in the heart of the coffee-growing country and, though not evident to the traveller, is reputedly one of the richest towns in the whole of Ethiopia.

Kaffa provides almost perfect conditions for the coffee plant, which still grows wild in parts of the region. Its rolling hillsides and valleys, at altitudes from 2,100 metres (6,900 feet) down to 1,300 metres (4,300 feet), receive just the right amount of rainfall — 1,500 to 2,500 mm (58.5 to 97.5 inches) a year — and have slightly acidic topsoils with pH values between 4.5 and 5.5. The people, too, have an established tradition of coffee cultivation, today harnessed to numerous cooperatives and to highly productive farms that make Ethiopia one of the world's leading exporters of highest quality *arabica*.

The **Jimma Oromo** — part of the giant group of people who began to move across southern Ethiopia in the sixteenth century, conquering and absorbing the local cultures — inhabit this area, living in small homesteads surrounded by a living euphorbia fence. Their houses are round, thatched, and surmounted by a clay pot.

The Bench

Another interesting group in the region is the **Bench** (formerly known as the **Gimirra**), who lived in semi-isolation in the heavily forested rainy Kaffa highlands. They were once a large kingdom of industrious cultivators, also known to the ancient world as 'great warriors and more esteemed than any of the black nations'. Tragically, their culture was virtually wiped out from the fifteenth to the mid-twentieth centuries, when they were persecuted, sold into slavery by the thousands, tortured, mutilated, and hunted down like animals in the forests — many groups suffering extinction in consequence.

Gimirra means 'honey collector' or 'tree climber', and they once inhabited a land rich in wildlife, cultivated fields and an abundance of honey. They appear to have provided a vital source of slaves for the great neighbouring kingdom of Kaffa, whose people sold them to Europe and Arabia. Other than that, little is known of them, as those who survived have seemingly forgotten their heritage.

Today, as they climb back to life, they are gradually losing the marks of distrust branded on them by decades of brutality. They are quite musical, and playing a set of pan pipes is one of their more cheerful pastimes.

The great forests have been much depleted by farmers and coffee merchants, but *enset, teff,* barley, and millet are grown in their place as agriculture is once again widely practised. Bees still have a special significance to the Bench, who remain great honey gatherers as well as hunters.

Their villages are strikingly picturesque, with each homestead having its characteristic elevated field-watching huts. The tree *Euphorbia amphiphylla,* used as a hedge, lines the pathways, and the same wood is used for the rafters of the houses, which are quite small with very low entrances. The thatched roofs are steeper than most and have a distinctly oriental look. Most interesting is the mural decoration used in the homes, a unique remnant of their lost culture. Walls are covered with mortar, which is modeled in light relief in simple designs with a triangle motif and coloured in orange or vermilion, charcoal, and cinders.

The peoples of the region often converge in the regional capital of **Jimma**, forty-four kilometres (27 miles) south-east of Agaro. One of the most important settlements in the west of the country and Ethiopia's most important **coffee-collecting centre**, it is a large urban town with many modern institutions. These include an **airport**, well-frequented **shops** and **hotels**, a **cinema**, a **college of agriculture**, an **institute of health sciences**, and an **agricultural research station**.

Places of particular tourist interest include the two-storey **palace** of Abba Jifar II (1878–1932), one of the most important local rulers of the past, the principal **mosque**, and the octagonal **church of Medhane Alem**, or Saviour of the World. The large Thursday **market** is also colourful and interesting. It is a good place from which to buy the famous three-legged Jimma **stools** and locally made **baskets**, as well as a wide range of local supplies, including coffee, which grows wild in the area.

The **museum** with its collection of

Above: *Enset* (false banana) is the basis of the Gurage economy, providing both food and the materials from which their homes are constructed.

Kaffa's traditional **wooden handicraft masterpieces** is also worth a visit, as are the many **coffee-cleaning units** in the town. A **park** by the river is the perfect place to sit and relax — perhaps with a cool drink, such as the delicious fruit juices available in the area or the famous local drink called *besso*, a non-alcoholic beverage made of ground barley. *Besso* can also refer to the common foodstuff made by mixing ground barley with water into a paste.

From Jimma, your journey back to Addis now heads **north-east** on a good **asphalt road** that runs through a highland zone of great scenic beauty.

First travelling through plains and valleys, usually spotted with large herds of fat cattle quietly grazing on the lush grass, you will follow the **Little Gibe River gorge** on the **left** as you climb up a mountainside before reaching the town of **Abelti**, recognizable by the huge box-shaped **stone** that juts up to the **east**. The 142-kilometre (88-mile) stretch of road between Jimma and the town of Abelti is also a good place to bargain for handicrafts made in the area, which are sold along the roadside by the local people.

The **road** then descends into the valley of the **Omo River**, which here, near its headwaters, is known as the **Gibe**. It then rises again to the edge of the great plateau, which — between **Welkite** on the **main road** and **Indibir** and **Hosaina** to the **south** — offers dramatic views of the surrounding countryside.

Curing waters

From Welkite the **road** continues **north-east** for forty-two kilometres (26 miles) to **Weliso**, also known as Ghion, which is built around natural **hot springs**. The Ethiopia Hotel here consists of one main building in which the bath tubs are the size of small swimming pools and a number of individual cabins built in the local *tukul* style. The hotel's **swimming pool** — surrounded by grassy lawns perfect for picnicking — is itself fed from the hot springs, the waters of which are said to have curative properties for almost every ache and pain.

And in case the waters don't work, a local resident, the Christian religious healer Abba Wolde Tensa'e, has for many years gained a great reputation for his cures — as well as the expelling of devils — which he usually carries out in public on Sundays and encourages sightseers.

Weliso has an exceptionally good **pastry shop**, which also sells refreshing fruit juices. Curios for sale in the town include a variety of **daggers**. To see some fine examples of **Gurage homes**, with roofs that all but touch the ground on each side, turn **right** at the **hotel sign** and follow the **road** for about two kilometres (just over one mile). From Weliso, you can also drive north to Wonchi crater lake near Ambo.

The Gurage

The area east of the Gibe River for hundreds of years has been the homeland of one of Ethiopia's most remarkable and industrious peoples — the Gurage. Of mixed Semitic and Hamitic stock, they probably migrated here from further north in the long-forgotten past. They have made themselves at home in the southern highlands and have evolved a uniquely vigorous and self-reliant economy.

The basis of this economy is the 'false banana' tree, known throughout Ethiopia as *enset*. Its cycle of growth determines the rhythm and special nature of the Gurage lifestyle, providing both their staple foodstuff and the materials from which their homes are constructed. Each house, tall and spacious with a high thatched roof, stands in its own garden of up to ten hectares (25 acres).

Around the house are rows of *enset* trees, the youngest plants further away followed by increasingly older and taller layers radiating inwards. Specific holes are reserved for trees of a specific age and the plants are rotated from hole to hole as they mature until, at the age of eight to ten years, they are ready to be cut down.

The bark and fibres of the felled tree are taken away to be used for building and rope-making, and the massive vegetative bulb is dug up, shredded, and then reburied, wrapped in leaves in a new line of holes close to the house. Here it ferments into a thick cheesy paste, which the Gurage use in unleavened form to bake into the grey, sour-flavoured waffle bread that constitutes the basis of their diet.

Beyond the *enset* plantation most Gurage farmers grow cash crops including coffee, *chat* (a mild stimulant popular in much of the Horn of Africa), tobacco, and eucalyptus trees (for firewood). These crops produce substantial revenues for the Gurage who, rendered self-sufficient for their staple food by the wonderful properties of *enset*, often become very prosperous. This prosperity is reflected in their well-furnished circular houses, which are supported by an imposing central mainstay and are divided within into sleeping, living, and cooking areas, with a large section to one side where the family's cattle and goats are kept. Mats and carpets cover the earth floor of the main living quarters, colourful baskets hang in precise rows along the walls, and beautifully fashioned pottery is arranged around the hearth.

A mixed community of Muslims and Christians, the Gurage live in what must surely be one of the most pleasant parts of Ethiopia. Their villages stand surrounded by grassy commons and meadows where horses graze beside thatched dwellings and where carpenters skilfully prepare the wicker frames of new homes.

About eighty-nine kilometres (55 miles) farther along the road back to Addis is the town of **Sebeta**. Just before the town, a **turning** to the **left** leads past the **Meta beer factory** to a little **restaurant** set in **citrus orchards** and a small **park** with two seasonal **waterfalls**. The restaurant serves national food and delicious *tej*. It is open for meals on Saturdays and Sundays only, but it is possible to get a drink and snacks on other days.

One can drive from here up to the

Overleaf: Neat thatched-roof Gurage homes are scattered throughout some of the most fertile lands of Ethiopia.

Above: Interior of the Adadi Maryam church just south of Addis Ababa, one of the southernmost stone churches similar to those at Lalibela and reputed to be the last that the king had built.

Menegesha Forest, and it is also a good spot from which the intrepid may make their assault on **Mogli**, one of the peaks of the crater mountain of **Wuchacha**. It is about a three-and-a-half-hour walk, and it is perhaps better to set out in the early morning before the sun gets too hot if you really want to get to the summit. (Your ascent is easier if you keep in mind the fact that the return journey is naturally somewhat quicker, and there are cold drinks and food at the bottom.) For the less ambitious there are many lovely walks near the restaurant — just to the top of the falls or into the woods which grace the hillside — or *ghari* (horse-drawn cart) rides to the main road and back.

Sebeta

The village of Sebeta itself lies in a tract of fertile country that produces cereal crops and vegetables and supports large herds of dairy cattle. Less than a half-hour's drive from the nation's capital, it is quite a popular weekend destination for Addis residents.

A number of wayside vendors have popped up in Sebeta, selling all manner of vegetables and fruit as well as baskets, stools, carvings, and other souvenirs.

Not far past Sebeta, the Ethiopian Highway Authority's **equipment yard** appears on the **left**, at **Alem Gena**. Turn **south** here on the **road** to **Butajira**, directly opposite the yard, for a number of interesting side trips.

Mount Furi

For the first of these, a trip to the top of **Mount Furi**, travel for about one kilometre (half a mile) **south** on this all-weather **gravel road**, and then turn **left** again onto a narrow **gravel road** that winds around and up the mountain for about ten kilometres (six miles). At first this small road is lined with a eucalyptus grove. The spectacular **panoramic views** on the way up and on top are a must for a visitor to Ethiopia; one can see for miles in all directions and appreciate the beauty of the volcanic mountains. Take a picnic lunch along and afterwards hike to the **grove of** trees that has earned the mountain its nickname of 'Crew Cut' or 'Toothbrush'.

For the more energetic a **spur** to the **north** of Furi lies on one's **left** as seen from the road to the top. The **west** side has been dug away to form a high wall with a V-shaped opening. Above this lies a labyrinth of man-made **caves**, thought to be inhabited until quite recently. Furi is also the site of a relay station, which should be avoided. It is sometimes windy and cool on top of the mountain, so take a sweater and scarf.

Back at the Mount Furi turnoff, continue to head **south** to the **bridge** over the **Awash River**. The **falls** near here are worth seeing; for the best view, climb down from the bridge along the little **track** leading to an **old watermill**.

Archaeological site

Just over the bridge, turn **right** to follow a **dirt road** to the **archaeological site** of **Melka Konture**. (It is best that you check with the Antiquities Administration in Addis first.) Since 1965, geologists and archaeologists have had a compound here, set up to excavate this area at the entrance to the gorge where, two million years ago, the earliest ancestors of mankind had a home. They left behind tools, as well as traces of meals and shelters. In the lowest levels pebble tools have been found and, in the higher levels, men of the Middle and Late Stone Age have left many examples of beautiful two-edged hand-axes, obsidian scrapers, and sets of 'bolas' — the round stones used together in nets to throw at animals. Fossilized bones of hippopotamus, rhinoceros, elephant, and various antelope have also been found here.

If you walk **upstream** along the banks of the river, some of these **Stone Age tools** can often be seen, particularly in the dry washes. Remember, however, that collecting of Stone Age artefacts is prohibited, and local citizens help to enforce this restriction.

While you are in this area, it is worthwhile visiting the nearby **Adadi Maryam church**, the southernmost stone church similar to those at Lalibela, although the workmanship is inferior. To reach the church, proceed five kilometres (three miles) beyond the **Awash River bridge** near the Melka Konture site and turn **right** on a **track** that is reasonably good in the dry season. There is a **sign** — in Amharic only — indicating the turn, which is amidst a small number of *tukuls* beside the road. From the turnoff, it is eleven kilometres (seven miles) to the church. It is helpful to have an Amharic-speaking person with you who can ask the local inhabitants for directions as you proceed on the track. At the church one must ask for permission to enter — as well as the key.

Twenty-six kilometres (16 miles) from the **signpost** pointing the way to Adadi Maryam you'll come to **Tiya** town, in the middle of which — in an open meadow — are many **prehistoric monoliths** or **stelae**. Considered as important an historic site as are Axum, Lalibela, and the like, the Tiya stelae are listed as a World Heritage Site and are partially administered by UNESCO.

To return to the capital, retrace your steps to the **Jimma road**. Turn **right**, and nineteen kilometres (12 miles) later, you'll be back in Addis. Just as you enter the town, you may wish to visit the **leprosarium**, which is reached by a long driveway to the **right**. You can purchase a variety of **handicrafts** produced by the patients here, including hand-knitted sweaters, socks, and toys. A bit further along on the **left** — by the 7-11 grocery store and before the Mobil petrol station — is a small outlet for goods actually made in Jimma: **stools**, **baskets**, and the like. Bargains may be had here, but you have to do just that — bargain.

PART THREE: THE CAPITAL

Above: The imposing façade of Africa Hall, home of the United Nations Economic Commission for Africa (ECA).
Opposite: The wide, tree-lined Churchill Avenue — with the distinctive City Hall at its top — is Addis Ababa's main thoroughfare.

Addis Ababa: The New Flower

Wide tree-lined streets, fine architecture, glorious weather, and the incongruity of donkey trains trolling along the boulevards make Addis Ababa, the capital of Ethiopia, a delightful place to explore. It is a city of surprises characterized by remarkable diversity and contrasts.

Abundant eucalyptus trees and crisp, clear mountain air endow Addis Ababa with the bracing atmosphere of a highland summer resort. Its cosy espresso bars and patisseries are reminiscent of Rome and the Mediterranean, and its bustling outdoor markets are colourful reminders of more traditional ways of life. The people, the bursts of music from cafes or shops, the aromas of spicy cooking, of coffee and incense, form a unique Ethiopian pastiche.

Vibrant Addis Ababa is as cosmopolitan as any of the world's great metropolises, and the architecture is as varied as the city itself. Tall office buildings, elegant villas, functional bungalows, flats, fashionable hotels, conference halls, and theatres — gleaming in their marble and anodized aluminium — vie for attention alongside traditional homes of wattle and daub, surrounded by cattle, sheep, goats, and chickens. There is no designated 'city centre' because, until very recently, there was no urban planning. Addis Ababa simply grew in a natural, organic way, and its present appearance reflects this unforced and unstructured evolution.

Set in rising countryside between 2,300 to 2,500 metres (7,500 to 8,200 feet) in altitude on the southern-facing slopes of the 3,000-metre-high (9,840-foot-high) Entoto mountain range immediately to the north, Ethiopia's largest city has grown at astonishing speed since it was founded just over a century ago. Covering 250 square kilometres (97 square miles), the city rambles pleasantly across many wooded hillsides and gullies cut through with fast-flowing streams.

Despite its proximity to the equator, its lofty altitude — the third-highest capital in the world — means that it enjoys a mild climate with an average temperature of 16°C (61°F). The hottest, driest months are usually April and May, when the days are pleasantly warm to hot and the nights are cool. During the main rainy season, from June to mid-September, both days and nights are cool by local standards. Between late October and mid-January night-time temperatures can drop to below 4°C (40°F), although day temperatures in the sun exceed 20°C (68°F). Visitors coming from the cold European winter, however, will probably find Addis Ababa's climate ideal.

The story of the city may be said to have begun in 1878 when the then king of Shewa, Menelik II, moved south from his old capital, Ankober, and established his camp on Wuchacha mountain, a strategic position to the west of the present capital. Three years later old ruins were discovered on Entoto mountain to the north of the present capital. Entoto was believed to have been the Ethiopian capital in the early sixteenth century, before the expeditions of Ahmed ibn Ibrahim, better known as Ahmed Gragn or Ahmed the Left-Handed, rolled the capital northward. Menelik, on learning of the finds at Entoto, is said to have declared, 'Since this discovery has been made in our time it is our duty to rebuild this town.' He accordingly transferred his camp from Wuchacha to Entoto.

Entoto's mountainous position was at first of considerable strategic value to Menelik, who was then afraid of possible attack or rebellion. From other points of view, the settlement's location was, however, far from satisfactory, and this became increasingly evident after Menelik consolidated his control over the country and had no need of a strategically placed capital. At Entoto firewood and provisions of all kinds were scarce and had to be carried up the mountain with very great effort.

The summit, moreover, suffered during the rainy season from a frightful climate, with heavy rain and frequent hail and lightning. Entoto, as a contemporary

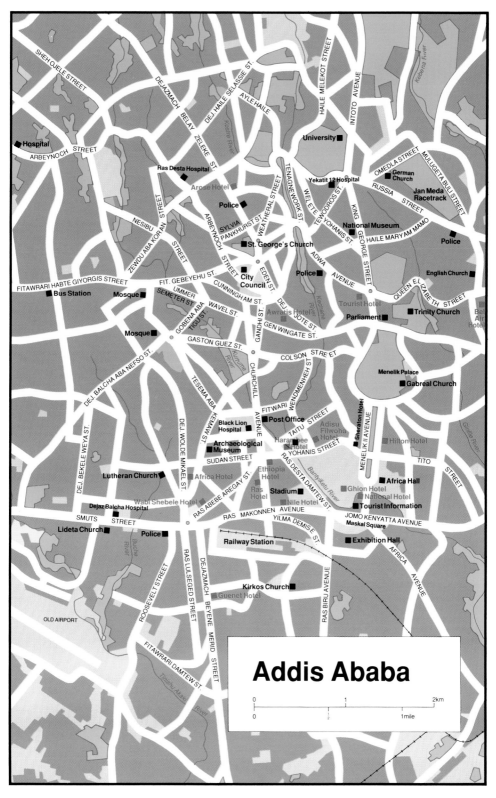

Addis Ababa

Opposite: Newest of the capital's three palaces, the National Palace — also known as Jubilee Palace — was built in 1955 to commemorate the first twenty-five years of the emperor's reign.

French observer, Charles Michel, commented, was thus an 'impossible capital'.

The Entoto foothills, which lay immediately to the south in the locality of the present capital, were on the other hand fertile, yielded abundant crops, and enjoyed an equable climate. The area was moreover the site of hot springs, which gushed out of the ground at a spot known as Filwoha, meaning 'Boiling Water'. Menelik's consort, Queen Taytu, and many of the courtiers spent much of their time travelling to these springs, where many of them camped for days or even weeks on end. There, one day in 1886, Queen Taytu asked her husband for a piece of land on which

to build a house. Menelik agreed and, following traditional Ethiopian royal practice, selected a place of some elevation as the site and allotted large stretches of land around it for the camps of his principal courtiers.

Taytu in the same year, 1886, gave the settlement its name: Addis Ababa, literally meaning 'New Flower' in Amharic. For several years Menelik and his courtiers divided their time between the two settlements, but by around 1891 Addis Ababa had definitely replaced Entoto as the more important of the two and thus emerged as the unquestioned capital of the realm.

From its inception Addis Ababa was

Above: Impressive interior of the National Palace, which can sometimes be seen by appointment.

clustered around two main centres: the palace to the east and the market, with Saint George's church, to the west. Together they generated so much activity that the capital grew and developed rapidly. The population was constantly increasing, particularly after Menelik's great victory over the Italians at the battle of Adwa in 1896, and more and more people flocked in from far and near.

What had started as a camp of tents soon emerged as a settlement of wooden and mud huts, and before long several hundred stone structures were also erected. Then, early in the twentieth century, the first shops and drinking houses sprang up. At about the same time corrugated iron roofing began to replace thatching.

The ceaselessly increasing population of Addis Ababa put a severe burden on the surrounding woodlands, which were being cut down to meet the capital's insatiable demand for timber and firewood. For a time it seemed that Addis Ababa, like Entoto before it, would have to be abandoned. With that in mind Menelik in 1900

travelled sixty kilometres (37 miles) to the west, where he contemplated establishing a new capital. Taytu shortly afterwards named this settlement Addis Alem, meaning 'New World' in Amharic. Menelik, following tradition, at once ordered the construction of a palace. The planned change of capital was, however, soon abandoned, for it became clear that the Australian eucalyptus tree, locally known as *bahr zaf,* or 'tree from beyond the water', which had been recently introduced, was growing so fast that it would soon meet the capital's demand for wood.

Menelik also realized that so much work and resources had by then been invested in the construction of Addis Ababa that the abandonment of that settlement would be virtually impossible. He therefore returned to Addis Alem in 1902 and gave orders that the palace then under construction be transformed into a church. This order symbolized his realization that Addis Ababa had come to stay.

The introduction of the eucalyptus tree, which had thus saved the city, also helped give it its distinctive character and charm.

213

At the turn of the century a British observer, A. B. Wylde, had described the capital as 'almost treeless', but a generation later a Georgian resident, Dr Merab, referred to it as a 'eucalyptopolis', or city of eucalyptus trees.

Addis Ababa was the site of most of the innovations associated with the reign of Menelik. Many of these were at first located in the palace compound, which measured almost two kilometres (1.2 miles) long by a kilometre and a half (one mile) wide. This area contained not only the monarch's personal quarters and a huge three-gabled reception hall capable of feeding over 5,000 diners at a single session, but also a stable, storehouses for supplies and provisions of all kinds, and a lion cage. It also housed the country's main arsenal; experimental gardens for growing eucalyptus and other trees; weavers', jewellers', and such-like workshops; a pharmacy and clinic; a mint for striking the emperor's newly introduced coins; a treasury; and a posts and telegraph station.

During the reign of Menelik the city also witnessed the establishment of many other new institutions, among them the country's first modern school and hospital, the first bank and printing press, and the first hotel and racing course — as well as the first modern roads and bridges, the first steam-roller, and the first two motor cars, one of which came from Germany and the other from Britain.

The growth of the city and the pace of its modernization increased greatly after the establishment of the Djibouti railway, which reached Dire Dawa in 1902 and the vicinity of the capital in 1915. The reign of Empress Zawditu (1916–1930) and the early part of Haile Selassie's reign (1930–1935) were characterized by the erection of many more new buildings. These included ministries as well as the first monuments, among them an equestrian statue of Emperor Menelik, the founder of the city,

and one of the Lion of Judah, the symbol of the ruling dynasty.

The Italian Fascist invasion of Ethiopia (1936–1941) resulted in a reign of terror, but later led to the construction in the city —as well as in the regional capitals of Gondar, Jimma, and Harar — of many new roads and buildings. The more important structures followed the grandiose architectural style favoured by the Italian dictator, Mussolini. The period also saw the removal of the Menelik and Lion of Judah statues.

The many post-invasion developments included the reopening of Ethiopian schools, the founding of colleges and later of a university, the establishment of Ethiopian Airlines and of a number of new banks and other institutions, and the opening of many modern hotels, restaurants, and cinemas.

In the late 1950s Addis Ababa entered the 'skyscraper age' and was recognized as the unofficial capital of Africa. Haile Selassie's pan-African diplomacy was crowned with success when the city was chosen in 1958 as headquarters of the United Nations Economic Commission for Africa (ECA) and, in 1963, as headquarters of the Organization of African Unity (OAU).

The capital later witnessed all the events associated with the Ethiopian Revolution of 1974, the deposition of Haile Selassie and later of Mengistu Haile Mariam, and the ensuing changes of government.

Today's Addis Ababa, which bears the imprint of many of these past developments, is a major metropolis, with an

estimated population approaching five million. (As there has been no recent census, Ethiopia's estimated population figures vary wildly. In 1987, two million was the generally accepted figure for the capital, but now people estimate that may have more than doubled because of the migrants coming in to the city at the time of the government changeover.)

Located at the centre of Shewa region, the city stands at the very heart of Ethiopia and enjoys excellent connections with all the country's economic zones. Addis Ababa is the unchallenged diplomatic capital of Africa, with more than seventy embassies and consular representatives clustered in the mountain location.

Historian Conti Rossini once characterized Ethiopia as a 'rich cultural mosaic'. He could have also been speaking about Addis Ababa itself. Each of the country's multitude of ethnic groups is represented somewhere in the capital, as are a large number of foreign residents from all parts of the world who contribute to the city's cosmopolitan atmosphere.

There is much to do and see within the capital, whether at night — at the variety of nightclubs offering all manner of music from traditional Ethiopian to modern pop, as well as dancing — or by day. The sports-minded should note that the Hilton and the Ghion (and soon the Sheraton, under construction in 1994) hotels offer tennis and open-air swimming in warm thermal water, the Addis Ababa stadium offers frequent inter-African and local football matches, and there are many opportunities for horse-riding, bowls, and other sports. (See 'Sporting Ethiopia', Part Four.)

Addis Ababa also has a flourishing cultural life. Lectures on subjects such as Ethiopian history and culture are given almost weekly at the Institute of Ethiopian Studies, the Alliance Française, the German and Italian cultural institutes, and at the Hilton Hotel, under the auspices of an independent 'Interest Group'. There are regular exhibitions of Ethiopian art at the Alliance Française, the National Museum, the Saint George Gallery, and the Hilton Hotel.

The Horticultural Society and the Ethiopian Wildlife and Natural History Society both hold regular lectures and organize frequent visits to gardens in and around the city, as well as trips to the countryside far and near.

There are many opportunities to experience Ethiopian music, song, and dance, and to go to the Ethiopian theatre, performances of which are mainly in Amharic. Cultural shows are usually given on Sunday afternoons at the Hager Fiker Theatre in the centre of the town, as well as on evenings during the week at the Hilton, Ghion, Ras, and several other hotels and restaurants. The Yared School of Music, near Sidist Kilo, presents occasional performances of Western as well as Ethiopian music. Concerts are also often presented at the Italian Cultural Centre.

Addis Ababa's cultural *mélange* has also resulted in a delicious assortment of restaurants. A wide range of European food (French, Italian, and Polish) is available, as well as Armenian, Turkish, Indian, and Chinese delicacies — not to mention unforgettably tasty Ethiopian cuisine. (See 'Eating Out in Addis', Part Three.)

The national language, Amharic, with its unique script, is widely spoken throughout the country and is predominant in Addis Ababa. The principal foreign languages are English, Italian, French, and Arabic.

Getting there

Addis Ababa, 578 kilometres (358 miles) from Bahar Dar, 453 kilometres (280 miles) from Dire Dawa and 1,005 kilometres (623 miles) from Axum, is well-served by many international flights. Domestic and regional air and road services link it with major centres in Ethiopia and the rest of Africa. A good rail service also runs from the capital through Dire Dawa to the Red Sea port of Djibouti.

Opposite: A large, modern, stone stylized Lion of Judah dominates Unity Square near the National Theatre.

When to go

The city is relatively pleasant all year round, but be prepared for damp and chilly air and almost daily rainstorms from July to mid-September.

Where to stay

The Hilton is top standard, likely to be matched by the Sheraton, under construction in 1994. Just below it are a number of two- or three-star government hotels, all adequate but not luxurious. The better of these include the Wabe Shebelle, the Ghion, and the Ethiopia hotels, while the Taytu Hotel — founded in 1907 — is still comfortable and full of character. An increasing number of private hotels, such as the Ibex, Yordanos, Plaza, and Extreme offer the visitor a combination of motivated service, a warm welcome, and very reasonable prices. There are many others with various degrees of quality and service. See Listings.

Sightseeing

The appearance and character of Addis Ababa owe much to the fact that the city evolved rapidly out of what was originally a military camp on the slopes of the Entoto mountains. The now extensive metropolis sprawls over a wide stretch of land descending from the Entoto heights in the north to much lower, flatter country in the south, in the direction of Zuqualla, about forty kilometres (25 miles) distant.

When orienting yourself, it also helps to keep in mind that the city is essentially divided into three main sections. To the **east** lies what may be termed the 'government and educational sector', where — running roughly from north to south — the university, the National Museum, the Menelik School, the first State printing press, the old Menelik palace, the Hilton Hotel, the Jubilee Palace, and Meskal (Revolution) Square are located.

The **central** sector is devoted largely to commerce but also houses some government businesses. This runs from Saint George's Cathedral, City Hall, and the television studio in the north to the railway station in the south — all by way of Churchill Road. Here you will also find the headquarters of the National and Commercial Banks; the main town sales office of Ethiopian Airlines; the Post, Telephone, and Telegraph Office; the main hospital; and the National Theatre.

Also much involved in trade is the **western** sector of the city, where the famous Mercato can be found, as well as the city's main mosque and many shops rarely frequented by foreign visitors. The south-west sector of the city, which developed later than the centre, is partly residential and partly industrial.

The **south-west** and **south-east** are also home to the majority of the **embassies**, clustered around the roads leading into the city from both the old (Lideta) and new (Bole) **airports**.

Happily the majority of Addis Ababa's principal thoroughfares take the form of wide, two- or four-lane avenues, with trees on either side and grass reservations in the centre. Many tourist attractions and important offices are found along the capital's main roads, making exploring the city by car easy and enjoyable.

But perhaps the best way to explore Addis is by foot, which allows you to take in much more of the local 'flavour' of the place and see some sights you would perhaps miss if you were in a vehicle. Be forewarned, however: walking about the city inevitably brings a certain amount of unwanted attention from beggars and from students hoping to practise their English or to 'exchange addresses' with you. If you are unlucky, you may encounter a team of pickpockets, whose mode of operation may be a sudden bump or distraction followed by a quick and hardly noticeable lightening of your pockets. But on average Addis Ababa is a much safer, more benevolent, place than most large cities throughout the world.

If you are using a map to get around, you should be aware that very, very few residents know the official names of the streets in the capital, nor are the streets marked with signposts. It is better to use landmarks for directions.

The huge and unmistakable **Meskal Square** (also still known as **Revolution**

Above: The Addis Ababa Museum, once home of Ras Biru Habtegebriel, a former Ethiopian Minister of War.

Square from Mengistu's time) is a convenient starting point for a trek through the city, as most travellers will pass this square on the way into Addis from the airport. The square, rebuilt and enlarged by the former Provisional Military Administrative Council, was inaugurated in 1975. It has a capacity of 100,000 persons and a dais that will accommodate 300 others.

Museum

Near the bottom of the road on the **southern** side of the square, although actually accessed from a small road off the Bole Road, is the **Addis Ababa Museum**. Opened in November 1986, it is the city's most recent museum. Its focus is on the political, cultural and architectural history of the capital; thus there are **photographs** of the first settlements in Addis Ababa, the first eucalyptus trees and the first cars, juxtaposed with modern views of the city showing the broad streets and high-rise blocks. The inauguration of the first school, telephone, and currency are illustrated, while upstairs there are examples of recent **artistic work**.

The building in which the Addis Ababa Museum is housed was the home of Ras Biru Habtegebriel, a former Ethiopian Minister of War. It was once rented out but in 1986 craftsmen restored its former glory in order to house the exhibits, which deal with all aspects of Addis Ababa's life from the city's founding. Not confined to items of historical interest, the museum also keeps residents and visitors up to date with current developments in the capital and one section focuses on the future. Next to the museum is an **exhibition centre**, which holds fairly regular events.

In addition to Ras Biru's establishments, other **houses** of aristocrats and businessmen from the time of Menelik's reign still can be seen in Addis. For information on the location of these unique architectural structures — a part of Ethiopia's cultural heritage — consult the **Ethiopian Tourism Commission** (ETC), whose offices are on the square. Here you can also pick up many brochures on the country's attractions, as well as a wealth of smaller 'foldups' on other tourist destinations. Next door a small ETC shop has maps, books,

Above: Each room of the Finfine Adarash Hotel, a building erected in 1902, features a large bathroom with one or two huge sunken tubs, in which you can relax in your own private mineral bath.

posters, and some souvenir items at reasonable prices.

Wildlife conservation offices

Heading toward the Addis Ababa Stadium, you can see on the far **left** corner of the square a six-storey building next to a Mobil petrol station. The **Ethiopian Wildlife Conservation Organization** offices are here on the **fifth floor**, where you can get information on the parks and make bookings for the guest house in Bale. Beware of the tricky elevator.

Take a **right** at the **light** at the far **west** end of the square and proceed **north-east** past the **China Bar and Restaurant**, the entrance to the **Ghion Hotel**, which features a large **thermal swimming pool** of sometimes dubious water quality, and the **National Tour Operation** (NTO) head office, which is also a source of travel information and a place to make bookings for the Historic Route and other tours. Across the street to your left you will see the 27,000-seat **Addis Ababa Stadium**, built in 1968. The arena, where Ethiopia

won the third Africa soccer cup, also stages athletics, cycling, and boxing as well as pop concerts and cultural festivals. Its entrance is actually off Ras Makonnen Avenue.

The next **corner**, where there is a **traffic light**, is an important hub. To the **right**, or **east**, is **Finfine Adarash**, one of the city's most attractive and lively restaurant/bars. It is also a fun **hotel**, with each room featuring a large bathroom with one or two huge **sunken tubs**, in which you can relax in your own private **mineral bath**.

Opposite the hotel is the public **Filwoha** ('boiling water') **Mineral Baths**, a good place for a hot bath or a massage. Standards of cleanliness and maintenance are less than perfect, even in first or second class — you might want to take along your own tin of scouring powder and a sponge.

If you turn **left** (**west**) back at the **traffic light**, you'll pass the **Ethiopia Hotel** and reach another large, five-rayed **intersection** dominated by the imposing round **Commercial Bank of Ethiopia** head office, adjoined to the tall **National Bank of**

Ethiopia. Near the **National Theatre** on the west side of this intersection, known as **Unity Square**, is a modern stylized stone **Lion of Judah**, the work of French sculptor Morris Calka. The 1,400-seat theatre, established in the early 1940s, focuses on the promotion of drama (local and foreign), modern and folk dancing, and music. Every Thursday afternoon a special **cultural programme** crams folk dancing, modern dance and jazz, a short drama, poetry reading, and acrobatics into two hours. Revival theatre, the bringing back of past dramas, has also been introduced.

The wide street intersecting the square at right angles is **Churchill Road** — one of the few roads in the capital that is known by its proper name.

Railway station

Heading **south** on Churchill, you'll pass the main **Ethiopian Airlines booking office** (although the one at the Hilton is more pleasant) on the **east** side of the road. Across the street is the National Theatre and the **Ras Hotel**, which boasts a **bar** with great atmosphere.

A series of **shops** and the **Telecomms office**, which offers a phone and fax service, are farther along on the **east** side of Churchill. After crossing **Ras Makonnen Avenue**, the road terminates at the **railway station**. A **bronze Lion of Judah** stands in the **square** immediately in front of the station, which was built by the French in 1929. The statue, taken to Rome during the Italian Fascist occupation, was returned after the liberation.

The recently renovated **Buffet de la Gare restaurant/bar** is here, providing simple food and disco music, but atmospherically it is a far cry from 'the good old days' when an incredible mix of nationalities met there to drink and dance to the colourful resident band, whose musical offerings ranged from old Italian songs through modern pop to traditional Ethiopian.

Back at the major **intersection** where the Commercial Bank of Ethiopia is located, head **north** on **Churchill Avenue** this time, which will take you up past the elegant main **post office** on the **east** side of the road. Attached to the post office is the **National Postal Museum**, which has a complete set of all the **stamps** ever printed in Ethiopia — a philatelist's paradise. The stamps, mounted on album pages, are clearly labelled in Amharic and English. The collection starts with the first Menelik issue of 1894 following the imperial edict of that year which established the Ethiopian Postal Administration. Ethiopian stamps were valid for internal use only until Ethiopia joined the Universal Postal Union in 1908. Some stamps printed immediately before the Italian invasion were withheld from circulation until the time of liberation, when they were embellished with a large red 'V'. (See 'Stamps of Ethiopia', Part Four.)

The museum, established in 1975, also has many of the **original drawings**, approved designs, examples of the printers' art, printers' proofs and other items unique to Ethiopian philately. The Ethiopian collection is permanent, but the museum also houses displays of stamps from other Universal Postal Union members, ranging from El Salvador to New Zealand, which are changed every six months. The post office also has a special philatelic section selling older stamps for collectors.

National Library

Not far away from the post office is **Saint George Gallery**, the country's first Ethiopian-owned private art gallery, which holds occasional exhibitions. Visitors can always see a wide range of the very best works of contemporary Ethiopian artists, as well as unique furniture designed by the proprietress, Saba Ellene. Across from the post office is the huge **Black Lion hospital,** with the **National Library of Ethiopia** between it and the National Bank of Ethiopia. For visitors interested in rare books on Ethiopia or those with legitimate research interests, this library, with its collection of more than 100,000 volumes, is an invaluable resource. Established just after the end of the Italian occupation, the library is organized into several divisions.

The National Library Division is responsible for the development of library services throughout the country. Its Ethiopian collection consists of **manuscripts, rare books, maps and engravings**, and books relating to Ethiopia published abroad — 20,000 books and manuscripts in total. Among the most valuable are the four **Gospels**, an early fourteenth-century **illuminated manuscript** — probably the oldest still surviving in the country — and the **Pauline Epistles**, a fifteenth-century manuscript found at the monastery of Lake Haik in Wollo region.

Other interesting manuscripts include an Old and New Testament Bible. It took five calligraphers five years and 500 sheepskins to produce this. A **silver-plated prayer book** belonging to a member of the royal family and the first book published in Amharic abroad are also in the collection.

Elderly gentlemen in charge of the ancient scripts, which are locked in a safe that would be the envy of any bank, painstakingly copy and restore old manuscripts in danger of deterioration.

The Legal Deposit Department of the National Library acquires three copies of all new publications printed in Ethiopia, even before the publishers have delivered the material to the clients or bookshops. A National Bibliography and National Periodicals Index records the number of titles published in the country each year.

The Public Library Service contains a sizeable collection of general, reference, and specialist books on a variety of topics, as well as literature in Amharic. It boasts 600 readers a day, mainly students.

Just above the main post office on Churchill is a series of curio shops, where can buy the same sort of swords, spears, shields, crosses, baskets, and other items that are to be found at the Mercato — but with a fraction of the hassle and at more or less fixed prices.

Continuing on up Churchill, you'll pass the **Lise Gebre Mariam School** on the **right** and some quality silver shops — across from which are excellent **cotton shops** — just below the **Tewodros Square** roundabout.

The Piazza

From this point, Churchill continues up to the **Piazza** area. As its name suggests, the Piazza is a legacy of the Italian invasion and still has a pronouncedly Italian character. Sprawling out along Adwa Avenue, it is an area of **gold** and **silversmiths, cake shops** filled with delicious pastries and doughnuts, **coffee bars** specializing in frothy capuccino, good quality Ethiopian leather shoes, **video libraries**, bespoke **tailors,** and all manner of **electronics retailers**. The area also houses, among other things, the **old post office**, a new three-storey complex of **small shops**, and **Castelli's Italian restaurant**, as well as the **Taytu Hotel** — featuring classic architecture and a funky bar — and the long **shopping street** that leads east to the **Ras Makonnen Bridge** and Arat Kilo.

At the centre of this area is **Menelik II Square**, dominated by a handsome **equestrian statue,** of the ruler, which was unveiled in 1930. The Italians, eager to forget their humiliating defeat at his hands at the battle of Adwa, pulled down and hid the statue when they invaded Addis Ababa in 1937. In 1941, when they were ousted by the patriots and Allied Forces, the statue of Menelik was restored to its proper place.

Facing the square is one of Addis Ababa's fine Ethiopian Orthodox churches, **Saint George's Cathedral**, a pre-World War II octagonal building set in pleasant wooded gardens. This elegant domed church contains several interesting modern **paintings** and **mosaics**, some of them by Ethiopia's leading modern artist, Afewerk Tekle. The church also has a small but interesting museum containing crowns and regalia from Haile Selassie's coronation, which was held here. The museum can be visited even if the church is closed.

On the **west-south-west corner** of the square is the **City Hall**, built to the plan of a three-cornered star. Opened in 1965, the building contains a marble-floored lobby, a **restaurant** and **bar**, and a **cinema**. The **City Hall Theatre** seats an audience of 1,000

Above: The architecturally magnificent Trinity Church, its large dome and slender pinnacles making it one of the landmarks of the city.

and is usually filled to capacity because of the high quality of the performances staged there. The building also houses Addis Ababa's television studios.

Just below City Hall to the **west** is **Abuna Petros Square**, named in memory of the Archbishop of the Ethiopian Orthodox Church who supported the Ethiopian patriots who fought against the Fascists during the Italian invasion of Ethiopia. Subsequently he was shot, and a **monument** describing the action can be seen within the square.

Continue **west** along this street past three major streets on the **left**. At the **fourth street**, where there is an unused **traffic light**, turn **left**, and shortly, on the **right-hand side** of the street, you'll see the **Al-Anwar Mosque**, the religious centre for Muslims in and around the capital. Addis Ababa has a number of mosques, but the two most interesting are the al-Anwar and the charming small, old **Nur Mosque** near the old post office. The sound of the *muezzin* calling the faithful to prayer is regularly heard on the western side of the city.

The Mercato

The Grand Mosque is actually situated in one corner of a fascinating attraction for first-time visitors to Addis: the fantastic **Mercato**, or Addis Ketema, meaning 'New Town'. This colourful **market**, the largest in eastern Africa between Cairo and Johannesburg, consists of an almost infinite number of sections devoted to such items as grain, spices, clothes, ironware, pots and pans, and the like. Many swords, spears, shields, crosses, baskets, and other curios displayed for the tourist are also on sale in the market.

Easily explored on foot, the Mercato is an amazing, crowded place with never-ending hidden pockets to discover. You never know what odd sort of economic activity you will observe. It definitely provides a lesson in recycling. Nylon cord is extracted from old tyres. Old tyres are made into sandals. Cotton waste is twisted into lamp wicks. Old tins are soldered up to make lamps. And so on.

The **butter and spice section** is of par-

Above: Small but colourfully painted shops of all descriptions line the capital's streets.

ticular appeal, with its myriad of colours and aromatic smells. In the two covered **main buildings**, known as the **'New Market'**, you can find **clothing**, **Harar cloth** (colourful voile shawls), and other **Ethiopian artefacts**. The New Market also has **souvenir shops**, but be warned: the owners are not above horrendous overcharging and there lurk many commission agents (*delalla*) who annoyingly intrude between shop owner and customer.

In general, when shopping in the Mercato, remember that the 'hard-sell' mentality dominates and that the first price you are offered is probably at least double or treble that which the vendor actually hopes to be paid. Do your best to lower the price, even if it all seems an unnecessary effort for a few birr. Above all, do not be discouraged. This is a place in which, the locals say, 'you can bargain for anything — even a new soul!' It takes some practise to be able to compete with the experts in such an art.

For a serious Mercato walkabout, it might be to your advantage to engage the guide services of an agreeable young per-son, benefiting from his or her knowledge — and protection.

One of the city's claims to fame is that it is the **headquarters of the Organization of African Unity** (OAU). To get there, head **south** from the Grand Mosque to **Patriot's (or Tekle Haymanot) Square**, where you go halfway around and take **Tesema Aba Kemaw Street** towards **Mexico Square**. (After crossing **Sudan Avenue**, there is a little confusion at the **stoplight**, but turn **right** and make a **left turn** at the next **stop sign**, which will bring you to the square.) Go halfway around Mexico Square to **Roosevelt Avenue**, taking this to **Damtew Ketema Street**, where you will see the OAU building on the **left**.

From back at Meskal (Revolution) Square, another route to the **north** offers a good tour of a different sector of Addis Ababa. On the square, on top of a **knoll** facing Menelik II Avenue, stands the contemporary **church of Saint Stephen** or Estifanos. Architecturally rather uninteresting — a cube topped by a dome — it nevertheless features a beautiful **mosaic** over the entrance of the martyrdom of

Above: The new Sheraton Addis with 295 rooms gives the visitor the choice between standard rooms, standard or deluxe suites and a presidential suite. Sheraton also offers ten self-contained villas, each complete with its own private swimming pool. There are twelve restaurants and bars including Italian, Indian, Chinese and grill restaurant with pizzeria — a night club, heated swimming pool and sports facilities to satisfy all tastes. The hotel also features excellent banqueting and conference facilities.

Saint Stephen, kneeling as the stones are brandished over his head. It is set on a background of gilt-toned file. Rows of small cross-shaped windows line the church façade and sides.

Heading **north** up **Menelik II Avenue**, you can't miss **Africa Hall** on the **east** side of the street, just across the **Finfine Bridge**. This seven-storey building houses the **United Nations Economic Commission for Africa** (ECA) and contains a **conference hall** that can seat 715 people. Dominating the foyer is the bold, modernistic **stained-glass window** depicting 'Africa: Past, Present and Future' — the work of Ethiopian artist Afewerk Tekle. The colourful designs on the outside of the building represent traditional *shamma* borders. Underneath Africa Hall itself is a round piazza, which often hosts small exhibitions and charity bazaars. This piazza also houses a small **book and gift shop**, **Ethiopian Airlines and Kenya Airways booking offices**, a branch of the Commercial Bank, a convenient **telecom office**, and a **post office**. Getting past the security at the main gate, however, is no easy task. The best way to get in is to find someone who works there and ask for an invitation to visit them during the lunch break.

National Palace

Across the street from Africa Hall is the **National Palace**. Formerly known as the **Jubilee Palace**, it is the newest of the city's three palaces and was built in 1955 to commemorate the first twenty-five years of Emperor Haile Selassie's reign. An ornate structure in a well-kept **garden**, the building was planned as a residence for important state guests, but the emperor, after giving the Genete Le'ul Palace to the university, used it as his personal home. Right next to the National Palace is a five-star Sheraton Hotel, without equal in Africa. The property is ultra-modern, with every high-tech telecommunication and conference facility and extraordinary

Above: Elaborate murals adorn the walls and ceilings of the city's principal Ethiopian Orthodox church, Saint George's.

comfort. The hotel is within easy reach of government offices and the UN conference centre.

After you cross an **intersection**, you will see the **Addis Ababa Hilton** on the **right**. The hotel has a wide range of **restaurants**, an **Ethiopian Airlines office**, an **NTO taxi office**, **duty free and gift shops**, a spectacular cross-shaped **swimming pool** with thermal waters, a **fitness centre** with sauna, a mini-golf course, and **tennis courts**.

The Gibbi

Up the hill the road curves around to the **left** as you skirt **Emperor Menelik's palace**, sometimes referred to as the **Grand Palace**, or *Gibbi*. Surrounded by a **stone wall**, the palace — the oldest in the city — is still the **Ethiopian government's main headquarters**, and taking photographs is not allowed. Inside the compound, which is closed to visitors, one may catch a glimpse of Menelik's three-gabled **banqueting hall**. Also in the compound is the **church of Kidane Mehret**, built in traditional *tukul* style with a thatched peaked roof.

To the rear of the compound stands the **Menelik Mausoleum**, a building surmounted by a large gilt crown, built in 1911 by the emperor's daughter, Empress Zawditu. The square building is made of gray stone with a central dome and four small cupolas, one on each corner. It houses the remains of the famous old monarch; his spouse, Empress Taytu; his daughter, Empress Zawditu; the Archbishop who crowned Menelik, Abuna Mateos; and Princess Tsehai, daughter of former Emperor Haile Selassie I. The mausoleum is open to the public for a small fee. Access is through the church at the rear of the compound.

Travelling **northwards** up the hill from the Menelik palace you'll see **Congress Hall** on the **east** side of the road. It was erected by the former Provisional Military Government headed by Colonel Mengistu Haile Mariam. Beside it is Ethiopia's first **parliament building**, with **clock tower**, built prior to World War II by Emperor Haile Selassie.

Before you reach the next roundabout of Arat Kilo, there is a main gate that leads to the **Selassie**, or **Trinity, Cathedral**, one of the most magnificent churches in Addis Ababa. Its large **dome** and slender **pinnacles** are one of the landmarks of the city. A handsome crystal **chandelier**, many notable **paintings**, **murals**, and beautiful **stained-glass windows** adorn the interior. In the church is the **tomb** of the former Empress Menen, and the **churchyard** is the burial ground of many patriots who lost their lives during the five-year occupation of Ethiopia, including Ras Imru, one of Ethiopia's principal commanders at the time of the Italian Fascist invasion. In front of the church is the **tomb** of British suffragette Sylvia Pankhurst. Her book, *Ethiopia, a Cultural History*, was the first comprehensive survey of Ethiopian arts and culture: music, painting, architecture, literature, philosophy, and theology.

Arat Kilo is the site of an **obelisk**, topped by a **Lion of Judah**, commemorating the country's liberation in 1941. The **Addis Ababa University Science Faculty**, the **Ministry of Education**, the **Natural History Museum**, **shops**, a **bank**, a **post office**, and the **Tourist Hotel** are all located at or near this roundabout.

Church of Saint Michael

If you turn right at Arat Kilo, a slightly longer side trip can be made to the rock-hewn church of Saint Michael, although it is best to inquire whether this area is open to tourists before making the excursion. Travel down Queen Elizabeth Street over the **Ginfile** and **Tesfa Aseged bridges**, where it becomes **Fikre Maryam Aba Techan Street**. You will pass the **British Embassy** on your **left** and then, just past the small **Yeka Park**, a **turning** on the **left** takes you up a **little road** leading to the **new Saint Michael's Church**. (If you get to the junction of Jomo Kenyatta Avenue, you've gone too far.) From the new church, a new road leads up the **hill** to the **old church**. Carved out of solid rock similar, though inferior, to the rock-hewn churches of Lalibela, the site is definitely worth a visit.

Just **north** of Arat Kilo, visitors interested in art may visit the **School of Fine Arts**, located in the **Menelik School** compound, where teachers' and students' **paintings** and **sculpture** are always on view.

Before you reach the next **intersection** — known as **Amist Kilo** — as you continue **north**, you will see the excellent **Forneria d'Italia** bakery on the **right** (try the *ciabatta* or the take-away pizzas). On the left at the corner is the Kidist Maryam church, which is the church of the Patriarch, the head of the Ethiopian Orthodox Church, who lives in the adjacent building.

National Museum

Immediately past this intersection is the **National Museum** on the west side of the street and the **Faculty of Technology** on the **east**. The collection of the museum, which is near the **University of Addis Ababa Graduate School**, was gathered largely from the northern regions by French archaeologists. Their **reports**, in French, may be purchased at the museum, as well as **postcards** of Ethiopia's **art treasures**. The museum displays a replica of the **early hominid 'Lucy'**, (the original being kept for security in a nearby safe), and a valuable collection of **historical artefacts, ancient coins,** and some **paintings** by modern Ethiopian artists. Upstairs there are stunning examples of traditional ceremonial dress, robes, and crowns and an enormous decorated throne. Guides are available for tours of this museum. There are no fixed fees for service.

The next roundabout is known as **Sidist Kilo**. Here the visitor will see an **obelisk** erected in memory of the citizens killed in the Italian Fascist massacre of February 1937. Just off Sidist Kilo is the entrance to the **Lion Park**, a rather sad and dilapidated miniature 'zoo' where a dozen or so full-grown **lions** and, especially in the spring, lion cubs can be seen pacing around in their small cages. There is a small admission fee. Around the 'zoo' are verdant **gardens**, a pleasant place for a coffee break.

Also near Sidist Kilo is the **Coffee House**, a popular nightspot for dancing and drinking just about anything *but* coffee.

North of Sidist Kilo is the **main campus** of **Addis Ababa University**. The university is housed in the city's second-oldest palace, that of Haile Selassie. Once known as the **Genete Le'ul, or Princely Garden Palace**, it is a dignified structure set in a formal **garden**. The edifice was built shortly prior to the Italian Fascist invasion as the abode of the emperor, who later presented it to the university.

The building, now open to the public, houses the **Institute of Ethiopian Studies Library and Museum** (where the emperor's bedroom is on view) on the second floor. This remarkable library, by far the most comprehensive collection on Ethiopia and the Horn of Africa in the world, contains old Ge'ez **manuscripts** and early works of explorers such as James Bruce and Richard Burton. It is a research, not a lending, library, but books can be read on the premises.

Ethnological Museum

The exciting Ethnological Museum provides an interesting overview of Ethiopian crafts, culture, and art. It is divided into two main sections. The Ethnological Section is arranged into areas of handicrafts. There are different types of clothing corresponding to the different regions of the country — Tigray, Harar, Jimma, Gondar, or Shewa. There is everyday clothing, warrior dress, festival and religious clothing. The looms and spinning mechanisms are also displayed, as well as some examples of jewellery and adornments. There are sections displaying tools and utensils, saddles and bits, boats and ploughs. The museum also exhibits old currency, coins, and postage stamps.

In the Art Section of the museum, you can see an extensive collection of classical Ethiopian religious art and artefacts, as well as more recent paintings reflecting the hunting and farming cultures of Ethiopia, folk legends, religion, and war.

A separate section of the institute containing **musical instruments** is housed in an old nineteenth-century **house** past the Menelik Palace, but it is open by

Above: Simple but colourful buildings of the Piazza area of the city, where one can find a wealth of interesting shops and coffee bars.

appointment only and you must take an escort from the Ethnological Museum with you.

Also located on the campus are the handsome and well-stocked **John F. Kennedy Library**, the **College of Social Sciences**, and several other units of the university. Opposite the university is the former headquarters of the Imperial Guard, now the Ministry of Planning and Economic Development, with an attractive modern circular meeting hall.

North-west of Addis Ababa University is another august **church** well worth visiting, that of **Medhane Alem**, or the Saviour of the World. This building is set amid beautiful trees in what is called the Ketchene area, a quarter of the city formerly largely occupied by weavers, potters, and blacksmiths.

Entoto

The road **north** continues on an uphill course that leads past the **United States Embassy** and on to the top of **Entoto Mountain**. From this beautiful height set in tall eucalyptus trees, the site of

Menelik's former capital, you can obtain a breathtaking view of modern Addis Ababa. To the **right** of the summit is the **church of Maryam**, or Saint Mary, which contains beautiful **mural paintings**, and within its precincts an interesting **museum** housing religious **manuscripts**, **crosses**, and other church paraphernalia, as well as the **vestments** of several kings and political leaders of the past. A five-minute drive to the **west** takes you to the somewhat older **church of Raguel**, an unusual pagoda-like edifice erected by one of Menelik's favourite craftsmen, an Indian called Hajji Khawas.

From Addis Ababa you can easily travel by road to many places of historical or cultural interest, as well as to a number of holiday resorts. (See 'Places and Travel', Part Two.)

Eating Out in Addis Ababa

Ethiopian food is like nothing you have eaten elsewhere. *Injera* is the national dish, and it forms the base of any meal — quite literally. This large, soft, pancake-like crepe is spread out on a large tray. The *wot*, or spicy sauces, are then dished out on it. Diners sit around the communal tray, tear off a piece of *injera* (with the right hand only) and scoop up the *wot* or meat or vegetables with it.

The tray on which the meal is served is placed on a *mesob*, a small round table woven like a basket, with a peaked cover and a depression on the tabletop where the tray is placed. Highly decorative patterns are often woven into these mesobs, and they are prized in the household. Many traditional Ethiopian restaurants serve food in this way.

In many restaurants a minstrel playing the one-string *massinko*, will make the rounds of the tables, singing songs composed on the spot and weaving in his own comments about one of the people to whom he is singing, often to the delighted amusement of others in the group. Or, late in the evening a dance troupe will entertain guests with songs and dances typical of the various regions of Ethiopia. Guests are usually welcome to get up and join in.

Especially striking is the *iskista*, a dance in which both men and women shake their shoulders forward and backward vigorously. This requires great skill and is very provocative.

Also distinctive is the Ethiopian traditional drink — *tej*. This is a honey wine, or mead, brewed with a hop-like woody shrub product called *gesho*. *Tella*, a dark beer brewed from barley, is a lighter, less alcoholic drink, while *araki* is a high-powered distillate made from *tella*.

Traditional restaurants abound in Addis Ababa. A good one can be found in the basement of the Hotel Afrique. The restaurant area is divided by draperies into little rooms that are suitable for intimate couples or even fair-sized groups. There is a good menu and selection of local drinks, but no music.

The Ghion and the Hilton hotels both have traditional nights, when they serve traditional food and have traditional music and dancing. Check to see which nights of the week.

The Karamara, on Bole Road toward the airport, is noted for its meat dishes and entertaining minstrels. The Addis Ababa restaurant, near Saint George's Church, also has a lot of local flavour and colour. Both restaurants are set in *tukuls* or rondavels, of a typical round shape, with thatched roofs and woven mats on the floor.

But there are myriads of tiny eating places, tucked away in residential areas. One serving delicious food has taken over what used to be a house, approached by a lane behind the Hilton. Ask local people for recommendations, if you'd like to venture off the usual paths.

After Ethiopian food, the next most popular cuisine is Italian — one of the many legacies of Italy's historical association with Ethiopia. The best known Italian restaurant is Castelli's, off the Piazza. The dining tables are set up in separate rooms of an elegant old house and the atmosphere is excellent — as is the food. The Castelli family treat you as guests in their own home and will be happy to guide you through the extensive menu. There are local and imported wines, and the restaurant's antipasto buffet is beautifully and temptingly laid out. A trip here is a must for any visitor to the capital who loves Italian cuisine — but be prepared to pay European prices for this luxury.

The Armenian Club, in the Amist Kilo area, has a sign on the door that says 'Members Only', but the rule never seems to be applied and everyone goes, although non-members are charged a twenty per cent supplement. Its Middle Eastern food is delicious, and economical. The kebabs served with either Armenian bread or rice, the yogurt, and the mint soup are outstanding items on the menu.

Also in the Amist Kilo area is Blue Tops, named for its twin bright blue pointed

Above: Addis Ababa has many top-class restaurants, like this one at the Hilton.

plastic rooftops. Under one peak is an Italian restaurant, serving at night; the other peak covers an open-air daytime snack bar, serving hamburgers, ice cream, and other Western-style favourites.

Another spot serving national food is the Patria, serving Polish dishes. A bit off the regular tourist routes in the Casa Inchess area, it is worth finding. The place is spotless, the decor and costumes are Polish — and the food is fine and moderately priced.

A very new and popular French restaurant in the Old Airport area is Le Petit Paris.

All the leading hotels have restaurants. The Wabe Shebelle Hotel's dining spot is high above the city, giving a panoramic view at night. The Kokeb, near the ECA headquarters, also commands a spectacular city view, especially good for a drink at sunset. The Hilton has several restaurants: the main one, featuring the Ethiopian night and other special nights, the Jacaranda, a coffee shop, and a pizza parlour.

Pizza is big in Addis Ababa, and a number of new pizza parlours have

recently opened: Vic's on Churchill, the Zodiac off Bole Road, and the tiny Roma, right on Bole Road, very close to the centre of town. Older and with lots of atmosphere is the Oroscopo in the Piazza area.

Chinese restaurants are ubiquitous the world over, and Addis Ababa has its three: the new Beijing, the China Bar and Restaurant, and the Hong Kong.

The Skyline Restaurant, known locally as 'The Captain's' as its proprietor is an Ethiopian Airlines pilot, offers superb fish (Nile perch) and chips, one of a wide range of choices. That and its cosy ambiance make it well worth the journey across the tracks on the Debre Zeit Road, after which you turn right on the road to Cherkos. The restaurant is on the left after you come up out of a dip.

To wash down your meal, try one of Ethiopia's beers, which, thanks to competition from the country's numerous breweries, have become quite good. The local wines are drinkable — Guder and Dukem are the best reds; Awash Cristal and Kemila the better whites — and make up in their very low price what they may lack in distinction.

PART FOUR: SPECIAL FEATURES

Opposite: Young and old alike take part in the country's many religious celebrations.

Above: A sea of brilliantly coloured bougainvillea in an Addis Ababa garden.

Wildlife: Uniquely Ethiopian

Ethiopia was long isolated from the rest of the world by its geography. An extensive montane fortress with a healthy, temperate climate and fertile soils surrounded by arid seas of semi-desert enabled it to thrive with little contact from the outside world. A civilization evolved in these mountains that subsisted on nature's bounty and subjugated the fertile highland plateaux over the ages.

There is little agreement amongst botanists as to what the 'natural' vegetation was really like. The same is true of the wildlife. However, vestiges remain at the extremes of altitude and climate. The extremes consist of the highest, coldest heights in the Simien and Bale mountains, and at lower altitudes wherever cultivation was not possible. In recent times even these natural barriers have been pushed back — by the sheer weight of people surviving as the result of widespread availability of medicine, by new methods of managing the land, by the demand for natural resources, especially firewood and charcoal, and by new strains of crops capable of withstanding either cold or aridity.

The origins of the geology of Ethiopia can be dated quite accurately. Around forty million years ago lava began to spill out of the crust of the earth, not as eruptive volcanic action, but a massive outpouring over some twenty million years, forming an extensive blanket of lava some two to four kilometres (1.5 to 2.5 miles) deep and 700,000 square kilometres (270,300 square miles) in extent. Towards the end of this time a second process began — the earth's crust weakened and split, forming the Great Rift Valley. The massive block of lava was split from north to south, through Ethiopia, Kenya, Tanzania, and southwards — and continues to widen at a rate of several centimetres a year. It is nowhere more evident than in the Danakil Depression — already more than 100 metres (328 feet) below sea level.

The two highland islands formed by this rift rise some 2,000 metres (6,560 feet) above the surrounding lowlands in most places, but at their extremes they are over 4,000 metres (13,120 feet) high. They form extensive plateaux that, in the more massive western block, have been shaped and worn by countless rivers, forming escarpments and *ambas* (open, steep-sided, and flat-topped volcanic plugs bordered by deep valleys), which mostly defy passage, whether human or animal.

Within these vertical kilometres can be seen a microcosm of Ethiopia, from desert to semi-arid to montane conditions; from the sun's glare and baking heat of the canyon's depths, to the mists, frosts, and even snow and ice of the highlands. This is the backdrop to the natural world in Ethiopia and what has survived the upheaval of the earth's crust, millenia of inclement weather, 8,000 years of glaciation, centuries of man's wresting a living from the soil, and long isolation by the surrounding sea of aridity from any similar forms of life and similar conditions.

Wildlife surprises

It is not surprising then that Ethiopian wildlife is so different and undocumented, like the **mountain nyala** — the last large mammal species to be named by science, in 1919 — and the **giant molerat**, found only in the Bale Mountains. Ethiopia continues to surprise scientists and visitors alike in the wildlife field, as it does all those who think they know Africa.

Millions of years of isolation of extensive areas with unusual conditions in the highlands of Ethiopia have led to the evolution and/or retention of unique species at all levels, especially those smaller species less able to travel or be carried across inhospitable habitat. Other species from temperate regions have found a habitat similar to their usual homelands and have established populations here.

Endemism is rife, particularly amongst large and small mammals, amphibians, reptiles, and fish. Endemic does not mean endangered — just limited to a geographi-

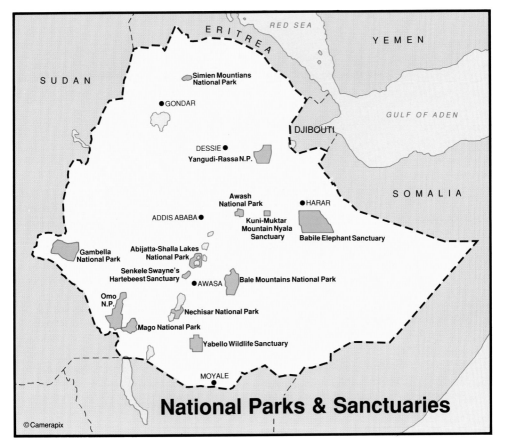

National Parks & Sanctuaries

© Camerapix

cal and nowadays political area. Ethiopia possesses a large and isolated area of unusual habitats within its political boundaries and is therefore endowed with more than a usual share of endemic species. The country, in fact, has a recorded list of 242 land mammals, of which twenty-eight are endemic.

Apart from the wildlife able to coexist with humans — such as **bushbuck, grey duiker, vervet monkey,** and **Anubis baboon** — in most of the highlands at 2,500 metres (8,200 feet) there is little wildlife to be seen. The rest of Ethiopia's animal kingdom is to be found either at the extremes of the highlands in the Bale, Simien, Arsi, and Ahmar mountains, or comprises the more usual East African wildlife in the more arid habitats of the lowlands.

Two of Ethiopia's wildlife conservation areas are in the highlands — the **Simien** and **Bale Mountains national parks** — and the rest either bordering or down the

length of the Rift Valley — **Yangudi-Rassa, Awash, Abijatta-Shalla Lakes, Nechisar, Omo,** and **Mago national parks** and **Senkele Swayne's Hartebeest Sanctuary** — or in the lowlands surrounding the edges of the highlands — **Babille** and **Yabello sanctuaries,** and **Gambella National Park.**

Swayne's hartebeest

Not all of Ethiopia's special wildlife is confined to the altitudinal extremes. **Swayne's hartebeest,** an endemic subspecies that once occurred from Somalia in a broad swath through the Ethiopian Rift, now lives in a few scattered populations: in Awash where it was reintroduced, Senkele, Nechisar, and Yabello. The **wild ass** lives in the remote desert confines of the **Danakil Depression** and is conserved in the Yangudi-Rassa National Park. In the west, in swampy Gambella, occurs wildlife from neighbouring Sudan, including mi-

235

grating droves of the **white-eared kob** and herds of the graceful **Nile lechwe** in inundated areas.

Omo and Mago are famed for their wilderness filled with the larger wildlife species expected of the African savannah — **giraffe, common eland, buffalo, elephant, ostrich, greater and lesser kudu,** and **Burchell's zebra**. Further north, Nechisar combines spectacular scenery bridging the two lakes of Chamo and Abaya with wildlife such as **Burchell's zebra, greater kudu, Grant's gazelle,** and **Guenther's dik-dik**. The lakes harbour great numbers of very large **crocodile** as well as **hippo**, easily seen from the safe vantage points along the steep escarpment roads.

Further north still, Senkele once safeguarded more than 2,000 **Swayne's hartebeest** in a very small area surrounded by farmland but the animal was hard hit when locals invaded the area in the anarchic period after Mengistu's fall. It is estimated that they now number only a few hundred. Nearby is Abijatta-Shalla Lakes National Park, part of the Rift Valley recreational area with neighbouring Lake Langano.

Both the lakes in the park are alkaline, but Abijatta is a shallow pan with no islands and its level fluctuates. Shalla is deep, steady in level, virtually fishless, contains many islands, and hot springs bubble to the surface along its shores. Abijatta feeds thousands of water birds, especially lesser **flamingos** and **great white pelicans**, while Shalla provides their nesting areas on the islands —a situation that leads to the sight of spiralling pelicans rising over the high isthmus between the lakes, only to make the return journey later with food for the young birds.

In Awash the Rift has opened out until the opposing walls cannot be discerned in the haze. Hot springs and rivers of crystal-clear waters well up in the north, lava blisters dot the plain, and Mount Fantale, with its huge crater and fresh black lava flows, dominates the landscape. These plains are inhabited by **Beisa oryx** in large numbers, **greater and lesser kudu, Defassa waterbuck, Soemmering's gazelle,** and **Swayne's hartebeest**.

Wild ass

Further north in the Rift, now a wide-open desert plain, is Yangudi-Rassa, which is stony and scrubby with acacia bushes and inhabited by camels, goats, and Kereyu and Afar tribesmen. This is the home of the **wild ass** and its desolate habitat around Lake Abbe, where sulphur fumaroles, salt mines, and wild and barren wastes abound. Also found here is a reasonable cross-section of other dry-area African fauna including **Grevy's zebra, greater and lesser kudu, oryx, lion, leopard, cheetah, Soemmering's gazelle, gerenuk,** and **hamadryas baboon**.

Far removed from this world and invisible in the bulk of the highlands lie the mountains. Simien, a sheer rugged mass of pinnacles and abysses, is likened to an upside-down table with its legs in the air. Bale, a solid bulk of high-altitude plateau studded with alpine lakes and the odd peaks rising from the Sanetti Plateau, is likened to a table the right way up. Both areas are mountainous in the extreme, yet each in its way is unique, separated by 700 kilometres (434 miles), six degrees of latitude, and the Great Rift Valley.

Eleven of Ethiopia's endemic wildlife species are recorded from Bale and eight from the Simien Mountains.

Walia ibex

Simien is unforgettable for its sheer verticality, and travelling around its 220 square kilometres (77 square miles) this is evident at every turn, from one viewpoint to another.

This is the home of the agile **Walia ibex**, the symbol of the Ethiopian Wildlife Conservation Organization. Rivalled only by the **klipspringer**, which is also here, the ibex was thought to be heading for extinction, but it appears to be surviving with the protection it is now given. The **Simien fox**, or jackal, has apparently been affected by the insidious invasion of its habitat here by humans in past decades, and numbers are now very low. **Gelada baboon** abound on the cliff tops, descending every night to secure cracks and ledges in the abyss edges.

Top: Large numbers of hippopotamus can sometimes be seen in many part of Ethiopia.
Above: Though difficult to spot, the majestic leopard is found throughout the country — even close to the capital.

Bale has seemingly infinite wide-open spaces and that incredible silence found only in vast mountains. Life here has to withstand immense contrasts, some 40°C (75°F) shift in temperature from night to day, -15°C to +26°C (5° to 80°F) in the dry season. One of the first visitors this century dubbed it 'the Sahara by day and Siberia by night'. It is no wonder that the plants and animals are so different.

Mountain nyala

The stately **mountain nyala** finds optimum habitat at relatively low altitudes, around 3,000 metres (9,840 feet), but can also be found on the plateau to the highest peak at 4,377 metres (14,356 feet) — Tullu Deemtu. Like a shaggy, stocky, greater kudu, to which it is probably more closely related than the nyala of southern Africa after which it was named, these antelope are at home in the juniper and hagenia woodlands and high grasslands to the north of the mountains.

The spiral-horned males tend to be in smaller groups or alone, as is the custom in this family, but on occasions more than ten can be seen together in the presence of females and juveniles. The hornless females and their young consort in larger groups, sometimes of more than a hundred, but more usually a dozen or so together. High in the mountains they are still very shy, but down in the woodlands they will stand and watch, the result of fifteen years of protection and familiarity with vehicles.

Simien fox

The Sanetti Plateau of Bale Mountains National Park is the best place to see the **Simien fox**. Variously known as the Simien jackal, Abyssinian wolf, and more correctly by its Amharic name of *kay kebero* — the red jackal — this animal is closely related to the jackal, is chestnut red in colour, and has long legs and a lope like a wolf. It feeds on the incredible numbers of rodents found on the 4,000-metre-high (13,120-foot-high) plateau. Its elongated snout hides hooked teeth interspersed with large gaps with which it holds wriggling rats.

Opposite top: The Simiens are also a favourite of the rock-loving klipspringer.
Opposite: Despite its name, the Simien fox is more likely to be seen in the Bale Mountains these days.
Top: Lion, the creatures most symbolically associated with Ethiopia, are found in the north-east and south-west of the country.
Above: Crocodiles abound in many of the country's waters.

Above: The petite grey duiker is likely to be seen in most of Ethiopia's national parks.

There are sixteen species of **rodent** recorded from the area, of which eight are endemic, but of greatest interest to both visitor and the Simien fox is the **giant molerat**. Weighing up to a kilo (2.2 lbs) and endemic to these mountains, this marmot-like creature lives underground but gathers its food above from a series of holes served by a network of tunnels. Rarely emerging more than half a body length, it gathers cheekfuls of vegetation before ducking below to deposit it.

Returning several times, it may only spend twenty minutes a day at the surface. The rest of the time is spent below, digging tunnels, plugging surface holes, and sorting the rubbish from the delicacies in what it has gathered. Its eyes, which are on the top of its head, give good vision — unlike that of its relative the common molerat — and are protected from the rough soil through which it digs by stiff, black eyelashes. The Simien fox has been recorded spending up to forty-five minutes motionless over a giant molerat hole, awaiting the eventual emergence of this delicacy, which, at a kilo a time, is effort well spent when compared with the eighty grams (three ounces) of the other rodents.

Amphibians

Although not as well known as the birds and mammals, Ethiopia's **amphibians** and **reptiles** present a rich array of species, many of them endemic to this country. Studies of the amphibians record fifty-four species, of which seventeen are endemic. However, this number could be as high as sixty-six species, of which thirty could be endemic.

Amphibians are usually creatures of wetter areas, hence the well-watered highlands exhibit the greatest variety and are the stronghold of the endemic species, because of their extent, their isolation, and the extreme conditions found there that are so unlike other nearby parts of eastern Africa. Thirty-two per cent of the **frogs** and **toads** and their relatives described from Ethiopia so far are known only from this country. This is an exceedingly high proportion, further illustrating the uniqueness of Ethiopia's fauna. On a recent expedition to the Bale Mountains **Harenna**

Above: The magnificent greater kudu, seen here in Nechisar National Park.

Forest area, four new species of frog were discovered in only a three-week period. This gives some idea of what is still to be learned about this area.

Not only are species unique but there are also several unusual adaptations. One recently described frog does not lay its eggs in water but in the moist soil among grass tussock roots, where the eggs swiftly develop into froglets. Another species specializes in swallowing whole snails. Yet another, *Balebreviceps hillmani*, known only from a very small area high in the Bale Mountains at the tree line, cannot hop, has no external ears, and has been found only underground beneath large rocks and tree roots.

Insects

To most people, the **insects** and other invertebrates are hardly considered a tourist attraction. However, few people can ignore a mass of **butterflies** fluttering at the water's edge, gliding through a forest clearing, or feeding on a beautiful flower. Ethiopia's forests in particular harbour a broad variety of colourful butterflies and moths, in addition to other insect forms. Though little studied, endemic species and forms have been recorded and described, and doubtless more will be found in the future.

Large, colourful, and strangely formed **beetles** exist in the drier woodlands, where their larvae, together with the **termites**, play a part in breaking down dead wood under conditions in which fungi and bacteria find it too dry to thrive. They in turn support a varied insectivorous bird life.

Walia ibex, Simien fox, gelada baboon, mountain nyala, snail-eating frog, giant molerat . . . these and many other creatures are all uniquely Ethiopian.

241

Bird Life: An Ornithological Paradise

Ethiopia's position, an extensive highland island surrounded by arid lands, has enabled the evolution of many birds of the region into unique forms and species. Ethiopia boasts 857 bird species, of which twenty-eight are considered endemic, limited within the confines of the Ethiopian borders. Not all these are limited to the highland massif, some being found in a surprisingly small area to the south with no apparent barriers to dispersal. The extremely varied birds of the Ethiopia and their spectacular habitats make them a must for every bird enthusiast.

Broadly speaking, Ethiopia can be divided into a number of habitats with respect to bird life — the Rift Valley lakes, the highland massifs, the lowlands, and the arid semi-deserts. Each of these is in turn a complex mosaic of terrain, soils, vegetation, and human use, all of which govern the avifauna found there.

It is difficult to single out specific sites especially good for bird-watching. However, many of the national parks provide areas less affected by human activity and where a broader range of bird species can usually be seen.

Many of the endemic species present on the western and south-eastern highland plateaux are common and surprisingly easy to see, even in the environs of a city. Endemic species include the heavy-headed **thick-billed raven**; the **wattled ibis**, with its raucous call and unsightly habit of clasping its partner's wattles and pulling; the **black-winged lovebird**, which whirrs through the sky like a miniature helicopter; and the **white-collared pigeon**, a delicate-grey bird with a neat white collar and white wing patches.

Songs of the forests

The highland forests are home to birds less easily seen. Their song is usually the first sign of their presence. The **Abyssinian catbird** has one of the most beautiful calls,
the male and female performing a duet in the seclusion of thick bush. The **black-headed forest oriole** has a distinctive call and its yellow colour shows clearly in the upper storey of the tall trees it favours.

Three endemics are found in the southern edge of the plateau, in the Yabello area. These are **Stresemann's bush crow**, the **white-tailed swallow**, and the colourful **Prince Ruspoli's turaco**. The latter is on the endangered species list.

Many endemics

The highland plateaux are home to many endemic species, and **Bale Mountains National Park** harbours sixteen of them. Among these are the **blue-winged goose**, whose closest relative is in the Andes mountains of South America. The **spot-breasted plover** is very striking and can be seen in large numbers at some times of year. The comical **Rouget's rail** is often seen in grass clumps near water, its tail flashing white as it is flicked up and down. The **yellow-fronted parrot** is usually first noted by its call and its typical fast parrot flight through the tall juniper trees.

The **banded barbet** is found over a large area; its chest is streaked with black. The **golden-backed woodpecker** has a striking golden colour and will be seen searching the bark of the St. John's wort trees in highland areas. On the other hand, the **Abyssinian long-claw** is ground dwelling, its bright yellow throat and chest a strong contrast to its black 'necklace'. The **white-winged cliff chat** has, as its name suggests, a white patch in the black wing and will be seen on cliffs or even on tall buildings in Addis Ababa.

Ruppell's chat is confined to the western highlands and is again seen on cliffs, often darting from the road as a car approaches, its white wing patches showing clearly. The **white-backed black tit** is often missed because it is small and likes the shelter of trees. Large parties of

Opposite: The ostrich is found in many parts of Ethiopia.

black-headed siskins are seen at high altitudes, often in the moorlands. White-billed starlings are in the red-wing group of starlings and are distinguished by their ivory-white bills. In the group of seed-eaters, or Serins, three are considered endemic, though there is some discussion over this. These are the yellow-throated of the Sidamo area and the Ankober and Salvadori's seed-eaters. Harwood's francolin is a little-known species found only in the gorges of the western highlands leading into the Blue Nile gorge.

It is the extensive high-altitude plateaux that form the quintessential Ethiopian habitat — for birds in particular, but also for other forms of wildlife. Most of the endemics are to be found here, as well as a considerable number of other species. Some of the richest areas are the small patches of natural forest on gorge edges, in inaccessible valley bottoms, and the often sacred groves on hilltops and around churches.

Above: The remarkable-looking Abyssinian ground hornbill.

Migrants

Here will be found a plethora of Palaearctic migrants at the right time of year. In addition, parties of chattering yellow and green white-eyes sweep through the undergrowth; mixed groups of firefinches, indigo birds, waxbills, and cordon bleu scour the ground for seeds, while the quiet, sedate dusky and spotted flycatchers plunge from their perches to snap up unsuspecting insects. The brilliant chestnut paradise flycatcher dives through the foliage followed closely by his long white tail streamers, while speckled mousebirds cluster on any ripening fruit.

In season several species of harriers sweep gracefully across the high-altitude grasslands, suddenly doing an impossible about-turn to drop back onto a rodent. Augur buzzards punctuate the skies, their cries carrying far in the clear open air. The delicate black-shouldered kite sits on a perch eyeing the undergrowth for prey, while its much-maligned relative the black kite, visiting in large numbers from North

Africa and the Middle East, gives sterling duty in towns and villages at all altitudes as sanitation squad member.

The pigeon group is represented here by the gentle dusky turtle dove and large flights of the endemic white-collared pigeon, which can often be seen on the airport buildings on arrival. Starlings here are represented by the red-wing starling and the slender-bill chestnut-wing starling at highest altitudes, feeding on the giant lobelias and striking red and yellow stems of the red-hot poker (*Kniphofia* spp.). Many other species in the mountains also gorge on the seasonal bounty provided by these flowers, and the Baglafecht weaver, olive thrush, and Tacazze and malachite sunbirds will all have bright yellow faces from the pollen.

High in the mountains in boggy patches — and elsewhere on the plateaux after harvesting — you may be lucky enough to catch sight of a stately wattled crane stalking through the stubble. Large numbers of visiting white storks can be seen in the same situation, especially if the stubble is

Clockwise from top left: The endemic wattled starling; Kori bustard; Augur buzzard; Rüppell's griffin vulture.

Above: Ethiopia is home to many species of weaver bird.

burnt off, when they will be joined by large numbers of the spectacular **carmine bee-eaters** from lower altitudes.

Bird life at the lakes

Ethiopia's lakes are famous for the sheer numbers of birds they harbour. In fact at each of two locations in the Rift Valley over fifty per cent of all Ethiopia's bird species have been recorded, because of the proximity of numerous aquatic and terrestrial habitats. These are the **Awash National Park** with Lake Basaka and the **Abijatta-Shalla Lakes National Park**.

Abijatta is a feeding ground for numerous **great white pelicans** and **greater** and **lesser flamingo**, as well as flocks of **little grebes**. The pelicans nest in very large numbers on an island in neighbouring Lake Shalla, which is almost fishless. Every day the birds have to thermal up and across the isthmus separating the two lakes to feed. Every few years Lake Abijatta's waters — now also affected by the recently established soda extraction plant there — recede spectacularly, causing a rise in alkalinity accompanied by major

fish die-offs and a change in the algal composition of the waters. The pelicans then have to fish further afield on lakes Langano, Ziway, Awasa, and even Chamo and Abaya, while the flamingos move further afield into neighbouring countries.

An island in Lake Shalla, a regular breeding ground for great white pelicans, is also known to be a nesting spot for the greater flamingo. The thousands of ice-pink birds coming and going over the water against the craggy backdrop of the lake shores are every bit as wonderful a bird spectacle as anywhere in the world. In the northern winters the shores of these lakes are ringed with all manner of waders — **ruff**, **plovers**, **sandpipers**, **stints**, and many other species well known to birdwatchers from the northern hemisphere. At the same time a large number of **ducks** will be found further from shore, particularly **garganey**, **shovellers**, and **wigeon**.

The waters of these lakes are especially rich as breeding grounds for the larvae of various lake fly species that in their turn attract thousands of **swallows** and **martins**

246

from the north. For the same reason the trees and shrubs around the lake edge are festooned in gossamer nets of dusty cobwebs as the spiders wait their turn for the hapless hordes as they hatch from the waters each day.

Fresher lakes produce a greater abundance and variety of fish. Here the day is punctuated by the haunting cry of the **fish eagle** soaring high above, with the occasional **osprey** in season. **Malachite kingfishers** flit like jewels along the banks and the **pied kingfisher** carries out its spectacular bombing runs on surface fish farther out. In nearby grasslands other kingfisher species plague the insects, the lovely duetting call of the **grey-headed** being typical of grasslands in drier areas.

The mouth of the Horacallo River, which flows from Lake Langano to Lake Abijatta, is an excellent site for bird-watching, as it provides 'fresher' water for birds to bathe. The **Goliath heron** and **marabou stork** await fish near the shore or, in the case of the latter, watch for weaker birds in the milling flocks. There are also the **black-headed** and **grey herons**, which can be found inland feeding on rodents in the grass and crops.

Egyptian geese are very common in these areas. (One inexperienced and bemused tour guide was heard to remark 'Madam, that is an Ethiopian goose, not an Egyptian one' — a comment that gives food for thought when we talk of 'European migrants'.)

Chestnut-bellied sandgrouse fill the air in their thousands near the lakes, leaving the water in groups that fly high and fast, wheeling and spinning, all the while giving their guttural calls. **Spur-winged plovers** are striking as they stand among the trees near the lakes, and the **crowned plover** resides closer to the shore here in more open grassland.

Lowland birds

It is in the lowlands that bird-watchers find more birds with which they may be familiar from neighbouring eastern Africa. These areas are especially rich in seed-eating and insectivorous birds, the vegetation dominated as it is by either dry grasslands

Above: Saddlebill stork.

or woodlands in areas too dry for fungi to break down the resulting detritus. Hence insects take their place and provide a plentiful food source for the birds.

The **weaver** group has taken advantage of these resources, and the lowland areas resound to their cries, especially of the **white-browed sparrow weaver** and the **white-headed buffalo weaver** with its brilliant red under-tail coverts. The related **red-billed buffalo weaver** builds its massive stick nests in acacia woodlands, which are in turn used by **chestnut weavers** and **cut-throat finches**.

Starlings too are well represented by a large number of species, as are pigeons. Massive flocks of the bizarre **wattled starling** rise from the ground at any disturbance, the males with their yellow and black wattles on an ash-grey body. Cheeky **Hildebrandt's starlings** take the place of the East African superb starling in many locations, the large **Ruppell's long-tailed**

247

Above: The colourful carmine bee-eater has a habit of using large animals and even the larger birds, such as the stately kori bustard, as mobile perches.

glossy **starling** shrieks from the trees, while **red-billed oxpeckers** throng the backs of animals, wild and domestic, in their hunt for ticks.

The dainty **Namaqua dove** is found throughout the drylands, although subject to local seasonal movements. The pigeon group is also represented by several other species whose gentle calls fill the air at dawn and dusk, although the deep cooing of the **speckled pigeons** scrambling and sliding on a corrugated iron roof at dawn will not endear them to late risers.

Kaleidoscope of colour

Larger insectivores can be just as colourful, as the **Abyssinian, European, lilac-breasted,** and **rufous-crowned rollers** demonstrate from their perches atop isolated acacia trees. The **bee-eaters** too make the woodlands and grasslands their home, their colourful flights and dives over the grass making them noticeable at all times. The **carmine bee-eater** is especially evident, not only through its colours, but because of its habit of using other larger ani-

mals such as **oryx, ostrich,** and the stately **kori bustard** as a mobile perch in the tall grasslands, swooping off their backs to hawk for insects their hosts disturb.

The arid and semi-desert parts of Ethiopia exhibit bird species in low numbers and with affinities to the neighbouring Arabian peninsula and north-east Africa. This area of Ethiopia is the 'funnel' where the Rift Valley between the two highland blocks is very wide and opens out to the Afar (Danakil) region across to the border with Eritrea in the north-east and Djibouti. The southern border of this lowland triangle is the Chercher Mountains. Because of its relative proximity to the Red Sea and the ocean, the area is fairly rich in marine avifauna, which is heavily augmented with Palaearctic migrants in the northern winter. But most bird life here comprises desert-adapted forms, including many **larks, ostrich, sandgrouse,** and various of the smaller and larger **bustard** species. The best way to visit this area is to drive along the road that runs between Addis Ababa and the Eritrean port of Assab.

Flora: Surprisingly Rich and Distinctive

Ethiopia has received much publicity over the years about its land degradation caused by loss of forests and natural vegetation. Though little is known about the true nature of the original plant cover, areas of natural habitat do exist, giving examples of the richness of this country. As in the animal world, many of the plants are endemic, and much has yet to be discovered. A 'Flora of Ethiopia' project is documenting the plants of the region.

Endemics

Some species endemic to Ethiopia are among the ones commonly seen in and around Addis Ababa, such as the **stinging nettle** (*Urtica simensis*) and the tall *Erythrina brucei* tree. The large yellow-flowered **senecio**, *Solanecio gigas,* is commonly seen as a hedge in towns and villages. In the Asela area a **globe thistle** is endemic: *Echinops ellenbeckii* with its large red balls of flowers. *Echinops longisetus*, also red-flowered and endemic, can be seen in Bale. The smaller, blue-flowered *Echinops kebericho* is seen only in the grasslands of Shewa and Gojjam.

Around September and October much of the highlands are coloured yellow by daisies collectively called the **meskal flowers** (*adey abeba* in Amharic), as they flower at the time of *Meskal*, or the Finding of the True Cross, celebration. Many of these are *Bidens* species, and six of them are endemic. In Bale carpets of flowers are seen, many being endemic. One of these is the small bushy *Alchemilla haumannii*. This is interspersed with a bright yellow-green herb, the endemic *Euphorbia dumalis*. Large areas may be populated with **red-hot poker** plants, *Kniphofia foliosa*, and the skyline at high altitudes is broken by endemic *Lobelia rhynchopetalum*, whose leafy rosettes stand two to three metres (6.5 to ten feet) high before sending up a spike of flowers — reaching six metres (20 feet) at times. The endemic *Plectocephalus varians* looks rather like a Scottish thistle at first but is soft to the touch.

Familiar flowers

A visitor used to European plants will find many familiar flowers in the highlands, some even the same species as those growing in more temperate climates. **St. John's wort** (*Hypericum* spp.) can grow as the familiar small herb in grassland or as a bush or tree, the large yellow flowers being seen in the dry season. There is only one **rose** indigenous to Africa, *Rosa abyssinica*, and its sweet foliage and creamy white flowers can be smelt and seen in many areas in the dry season. The tiny **pimpernel flowers** of Europe will be seen in short grass areas of the highlands. *Anagallis serpens* is a pale pink colour, but there are also red and blue species. **Heathers** of the genus *Erica*, which cover large areas at high altitude, will grow to form substantial trees ten metres (33 feet) tall if left undisturbed.

On the high plateaus at 4,000 metres (13,120 feet), clumps of white and mauve **gentians** (*Swertia* spp.) of many varieties bespeckle the ground, many of these yet to be named scientifically. Carpets of small blue **lobelia** and mauve and pink **clovers** carpet the sides of the roads. There are many different species of yellow-flowered everlasting flowers, *Helichrysum* spp., and groundsels, *Senecio* spp. One of the most common is *Helichrysum splendidum*, whose grey bushes cover large areas of the high plateaux, bursting into yellow flowers before the beginning of the rains. *Alchemilla* or **lady's mantle** plants cover the ground profusely, many species intermingling in the rich sward found here.

Trees found in the highland areas are often **juniper** and **hagenia**, or *kosso* as it is called in Amharic. Other trees of the highlands include the **African olive** (*Olea africana*) and several species of *Maytenus* with their striking red and white seeds.

The forests of south-eastern Ethiopia on the slopes of the Bale Mountains are relatively untouched, their remoteness being

Above: Characteristic high-altitude flora, a giant heather towers above clumps of *Helichrysum citrispinum* in Bale Mountains National Park.

their salvation. A journey through the forest here shows the altitudinal zonation, starting with **heather** trees at the top, with carpets of wild flowers beneath, to other species such as **bamboo** (*Sinarundinaria alpina*), **podocarpus, milletia, celtis,** and so on, until at 1,500 metres (4,920 feet) the level of lowland woodland is reached, with trees and shrubs such as *Combretum, Terminalia,* and *Commiphora* spp. On these southern slopes of the mountains there is no juniper, and on the north there is no podocarpus, though the two are seen together in other areas.

The most extensive areas of natural forest still left are in the west and south-

west. Although not as rich in species as their equivalent in neighbouring countries, there are important timber species such as *Aningena* spp. and a number of endemic herbs, including the spice crop *Afromomem koririma.* These forests are the home of Ethiopia's major export crop, arabica coffee.

In drier areas, such as down the Rift Valley and to the south, there is less that may be familiar. **Acacia** trees and bushes fill large expanses of country, the latter so thick in areas that it is difficult to pass through. Other species are adapted to harsh conditions, such as *Dobera glabra* with its leathery shiny green leaves and

Above left: Delicate white blossom of the beautiful, endemic Abyssinian rose, *Rosa abyssinica*.
Above right: An aloe plant has many therapeutic properties.

Balanites aegyptiaca, with large green spines and green stems taking over the function of leaves. Along rivers there will be large acacia trees, as well as **figs** and **tamarind**, both of which are favoured foods of baboons, other animals, and numerous birds. The smaller **herbs**, such as *Blepharis edulis*, are often very spiky with flowers that bloom as soon as the rains fall, only to disappear again as the soil dries up.

Ubiquitous eucalyptus

Around Addis Ababa the most striking aspect of the vegetation is the profusion of **eucalyptus** trees that surround the city. It is these trees that were and are the salvation of Addis. They were introduced by a Frenchman at a time when firewood in Addis was so scarce that plans had been made to move the whole city fifty kilometres (31 miles) to the west. The fast and continued growth of the eucalyptus has meant that even when no other fuel is available the people can cook, and the many small fires often cause a pall of

smoke to hang over the city. Eucalyptus is also used extensively in building, both for the rickety trellis of scaffolding and the actual construction, such as in the roof timbers.

The climate of Addis means that many European species can be grown here, and gardens of roses mingle with the odd remaining juniper and hagenia trees. To the north of Addis are extensive areas of seasonally swampy highland grassland where agriculture is not practised, with clumps of eucalyptus trees marking each settlement.

Few books exist that are helpful in identifying plants. However, there is an excellent small, locally produced book by Sue Edwards called *Some Wild Flowering Plants of Ethiopia*, and ETC has recently published the informative *Some Endemic Plants of Ethiopia* by Dr Mesfin Tadesse. For the serious student of plants, the first volume of the *Modern Flora of Ethiopia*, Volume 3, is available from the National Herbarium, and three more volumes will appear before the end of 1995.

An Angler's Paradise

Conditions for sport fishing could hardly be better than they are in Ethiopia. Rivers and lakes are full of a wide variety of fish, some of extraordinary size. Less than one-hundredth of one per cent of the country's population are anglers, as compared with more than eight per cent in the United Kingdom. A typical day's fishing may also include the bonus of seeing giant crocodiles, families of hippo, pink clouds of flamingos, exotic tropical fruits ripening on the trees near the water. Trout may be caught in mountain streams situated quite close to the equator.

Ethiopia boasts more than 200 species of freshwater fish including Nile perch, immense catfish, tigerfish, and brown and rainbow trout. Angling techniques that may be used include fly-fishing, threadline spinning, bait fishing with float and leger, freelining, and even trolling. Facilities, however, are limited. Those planning a trip need to be as self-contained as possible.

The largest of Ethiopia's lakes, Lake Tana, is one place to start a fishing safari. The grounds of the Ras Hotel in Bahar Dar run down to the lake shore, enabling you to fish in comfort for the barbus, catfish, and tilapia so numerous here. Boats are available for hire nearby, permitting the exploration of more remote fishing grounds; barbus fishing in the upper reaches of the Blue Nile can be superb. In the clear water conditions, barbus and catfish of truly enormous size may be seen in the fast runs above the Blue Nile Falls (*Tis Isat*) which are a sight to see themselves. (See 'The Historic Route: Mountains and Gorges, Mystery and Grandeur', Part Two.)

Tilapia and barbus are the main species of fish in the beautiful Rift Valley lakes of Ziway and Langano. Further south in the Rift, Chamo and Abaya lakes, near the town of Arba Minch, also offer good fishing. The Baro River, in the west of Ethiopia with access gained at the town of Gambella, is noted for the giant size of its Nile perch — and the great density of the crocodile population as well. The ubiquitous tilapia is found in most of the country's lakes and rivers. Normally a shoal fish, the largest on record was just over five kilos (12 pounds).

There are several species of catfish in Ethiopia, although the most common is *Bagrus docmac*, known to achieve weights of eighteen kilos (40 pounds) or more. Another interesting fish you may come across is the revolting-looking electric catfish, *Malopterurus*. Although it grows to more than one metre (three feet) in length, it has the unfortunate habit of delivering an electric shock to anyone handling it. An average-sized fish can send 100 volts and enough amperage through your system to knock you over. If you don't relish the idea of catching such a specimen, then limit your fishing to daylight hours, as the species is mainly nocturnal.

Of the many species of barbel found in the country, two are of great interest to the angler. The rhino-nosed barbus, *Barbus mariae*, is the largest of the family, achieving weights in excess of eighteen kilos (40 pounds). *Barbus tanensis* is more heavily built, somewhat humpbacked, and there is a pronounced spine on the leading ray of the large dorsal fin. Maximum recorded weight is around fourteen kilos (30 pounds).

The tigerfish, a voracious predator with a remarkable set of teeth quite capable of biting a chunk from an angler's hand, averages about one-and-a-half kilos (three pounds) in weight, although much larger specimens have been recorded — up to a fantastic sixteen kilos (35 pounds).

Nile perch are likely to be the prime objective of many anglers, with their potentially vast size and excellent fighting capabilities. They are usually found in deeper water close to weeds and reeds. Although fast, strong and seemingly tireless, the Nile perch rarely runs more than forty-five metres (150 feet) before it can be turned and prefers to fight in open water rather than seek out obstructions.

The fight is often long but light tackle usually proves adequate.

Trout

By far the biggest sport fishing attraction in Ethiopia is the superb trout fishing waters to be found in the beautiful Bale Mountains in the south-west of the country. To reach Bale, you have to organize four-wheel-drive vehicles for the 400-kilometre (248-mile) journey from Addis Ababa to the Bale Mountains National Park, where there is self-service accommodation at Dinsho, or a further eighty kilometres (50 miles) east to the provincial capital of Goba, where there are several hotels.

For the keen trout angler, there are three quite spectacular rivers that flow out of 3,800-metre-high (12,464-foot-high) Sanetti Plateau, the highest massif within the Bale Mountain range, which stretches over 140 kilometres (87 miles) on the eastern side of the Great Rift Valley south of Addis Ababa.

Above: Tranquil setting for trout fishing enthusiasts.

The Bale Mountain waters offer a challenge few fly-fishers can resist. Notable among the many options are the pools below the falls of the Upper Web and the long, placid stretches where it flows across the moorlands. There are also abundant trout in the Shiya and Danka rivers. The self-help lodge at Dinsho is the headquarters of the Bale Trout Fishing Club. Government regulations specify fly-fishing — spinning rods are forbidden.

The Danka is really a tributary of the Web, and both these rivers are easily accessible from Dinsho. Some stretches of water that flow through the national park are closed to sport fishermen to encourage breeding. However, there is plenty of open water well stocked with brown and rainbow trout.

The rivers are easy to fish, flowing through upland hillsides covered in heather, interspersed by tumbling cataracts with plenty of good water for the fish. The bag limit of ten is easily achievable, especially for those with the stamina to walk deep into the Web gorge proper. This is idyllic trout fishing country, and infrequently visited.

The largest of the three rivers is the Shiya, bordered by open grassland. The river is distinctive because of its huge holding pools along the thirty kilometres (19 miles) of fishable water. The fish are mainly rainbow — all indigenously bred since the rivers were stocked by Kenyan sport fisherman in the late '60s — and are powerful fighters. One- and two-kilo (two-to four-pound) rainbow are common, and others up to three kilos (seven pounds) in size have been caught with some regularity. Brown trout will normally average around two kilos (four pounds), with potential maximum weight about twice this figure.

The Shiya's vast deep pools are interspersed with tumbling, rock-filled rapids and the banks are generously covered with weed, grass, and water weed — ideal hiding spots for trout as food abounds. The weather is cold at night, dropping to freezing. Fishing cannot take place in the rainy seasons of June to August and November–December. It is best just before and after the rains, from mid-December to March and September–October.

Camping in Ethiopia: A Truly Great Outdoors

Camping in Ethiopia is almost the only way to visit the most beautiful, undeveloped, and unspoilt areas of the country. These days most road towns have acceptable cheap hotels, so camping is really a strategy for those driving to the more remote parts of the country or for those heading off-road, either to national parks or to other rural areas.

The national parks

Awash National Park has shady riverside designated campsites, but you must bring all equipment and supplies, including water and firewood. The latter is obtainable along the road between Nazaret and Metahara. The canopy of tamarind and ficus draws a wonderful variety of birds.

Be warned that the resident vervet monkeys are fond of picnics and will enter any open vehicle or tent in a flash. Game scouts are available to guard the camp for those who wish to go off on game drives or walks to the falls and nearby gorge.

In Bale Mountains National Park, some pleasant campsites are laid out near the Dinsho headquarters and are even furnished with rough benches and tables. Mountain nyala have become very tolerant and will often stroll through the campsites, stopping to browse or horn the earth. For trekking in the park, camping is the only option, and excellent sites abound. The Bale Mountains are often wet and cold, so good equipment is essential.

The sites at Mago National Park may seem rather dark and claustrophobic but do have the benefit of being a three-minute walk to the clear cool waters of the Neri River. Beware of the possibility of encountering buffalo or elephant.

Omo National Park has one large open campsite under some huge fig trees. For the camper who does not mind sharing the clear deep pool in the Mui River with a dozen five-foot crocs, the bathing is refreshing. In 1994, the Maji-Omo National Park road was being rebuilt in a food-and-tools-for-work programme using ex-Dergue soldiers. When completed, this road will at last make Omo National Park accessible by four-wheel drive via Jimma.

In Simien Mountains National Park, camping is allowed anywhere at present, although some sites, by virtue of flat terrain and availability of water, are used regularly.

With an increasing number of visitors, the park authorities would be well advised to educate their staff and visitors on the principles of maintaining a proper campsite. All burnable waste should be burned, while organic waste should be buried, and all hard trash carried out to the road for disposal in town rubbish pits.

It would also be nice to see more care taken in the disposal of human waste. At present the best practice is for each group of campers to carry a small spade. This, when needed, is taken off to a suitably distant spot, where a quick excavation and subsequent burial, cat style, will make sure that human waste and toilet paper do not disfigure the area or pose a health hazard.

Other national parks also have campsites, and enquiries may be made at the respective headquarters.

Elsewhere

Lake Langano, 205 kilometres (127 miles) south of Addis Ababa and five kilometres (three miles) off the main road, is a popular weekend resort area for Ethiopian residents. Both hotels on the lake charge moderate fees for putting up a tent. The lakeside sites are on sandy ground shaded by gnarled acacias. On weekends and holidays the sites tend to be crowded and noisy, but the swimming is always great and fine walks may be enjoyed along the lake shore.

In the arid lowlands of the south-west, the sites used by car campers are few and are usually determined by the availability of reliable water. The better-watered highlands offer a choice of more sites, although these may be near villages or cultivation. Most country people are happy to have

Above: Campsite in Mago National Park is well situated in a shady fig tree forest near the park headquarters.

campers on their land as long as simple rules of courtesy and common sense are observed, like not trampling through their barley fields.

Security

In the national parks and most highland areas, campers may pitch a tent, climb in, and enjoy a good night's sleep, untroubled by worries of unwelcome night visitors intent on thievery or worse. Country people are, for the most part, pacific, hospitable, and cooperative. They are not immune, however, to curiosity and campers should not be surprised to have an audience as they go about their bizarre business of tents, camp stoves, and air mattresses. In any case, it is wise to leave no portable items outside the tent after turning in for the night. Some campsites on the south-west road circuit have been occasionally subject to harassment or theft by undisciplined youths, in spite of hiring some of them as watchmen.

Other road routes — for instance, in the direction of Harar and Dire Dawa — have questionable security and may be unsuitable for camping. Before leaving Addis Ababa seek informed local opinion on current conditions.

Ethics

The sensitive visitor to Simien or Bale will surely feel pangs of conscience as many people bring in loads of that scarce commodity, firewood. Dead stumps and twisted tree trunks are depressing reminders of the insatiable demand for firewood that has denuded most of the northern highlands. Visitors may make a small stroke against the tide by bringing camp stoves and fuel. Camping gas stoves or kerosene pressure stoves are options, both of which are usually available in Addis Ababa.

Maybe someday Ethiopia's Wildlife Conservation Organization, together with the international conservation community, will instigate some programmes to promote firewood plantations to relieve the pressure on indigenous trees in critical areas like the Simien National Park.

Above: Scenic camping spot in the beautiful Bale Mountains.

Health and safety

Stomach problems while camping may be avoided by the faithful use of iodine tablets or solution to purify drinking water. Water filters of various degrees of durability, cost, and effectiveness are available in first-world shops, and these produce potable and tasty water.

Some campers like to sleep in the open air when weather conditions allow, but this habit is definitely unwise in areas with hyena, as these bold scavengers have been known to help themselves to the inviting, exposed tender parts of sleeping humans.

Equipment

If you want to go off camping on your own, come fully prepared with everything you need, as there is virtually nothing for hire in the country. (See 'Trekking in Ethiopia: Trails of Adventure', Part Four, for packing suggestions.)

Alternatively, you can use one of the reputable tour operators who run camping safaris, such as Orooro, Yumo, and Nile Touring Company. The government-run National Tour Operation (NTO) organizes car camping trips with everything provided, including equipment, a guide, a cook, and the vehicle.

Trekking in Ethiopia: Trails of Adventure

Blessed with a temperate climate, grand mountain scenery, and a tradition of generous hospitality, the Ethiopian highlands offer superb trekking opportunities. Horses, mules, and donkeys are universal means of transport, so horse trekking has been a natural development.

Trekking can be interpreted in many ways, but it is usually walking or riding a mule or horse, or a combination of the two. The animals can be used just for carrying a load or can be ridden part of the time. The usual group will have pack animals for baggage and some riding animals, which the group can use in turn.

Trekking in Ethiopia does not involve any necessary skill, although it obviously is best if you are physically fit. The terrain is usually steep for only short periods, when walking rather than riding may be necessary. Much of the time it will be walking, although this may be at an altitude as high as 4,000 metres (13,120 feet). A slow pace is recommended, which is not difficult as there is so much to see and wonder at. Trips can be tailored to meet all individuals' needs, whether they be day trips around Dinsho in Bale, or ten-day hikes around a whole park. Patience will be needed as there is little one can do to change the accustomed pace of life.

Where to go

The principal, well-established areas for trekking are the Simien and Bale Mountains national parks (See 'Places and Travel', Part Two). More recent, lesser known trekking areas, some only recently reconnoitred, are in the remote south-west highlands east and west of the Omo Valley, where strong and colourful cultures complement the appeal of scenery, flora, and fauna. Other suitable and beautiful areas include Mount Chilalo and the Arba Gugu area in Arsi, and the Chercher Mountains in Harerge.

Treks have been organized on and off in Simien and Bale for the last three decades. In Simien, the attractions include spec-

tacular views from the northern escarpment, the presence of the endemic Walia ibex, gelada baboon, and Simien fox — as well as Ethiopia's highest peak, 4,543-metre (14,901-foot) Ras Dashen, outside the park to the east.

Bale has a less inhabited, richer mosaic of high-altitude plateau, heather moorlands, and dense juniper forest, with an easily seen population of mountain nyala and Simien fox — and some fabulous birds, many of them endemic. For dedicated climbers, Bale has Tullu Deemtu at 4,437 metres (14,553 feet) and Mount Batu at 4,207 metres (13,799 feet), although these are just the highest 'bumps' in the already very high Sanetti Plateau.

When to go

The best time to arrange trips varies slightly, depending on where you are going, but in general it is wise to avoid the rains. In Simien, November through March is a reliably dry period. December to February is the best season to trek in Bale, while in the south-west highlands, which are more temperate than the Bale or Simien mountains, any time between October and March is good.

Trekking arrangements

In Bale and Simien, treks of any duration may be arranged through the park offices. Staff supervise the hiring of guides, horses, mules, and muleteers. Rates for all these are fixed and reasonable. The arrangement spares the visitor the hassle of haggling and, if followed faithfully, keeps the interface of tourism and local interest from degenerating into one of exploitation and venality.

Trekking parties are normally accompanied by park rangers who help with the mules and are generally sharp-eyed and knowledgeable about flora, fauna, and terrain.

Experienced English-speaking guides, at least in Simien, are assigned on a rotation basis and are responsible for communi-

Above: Ethiopians have long been known for their equestrian skills.

cating with the visitors, helping to plan the itinerary, as well as providing information on Ethiopian history, natural history, and culture.

As of February 1994, the national park trekking fees were fifty birr for park entry (per forty-eight-hour period), twenty birr for camping (per forty-eight-hour period), ten birr a day for each horse or mule, ten birr a day for each muleteer, forty birr a day for each guide, and twenty birr a day for a park ranger. These rates, of course, are subject to change and are payable in advance at the park office, which dispenses them to the guide, rangers, and muleteers after the successful completion of the trek.

Saddle and pack animals

In the Simien Mountains mules are the preferred 'beast of burden', whereas in Bale horses are used. Any pack or riding animal for hire should be thoroughly checked, with the saddle off, for saddlesores, lameness, or other defects. Avoid nervous and flighty animals, and give saddle mounts a trial ride. Pack and riding saddles should be inspected and adjusted. Ethiopian riding saddles tend to be small, wooden, and hard and a sheepskin or cushion thrown over them provides some welcome padding. Stirrups are tenuously held up by tatty thongs and likely to break under too much weight. Saddle girths are neither robust nor tightly cinched, so to avoid a sudden and disconcerting bellyward rotation when mounting, a colleague should hold the saddle firmly.

Ethiopian horses and mules, however, are extremely sure footed and trail wise, and tend to follow in line with little guidance. The accompanying guides will instruct visitors in the art of conveying to the horse or mule the required direction, but there are some general guidelines to follow. The pace may be quickened with a forceful shout of *Mich!* (for mules) or *Che!* (for horses), accompanied by a nudge with your boots and, as a last resort, a flick on the backside with a switch. A tap on the neck with same will suggest to your steed a turn in the direction of the opposite side.

Many mounts may be ridden without bits, sometimes without any kind of bridle even. You will often find a mount is guided

Above: Rough terrain of the towering Simien Mountains requires exploration on foot, mule, or horse.

by a single rope wound around the animal's lower jaw and then held lightly. If your mount is fitted with this harsh local bit, this is best left alone, except to order a halt, for which a gentle pull will usually suffice. Mules go up surprisingly steep slopes without hesitation. It is rarely necessary to dismount, but a firm grasp on the animal's mane while leaning forward will help prevent the saddle from slipping tailward or farther. Lastly, at all times exercise caution when moving behind a horse, donkey, or mule, as a kick can cause serious harm.

Packing

The ideal container for tents, clothes, and other gear is a flexible waterproof bag that will repel both rain and horse sweat. Next best is a sturdy water-resistant duffle. In extremis, pack all your gear in multiple plastic bags and stuff it all in locally available gunny sacks.

The constant jarring and shaking inflicted on horse-borne loads is a real test of packing; glass jars or bottles should be carefully taped and wrapped in soft mate-rial. Fragile items such as kerosene lamps should be hand carried by the muleteers. Kerosene should be confined to leakproof containers and kept well away from food or clothing. Some extra straps or rope may well come in handy. Provisioning for the trek is best done in Addis Ababa, where a great variety of local and imported products is available.

All requirements for the journey must be taken. The weather changes fast because of the high altitude and steep slopes. On a still, sunny day it may be warm enough to have a relaxed bathe in a river but after dark it can quickly drop to a few degrees below freezing. Layering with wool or polypro or pile clothing for warmth is recommended. Polypro whisks away perspiration and dries out quickly when washed. Cotton is comfortable but does not provide much insulation, especially when wet. It helps to remember that once the pack horses or mules are loaded for the day it is difficult to reach possessions, so a day pack is necessary to carry all the day's requirements, such as packed lunch, water, and clothing.

Above: Horse trekking in the Web Valley, Bale Mountains National Park.

Equipment should include enough food and cooking utensils for the whole trip, a jerrycan to carry water from the nearest source, tents and bedding, personal items and clothing, a comprehensive medical kit, sunscreen, and hat. The medical kit should include painkillers, a broad-spectrum antibiotic, an anti-diarrhoeal preparation, throat lozenges, treatment for cuts, and other simple remedies. Availability in Ethiopia is variable, so these items should be obtained prior to arrival.

In some areas there is little or no firewood, so a camp stove is necessary. However, supplies of fuel are variable. Although the two-kilo refillable camping gas cylinders are available, disposable types are not. A multi-fuel stove is advised. Remember that kerosene or butane may not be carried on planes. Kerosene is available in all towns. Other items to remember are torch, penknife, plastic bags (for food storage, keeping clothes and other items dry, rubbish, and so forth), and toilet paper. Water at high altitudes, far above all human habitation, is usually safe to drink, but if in doubt it should be boiled or treated.

Treks vary from day trips to two-week expeditions. Consult a reputable tour operator for recommended itineraries. Experienced outfitters capable of providing fully equipped and catered treks to Bale, Simien, and the south-west include Remote River Expeditions, Orooro, and Mountain Travel — Sobek. (See Listings for Tour Agents.)

A typical trek day begins with an early morning wake-up to light the fire or stove for a bracing pot of coffee and breakfast, while the muleteers collect the steeds from their nearby grazing. The mules are usually tied to trees, stakes, each other, or hobbled in some way. After breakfast, when tents are down and gear packed up, the muleteers make short work (after the first day anyway) of balancing and tying down the loads with strong, supple leather straps. Then the party sets off, following ridges, crossing stream valleys, or meandering between banks of everlasting and St. John's wort, staying on the lookout for wildlife.

Lunch may be by a stream, at a viewpoint, or in a sheltered piece of meadow. It is nice to reach a site by mid-afternoon to allow time for setting up camp, cooking, and a sunset stroll. At higher altitudes in Bale and Simien the temperatures plummet to below freezing, so early evenings are the rule, although a brilliantly clear night may keep you up star-gazing.

Avoiding dehydration and sunburn at such high altitudes is especially important. Keep a water bottle filled and handy and try to drink frequently. Flavouring the water with lemon juice or commercial preparations may increase the incentive to drink. A wide-brimmed hat will ward off the sun, and any areas not covered by clothing should have regular applications of sun block.

Most trekkers going to Bale or Simien will have had the benefit of several days at an elevation of 2,500 metres (8,200 feet), so a reasonable level of acclimatization will have been attained before ascending to higher areas. However, high-altitude sickness is a threat and warning signs should be known. These include shortness of breath, headache, nausea, vomiting, and insomnia.

If these become severe, or are accompanied by bubbly sounds in the chest, a persistent cough, or blueness of the lips, then the case should be taken seriously and the patient **immediately** taken to lower altitudes where recovery is usually prompt.

Suggested Trekking Equipment List for Bale and Simien

Clothing

- long-sleeved shirts for sun protection and warmth
- short-sleeved shirts (or T-shirts) for warm days
- medium-weight wool, pile, polypro, or other sweater
- insulated parka or pile jacket, big enough to go over shirt and sweater (hooded jackets keep head and neck warmer)
- long trousers for warmth and/or sun protection
- shorts for warm days
- cap with visor or wide-brim hat for sun
- ski cap or similar for warmth
- mittens or gloves for cold nights before retiring
- light boots for trek
- tennis or running shoes for camp
- appropriate socks — polypro or wool is warm
- rain jacket or poncho (rain is possible even in the dry season)
- rain pants (optional)

Miscellaneous necessities

- sleeping bag, warm enough for a few degrees below freezing
- Thermarest or equivalent sleeping pad
- day pack big enough for jacket, lunch, water bottle
- sunscreen, sunglasses, lip cream with sunblock
- personal first aid and toiletries
- toilet paper
- flashlight with spare batteries and bulb; headlamp optional
- light towel
- water bottle
- binoculars

Personal medical kit

- Bandaids/plasters
- flexible adhesive tape (Elastoplast) for anti-blister
- your favourite painkiller
- broad-spectrum oral antibiotic to which you know you have no allergy
- antihistamine (if you react to insect bites)
- vitamin C and other vitamins (to help ward off colds while travelling/trekking)
- Pepto-Bismol or similar for upset stomach or digestive disturbances

Optional

- camera
- reading material
- moist towelettes
- bottles or flasks of spirits/champagne
- pocket knife/Leatherman tool
- playing cards or Scrabble set
- fluorescent camping light for tent
- special snacks you might like to munch on the trail
- umbrella

Shooting the Rapids: White-Water Rafting in Ethiopia

Born in the USA's Grand Canyon in the '60s, white-water rafting has expanded rapidly to become a hugely popular activity enjoyed on all the continents. Ethiopia's rivers, perhaps surprisingly, played an important role in the internationalization of this blend of sport, ecotourism, and adventure.

The Omo River was the main attraction for the group of intrepid young Colorado River guides who arrived in Addis Ababa in March 1973 with some well-used equipment, a shoestring budget, and boundless enthusiasm. Their objective was the Omo, which tumbles its way some 350 kilometres (217 miles) through a steep, inaccessible valley and mellows its pace as it nears the lowlands, finishing up as a torpid meander through flat, semi-desert bush, where it finally feeds into Lake Turkana.

Without aerial reconnaissance and little first-hand information, the hazards presented by rapids, falls, wildlife, and potentially hostile people were largely unknown. To placate the crocodiles at least, the group adopted the name of the ancient crocodile god of the Nile, Sobek, and made a successful descent of the river from the Gibe Bridge all the way to the Mui River confluence by the Omo National Park.

Inspired by their experience, the guides never looked back. The first commercial trip down the Omo took place in November 1973 and since then Sobek's pioneers have reached Peru, Chile, India, Pakistan, China, New Guinea, Tanzania, Zambia . . . to name only a few countries.

Since 1973, the Omo has been run every year but for '78, '91, and '92, attracting a small number of motivated clients of many nationalities. The season for Omo trips is between September and October, when the river is still high from the June–September rains and the weather is starting to dry out. Spirited rapids, innumerable side creeks and waterfalls, sheer inner canyons, hot springs, abundant wildlife, and exotic tribal peoples combine to make the Omo one of the world's classic river adventures. And it is still wild and remote, with only one possible motorable track between the start and kilometre 525 (mile 325). At some points, a walk out could take three days to the nearest village, a week to the nearest road.

The trip starts at the Gibe Bridge, 185 kilometres (115 miles) south-west of Addis Ababa on the road to Jimma, at an altitude of 1,100 metres (3,608 feet). The river, known there as the Gibe, lies in a deep valley, whose steep sides hold small trees in dense stands of tall grass. A belt of riverine forest at the water's edge shelters black-and-white colobus monkeys, whose growling calls reverberating up and down the river herald the dawn of each new day. High above, patchwork fields and plumes of smoke mark the homes of highland farmers — Janjero, Gurage, Kambatta, Wolayta. Coffee smugglers, marketgoers, and people on their way to visit relatives do descend the valley to cross the river, paddling across while balancing on tightly inflated goatskins. In this section, crocodiles are not a menace. But the threat of malaria and tsetse flies, the heat, and the steepness of the terrain have kept the lower slopes of the valley free of habitation.

Challenge

Here and there narrow black basalt inner gorges constrict the waters, forming numerous short but violent rapids — Haystack, Henderson's Hydraulic, Double Trouble, and Tewodros — building up to the first serious challenge at Gypsy's Bane. There the river curls over a submerged shelf, accelerates as it is squeezed to the right into a series of big waves that converge at the bottom to a soaring rooster tail that drops into more big diagonals below.

It's not over yet, though, with a submerged boulder creating a sharp and awesome hydraulic 'hole', one that's been known to grab and hold a five-metre fully

Above: Adventurous rafters negotiate one of the Omo's biggest rapids, Potamus Plunge.

loaded Avon Pro in its rinse-and-agitate cycle for several long minutes. However, a careful scout allows the guides to chart a safe course through the obstacles, a last-minute pivot and pull avoids the hole, and the boats push on, with everyone exhilarated by the power of the rapid, the gallons of water cascaded over all, and a close but far-enough view of the nasty keeper hole.

Actually, most of the Omo's rapids are rated at a fairly non-threatening 3-4, with the latter figure applying to one or two rapids at certain water levels. This is not the Zambezi, where flips are routine and rapids have been known to wrench the floor right out of a boat. But boats have flipped on the Omo, rapids change, and the river may always have a surprise for the unwary or overconfident boatman.

Downstream from Gypsy's Bane, two big, long rapids — Snake Pit and Bovine — offer a different ride: a roller-coastering gradual S-bend on huge standing waves, between which the boats disappear completely. Past these rapids (by about day 4), the river widens a little and near the confluence with the Gojeb the valley opens up,

affording grand views to the range of mountains south of the Gojeb.

On the west bank, a 300-metre-wide (984-foot-wide) strip of old river bed, still watered by the major floods, has produced a wonderful open gallery forest — mostly big tamarinds and figs.

Wildlife spotting

Under the canopy, which is alive with colobus, it's refreshingly cool, even at midday, and a stroll may turn up an interesting bird like the blue-breasted kingfisher or send monitor lizards scuttling noisily off through the dry leaves littering the floor.

Away from the river, above the forest, a shelf of hippo-grazed savannah slopes gently toward the mountain wall, a good place for waterbuck and bushbuck in the occasional thicket, as well as Abyssinian ground hornbills.

All this, plus a beautiful and comfortable sandy camp with good parking, plenty of firewood, and lots of space make it a unanimous choice for a layover — two nights here — and time to bake bread in

Opposite: Quietly gliding through an Omo River gorge can be just as rewarding as 'shooting the rapids'.

the cool of the evening in a well-embered Dutch oven, while watching the brilliant sky for flaming meteorites.

The good grazing in the ten kilometres (six miles) above the Gojeb supports a dense hippo population, and without high water, it requires care — and maybe some warning shots from a flare gun — to get past the 200 or so that inhabit this section, which is also rich in plant and bird life.

Hippo Alley

At the end of 'Hippo Alley', where the Gojeb comes in from the right, the Omo re-enters a steep-sided valley whose walls frequently top out in red stone cliffs, over which curl some mesmerizing long, slow-motion falls. Other falls are located close to the river and reward a creek-bed clamber with a good shower and pool. At one creek, the forceful current pours in a groove over a smooth ledge and plunges into a deep pool, creating a safe but exciting waterslide.

The last camp before the track and Bailey Bridge that link the towns of Soddu and Waca is on a shelf of clean sand shaded by overhanging trees festooned with jasmine. As a frequently used ford is nearby, there's a trail leading west up to the top, where Wolayta people grow grain crops, false banana, sweet potatoes, and coffee. Their thatched houses are large and well made, and the appearance of visitors quickly elicits an invitation to come inside and rest, while the woman of the house stokes up the fire to roast, grind, and brew the most delicious coffee, served of course in the universal, handleless Chinese-type cups. As sugar is a luxury, coffee is not uncommonly flavoured with salt, and the camp at the base of the trail goes by the name 'Salt Coffee'.

At the bridge (day 9 or 10), outgoing and incoming participants are exchanged (you can opt to do just the first or the second half of the trip if you wish). Fresh fruit, vegetables, ice chests are delivered — maybe even ice cream and some cold beers — before the group pushes on downstream, glad to leave behind the sound and smell of cars, the intrusion of the outside world.

South of the bridge, the valley becomes less steep, the inner gorges less frequent and constricting, and the river mellows, with long tree-lined straights, and curves around enormous rock bars. Two of the Omo's biggest rapids, however, are yet to come, and those who join the trip at the bridge get their money's worth from Potamus Plunge and B-Team (days 11 and 13). The latter is a long and challenging three-part roller-coaster that definitely calls for an experienced team on the oars. Only at low water may a boat be entrusted to a trainee or talented client. The big crocs circling in the eddy way below do nothing to relieve the pressure either.

Superb vistas

Once past B-Team, there are superb vistas of distant peaks and hikes to highland farms lead to more and more remote

groups — Gemo, Gofa, Zala, Kulo-Konta. The campsites exude signs of the wild, with lion, leopard, or buffalo spoor embedded in the sand.

Now the sides of the valley start to drop away, the nights become warmer, and near the confluence with the Dincia (about day 16) the first riverside farms become visible. These belong to the Bodi, a small tribe who come to the Omo every September and October to grow sorghum, clearing and planting suitable mud banks as the annual floods retreat.

The Bodi are of Nilo-Saharan stock and pastoralist background. Although no longer pure pastoralists, their culture is very much cattle centred, with livestock playing an important role in marriage, divination, and name-giving rituals. The Bodi classification of cattle is complex, with over eighty words to denote different colours and patterns. Dress is simple. The women wear goatskins tied at the waist and shoulder, while men fasten a strip of cotton or bark-cloth around their waist.

For adornment, the women wear numerous brass or copper bangles and sometimes a wooden plug inserted in a hole pierced between lip and chin, while the men favour a simple string of beads. They also may carry an old Italian or British rifle, although AK-47s are increasingly common.

For the last five or six days of the trip, on a wider, slower river, with good campsites fewer and farther apart, the boats are tied together and a Yamaha 9.9 hung over the back happily pushes the whole rig along, producing a light refreshing breeze while still allowing a good look at a Pel's fishing owl in its daytime roost on an overhanging branch.

Frequent stops give an opportunity to visit riverside settlements to exchange news, give limited medical help, take photos, and bargain for baskets, bangles, or carved headrests.

Birding is rewarding too. Goliath herons stalk the shallows where African fish eagles study the opaque waters from riverside rocks as black kites wheel overhead. Crimson wings flash as white-cheeked turacos swoop through the riverine forest. In the background may be heard the soft lament of the emerald-spotted wood dove, the bubbly purr of the white-browed coucal, and the raucous cawing of silvery-cheeked hornbills.

Lower Omo cliffs are densely perforated with the nesting holes of red-fronted bee-eaters, and noisy colonies of black-headed weavers build their nests in bushes and trees overhanging the water. A short walk from any campsite will produce other sightings, be they of cuckoo, shrike, or barbet.

Unique cultures

Other tribes encountered after the Bodi include the Kwegu, the Mursi, and the Bume. The Mursi are well known for the large clay discs that the women wear, inserted in their slit lower lips. Mursi men wear very little, although a cotton wrap is becoming more and more common. Their way of life is similar to that of their traditional enemies, the Bodi, depending on sorghum and cattle.

The Kwegu, thought to be the remnants of a hunter-gatherer tribe, live scattered along the Omo, existing in an interesting symbiosis with the Bodi and the Mursi. The Kwegu are experts in making and piloting dugout canoes and also in hunting. But their Mursi and Bodi neighbours do not allow them to keep cattle. Each Kwegu man attaches himself to a Bodi or Mursi patron, for whom he provides ferry services across the Omo and, occasionally, hunting products like meat, skins, or ivory. In return, the patron protects his Kwegu client against the depredations of other Bodi or Mursi. Also, in order for the Kwegu to marry, the patron must 'loan' his client enough cattle to satisfy the bridewealth requirement that even the Kwegu have — a peculiar and fascinating arrangement in this far-away, disappearing world.

The Bume, close relatives of the Turkana, share both the language and many cultural practices. They live on the west bank of the Omo, growing sorghum and keeping cattle, sheep, and goats. It's in Bume country, at the bend in the river known as Pongoso, where the Omo trip comes to an end after twenty-three days and 600 kilometres (372 miles), with a walk or drive twelve kilometres (seven miles) across the open thornbush to the border settlement of Kibish. There a good airstrip receives the DC-3 or Twin Otter for the return to Addis Ababa.

Awash River

Bordering the Awash National Park, a twenty-eight-kilometre (17-mile) stretch of the Awash River offers a superb one- or two-day trip, featuring lots of spirited rapids, wildlife and impressive rugged cliffs and side canyons. The trip starts at Awash Falls, with a paddling drill in the foaming pool below, and the rapids follow one after another, with sharp drops, narrow channels, and fast current. It's all 'read-and-run' until Haile Selassie I Rapid, where a quick scout can help avoid a possible wrap on the big boulder obstructing the main channel.

Colobus and vervets stare down from the tamarinds and figs lining the banks, and baboons, waterbuck, warthog, and lesser kudu come down to the river to drink. A few crocodiles share the river and monitor lizards scurry along the banks.

A sacred hot spring (where Kereyu offerings of coloured string, cloth, brass bangles, and cowries hang in the gnarled trees that shade the bath-temperature rocky pool) is a great place for an overnight camp. Alternatively, the group can push on for the remaining two hours or so to the take-out at the beach below the town of Awash Station, where the historic Buffet de la Gare provides cold beers and delicious Greek and Italian cuisine.

The Blue Nile

The famous Blue Nile River has attracted various expeditions, some farcical, some well organized and successful, with Swede Arne Rubin's 1965 nine-day solo paddle in a Klepper canoe from the Shafartak bridge to Roseires in the Sudan an especially notable effort. Later expeditions have had trouble with bandits, and any aspiring boaters should have strong assurances that all is peaceful in the Blue Nile Valley before attempting a river trip.

Sporting Ethiopia

Lack of a sizable middle and upper class has perhaps inhibited the development of modern sports facilities in Ethiopia. Sports, however, are becoming increasingly popular, and now that the private sector has been encouraged to invest, gyms, fitness centres, and sports clubs are burgeoning.

By far the most popular sport is football, played in school yards, pot-holed city streets, or rural pastures with balls ranging from the official leather one to home-made spherical bundles of old rags. At the pinnacle of the local game, interclub and international matches draw full crowds of enthusiastic partisans to Addis Ababa Stadium.

The greatest Ethiopian sports heroes and heroines have won their laurels in long-distance running, in which both men and women have excelled at the highest levels of the sport. It is not infrequent to see runners training in the streets or outskirts of Addis Ababa. Visitors with a compulsive or merely occasional inclination for jogging may find it most pleasant early in the morning when the streets are empty of obnoxious children and fumes from the rapidly increasing vehicle population. Or join the Hash House Harriers weekly run. Check at the Hilton for times and places — but remember, if you are not accustomed to the 2,400-metre (7,800-foot) altitude, take the jogging easy.

Other sports played by many Ethiopians are basketball, volleyball, and table tennis. The latter is a real growth industry with locally made tables set up at numerous roadside locations in the capital and even on minor road towns. The table, rackets, and ball are available as a pastime for the local youth at low hire rates.

Of course, it is no surprise that certain bourgeois sports fared badly during the Marxist era. Golf was played at a nine-hole course until 1978 when the club was requisitioned as the staging ground for parades of the newly formed 80,000-strong militia. The first fairway became the site of a 100-

Above: Ethiopian Belayneh Dinsamo achieved the world record in the 1992 marathon. In 1988 Dinsamo ran the Rotterdam marathon in the record time of two hours, six minutes and fifty seconds.

Above: Top-quality tennis courts and thermally heated swimming pool at the Addis Ababa Hilton.

metre (328-foot) latrine trench (still marked by an unusually green strip of grass) and the clubhouse was enjoyed mainly by Russian military advisers. However, another nine-hole course on the British Embassy compound still exists, and one can play by invitation from a member of the Embassy Golf Club.

Fuel rationing put paid to any hopes for car rallying, which had been popular in the 1960s when intrepid residents like Carl-Gustav Forsmark would drive his well-worn Saab to Nairobi for the East African Safari Rally, which was probably an anticlimax after the punishing tracks of southern Ethiopia. Happily, the local rally scene is now coming alive again, with the first being held in early 1994.

Tennis

Tennis is a sport in which a tourist can easily participate. Even under Mengistu, who was said to play frequent singles matches at the Palace Court, tennis continued to flourish in a modest way and Ethiopian juniors are now doing quite creditably on the African circuit, in spite of the lack of a serious talent development programme.

Excellent clay courts at major hotels are available to visitors and usually have resident pros who give coaching sessions at very low fees. The Hilton, Ghion, Genet, and Taytu hotels all have courts. Clubs offering court space and coaching are the Addis Ababa Club, located behind the NTO office near the Ghion; the Commercial Graduates Association, off the Bole Road near the Pilots' Club; and the International Club in the old airport area.

If you want a game, bring your gear, making sure the balls are for high altitude — at Addis Ababa's 2,400-metre (7,800-foot) elevation, normal balls are barely playable. A relaxed evening of ten-pin bowling may be enjoyed at both the Genet Hotel and the RECE bowling centre off the Debre Zeit Road.

Swimming enthusiasts may choose between a pricey temporary membership at the Hilton or a modest entry fee at the Ghion Hotel's Olympic-size pool. Both pools are comfortably warm, having as their source the thermal waters of Finfine,

268

Above: Used for both sport and transport in Ethiopia, the horse is popular with all ages.

which was an important factor in the establishment of Addis Ababa.

Farther afield, Lake Langano's slightly alkaline waters and pebble beaches provide safe swimming — no bilharzia, no crocodiles, only the odd over-powered outboard — in surroundings of exceptional tranquillity and scenic beauty. Sailboat and sailboard owners work the fresh afternoon breezes that blow down off the Arsi mountains, but to date, no equipment is available for hire.

Genna and gugs

Indigenous sports include 'genna', a wild, free-form country hockey played over vast distances, in which teams from rival villages try to drive a puck into their neighbour's territory. The interested visitor may look for this at the time of Ethiopian Christmas (7 January) — from which the sport takes its name.

'Gugs' is an expression of equestrian exuberance that tends to break out at big holidays like New Year (11 September) and *Meskal* (27 September). Riders dressed in traditional white, mounted on gaily be-decked horses, chant boasts and challenges and spur their mounts, inciting rivals to take off in pursuit.

When the pursuer draws close enough, he hurls a wooden club at his adversary who, if necessary and possible, fends it off with a round hide shield. The plains of Sululta, along the Gojjam road on the north-east side of Entoto, is a good place to see gugs.

More familiar sorts of horse riding may be indulged at the Equestrian Centre near the International School in the Old Airport area of Addis Ababa and at the stables near the British Embassy, where one can rent horses and go out with a guide. The hills around the city are well suited to cross-country riding, with no fences and many trails leading from farm to farm, and eventually over the top of the ridge toward Sululta. Show-jumping competitions and polo matches are occasionally held at the Jan Meda playing field.

Ethiopian Traditional Dress

International trade and mass production are conspiring to eliminate traditional attire all over the world. Ethiopia is no exception. Fortunately, however, in spite of deposed dictator Mengistu's serious attempts to oblige citizens to wear khaki or blue clothes of Korean design, the process has not yet made much impact. The greatest effect is in the larger towns where Western style clothes are nearly universal, often taking a transitional form in the cool of evening when men wear a *gabbi* cloth around the shoulders and over the jacket. In the daytime you will often see poorer citizens in a combination of Western jacket and traditional Ethiopian trousers.

Beyond these recent developments, however, traditional culture has been preserved. At ceremonies and festivals, both public and private, the streets and gathering places are transformed into a sea of white as finely woven cotton dresses and suits are donned, jewellery glints in the sunshine and colourful umbrellas fan out.

The women's dresses, tight bodiced and full skirted, are bright white with coloured embroidery and woven borders, and the men are resplendent in white jodhpurs and tunics. Although originally most of the border designs were based on the varied designs of the Ethiopian cross, nowadays you sometimes see more modern motifs — flowers, birds, and even aeroplanes.

Religious occasions

Major national occasions, such as New Year's Day or the Festival of *Meskal*, both in September, or the Ethiopian Christmas, *Genna*, in January demand the wearing of traditional costume. If your visit does not coincide with one of these, you should rise early on Sunday and mingle with the worshippers around one of the many Ethiopian Orthodox churches in Addis Ababa or direct your steps towards one of the several mosques on Friday when the Muslim population will be assembled.

Traditional Muslim dress for an Ethiopian woman is a light, full-length, cotton dress over a full embroidered underskirt (*gorgora*) and usually also embroidered velvet tight-fitting trousers. A light cotton, coloured cloth is worn over the head and shoulders.

Traditional costume is most often seen in the countryside, where imported alternatives are few and where locally made clothing is worn in the market place. Markets are arranged between the villages so that there is a market on each day of the week. These are the places to purchase cloth of various qualities and styles, much of it homespun and hand-loomed, and also made-up dresses and accessories.

At the market

In the market, which serves as a place for regular social gatherings as well as the exchange of produce, it will become clear, wherever you are, that there is no such thing as Ethiopian national dress. It is usual to see traditional costumes of at least two or three of Ethiopia's ethnic groups. In the markets along the road north of Addis Ababa, where the great escarpment separates highlands and lowlands, Amharas and Tigrays from the highlands mingle in white cotton robes with Afars from the desert plains and Oromo from the slopes of the escarpment, attired in brightly coloured cloth from the coast. In the market places leading south from Addis Ababa along the Great Rift Valley, the visitor will encounter Sidamo girls in their finery of gay black, red, yellow, and white striped material; Oromo and Bale people, whose leather, bead-encrusted garments reflect their economy, which is based on livestock; as well as a Gurage farmer and his wife in the heavier off-white cotton and

Opposite (clockwise from top left): Typical male dress consisting of gleaming white jodhpurs and tunic; Women from Tigray traditionally wear their hair plaited and braided to the head and fuzzing out at the shoulders; Oromo woman from the highlands of Bale; A deacon of the Ethiopian Orthodox Church wears richly embroidered cloths and carries an umbrella.

black headscarf. On Saturday at the weekly markets in the larger centres, there is almost the varied glamour of a fashion show.

Although the fashions of the larger groups — for example, the Amhara and Tigray highlands — may be similar they are not identical, particularly in the way the cloth is worn. The most obvious identification is in the jewellery and the hair styles and in the embroidery of the dresses. The hair of Ethiopian people varies from baby peppercorn and Afro fuzzy to black wavy locks, and it is cut, brushed, plaited, and sculpted into a hundred fashions.

The women of Amhara and Tigray wear dozens of plaits (*sheruba*) tightly braided to the head and fuzzing out at the shoulders; The women of Harar part their hair in the middle and make two large buns behind the ears; Hamer, Geleb, Bume, and Karo men form a ridge of matted hair and clay to hold their feather head decorations (and as a result must sleep with their neck on a wooden headrest); Arsi women have a fringe and shortish, bobbed bushy hair; Bale girls the same but covered with a black headcloth, held in place with a white headband decorated with fine dangling chains or coins.

Young children often have their heads shaved, except for a tuft or a small tail of plaits, which are left so that if God calls them 'He will have a handle by which to lift them up to Heaven'.

Adornments

Jewellery worn by both Muslims and Christians is mainly of silver and gold and is made up of moulded beads, chains and links, and filigree work, often with amber or glass beads incorporated into necklaces and earrings. In warmer climes, heavy brass, copper, or ivory anklets and bracelets are worn. Where clothing is minimal, in addition to massive bead necklaces, body and hair decorations flourish. Accessories, like brightly coloured umbrellas and sunshades woven from grass and fibre, are also distinguishing signs.

Costumes also respond to a great range of climatic conditions. Heavy cloth capes and wrap-around blankets are needed on the highlands, particularly at night. In the great heat of the lowland plains a thin cotton skirt and bare torso is more appropriate for men and women alike. Men protect their heads from the heat of the sun by means of the thick, combed out mass of woolly hair, but the women wind a long length of black or indigo cotton around their heads.

Elsewhere in the lowlands, where livestock are common, over wide areas of Sidamo, Bale, and Arsi, leather forms a major part of clothing, particularly for women. The leather is tanned till it is soft and pliable and then embroidered with red, white, and blue beads and cowrie shells. But in the plains of Ogaden, inhabited by Somalis, white cotton cloth is the rule.

A distinctive style of dress is found among the Oromo horsemen from the central highlands. On ceremonial occasions, such as New Year's Day and the *Meskal* festival, large groups of horsemen, attired in lion mane or baboon skin head-dresses, carrying hippopotamus hide shields and spears, ride down to the main squares of the city where they participate in the parades. The horses are also gaily caparisoned on these occasions.

Then there are the special groups with their own particular costumes and regalia. On festive occasions such as the anniversary of the Battle of Adwa, which is held on 2 March, the traditional costumes of the Ethiopian warrior may be seen. These, naturally, become more elaborate and decorative up the scale of army rank and aristocratic status. Beneath impressive head-dresses, the warriors glisten and shine with decorations and embroideries on capes and blouses.

Over white jodhpurs the tunic is usually black and yellow striped satin, and over that, in lieu of the *gabbi*, an embroidered shoulder cape is worn. This has five long appendages hanging from it, which are based on the four limbs and tail of an animal skin.

Festivals

More frequently seen, as church festivals occur regularly throughout the year and between come marriages and funerals, are the very elaborate costumes of the priests of different ranks in the hierarchy of the Ethiopian Church. At the greatest of these occasions, the baptism feast of Epiphany (*Timkat*) all are present from the Patriarch down. The *tabot* (the Ark of the Covenant) is paraded beneath richly embroidered cloths and a sea of gold-embroidered velvet umbrellas and processional crosses, all carried by church officials in equally elaborate robes. These are costume occasions not to be missed.

Ethiopians are extremely proud of the range of their traditional costumes and there are frequent occasions when these may be seen on national dance programmes on television, in several national theatres, and in the Ethnographic Museum of Addis Ababa University.

The larger hotels also dress their staff in national dress, either to serve local food and drink or on festive occasions. The cabin crew of Ethiopian Airlines have their own version of traditional costume, which will introduce the traveller to its charm. The workshops of the Tourism Trading Enterprise also produce a range of dolls in traditional costumes, which are for sale in larger shops.

Above: Distinctive hairstyle and dress of a woman from Tigray.

Glossary of terms related to dress:

Buluko	heavy cotton blanket also used a wrap during daytime; usually with two thick layers. Natural greyish-white colour and often with a black or red stripe at the ends of the length
Burnos	cape, usually of heavy black woollen cloth. One type was traditionally designed to cover a slung rifle
Chama	shoes
Gabbi	thicker than a shamma or natala and larger; worn over basic clothing for extra warmth usually by men
Kemis	woman's dress with full skirt
Kuta	Two-layer thick cotton covering as a shamma, but usually worn by women
Libs	used for both cloth and dress and also when qualified by another term, having a special sense, e.g. *bird libs* ('cold' clothing; blanket) *alga libs* (bed cloth; bed cover); *terapesa libs* (table cloth)
Natala	one-layer shawl with matching tibeb border worn with a kemis
Shamma	shawl worn over a male costume (*waya* in the Oromo language)
Shash	headcloth worn by women
Shemis	shirt worn by men
Sheruba	distinctive hairstyle plaited tightly on the head and frizzed out
Shirit	skirt worn by Somalis and Afars
Surri	trousers; different styles produced by various nationalities
Tibe	coloured border to kemis or shamma

Tastes of Ethiopia

Like much else in Ethiopia, the country's cuisine is unique, and partaking of a traditional Ethiopian meal means participating in what resembles another of the country's colourful and fascinating ceremonies.

A formal meal in Ethiopia begins with the washing of hands. A decorative metal or earthenware jug is brought to the table and water is poured over the guest's outstretched hands into a small basin. This small ceremony is sometimes followed by a short prayer or grace.

The first course, served immediately after the washing of hands, is often a mild dish of curds and whey, giving no hint of the spicy feast about to come.

Spicy speciality

The national dish of Ethiopia is *wot*, a type of spicy stew that comes in many varieties. It is invariably accompanied by *injera*, a fermented pancake-like bread made from *teff*, a locally grown grain, and water. The mixture is left to ferment for three or four days until ready for baking, which is done in a covered flat earthenware griddle.

The *injera* is placed in layers on a special 'basket table' or *mesob*. Resembling colourful mushrooms, the finest of these tables are produced in the Harar region and are notable for their elegant, tightly woven geometric patterns.

Dollops of different types of *wot* are artistically placed on top of the *injera* in the *mesob*. All you need to do now is tear off a piece of *injera* and dig in, wrapping the bread around chunks of meat or using it rather like an Indian *chapati* or Mexican *tortilla* to scoop up the savoury sauce.

Often, as a sign of affection or respect, an Ethiopian diner will choose a particularly appetizing morsel and place it in the mouth of a companion at the table. In some regions, the meal does not begin until the head of the household (or a priest, if present) has torn off a piece of *injera* for each person present, which is done in a strict order of precedence.

The fiery, peppery *wot* is a spicy concoc-tion of meat, fish or vegetables simmered in an onion and spice sauce. *Doro* (chicken) and beef are the most common bases for *wot*. The secret of a good *wot* lies in the *berbere*, a mixture of red pepper, herbs, spices, and other flavourings — such as black pepper, garlic, onions, cloves, nutmeg, cardamon, fennel seed, coriander, and fresh ginger.

For those who simply can't handle such 'hot' food — and be warned, it *is* hot — you would be advised to try *alicha*, a much milder but equally delicious dish, usually based on chicken or lamb and flavoured with onions and green ginger. *Alicha* never contains *berbere*. In either case, the mildly sharp taste of *injera* offers an ideal contrast to the rich, succulent flavours of the *wot* or *alicha*.

Lenten offerings

The ingenuity of the talented Ethiopian cooks really comes into play during the lengthy Ethiopian Lent, when all forms of animal products are forbidden to members of the Orthodox Church and only vegetable dishes are eaten.

Weeks before Lent begins, large quantities of *mitin shiro*, which will be used as the basis of fasting *wot*, are prepared. *Mitin shiro* is a mixture of dried peas, lentils, beans, and chick-peas, which, after being lightly boiled, roasted, and ground, is then combined with *berbere* and a host of other herbs and spices. Then the mixture is ground very fine and stored in a cool, dry place to be used as needed. The *wot* made from *mitin shiro* is made with vegetable oil instead of butter and is generally eaten cold.

There are fasting variations of *alicha* too, usually with a basis of pea flour, potatoes, or split peas. One very popular version includes carrots, tomatoes, cabbage, and green peppers.

An interesting feature of fasting cooking is the fashioning of 'fish' and 'eggs' from a dough of chick-pea flour. These are cooked in and served with a variety of spicy onion-based sauces.

You would normally wash down a traditional Ethiopian meal with either *tej*, a type of mead or honey wine with a light, wine-like taste, or *tella*, a light local home-brewed beer made from malted barley or some other grain. Once reserved for the monarchs and their guests, *tej* is now enjoyed by everyone and can be bought in special shops, bars, and restaurants in all parts of the country.

Ethiopia's commercially brewed beers are also tasty, as are the very palatable yet inexpensive wines: try Guder and Dukem if you like red; Awash Cristal and Kemila are the better whites.

Regional delights

Different regions of the country have their own special delicacies. In the Harar region you may be offered a *biddena*, another pancake-type bread made of millet, which has a slightly sugary taste because the dough is not fermented. A much-esteemed Harari speciality is the *kwalima*, a beef sausage. The beef is mixed with onions and highly spiced with pepper, ginger, cumin, basil, cardamon, cinnamon, and cloves, and coloured with turmeric. The sausages are smoked and dried and may be eaten either raw or cooked in soup for a few minutes. They are generally considered a festival food, eaten at marriage feasts and similar celebrations.

A popular drink in the Harar region is the tasty *hojja*, a sort of tea made from the dried leaves of the coffee tree, which is served with salt and milk.

An Ethiopian meal is not usually followed by dessert, but in many areas honeycomb dripping with fresh honey is served. The soothing sweetness of the honey somehow seems to 'put out the fire' of the spicy meal you've just enjoyed.

An Ethiopian meal simply wouldn't be complete if it wasn't rounded off in the traditional fashion with coffee — a drink that was 'born' in the country. It is still possible in many restaurants throughout the country to watch the elaborate and charming coffee ceremony take place at the end of the meal. (See 'The World's Favourite Drink', this section.)

There are many excellent 'national restaurants' in Addis Ababa (See 'Eating Out in Addis', Part Three), offering the visitor a perfect opportunity to experience a wonderful Ethiopian meal.

Left: Ethiopian food is traditionally served on a brightly coloured woven *mesob*, a basket table.

The World's Favourite Drink

The word for coffee throughout most of the world is similar: 'café', 'kofye', 'kahawa', 'kaffa', 'kave,' and other cognates. But in Ethiopia, where it all started, the word is 'buna'.

Yes, coffee, one of the world's most popular beverages, originated in Ethiopia. Its spread from a plant known only locally to a worldwide commodity makes an interesting story.

The drink was taken from Ethiopia to Yemen in the fourteenth century, where it acquired its Arabic name, *qahweh* — possibly a colloquialization of 'Kaffa', the Ethiopian region in which the first plants were discovered.

Legends as to the actual discovery of coffee are numerous, but perhaps the most attractive is that of the 'dancing goats'. According to tradition, Kaldi, a young Ethiopian goatherd from Kaffa, was surprised that his lazy and sleepy charges became suddenly invigorated and began to prance about excitedly after chewing certain berries. He tried the berries himself and found them stimulating — indeed in large enough quantities they produced a mood of merriness akin to intoxication.

The legend has it that a monk from one of the many monasteries nearby came upon Kaldi in this happy state and decided to try the berries too. That night, during an arduous session of prayer, he discovered that he remained wide awake with his mind more active and acute than it normally was on these occasions. Accordingly he passed on the coffee secret to the brothers of his order and soon all the monks in Ethiopia were chewing the berries, rendering up their devotions without the troublesome interference of sleep.

For many centuries after its discovery, coffee was eaten and not drunk. Berries were either taken whole or crushed and mixed with ghee (clarified butter), a practice that persists in the remoter regions of Kaffa and Sidamo provinces to this day. Later refinements included a variety of wine made with fermented pulp and another concoction produced from the dried fruit and beans. It was not until the thirteenth century that the practice of brewing a hot drink from roasted beans was introduced, but this soon acquired widespread popularity.

Ceremonial honours

Coffee is widely drunk in Ethiopia, and it is treated with the respect properly due it. It is one of the country's big earners of foreign exchange. But the honour bestowed upon it in the Ethiopian home has nothing to do with that. It is simply because the drink is appreciated.

A typical delicious Ethiopian meal is followed by an elaborate coffee ceremony. While the guests are replete after their *injera* and *wot*, a woman of the household quietly starts the ritual. She scatters freshly cut grass on the floor in one corner of the room to bring in some of the fragrance and freshness of the outside. She seats herself in that corner on a low stool beside a charcoal brazier. She lights incense, further enhancing the pleasant setting. She usually produces something to nibble on, often popcorn, which she passes around to the guests. Then she roasts the green coffee beans, shaking them on a concave pan to turn them and roast them evenly.

When they are toasted just right, she brings the pan with the roasted beans around, shaking it in front of each guest, to give all the pleasure of smelling the fragrant odour. Then she disappears into the nether regions of the house. From there comes the sound of pounding as the beans are ground by mortar and pestle.

She comes back with a traditional clay coffee pot, round and plump at the base, usually with a long narrow neck ending in a pouring spout at the top. She heats the water in the pot, puts in the coffee, and brings all to a boil. Then she pours the coffee into little handleless cups, adds sugar and often a sprig of rue. And serves.

The coffee is delicious — full-bodied but not the least bitter.

276

Above: A typical Ethiopian meal is followed by an elaborate and charming coffee ceremony.

After everyone has drunk and enjoyed, she collects the cups, adds more water, and brews a second round, using the same grounds. Tradition calls for even a third round, if the guests wish. Ethiopians say the first round, the strongest, is for the fathers, the second for the mothers, and the third, weakest, for the children.

Indulging in all three rounds is tempting, as the brew is so tasty and satisfying after a hearty meal. But the coffee is strong, and the unwary can lie awake, wide-eyed throughout the night after such an indulgence.

A Treasury of Arts and Crafts

Ethiopia's involvement with the tourist industry is comparatively recent and, except for the brief period of partial Italian invasion, does not involve a colonial experience with its accompanying large numbers of long-term resident expatriates.

The outcome, of great benefit to visitors seeking new experiences, is that there is no long-established system of production of indigenous artefacts for a wider market, in contrast to most other African countries.

The largest customers for Ethiopia's arts and crafts are Ethiopians themselves. Most objects are functional and put to daily use. The visitor seeking a souvenir will find it easy to obtain articles that have practical use as well as artistic and cultural values. So much of Ethiopia's skill, ingenuity, and sense of design is employed in the production of useful items that the Handicraft School in Addis Ababa is well patronized by Ethiopians furnishing their homes.

On the other hand, the more recent development of a tourist industry in Ethiopia has permitted a careful and systematic approach to the production of cultural souvenirs and 'antiques', especially for visitors. Modern technology is allied to the vast stock of Ethiopian traditional design and craft experience and to the range of raw materials available locally. The lead has been provided by the Ethiopian Tourism Commission and its Handicraft Production Centre near Bole Airport, where trained artists and craftsmen produce a wide range of items that incorporate traditional design and decoration. This modern output is a genuine Ethiopian product that does not compete with, but rather complements, the range of articles produced by peasant artisans.

Visitors should also bear in mind two important aspects of Ethiopia's culture. The first is its long recorded history and its very much longer unrecorded history. Although Ethiopia is only now being opened up to modern tourism, it has for long been a destination for the determined traveller. It is now thought that the gold in jewellery found in Tutenkhamun's tomb probably came from the western provinces of Ethiopia. Early visitors returned with the detailed information seen on fourteenth- and fifteenth-century maps of this part of Africa. In the eighteenth century, tales of Ethiopia's highland civilization were brought to England by James Bruce, whose audiences found it difficult to believe that the Abyssinians had musical instruments similar to those in Europe.

Ethiopia's cultural history stretches back over the unrecorded centuries and millennia to 'Lucy', the earliest hominid discovered so far. Somewhere between Lucy and the beginnings of recorded history, several hundred years before the birth of Christ, Ethiopians were using ploughs for cultivation, perhaps the first to do so. The Christian religion arrived around 300 AD, long before its advent in many parts of Europe.

Its influence on the arts and crafts is obvious to today's visitor and is responsible for many basic design forms. No other country in the world has such an incredible range or intricacy of cross designs. Modern Ethiopian art's deep foundations stem from 1,700 years of experience accumulated in the creation of church murals and manuscript illustrations.

Ethiopia's second cultural attribute is its diversity and complexity. Few countries encompass such a range of ethnic groups and their particular cultures, developed in environments that differ widely. Ethiopia's cultural heritage is based on a kaleidoscope of arts and crafts developed by various ethnic groups. These range from the shepherd boys of the high mountains, who craft woollen hats from the hair of mountain sheep and ornament them with patterns based on the range of colours in the fleeces, to the Anuak women of the low borderlands with Sudan, who produce finely decorated and thin-shelled kitchen potteryware. Other crafts range from the Harari basket makers, who use

Top left: Decorated gourds of the Nuer people in Gambella.
Top right: Highland shepherd boys making sheep's wool hats.

Opposite: Falasha pottery, near Gondar.

the grasses of their extensive grazing lands, to the silversmiths and goldsmiths of Jimma, who add to their raw materials intricate value of great worth.

And there are many specializations within the various crafts. Thus, pottery embraces the distinctive figurines produced by Falasha craftsmen in the Gondar region and the graceful coffee pots from the lowlands further north. Leatherwork includes the saddlery of the Bale region and the curved knife scabbards of the Afar people. Boat builders in the highlands produce papyrus *tankwas* for Lake Tana, while in the deep south, along Lake Abaya, they fashion boats from the balsa-like wood of the *ambatch* tree.

Ethiopia's arts and crafts are found in a wide spectrum. At one end is the sophistication of the in-house shops of the international hotels. There, although you pay more for the privilege of buying off the front doorstep, you have access to the highest quality, and the shop may be authorized to receive your foreign currency.

At the other end of the spectrum is the farmer's son or daughter by the roadside far from Addis Ababa, offering wonderful examples of peasant crafts from practical wide-brimmed sunhats, woven from grass, to the imaginative use of pith stems in the manufacture of toy houses and churches. In Addis Ababa, if you are tough, persistent, and wary you may acquire a bargain from a street trader, but the haggling will be lengthy and your purchase will have no provenance.

'Tourist shops' scattered along the main streets of the capital sell a wide range of goods from jewellery to clothing. In most cases prices are not fixed and it may be as well to go from one to the other to compare offers. Some shops are specialized. There are outlets for the local weavers, and shops on the streets around the Piazza sell gold and silver articles produced in small workshops behind. There, the prices are fixed.

The Addis Ababa Mercato in Tekle Haymanot district is reputed to be the largest in Africa and visitors would do well to use the services of a reliable local guide to lead them through the maze of stalls and shops. A visit is to be regarded as a rich and never-to-be-forgotten experience, but leave all but your basic essentials in safe-keeping. There are specialized areas devoted to every kind of product and trade goods. One area specializes in arts and crafts and other objects assembled as a tourist or *ferenge* (foreigner) attraction. There you will find examples from all over the country. The Tekle Haymanot market is the centre of a spider's web of communications stretching to all corners of Ethiopia. But, be warned. You must be prepared to bargain — lengthily — and an Ethiopian friend to assist is probably essential.

The first steps towards an overview of Ethiopian cultures may be obtained by the serious traveller from a visit to the Institute of Ethiopian Studies, within Addis Ababa University at Sidist Kilo, which has an Ethnographical Museum where an excellent collection of traditional crafts and other items are assembled. Also, a visit to the National Museum at Amist Kilo, under the Ministry of Culture, provides a useful systematic review of the development of various cultures in Ethiopia. In addition, the Ethiopian Tourism Commission has a number of publications that delve deeper into the culture, under such titles as *Ethiopia: Design & Decoration, Ethiopian Costumes,* and *Ethiopian Houses.*

Basketry

The best known and most colourful baskets are from Harar, where visitors may see them being made. The largest (and the most expensive) are the *mesobs* — round tables on which the meal of *wot* and *injera* is placed. A decorative lid is provided to cover the remains of the feast.

Traditional paintings

Traditional paintings are made on canvas, skin, or parchment. The best known on canvas are the 'comic strip' presentations of the story of Solomon and Sheba. Rural scenes and traditional representations of Saint George and the Dragon are painted on smaller squares of sheep and goat skin. Paintings on finer parchment may be used to make lampshades.

Above: Harari baskets are distinctive, colourful, and very collectable.

Musical instruments

To avoid the incredulity that faced James Bruce, it is possible to purchase an Ethiopian lyre (the *krar*) or a one-string fiddle (the *massinko*), which is the accompaniment to much modern singing. Or you may fancy a bamboo flute (*washint*), a small drum (*atamo*) or a traditional church instrument, the sistrum (*tsinatseil*). It is also possible to find miniature sets of all Ethiopian musical instruments.

Pottery

There are two categories of pottery: modern pots fired in electric ovens and traditional peasant pottery. The former are available in shops at the top end of the souvenir market in the large hotels and around the Ras Hotel in Addis Ababa. The latter are available in local market centres on market day and at points along the roads leading out of the capital, for example, on the road west towards Ambo. There a range of items may be obtained, from large flower pots and planters to small ashtrays and soup bowls. Be aware, however, that this red pottery is fired in a very rudimentary fashion and is therefore fragile. Originals or copies of the Falasha figurines from Gondar may be found at these sales points.

Above: Dorze weavers are known for their special quality of homespun cotton cloth.

Wood carving

Ethiopia had substantial forests of various tropical and temperate hardwoods, and many attractive items of furniture have been carved from the round. The traditional three-legged Jimma stools and the curved-back chairs from western Shewa are examples. Trees large enough for this work, however, are now in short supply and the items scarce.

One problem with woodwork has been inadequate seasoning of timber. However, the articles manufactured by trained craftsmen at the Tourism Commission workshop and the Handicraft School are made of fully seasoned timber. There are some very attractive traditional designs with carved decoration. Examples may be seen in use in the international hotels, the UN Economic Commission for Africa, and the Lalibela Restaurant in Addis.

Metalwork

The hand and neck crosses of Ethiopia are well known throughout the world. They are much sought after, but a full range —

large and small, old and new, silver and gold, brass and wood, intricately fashioned or simple — is found without trouble in Addis Ababa, with a corresponding range of prices. A great deal of time may be spent admiring and selecting. There is also a flourishing output of large brass crosses from small workshops in the Mercato. These are more crudely fashioned but make attractive wall decorations.

The small shops and street sellers have a selection with examples of Gondarine, Lalibela, and Axum style crosses. A comprehensive collection of Ethiopian crosses has been assembled in the Institute of Ethiopian Studies at the university and there are related publications for these exhibits. The metalwork from Ethiopia's Christian culture is rivalled by beautifully crafted metalwork from the workshops of Muslim artisans in Harar. This silverwork, just as attractive as jewellery from Yemen across the Red Sea, includes the elaborate collars and chest decorations and delicately crafted charm boxes and bracelets.

Other items often found on sale, either at markets in the region or in Addis Ababa

Above: Ethiopian potter adds finishing touches to her latest creation.

emporia, are the heavy metal bracelets made by the Oromo people. These are frequently plain but many have attractive inscribed designs.

Beware, however — airport customs officials have become very strict as to the necessity of a 'museum permit', technically required for silver crosses as well as bibles, icons, or anything else that looks old. Shop owners are usually willing to obtain (probably fraudulently) these permits for their customers.

Weaving

This is another large area of multi-ethnic interest. The Konso people from south-west Ethiopia make very heavy blankets called *buluko*; the lighter cotton cloth used for women's dresses has a wide demand and is the base of a widespread domestic industry with material of special quality made by Dorze and Gurage weavers.

Special skills are necessary for the weaving of the multicoloured design strips, called *tibeb*, which are added to the borders of women's garments. Lengths of woven *tibeb* are on sale and may be used effec-tively by dressmakers anywhere.

The heaviest weaving is in the making of wool carpets, produced with a thick pile or in flat weave form. The designs are based on natural wool colours. Very large carpets are made but smaller rugs and runners are available. For those with limited baggage, small but attractive mats with striking pictorial designs, measuring about fifty centimetres (20 inches) square, are appropriate souvenirs. Debre Birhan, north of the capital, is an important centre of manufacture.

Leatherwork

Ethiopia has more livestock than any other country in Africa and leather of all kinds is plentiful. Since the establishment of a modern tannery in the Rift Valley, south of Addis Ababa, the production of a range of modern leather goods has been initiated.

Belts and bags of various kinds of excellent quality and reasonable price are widely available. A traditional product of some interest is a leather-covered basket with lid called the *agelgil*, used by travellers in the highlands to carry supplies

Above: Dorze weavers making the *tibeb* (brightly coloured *shamma* border).

of precooked meals of *wot* and *injera*. Used as a wall decoration or in their true function as picnic baskets, these are most attractive.

Hornwork

Another raw material from livestock, cattle horn, is often fashioned into drinking mugs and shoe horns. Hornwork is also often incorporated in the manufacture of reading lamps, flower vases, combs, and representations of animals and birds.

Art

Out of the traditional art forms found in ancient manuscripts and church murals has grown a live body of more recent artwork. In the traditional sector these take the form of religious subjects on skin or canvas, including the Solomon and Sheba story and lively portrayals of great battles of the past. Some artisans have also continued the painting of traditional subjects on wood, sometimes in the form of triptychs.

There is also a growing body of modern Ethiopian artists whose work without exception is strongly influenced by the national culture, although it is at the same time very personal. This is no place to attempt even a summary evaluation and identification. Well known are the names of Zerihun Yetemgeta, Gebre Kristos Desta, and Skunder Boghossian.

There are frequent exhibitions of their work and that of others in various cultural institutes, in the City Hall, or in the university.

Wildlife products

It is possible and legal to buy ivory, game skins, and similar items in Ethiopia. However, they are not exportable and are subject to being seized at the airport — not just in Addis Ababa but also on your arrival in Europe or North America. It is also highly likely that 'legal' ivory or game skins were improperly obtained. It is best not to buy them in the first place.

Opposite: The beautiful stained glass work of Ethiopian artist Afewerk Tekle dominates the foyers of Addis Ababa's Africa Hall.

The Enchantment of Ethiopian Music

Ethiopia has a rich tradition of both secular and religious music, singing, and dancing, which together constitute an important part of Ethiopian cultural life.

Throughout Ethiopian history *azmaris*, or wandering minstrels, formed a noteworthy feature of the country's social scene and resulted in a wide range of folk songs. *Zefen* (folk songs) accompany *iskista* (dancing). *Fukara* is sung by warriors when boasting of their heroic deeds. *Musho* and *lekso* are sung to express sorrow at funerals.

Singing forms the accompaniment of many agricultural operations. It comes to the fore at religious and other festivals, as well as at many events in the life cycle: births, marriages, and deaths.

Instruments

Traditional musical instruments in widespread use include the *massinko*, a one-stringed violin played with a bow; the *krar*, a six-stringed lyre, played with the fingers or a plectrum; the *washint*, a simple flute; and three types of drum. The *negarit*, or kettledrum, is beaten with sticks; the *kabaro* is usually played with the hands; and a smaller instrument, the *atamo*, is tapped with the fingers or palm.

Other instruments include the *begena*, a huge, multi-stringed lyre often referred to as the Harp of David and used on sacred occasions; the *tsinatseil*, or sistrum, which has its origin in ancient Egypt and is used in church music; the *maeeket*, a long trumpet without finger-holes; and the *embilta*, a large, simple one-note flute used on ceremonial occasions.

The *massinko*, essentially a square or diamond-shaped wooden soundbox with a string made from strands of horsehair, is thought to be related to a biblical prototype. Though simple and sometimes even crudely made, the *massinko* in the hands of a skilled musician will produce a wide variety of melodies. Today the tones of the *massinko* can be heard most frequently in eating houses, where it is played by wandering minstrels who compose extemporaneous songs about the diners.

The rousing rhythms of the *negarit* were used in times gone by to accompany important proclamations, including declarations of war. Likewise, when chiefs were on the march they would be preceded by a group of as many as thirty men, each beating a *negarit* carried on a donkey — a custom that ensured no one would be in any doubt as to the importance of the dignitary who could command such a performance. The tiny *atamo* is most frequently played at weddings and festivals to lead the rhythmic beat of folk songs and dances.

Modern-style bands have come into

Above: Ethiopian woman dances to music from the traditional *massinko*, a soundbox with a string made from strands of horsehair.

Above: Ethiopia's interesting variety of traditional musical instruments give the country's music its distinctive sound.

existence in recent decades, and there are noted Ethiopian jazz musicians, among them Mulatu Astatke, who has played in many parts of the world.

Religious music

Music is no less significant in the religious field. *Zema*, or church music, is still a major subject of the traditional church education. Music is heard in all Ethiopian church services and most of the liturgy is chanted.

Ethiopian church music, which was introduced many centuries ago, is said to have been invented in the sixth century by a churchman known as Yared the Deacon. He is believed to have introduced a complex system of musical notation that to this day is used to write down the haunting songs and chants that form the basis of all the music performed in the Ethiopian Orthodox churches.

Many of Ethiopia's traditional instru-ments can be heard accompanying important church processions, such as those at *Timkat* and *Meskal*, in which many members of the public join in.

It is during such ceremonies that the visitor to Ethiopia will have the best chance to experience the enchanting music of this ancient country in its full range and vigour. Everyone joins in with one kind of musical instrument or another, there is much singing and clapping of hands, and the excited ululations of the women contribute to the timeless atmosphere.

Watching and listening to such a musical spectacle, no visitors who know their Old Testament could fail to be irresistibly reminded of the great scene described in Chapter Six of the *Book of Samuel*, in which 'David danced . . . with all his might and all the house of Israel played before the Lord on all manner of instruments made of fir wood, even on harps and psalteries, and on timbrels and on coronets, and on cymbals.'

The Stamps of Ethiopia

The history of philately in Ethiopia is intrinsically linked with the history of the railway (See 'The East: Railway to the Sea', Part Two) and has certainly had as many ups and downs.

Before a railway was even thought of, Ethiopians forwarded their correspondence by special couriers, called *melektegnas*, who rode on horses, mules, and camels, or went on foot. The messengers, under imperial protection, bore the letters visibly, attached to a stick, and it was strictly forbidden to trouble them. Official and urgent messages were delivered by express couriers who had the right to requisition any form of transport to complete their mission. People owed them complete hospitality.

After the coronation of Menelik II as Emperor of Ethiopia, Swiss engineer Alfred Ilg, who was in Menelik's service at the time, began to lobby for a railway, as well as functioning postal, telegraph, and telephone systems. Menelik accepted most of Ilg's modern ideas, including, in 1892, the suggestion to have printed stamps, bearing Menelik's own picture. Thus an order was made with the world-renowned engraver E. Mouchon in Paris for the first set of Ethiopian stamps, which was printed in Paris and consisted of seven values: 1/4, 1/2, 1, and 2 guerch — with the picture of the emperior — and 4, 8, and 16 guerch showing the heraldic lion. Post cards of 1/4, 1/2, and 1 guerch values were also printed.

Officially established

But it was not until 9 March 1894 that the Ethiopian postal system was officially established by an imperial edict. The first postal experiments began with the sale of stamps at Harar in January 1895. After a successful start there, it was the intention that the Ethiopian postal system be organized gradually, town by town, over the entire country.

Politics, however, intervened. Diplomatic relations with Italy grew more and more strained. The Italians were irritated that Emperor Menelik applied to French and British post offices for the forwarding of the Ethiopian foreign post. The 'straw that broke the camel's back' came when the emperor formally requested membership for his country in the Universal Postal Union (UPU) at Berne. War was inevitable and culminated in the famous battle at Adwa on 1 March 1896, when the Italian army was defeated.

Post-war

After the war, Ilg once again took up the task of organizing the post, telegraph, and telephone establishments of Ethiopia. The first three post officers arrived from Switzerland and from 22 August 1899 they organized regular postal distribution. Gradually as the railway works proceeded, the post couriers used the ready part of the line for the transport of post bags. The receipt and despatch of these sacks were incumbent on the Governorate of Harar until 1904, when the railway line reached Dire Dawa and an Ethiopian post office was opened there.

At the world exhibition in Paris in 1900 stamps of the first issue were sold in the Ethiopian pavilion as propaganda for the country and its recently started railway.

While the circulation of stamped letters was perpetually increasing, the sale of the stamps in the post windows decreased. This was largely because people who speculated in Ethiopian stamps bought these in Paris for a subcost and sold them in Ethiopia with a profit of three francs per set. To avoid another loss for the Ethiopian Post Office Department it was resolved by an edict of 18 July 1901 that the old stamps were no longer valid without a countermark put upon them.

Every year up to Ethiopia's entrance into the UPU in 1908 the surcharges, which had different bearings and importance, were exchanged. In 1901, the stamps were furnished with a small aniline overprint with the name of the country in French ('Ethiopie'). In 1902, the surcharge of 'Bosta' meant 'Post' and in 1903 'Melekt'

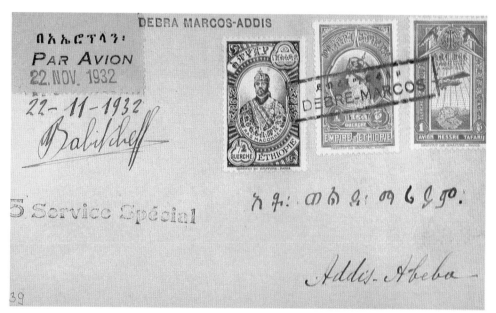

Above: Three stamps from a July 1931 issue show Ras Makonnen, Emperor Haile Selassie's father; the empress in coronation robes; celebrating the arrival of the first airplane in Ethiopia on 8 August 1929.

meant 'Letter'. In the latter the first Amharic symbol was incorrect, so it was corrected in the surcharge of 1904. In the years 1905 and 1906, the stamps were furnished with the emperor's own name, 'Menelik'.

After its admission into the UPU on 1 November 1908, a new era for the Ethiopian Post Office Department began. To celebrate this event a fresh set of stamps was ordered from the official French printing office in Paris. These stamps, which were issued in February 1909, were provided with the inscription 'Postes Ethiopiennes' — a philatelic piece of news. When Empress Zawditu was crowned in 1917, Ras Teferi Makonnen became Regent and Heir to the Throne. To mark this event a great number of the 1909 stamp sets were overprinted with the names 'Zawditu' and 'Teferi' in Amharic above the date of '11/2/1917'.

In 1918, the Ethiopian Post Office Department ordered new stamps from the official French printing office, which this time were principally motifs from Ethiopian fauna, using drawings by Ethiopian artists. The French office, however, had to decline the order because of its involvement in World War II, so the order went to

neutral Switzerland. The Ethiopian drawings for the stamps were modified and shaped by the Swiss artist Walter Plattner. A complete set consisted of fifteen stamps in values between 1/8 guerch and ten dollars.

On 1 September 1928, a new set of stamps was again ordered from the official French printing office in Paris, with motifs of Empress Zawditu and Ras Teferi. The Amharic texts on the two portrait stamps runs in translation, 'Ethiopia stretches her hands to God' and 'Conquering lion of the tribe of Judah.' The thaler symbol was taken away and in its place was the more national expression of 'thaler', which from then on was divided into sixteen *mehaleks* instead of guerches.

New post office

September 1928 also marked the inauguration of a new post office in Addis Ababa, and to celebrate this occurrence ordinary stamps provided with an Amharic surcharge were issued. On 7 October, Ras Teferi was proclaimed king, and a new set of stamps was issued. The portrait stamps of Ras Teferi from September 1928 were overprinted by a large royal crown, under

289

which could be read 'Negus Teferi' in Amharic.

To celebrate the arrival of the first airplane in Ethiopia, the stamp issue of 1928 received a heavy aniline overprint showing an airplane.

Coronation

After Empress Zawditu died and Negus Teferi mounted the throne as Emperor Haile Selassie I, the 1928 stamps were provided with an aniline surcharge that read 'Haile Selassie I: April 3, 1930' in English and Amharic. Another surcharge was put on the ordinary stamp in November 1930 to commemorate the emperor's coronation. Special coronation stamps, ordered from l'Institut de Gravure in Paris, didn't arrive until the coronation was over. These beautiful stamps, produced by intaglio (recess) printing, featured old Ethiopian symbols in a concentrated shape: the Lion of Judah, wearing the old king's crown, rests with a paw upon the orb and the sceptre, while the shield of Solomon can be observed in the background.

The next set of ten ordinary stamps, which appeared in July 1931, showed pictures of the emperor and the empress in coronation robes; Ras Makonnen, the emperor's father; the equestrian statue of Emperor Menelik in Addis Ababa; and the railway bridge across the Awash River. For the first time, 'Empire d'Ethiopie' was indicated on the stamps. At the same time a set of seven air mail stamps was put into use on the weekly air connection between Ethiopia and the French port of Djibouti.

In January 1936, the Ethiopian Post Office Department found time to distribute a last temporary stamp before the war and occupation. This set, consisting of five stamps of the 1931 issue, was provided with surcharges of the new centimes values.

The war caused great material damage, and a dark period in the postal history of Ethiopia followed. Even at an early stage the Addis Ababa Post Office was bombed, the archives were spoilt, and old stamp stocks were lost. What remained of the old stamp issues was taken out of the country by Italian soldiers when they returned home. When, after the invasion, the Ethiopian post officers returned to their places, they found everything devastated.

By 1942, however, things were beginning to return to normal. Haile Selassie I had triumphantly returned to his country the year before, and in March three stamps — printed at Nasik in India — were issued showing a portrait of the emperor in coronation robes, with the values of 4, 10, and 20 centimes.

As early as the end of 1942, the first set of portrait stamps was increased by a set with the same engraving but with an increased number of values. In November 1943, a jubilee set of five stamps — known as the 'Obelisk' stamps — was issued to commemorate the thirteenth year of the emperor's coronation.

On 31 December 1944, the 'Menelik' set appeared. This was printed by the Imperial Post Office in Addis Ababa and consisted of five stamps in the values of 5, 10, 20, 50, and 65 centimes. It commemorates the centennial of the birth of Emperor Menelik II on 18 August 1844.

Ethiopia also has her 'V' — Victory — stamps. These stamps, commemorating the Allies' victory, appeared in August 1945. The set consists of the values 5, 10, 25, and 50 centimes and 1 thaler. At the end of 1946, a temporary air mail set of three surcharged stamps was issued, and in early 1947 the 'Roosevelt' stamps appeared, consisting of five values: 12, 25, and 65 centime ordinary stamps and 1 and 2 dollar air mail stamps.

Post's half centennial

On 18 April 1947, somewhat belatedly, stamps were issued to celebrate the half centennial of the Ethiopian post: 1894-1944. The values were 10, 20, 30, 50, and 70 centimes. Illustrations symbolized the development of the post office and included postal mules on one half of the 30-centime stamp with a post bus going up a mountain road on the other half.

Ethiopia's first express stamps also appeared on 18 April 1947. The two-stamp set included, on the lower value, an Ethiopian motorcycle leather 'Jack' who, loaded with express letters, takes a curve at a breathless speed with his machine.

Above: To this day, Ethiopian stamps remain sought after by collectors the world over.

A new jubilee set was issued in May 1947 to celebrate the 150th anniversary of the birth in 1795 of Negus Sahle Selassie, great-grandfather of the emperor. Later in the year two extremely beautiful sets appeared — one set consisting of twelve stamps of various values, and the second an air mail set of eight values. The motifs were taken from Ethiopian nature and were also provided with the emperor's portrait medallion.

Another jubilee set was issued in 1949 to commemorate the sixth anniversary of the end of the invasion and in 1950 Ethiopia celebrated the 75th anniversary of the UPU by the issue of four stamps. Various other stamps issued in subsequent years included commemorations of the 20th anniversary of Their Imperial Majesties' coronation, the bridge built across the Blue Nile, the battle of Adwa, the 60th birthday of Haile Selassie, and the occasion of the Ethiopian Province of Eritrea being handed back to the motherland.

Throughout the years, Ethiopian stamps have been much sought after by collectors and traders around the world.

Museum

Attached to the Addis Ababa post office, the National Postal Museum has a complete set of all the stamps ever printed in Ethiopia. The stamps, mounted on album pages, are clearly labelled in Amharic and English. The collection starts with the first Menelik issue of 1894 following the imperial edict of that year that established the Ethiopian Postal Administration.

The museum, established in 1975, also has many of the original drawings, approved designs, examples of the printers' art, printers' proofs and other items unique to Ethiopian philately. The Ethiopian collection is permanent, but the museum also houses displays of stamps from other Universal Postal Union members, ranging from El Salvador to New Zealand, which are changed every six months.

Ethiopian Coins: A Fascinating History

Like many other aspects of Ethiopia, the history of the country's coinage is unique and intriguing.

In very early times in the region that is present-day Ethiopia, an advanced system of coinage was developed by the Axumite kingdom, which was centred around the holy city of Axum in Tigray.

The first coins were struck by King Endybis (c. 270–300 AD) in gold, silver, and bronze and depicted the ruling monarch on both sides. The coins were inscribed in Greek, the common language of the commercial traders in the Red Sea area. Ge'ez, Ethiopia's ancient language, was substituted on many of the later coin issues. The time periods of this coinage spanned 450 years and included the output of over twenty-five different monarchs. These small treasures have proved to be a blessing to historians studying the Axumite culture, as the coinage has often provided the only source of information about some of the monarchs.

As the Axumite kingdom flourished, trade extended to Egypt, Persia, India, Arabia, Rome, and Byzantium. The coinage facilitated trade with neighbouring kingdoms and increased commerce within by giving the country a useful medium of exchange.

Salt money

With the demise of the Axumites and their coinage, Ethiopians turned to barter and primitive money forms, including cloth, iron, gold, beads and — most importantly — salt bars.

Amole, or salt bar money, was first referred to in recorded history by an Egyptian monk, Kosmos, around 525 AD. A tribute to its longevity is the fact that a thousand years later, a visiting Portuguese priest, Francisco Alvares, observed that salt was used as money in all parts of the country and that 'whoever carries it finds all that he requires'.

The name *amole* derived from the Amole people, who once inhabited the torrid Afar (Danakil) region where the salt bars were quarried. The mining was done at Lake Karum, an often-dry lake containing extensive deposits of ready-to-use salt accumulated over countless millennia. The work was accomplished during the dry season by a few hundred Afar men who had become accustomed to toiling in the oppressive heat. Using wooden poles, they pried loose large blocks of salt from the lake bed, cut the slabs into rough bricks with hand axes, and then smoothed the salt blocks into their final shape.

Once fashioned, the salt bars had to be transported throughout the country by porters and pack animals. Because of the mountainous terrain, river crossings, and virtual absence of roads, any caravan faced a perilous journey. In every province the caravan passed through, it was stopped, the cargo assessed, and a tax levied by the local *dejazmach*, or chief. Payment was usually obtained by relieving the pack animals of a portion of their *amoles*.

Salt bars were popular because salt was a scarce commodity in the highlands, desired by every Ethiopian household for cooking. Because transport was difficult, salt bars increased in value the further they were carried from their original source. Salt bars were utilized as currency in Ethiopia for at least fifteen centuries and were reported by travellers to have been used as late as the 1960s in Tigray province.

Maria Theresa thaler

A new medium of exchange and the first modern coin to gain major acceptance in Ethiopia was the Austrian Maria Theresa thaler (or dollar). Maria Theresa, who reigned from 1740 to 1780, was the last empress of the Holy Roman Empire. Her coin, also called the 'Levantine thaler', originally gained prominence in the Arab world around the Red Sea coast for use in the slave trade and for other commercial transactions. It was introduced into Ethiopia towards the end of the eighteenth century but was only gradually accepted by the population. However, by the 1850s it was reported to have become prevalent throughout most parts of the country.

Ethiopians were extremely particular about which thalers they would accept. Samuel Baker, a mid-nineteenth-century British explorer, noted that only coins bearing a 1780 date and showing a 'profusion of bust' in the Empress's image were acceptable. P. H. G. Powell-Coton, writing at the turn of the twentieth century, stated, 'Every piece offered is carefully scrutinised, two or three friends being often called in for their opinion. A new one, or one that is much worn or one on which the ornaments of the neck, especially the points of the star (brooch), are not clear, is at once rejected.' It is evident that a coin's acceptability to an Ethiopian was greatly dependent on personal whim.

The Maria Theresa coin became entrenched in Ethiopia's economy for use in commerce — and also for jewellery. Some were used intact for necklaces, pendants, pins, and the like, while others were melted to make crosses, rings, earrings, bracelets, head scratchers, and ear cleaners. C. F. Rey, writing in the 1920s, noted the skilled craftmanship of the Ethiopian silversmith: 'Their outfit is simple — a hammer and anvil, a pair of pincers, a charcoal fire and a goat-skin bellows. With this primitive equipment they certainly produce some very attractive things.'

Modern coinage

Emperor Menelik II established Ethiopia's modern coinage in 1893. The first coins were struck at the Paris Mint and seven denominations were authorized, four silver and three copper. The new thaler, called a birr (which means 'silver' in Amharic) had Menelik's portrait and the inscription 'Menelik II, King of Kings of Ethiopia' in Amharic. The reverse displayed the traditional lion and was inscribed 'He is the Conqueror, the Lion of the Tribe of Judah'. An edge intonation read 'Ethiopia Stretches her hands to God'.

Coins of Ethiopia's ancient Axumite kingdom. Top: A gold coin of King Endybis. Above: A silver coin of one of Endybis's successors, King Ezana (c. fourth century AD).

Only a small quantity of these birr coins and their fractional counterparts were minted. Following the Ethiopian victory over the Italians at Adwa in 1896, a somewhat larger quantity of the Menelik coins was produced. Italy paid Ethiopia ten million lire in war reparations and part of the money was used by Menelik to strike more coins.

Mint established

It is believed that Menelik had an affinity for technical matters and in 1903 he established a mint in Addis Ababa. Among the coins produced were three beautiful gold ones bearing his visage, called a *werk* (meaning 'gold' in Amharic), and fractional half and quarter *werks*. They were used both for presentation purposes and for trade. They were carefully weighed when they changed hands, as the weight of any two pieces of the same denomination could vary widely.

In 1905 the Bank of Abyssinia was created and a decade later a series of banknotes was issued for circulation. Paper money was slow to achieve acceptance among the Ethiopians, who preferred 'hard' money. The banknotes were used mainly by Europeans in the capital to facilitate large commercial transactions.

Above: Austria's Maria Theresa silver thaler was popular with commercial traders throughout the Middle East and Ethiopia. It endured from the beginning of the nineteenth century until the end of World War II.

Following the accession of Emperor Haile Selassie I to the throne in 1930, a new coinage, the *metonya*, based on the centime or one-hundredth part of the dollar, was established. There were five denominations issued: copper 1 and 5 *metonyas* and nickel 10, 25, and 50 *metonyas*. Struck chiefly at Addis Ababa, the issue was poorly received because of the coins' low metallic worth, and short lived because of the Italian invasion in 1935–1936. A new Bank of Ethiopia was also established at this time, replacing the old Bank of Abyssinia, which issued a new series of currency.

During the Italian intervention from 1936 to 1941, the Italian lira was introduced into Ethiopia but was largely rejected by the populace. They preferred the old, established Maria Theresa thaler, and the Italians had to import a substantial quantity of the thalers to satisfy the demand. Following the ousting of the Italians with the help of British Commonwealth forces, the coinage of British East Africa was used for a short period.

In 1944, with Emperor Haile Selassie restored to the throne, a new coinage was struck at the United States Mint in Philadelphia consisting of five denominations: copper 1, 5, 10, and 25 cents and silver 50 cents. The coins featured a more modern design, portraying a profiled, bareheaded bust of the emperor on the front and the traditional Lion of Judah on the back. In addition to the coins, a new issue of banknotes was produced, ranging from one Ethiopian dollar to five hundred Ethiopian dollars.

Uniform system

This time, the new issues gained wide acceptance by large segments of the population. Experts attributed this to the presence of Haile Selassie's image on the coins and notes. Though the British East Africa money was retired, the English terms 'shilling' and 'pound' thereafter attached themselves to the Ethiopian silver fifty-cent coin and ten-dollar note, respectively. The post-war national currency issues may have been the most important for Ethiopia, because for the first time the country had a uniform monetary system with coins and notes that were issued in abundance and recognized and accepted by nearly all of the people.

The Haile Selassie money endured until 1977 when it was replaced by the new Socialist government. Five new coin denominations of 1, 5, 10, 25, and 50 cents were struck in various base metal alloys.

All of the coins portray a lion's head on one side and a variety of themes on the reverse. The ten-cent piece depicts Ethiopia's endangered antelope, the mountain nyala, while all of the other denominations are thematic of people working in farming, industry, and military.

The National Bank of Ethiopia also introduced a new series of banknotes with denominations of 1, 5, 10, 50, and 100 birr, inscribed in both Amharic and English. All of the notes were attractively rendered, each in a different colour scheme, representing various themes and endeavours in Ethiopian life. The 100-birr note, for instance, depicts a contrast between old and new; the front portraying an old Ethiopian warrior in traditional dress, carrying spear and shield, and the back of the note showing a scientist peering through a microscope.

Finally, from 1978 through to 1984, Ethiopia issued a series of commemorative coins intended for collectors. Notable are two silver coins and one gold struck as a conservation issue made in cooperation with the World Wildlife Fund (WWF). Net proceeds from the sale of coins were given to finance conservation programmes in Ethiopia. The silver 10 birr shows a bearded vulture and the silver 25 birr a mountain nyala. The gold 500 birr displays a rare Walia ibex atop a craggy rock formation. Other issues celebrated the UN-sponsored International Year of the Child (1980), International Year of Disabled Persons (1981), the World Football (soccer) Games in Spain (1982), and the Decade for Women (1984).

From the ancient to the modern, from coins to salt to banknotes, the money of Ethiopia continues to interest the general observer as well as the historian or numismatist.

Above: Front (top) and back (above) of a silver quarter-birr coin (1897) depicting Emperor Menelik II and the Lion of Judah symbol. It was struck at the Addis Ababa Mint founded by Menelik.

Ethiopian Airlines

The story of Ethiopian Airlines is one of the most incredible success stories in Ethiopia's, and Africa's, history.

Aviation was first introduced to Ethiopia in August 1929, when a French Potez 25 made a triumphant landing on a plain near Addis Ababa. From that moment on, the face of transportation in the country was changed forever.

The major forms of transport known to Ethiopians prior to the airplane's arrival were horses, mules, and the railway line between Djibouti and Addis Ababa. The advent of the airplane, which was considerably faster and required no roads, bridges, or rails, was welcomed with open arms.

It wasn't long after that first landing in 1929 that Ethiopia's first pilots were being trained and its first fleet was being mustered.

First airline

Although aviation in Ethiopia, like almost everything else in the country, suffered a severe setback during the Italian invasion, things were put back together after the Fascists were driven out in 1941. In 1945, the Ethiopian Air Force was formed, which was to pave the way for the birth, on 8 September 1945, of the country's first commercial airline: Ethiopian Air Lines, Inc. (EAL).

The airlines' first executives made a trip to Cairo to purchase a fleet of DC-3s from the stock of World War II surplus aircraft held in the Egyptian capital.

The first few runs for the company mainly involved currency transfer flights to Nairobi and back. But the aim was to entice passengers as well, and EAL let prospective flyers ease into the modern age of flying by introducing 'Scenic Flights' over the Ethiopian countryside.

This led to the big day, on 8 April 1946, when a scheduled international passenger service was inaugurated with a record-setting ten-hour flight from Addis Ababa to Cairo. With this flight, EAL established a same-day link between the two north-east African capitals that never existed before.

Bringing Africa together

It was only a sign of things to come. The next year EAL began scheduled flights from Aden to Bombay and more local flights were added. The airline rapidly became known as a pioneer in its effort at 'Bringing Africa Together' (its slogan), and for bringing Africa closer to the rest of the world.

The coming of a new decade saw EAL expand not only its route network but its fleet. In 1950, the airline, seeking to improve its international service, marked the arrival of two new 36-seat Convair-240s. A third was added in 1955, followed not too long after by two Douglas DC-6Bs. With a full complement of modern aircraft, Ethiopian Airlines began to expand its already growing route network — both domestic and international.

The 1960s saw the airline establish its own aviation training centre and marked the ushering in of the jet age for EAL, with two Boeing 720Bs joining the fleet in 1962. In 1965, the airline changed its legal status from a corporation to a share company and become known as Ethiopian Airlines (two words), or Ethiopian.

Route expansion and fleet modernization continued into the '70s, with China added as a destination in 1973. At the end of the decade, the airline purchased three 727Bs to help out on the ever-expanding route network.

Expanding fleet

In 1984, Ethiopian was the first airline in the world to take delivery of the first of its three Boeing 767 Extended Range versions. The following year, five Twin Otter 300s were delivered to help cope with Ethiopian's expanding domestic route network, and the last part of the decade saw the acquisition of two technologically advanced ATR-42s and two twin-jet Boeing 737s. Two new specialized freight aircraft,

Above: The modern Boeing 767 added a new dimension to Ethiopian's already renowned in-flight service.

Lockheed L-100-30s, also arrived during this period.

In late 1990 and early 1991, Ethiopian took delivery of the first of its fleet of passenger and cargo Boeing 757 jets. Technical and commercial contract services were enhanced in 1994 with the acquisition of a jet engine test cell and a B767/757 simulator. In the cards for the future are plans to construct a modern cargo terminal and wide-body aircraft maintenance hangar — as well as the continuing modernization of the fleet.

The airline's system-wide destinations are now sixty-eight. It remains the only airline with a daily east-west flight across Africa, and it serves three routes across the continent.

Alongside its continual fleet and route expansion, Ethiopian's reputation for efficiency and operational success has blossomed over the years. The airline has turned a substantial profit for almost all the years of its operation. It has a balance sheet and debt-equity ratio that would be the envy of many airlines.

From its meagre beginnings, Ethiopian Airlines has grown into a company that remains the pride of its employees — and the pride of Ethiopia.

Religion in Ethiopia

Orthodox Christianity and Islam, the two main religions in Ethiopia, have coexisted since Mohammed's time. The first believers in Islam were converted while the Prophet Mohammed was alive and the first mosque was built in the eighth century. However, culturally the Orthodox Church has dominated the political, social, and cultural life in the highlands, as it has been the official religion of the imperial court and hence also of the feudal establishment until Haile Selassie was deposed in 1974. Since then religion and state have been separated.

Islam

Ethiopia has long enjoyed the most intimate relations with Islam. Some of the earliest disciples of the Prophet Mohammed, when persecuted in Arabia, found refuge at Axum, which was then ruled by King Armah. When one of the refugees,

Above: Entrance to an ancient Harar mosque.

Umm Habibah, was to marry Mohammed, Armah sent her a golden dowry. The Prophet later prayed for the Axumite king's soul and instructed his followers to 'leave the Abyssinians in peace', thus exempting them from a 'holy war'. Many words in Ge'ez, the classical language of the Ethiopians, are to be found in the Holy Qur'an. The first *muezzin* calling the faithful to prayer in the Prophet's time was an Ethiopian named Bilal, as his compatriots recall with pride to this day.

Ethiopia has an extensive and very active Muslim population, who have played an important role in Ethiopian life, particularly in the field of commerce, for over a millennium. The majority of Muslims inhabit the eastern, southern and western lowlands, but there are also many followers of Islam in Addis Ababa and in all Ethiopian towns — even in the so-called Christian highlands. Mosques, however, were for the most part constructed only within the last century or so; they are now found throughout the length and breadth of the country.

Ethiopia's earliest and most holy Muslim centre, according to tradition, is at Nagash, north of Wukro in Tigray, where there is a fine mosque of considerable antiquity.

Perhaps the most important Islamic centre since medieval times, however, has been the famous walled city of Harar. One of the principal holy cities of Islam, it has long been renowned for its religious learning, as well as for its mosques, many Muslim shrines, and tombs of several holy Muslim leaders of the past.

An important centre of Muslim pilgrimage today is the town of Shek Husen in Bale region. The faithful flock there twice a year from all over Ethiopia, as well as from neighbouring countries.

The Orthodox Church

The Ethiopian Orthodox Church was established at the beginning of the fourth century, making it one of the oldest established churches. The coming of Islam into the Middle East and North Africa only three centuries later isolated it from the rest of Christendom. The Ethiopian highlands at that time were primarily Christian in the north-east, Judaic in the north-west and mostly animist in the south.

The Church also believes the Christian parts of the country had been Judaic before they were converted. This combination of facts perhaps explains the strong Judaic elements in the Ethiopian Orthodox Church. Most notable among these are food restrictions, including the way animals are killed, consistent with the rules set out in the Old Testament — but not the prohibition of mixing milk and meat. Another similarity is the strict observance of naming (christening) eighty days after birth for girls and forty days for boys.

The most striking feature of the Ethiopian Orthodox Church with its root in Judaism is the presence of a replica of the Ark of the Covenant in the 'holy of holies' of each church, called the *tabot*, which only priests are allowed to see and handle.

The most colourful pageant in the year is when churches parade their *tabots* to a nearby body of water. This is *Timkat* (Epiphany), the commemoration of Christ's baptism, which falls on the nineteenth of January. The *tabot* is taken out in the afternoon on the eve of Epiphany and stays overnight with the priests and faithful congregation. The following morning the water is blessed and splashed on everyone in a ceremony where the faithful renew their vows to the Church. If the body of water is large enough, some people will immerse themselves. Women who have been unable to have children participate in the ritual for fertility. After this ceremony, the *tabot* is paraded back to its church accompanied by much singing and dancing.

Timkat is but one of many religious festivals observed by the Ethiopian Orthodox Church. Another prominent one is *Fasika* (Easter), which follows a fast of fifty-five days. During this time, no animal product is eaten. The faithful do not eat anything at all until the daily service is finished at around three o'clock in the afternoon. From Thursday evening before Good Friday, nothing is eaten until the Easter serv-

ice ends at three o'clock in the morning on Easter Sunday, when animal products can once again be taken.

Buhe, which falls on 12 July in north-eastern Ethiopia and 21 August in other parts of the country, commemorates the flogging of the disciples. Traditionally boys make long whips and crack them as loud and as often as they like. This goes on for about a week. A special holiday for young girls, who get together in their best clothes to dance and sing, is *Filseta*, which celebrates the Ascension of Mary. It falls in the middle of the rainy season on 24 August.

Ethiopian New Year's Day is called *Kidus Yohannes* or *Enkutatash*, and is celebrated on 11 September. It is primarily secular and a time for people to put on new clothes if they can and visit friends and relatives.

Another major religious celebration is *Meskal*, said to be in memory of the Finding of the True Cross by the Empress Eleni. This is as colourful an occasion as *Timkat*. However, instead of water, the focus of celebration is a bonfire topped with an image of a cross, to which flowers are tied. Priests in full regalia bless the bonfire before it is lit. This festival coincides with the mass blooming of the golden yellow '*meskal* daisies', called *adey abeba* in Amharic.

Christmas, called *Lidet*, is not the primary religious and secular festival that it has become in Western countries. Falling on 7 January, it is celebrated seriously by a church service that goes on throughout the night, with people moving from one church to another. Traditionally, young men played a game similar to hockey, called *genna*, on this day, and now Christmas has also come to be known by that name.

One indication of the influence of the Church in everyday life is the fact that the thirteen major saints' days in each month are named by their saint, while others are referred to by date. Each church is dedicated to one saint, and on that saint's day once (and sometimes twice) a year the *tabot* is paraded in front of the congregation by taking it around the church three times. It is also a special feast day for the

Above: *Timkat* (Epiphany) is celebrated with much ceremony throughout the whole of Ethiopia.

community associated with that church, and friends and relatives from far and near will come to join in.

Many Orthodox Christians have religious associations dedicated to a particular saint whose members meet once a month on that saint's day, with rotating venues.

Visiting a church

Priests are always happy to welcome visitors to their church to attend a service or at other times, if they are available to open the building. They are usually very pleased and proud to put on their vestments and bring out any special treasures for visitors to view and take photographs. However, most priests do not speak English and it is advisable to take a guide with you.

Each church has three or four entrances: that to the east leads to the holy of holies and is only for priests, that to the south is only for women, and that to the north only for men. A western entrance can be used by both men and women, but once inside, men go to the left (north) and women to the right (south). Outside of service hours, visitors can use any of the entrances except the eastern one, and they do not have to segregate by sex.

Visitors are advised to observe the following practices when visiting a church:

- Only priests are allowed anywhere near the holy of holies where the *tabot* is kept.
- One should never smoke anywhere near a church.
- Shoes must be removed before one enters the building.
- If you wish to attend a service, you are expected not to eat beforehand.
- Both men and women are expected to wear clothing that covers their body completely, and it is preferred if women cover their heads.
- Outside the main tourist centres, churches do not charge an entrance fee, but a donation to the church is much appreciated.

Opposite: Beautiful murals, like this one in Saint George's Church in Addis Ababa, attest to the country's strong faith.

The Ethiopian Cross

The cross as a symbol of Christianity is omnipresent in Ethiopia. There are pectoral and neck crosses for everyday use, small hand crosses carried individually by priests and larger ones used in church celebrations to bless the faithful, large processional crosses, and apex or pinnacle crosses on the roofs of churches. The cross also appears as a staff cross of pilgrims, is included in architecture, painted on walls, incised on manuscript bindings, embroidered on dresses, tattooed on the body, and used as a decorative element within manuscripts.

Nowhere in the Christian world has there been developed such a multitude of types and shapes of crosses as in Ethiopia — and perhaps nowhere can the cross be considered such a work of art.

Crosses have been represented in flourishing varieties in the country for centuries, with craftsmen elaborating on forms and sophisticated clergymen concentrating on symbols. To appreciate just how wide a variety of crosses exist, one should visit the Institute of Ethiopian Studies in Addis Ababa, which has a collection of some 3,000 neck crosses alone, each different in shape. Yet this collection is still not representative of all the existing variations of this single symbol, the cross.

The materials used in the manufacture of Ethiopian crosses are of wide range. Processional crosses are occasionally wood but most often are made of metal: iron, copper, bronze, silver, and rarely gold. Hand crosses are made of metal, usually silver or brass, but also iron and rarely copper. Stone and wood are also used for this type of cross. Pectoral and neck crosses can be found in silver, gold, stone, or wood. Combinations of materials are also used.

Most of the early processional and neck crosses were made in the 'lost wax' technique. The model, first made of wax, was then covered with fine clay, leaving two small channels open. The clay was heated so that the wax melted and ran out. The empty core of the baked clay then had the negative shape of the cross. Afterwards the molten metal was poured into this mould. Once the metal had cooled and set, the clay mould was broken and removed. Thus every cross made in this way is unique.

For neck crosses, the half-mould technique could be used: a wax model was made on a flat surface and then covered with clay, so that when the wax ran out after heating, the clay mould retained a cross-shaped indentation on its surface. This type of mould could be used more than once. The half-mould crosses are characterized by a rounded face and a flat reverse. Another method, used with some processional, hand, and neck crosses, was to trace the image of the cross on a sheet of metal and then to cut or punch it out. Iron crosses mostly were forged; wooden and stone crosses carved. Decorations added later could be incised, stamped, or, in the case of a wooden body, painted.

Ethiopian crosses are traditionally represented in six basic forms: the Mesopotamian or 'paw' cross, often encircled; the Greek cross, or *crux quadrata*; the Egyptian cross, or *crux ansata*; the Indian cross (swastika), or *crux gammata*; the 'Tau' cross (Saint Anthony cross), or *crux commissa*; and the Latin cross, or *crux immissa*. The Egyptian and Indian cross types are not found as often as the other types. The 'paw' cross has melded over time with the Greek cross, which is by far the most widespread of the basic cross shapes.

Local preferences for specific cross patterns seem to have evolved in the course of history. A pear-shaped encircled Latin cross has come to be called a 'Lalibela cross' because of its wide distribution in Lalibela and surrounding areas. The Tigray hand cross style is characterized by an elongated shape, two parallel horizontal arms of different length (interpreted as a combination of a Greek and a Latin cross) and sometimes a quadrangular 'chapel' replacing the more usual square tablet at the bottom.

Ethiopian crosses can often be combinations of several crosses of various basic shapes. Such combinations are not

Above: Ethiopia's unique and intricate crosses each have a story to tell.

only formal diversions, but symbolic expressions. Symbolism, in fact, abounds in Ethiopian crosses. For example, the rectangular base of the hand cross has been interpreted as symbolizing the tomb of Adam, important in the Christian Ethiopian faith. (One of the carved-out rocks in Lalibela is said to be Adam's tomb.) Another explanation given is that it represents a *tabot*.

In some cases, the handle is anthropomorphic. The figure represented is crudely naturalistic or stylized, the arms often lifted to carry the cross. An Ethiopian legend tells that the cross of Christ stemmed from the tree of paradise. The cross is also seen as the tree of life, which has been planted in the centre of the world.

The hand cross is sometimes treated like an icon, with representations including the Trinity, the crucified Christ, Mary with child, archangels, saints, and the four living creatures of the *Book of Revelation* 4: 6-11. In some cases, there is an obvious correspondence between the pictorial arrangement and the symbolism of the cross, whereas in other cases it is completely lacking. There are examples in which the reverse side of the cross expresses the symbolism of the cross: the face is treated like an 'icon', in either bas-relief or carving, or by colour application.

For example, a wooden hand cross from Wollo shows, on the face, carved iconographic representations of Mary with child and the Trinity, surrounded by the four living creatures. The reverse of this cross is decorated with geometrical designs.

Explanations and interpretations of crosses are continually being collected from priests, monks, and nuns in the hope of better understanding the fascinating range of symbols, combinations, variations, art, and manufacture of the unique crosses of Ethiopia.

Overleaf: Commercial Bank of Ethiopia in Addis Ababa.

PART FIVE: BUSINESS
ETHIOPIA

The Economy

The Ethiopian economy is typically agrarian. More than forty-eight per cent of the country's GDP originates from agriculture, and other components of the GDP are directly or indirectly dependent on it. Modern manufacturing accounts for no more than six per cent. Small-scale industry and handicrafts make up about four per cent of the GDP. Services of all types, including distribution, public administration, defence and financial services, have a significant share of more than thirty-seven per cent of the GDP. The average value of the GDP at constant prices over the last three years was about 8.8 billion birr.

Apart from its large population, which is estimated at 55 million, the country's main real and potential natural resources are land, water, hydropower, animals, forestry, natural gas, and other minerals. The total area of the country is 1.112 million square kilometres (430,000 square miles). Only about fifteen per cent of the total area is currently under cultivation, although it is estimated that close to sixty-five per cent of the total area is arable.

Ethiopia's water resources are immense. It has fourteen large and medium-sized river basins, including the Blue Nile, Gibe, Baro, and Takazze. It is estimated that some 115 billion cubic metres (150 billion cubic yards) of water pass annually through these river basins. Hence, the country's hydropower is also great. It is believed that some sixty billion kilowatt hours of electricity could be generated from the country's numerous rivers. Current electricity generation, however, is only about one billion kilowatt hours.

Ethiopia ranks first in Africa and tenth in the world with respect to animal resources. The cattle population is estimated at about twenty-seven million, while that of sheep and goats stands at around forty-two million. However, the picture of the country's forest resources picture is rather gloomy. Some estimates indicate that about one hundred years ago roughly forty per cent of the country's total area was covered with forests. Now the estimate is less than three per cent. Even so, Ethiopia's forest resources are still important and could be developed into a major economic resource. Another natural resource worth mentioning is natural gas, of which a very large amount has been found in the Ogaden region. Trial production is currently under way. Other potential natural resources of significance include geothermal energy, iron, tin, lignite, and potash.

Infrastructure

Despite its geographical diversity, Ethiopia has a fairly well developed system of transport and communications. An extensive road network (although of sometimes dubious quality) connects the capital, Addis Ababa, with various regional and urban centres as well as Assab, a principal Red Sea port. There is also a road from Addis Ababa to Nairobi, Kenya — although the northern Kenyan portion of the road is of very poor quality. A railway system links Addis Ababa with the port city of Djibouti to the east of the country. Ocean transport is provided through Ethiopian Shipping Lines. Ethiopian Airlines links the capital to most major commercial centres in the country and most countries in Africa, Asia, and Europe.

Telecommunication services in major urban centres are served through a microwave system. Excellent international communications are also maintained through two satellite earth stations.

External trade

Ethiopia's major export commodity is coffee, which accounts for more than fifty per cent of total export earnings. Other important export products and sources of foreign exchange include gold, leather and leather products, fruits and vegetables, sugar and molasses, pulses, oilseeds, live animals, textiles, and spices. Main destinations for the country's exports are Germany, Japan, France, Italy, Djibouti, Belgium, Netherlands, the UK, the USA, and Saudi Arabia.

Ethiopia's major imports are generally similar to those of any non-oil-producing African country. They include petroleum; transport, agricultural, and industrial machinery and equipment; chemicals and fertilizers; private motor vehicles; other consumer durables; processed food products; pharmaceuticals; and textiles. Major countries of origin for Ethiopia's imports are the USA, Japan, Saudi Arabia, Germany, Italy, Netherlands, France, the UK, and Kenya. Ethiopia has always had a large trade deficit, financed by net private and official transfers and foreign loans.

Public finance

About sixty-nine per cent of the country's total domestic revenue originates from taxes and the remainder comes from non-tax sources. Direct taxes include those on personal income, rents, business profits, and agricultural products. Indirect taxes comprise excise and sales taxes and stamp duties. Taxes on foreign trade are composed of import duties and export taxes — the latter now levied on coffee only. Non-tax sources include surpluses from government-owned enterprises, capital charges, pension contributions, and various other charges.

Total government domestic revenue is not sufficient to cover total public expenditure, so the country incurs a significant overall annual fiscal deficit, which in recent years has been equivalent to slightly over ten per cent of the GDP, excluding that part of the deficit financed outright by external grants. The budget deficit after external grants is covered by domestic and external borrowing. For the latest year for which figures are available, this was equivalent to 5.8 per cent and 4.5 per cent, respectively.

The government maintains separate current and capital expenditure accounts. The biggest expenditure items on the current account are defence, public order and security, general services, various economic and social services, pension payments, and interest payments. As the name suggests, the current budget is appropriated to cover costs of an operational nature, whereas capital expenditure pertains to costs associated with new investments or expansion of existing ones and substantial renovation or repair work. The largest capital budget allocations are made for agriculture, water, and natural resources development; mining, industry, and commerce; and roads, transport, and communications.

Money

The unit of Ethiopian currency is the birr, containing 100 cents. Two official exchange rates are maintained vis-a-vis the US dollar — the country's reference currency. One has been officially fixed at five birr to the US dollar since the fifty-nine per cent devaluation in October 1992. The other oscillates above the base rate of five birr per US dollar and is determined by the outcome of a foreign exchange auction held every fifteen days.

As in many other countries, money in Ethiopia is defined as 'narrow' and 'broad'. Narrow money is made up of currency outside banks and demand deposits. As the name suggests, broad money comprises not only narrow money but also savings and time deposits. The main determinants of money are domestic credit and the outcome of the country's balance of payments. For many years the cause of monetary growth had been domestic credit expansion, but recently nominal balance of payment surpluses are also coming into the picture. The annual growth rate for broad money in recent years averaged about 15.5 per cent, substantially higher than the growth rate of the real GDP.

External debt

Ethiopia's outstanding external debt, including ruble-dominated debt, is about forty-three billion birr. The country has accumulated arrears in recent years amounting to nearly five billion birr. Major creditors are the former Soviet Union, IDA, ADB/Fund, the USA, Italy, and Libya. The debt:service ratio has exceeded eighty per cent in recent years. Paris Club creditors have cancelled and rescheduled a portion of the country's debt, but the concession is not enough to remove the constraining impact of the overall debt on future economic development.

Employment

Data on employment and unemployment are extremely tentative and fragmentary. It is estimated that more than eighty-five per cent of the country's labour force is employed in agriculture. The cumulative number of unemployed people in major urban centres as of the latest date for which figures are available is about 800,000. However, some estimates put the rate of urban unemployment as high as forty per cent. This is claimed to be partly owing to the government's workforce retrenchment programme, which has left thousands of people without means of subsistence. It is estimated that most of Ethiopia's 55 million people have a per capita income of less than US$ 100 a year.

Economic changes

After the Dergue — the military government that came to power in 1974 — was overthrown by the Ethiopian People's Revolutionary Democratic Front (EPRDF) in May 1991, the Transitional Government of Ethiopia (TGE) was established. One of the government's first moves was to initiate an Emergency Recovery and Rehabilitation Programme (ERRP) towards the end of the 1991/1992 fiscal year as part of various short-, medium-, and long-term strategies and policy measures devised to tackle the chronic as well as the immediate economic problems of the country.

The programme was started with two basic objectives: to repair or reconstruct the basic economic and social infrastructures either damaged or destroyed during the civil war, and to rehabilitate those sectors of the society whose normal lives were disrupted as a result of various man-made and natural calamities during the previous seventeen years.

The operating capital of the ERRP, which amounts to US$ 657.5 million, was provided by various international donor and creditor countries and organizations in the form of grants or loans, as well as by the TGE. Under the programme, forty-six per cent of the total fund was allocated to the production sectors of the economy to meet the need for raw materials and necessary equipment in the agricultural and industrial fields.

Some twenty-two per cent of the fund was allotted to the social sector, mainly to be used to purchase medicines and medical equipment and to repair or rebuild educational and health facilities destroyed or damaged during the war. The remainder of the fund was assigned to the rehabilitation of the basic infrastructural facilities in the sectors of transport and communication, energy, and construction. The ERRP became fully operational in the 1992/1993 fiscal year. Although much remains to be done to bring all the projects in each sector of the economy to completion, the overall annual economic growth of 7.6 per cent scored by Ethiopia in 1992/1993 would have been unthinkable had it not been for the programme, which provided the necessary raw materials, spare parts, and modern agricultural inputs to the productive sectors.

New economic policy

The restoration of peace and stability in the country during the first year of democratic rule in Ethiopia made it possible for the Transitional Government to address the scores of economic and social agonies that the country faced as a result of the protracted civil war, recurrent drought, and what the TGE calls 'the misguided policies' of the past regime.

One of the major policy measures instituted to put the country's beleaguered economy on the road to recovery was the New Economic Policy for the Transition Period. In its long term, the economic policy focuses on transforming the centrally controlled economic system into a market-oriented one through various policies of adjustment and economic reform programmes.

Some of the pillars of the New Economic Policy are:

- altering the role of the state in economic activity by limiting its participation to those fields that cannot be operated by private capital for various reasons through joint ventures or on its own;
- creating an atmosphere conducive to the participation and strengthening of external and internal private investments;
- increasing the capacity to obtain and effectively use external loans and grants to achieve fruitful results in the building of the country's economy;
- designing and implementing a coordinated and harmonious general and sectoral economic policy compatible with the New Economic Policy; and
- sharing with the newly founded regional administrations the power of decision-making on economic management and assisting them to become the owners of their resources as well as obtaining the means of deciding on economic matters in their regions.

Various economic reform measures put into effect under this policy have already reduced the level of government expenditure, adjusted the interest rates upwards, and devalued the foreign exchange rate of the birr. A labour code providing for the liberalization of the labour market was issued and a new investment code to encourage domestic and foreign investors was proclaimed. Trade regulations and tariff improvement laws were announced, various restrictions previously imposed on the marketing of

agricultural products and price control of such commodities have been lifted, and the markets for agricultural and industrial commodities are being liberalized. Public enterprises have been granted management autonomy under their own boards.

As part of the economic reform and structural adjustment, an agricultural-development-led industrialization is foreseen that visualizes export-led growth feeding into an interdependent agricultural and industrial development endeavour as a long-term economic development strategy. The strategy also concentrates on building the industrial sector by improving farmers' productivity and using domestic raw materials as well as workforce.

Other commendable achievements brought about by the structural adjustments and new policy measures include a considerable decrease in the inflation rate, operation of most factories at nearly full capacity, significantly improved agricultural production, and the growth of the official foreign currency reserve of the country — earned from foreign trade — and the volume of export commodities. The value of the US dollar in the black market, which was rising day by day, is expected to be neutralized at near the official price rate in the country.

All these clearly point to the fact that the economy is indeed recovering and the policy measures are also working. Although it will take a fair amount of time before the full effects of these reform measures on the performance of the economy are seen, the encouraging results thus far could serve as a strong foundation for future activities.

Investment

Given its vast land mass, hard-working people, and virtually unexploited natural resources, Ethiopia has considerable potential for development, particularly in agriculture, agroprocessing, mining, energy, tourism, and construction. The democratization process is currently under way and a liberal market-oriented economic policy is being developed.

Data on investment are still rudimentary. What are available indicate that in recent years total investment (both public and private) as a percentage of the GDP averaged about 10.6 per cent, which is considered far too low compared with the twenty-five per cent recommended by international financial and development organizations if any appreciable real growth in per capita income is to be realized. Slightly outdated estimates suggest that more than eighty per cent of the total investment is attributable to the state, while the private sector accounts for the remaining twenty per cent. This situation is likely to change somewhat under the new economic reform programme currently being implemented, although from the current government's pronouncements on the role of government in the economy the share of public investment is expected to remain quite large.

The government issued a reasonably attractive Investment Code in May 1992. With the exception of a few sectors, which at any rate are not generally of interest to the private sector, private investors are allowed to participate in all areas of economic activity. Incentives include land allocation, various tax exemptions, fund remittance rights, and investment guarantees and protection.

Areas of investment reserved for the public sector include defence industries, post and tele-communication services; large-scale production and supply of electric energy; large-scale transport services; insurance, banking, and large-scale financial services; and certain critical import-export services.

Opportunities

Agriculture and agroprocessing

Ethiopia is a predominantly agricultural economy, engaging more than eighty per cent of the population on less than twenty per cent of the arable land currently under cultivation. The country is first in Africa and tenth in the world in the size of its livestock resources. Although the contribution of the livestock industry to the country's total production is at present very low compared with its potential, it holds great promise as a source of export diversification for the future. Areas in this sector that have substantial opportunities for new investments include production and processing of oil crops and cotton; plantation crops (such as tea, coffee, and tobacco); horticulture and floriculture (fruits, vegetables, flowers); livestock and poultry; fish farming; and forestry and forest byproducts.

Banking and insurance

In early 1994, the government announced that Ethiopian citizens are now allowed to own banks and insurance firms under a share-option system. The businesses, previously a government monopoly, are open only to Ethiopian nationals at present, although officials say that as the economy of the country improves, the participation of foreign banks may be considered.

Ethiopians planning to set up a private bank are required to produce a minimum of ten million birr (US$ 2 million) paid-up share capital. Each shareholder in a private bank is limited by law to own not more than twenty per cent of the share capital, a move intended to avoid monopoly of the bank by a group, a family, or an individual.

Manufacturing

The manufacturing sector has yet to grow to claim its share in the country's GDP. Manufacturing

activities fall mostly under light industry production. The existing potential for industrial growth, especially in medium- and large-scale industries, has prompted the country to accord high priority to the development of industrial infrastructure and promotion of new investments in these fields. Areas ripe for investment in this sector include food and beverage industries, textiles and clothing, leather and leather products, fertilizers and chemicals, drugs and pharmaceuticals, paper and paper products, electrical and electronic products, automotive components, building materials, and synthetic products.

Mining

The mining sector of the economy has immense potential for development. Limited scale gold, tantalum, and platinum mining is currently being undertaken. In addition, exploration for oil and natural gas is under way in the south-eastern part of the country. Resources such as copper, potash, zinc, nickel, iron ore, coal, and geothermal energy are also known to exist, providing opportunities to the investor for exploration and exploitation. Investments in this area are to be determined by the relevant mining law.

Service industries

In the service sector, areas that have substantial opportunities for new investments include marketing and promotion of export goods, medium- and large-scale construction, and hotels and tourism.

Foreign investment

Despite relatively attractive investment incentives, foreign investment is still negligible, although the new Investment Code is designed to give this area a particular boost. Foreign investors are especially encouraged to invest or participate in areas that assist the transfer of new technologies and procedures that will assist the rehabilitation and reconstruction efforts of the country. Such investment is particularly welcome in most production sectors with the purpose of predominantly using local raw materials, substituting for resource-based imports, supplying industrial crops, carrying agro-industry, exporting — or any combination of the above.

Foreigners are welcome to invest on their own or jointly with local investors and may set up various forms of business organizations such as private limited companies, ordinary partnerships, general partnerships, limited partnerships, and joint ventures. The government hopes to expand these to include share companies within the year.

The minimum entry requirement for foreign investors is US$ 500, 000, or equivalent in any other convertible currency, per project. The investor is required to deposit twenty-five per cent of the initial investment, which will be released when the project is formally established or ready to be implemented.

Investment protection

The government fully guarantees that no assets of a foreign or domestic investor shall be nationalized except in accordance with due process of law and upon payment of adequate compensation. Ethiopia has recently become a member of the Multilateral Investment Guarantee Agency (MIGA), which is the newest member of the World Bank Group. MIGA provides protection for all investments against losses resulting from non-commercial risks such as currency transfer delays, expropriation, war, revolution, civil strife, or breach of contract.

Remittances

Remittances in freely convertible currency shall be permitted to foreign investors with regard to
• profits and dividends;
• payments for debt servicing;
• fees and royalties for technology and know-how;
• payments from the sale or transfer of any rights on investment; and
• income from liquidation of an investment enterprise.

In addition, expatriate employees involved in an enterprise may remit their salaries in accordance with the Foreign Exchange Regulations of Ethiopia.

Incentives

The Investment Code offers a comprehensive package of incentives for projects in qualified areas.
Fiscal incentives include:
• exemption from import duties and taxes on capital goods such as machinery, equipment, and spare parts up to fifteen per cent of the capital invested, provided these goods are not available locally;
• exemption from income tax for three years from the beginning of operation for a new operation;
• exemption from income tax for two years from the beginning of any expansion;
• possible additional tax exemption for three to five years for investments in specific regions or in areas of priority;
• the carrying forward for one year following the expiry of the exemption period any loss incurred within the exemption period;
• exemption from income tax for up to three years for new investments and for two years in the case of expansion for investors who reinvest profits;
• exemption from payment of import duties on raw materials used for production of export commodities;
• exemption from export taxes and other duties;
• exemption from payment of tax on proceeds from the sale or transfer of shares or acquisition of an enterprise by a domestic investor.
Other incentives include:
• transfer of capital goods and equipment imported

without payment of duties to investors having similar privileges;
• opening and operating a foreign currency account if an investor or enterprise earns foreign exchange;
• retaining a portion of any foreign exchange earnings to purchase such things as machinery, equipment, or raw materials.

Applications for new investments

The Investment Office of Ethiopia (IOE) was recently established as a 'one-stop-shop' for all foreign investors and will arrange for all approvals, licences, permits, and authorizations required for new investments and expansions. The IOE also provides foreign investors with
• data and information on projects and subsectors of particular interest to potential investors;
• project profiles in selected areas;
• assistance in searching for and approaching potential local partners in proposed joint ventures.

Foreigners intending to invest in Ethiopia should obtain an application form (available from Ethiopian embassies abroad or from the IOE) and send it with the additional documents specified on the form to the Investment Office of Ethiopia, P.O. Box 2428, Addis Ababa, Ethiopia. (Tel. [251-1] 510033, 514443, 157962, 150223; telefax [251-1] 517988; telex 21368 OSCFER ET.)

PART SIX: FACTS AT YOUR FINGERTIPS

Visa and Immigration requirements

Visa applications may be obtained at Ethiopia diplomatic missions located in Abidjan, Accra, Beijing, Bonn, Brussels, Cairo, Dakar, Djibouti, Geneva, Harare, Jeddah, Khartoum, Lagos, London, Moscow, Nairobi, New Delhi, New York, Ottawa, Paris, Pyongyang, Riyadh, Rome, Sanaa, Seoul, Stockholm, Tehran, Tel Aviv, Tokyo, Tripoli, Vienna, and Washington DC.

Visas are required for all visitors to Ethiopia, with the exception of nationals of Djibouti, Eritrea, Kenya, and Sudan. Visas should be applied for well in advance of any trip as applications can take time to process.

Except in the case of a few nationals, passengers in transit in Ethiopia holding confirmed onward bookings within 72 hours can obtain transit visas on arrival for a fee of Ethiopian birr 20. However, in this case, passports are held at the airport until departure and a pink-coloured receipt card is issued.

Any visitor intending to take up work or residence in Ethiopia must have a work permit from the Ministry of Labour and Social Affairs and a resident permit from the Department of Immigration in the Ministry of the Interior. A visitor on a tourist visa cannot take up work or get a work permit. It is best to have all formalities cleared before you enter Ethiopia and come in on a working visa.

Health requirements

All visitors (including infants) are required to possess a valid yellow fever vaccination certificate. Vaccination against cholera is also required for any person who has visited or transited a cholera-infected area within six days prior to arrival in Ethiopia. Your doctor may also recommend gamma globulin shots or refresher vaccines of typhoid and polio before you go. Hepatitis, typhoid, meningitis, and other communicable diseases do exist in the country, but most tourists will run little risk of coming in contact with them.

Malaria is endemic throughout the country — even at altitudes as high as 2,000 metres (6,560 feet). Visitors should begin taking a recommended chloroquine-based prophylactic two weeks before their arrival and continue taking them for six weeks after their departure. Medication for chloroquine-resistant malaria is also a wise precaution, especially when in a malarial area.

Bilharzia (schistosomiasis) is common throughout Ethiopia but is easily avoided by drinking treated water — tap water in Addis Ababa is treated and safe to drink — and by not swimming in lakes and rivers, with the exception of lakes Langano and Shalla, which are known to be bilharzia free.

International flights

Ethiopia is served internationally by Ethiopian Airlines, Lufthansa, Kenya Airways, Puntavia (Air Djibouti), Saudia, Sudan Airways, and Yemenia.

Ethiopia's major point of entry by air is Addis Ababa's Bole International Airport, which is modest but does provide full passenger facilities — currency exchange, postal services, banking facilities, telephones, a duty-free shop, gift shops, and a restaurant and bar service.

Taxis and rental cars are available at the airport for transport into Addis Ababa.

Air fares

The usual range of fares is available: first, business, and economy class; excursion fares, bookable any time for stays of between fourteen and forty-five days; an APEX fare, bookable one calendar month in advance, allowing for stays of between nineteen and ninety days. The price of cheaper APEX fares varies according to the season. Stopovers en route are possible when arranged with the airline for all but APEX fares. Reductions are available for children.

Departure tax

As of mid-1994, the airport departure tax was US$ 10, payable in any convertible currency. Traveller's cheques are not acceptable. On local flights, there is a 'boarding charge' of five birr for residents and non-residents.

Arrival by rail

The sole point of entry into Ethiopia by rail is at Dewele on the Ethiopia–Djibouti border. Arrivals undergo full customs and immigration checks.

Arrival by road

There are four 'official' points of entry by road into Ethiopia from the country's neighbours. Moyale serves as the border post from Kenya, Sudan has border controls to Ethiopia at Humera and Metema, and Dewele is the point of entry from Djibouti. All have full customs and immigration checks.

Visitors intending on driving their own vehicle into Ethiopia should first obtain the necessary permit by writing to the Ministry of Transportation and Communication, PO Box 1238, Addis Ababa.

Customs

Besides personal effects, a visitor may import duty-free spirits (including liquors) or wine up to one litre, perfume and toilet water up to half a litre, and 250 grams (half a pound) of tobacco (up to 200 cigarettes or fifty cigars).

If you are carrying a video camera, laptop computer, or any other pieces of sophisticated electronic equipment, it is usually entered in your passport to ensure that you take it with you when you go and do not sell it while in the country. You do not need to declare still cameras, small shortwave radios, calculators, and similar small electronic devices. Professional journalists and photographers must report to the Ministry of Information to get a permit.

Permit is given for temporary import of certain articles — such as trade samples or professional articles — which must be produced on departure or duty will be paid.

Visitors may import up to Ethiopia birr 10 and an unlimited amount of foreign currency, providing declaration of such currency (on the appropriate blue-coloured form) is made to Customs on arrival. This currency declaration form will be required by Customs on departure.

Permit is required for export of antiques and wildlife products from the appropriate authorities.

Domestic air services

Ethiopian Airlines operates a comprehensive network of regular daily flights between Addis Ababa and Axum, Bahar Dar, Dessie, Dire Dawa, Gondar, Humera, Jimma, Lalibela, and Makale, as well as several other flights each week to many other towns. The airline flies to forty-three airfields and an additional twenty-one landing strips within the country. Charter companies also offer flights to all main airports and to many landing fields not served by the national airline.

Road services

There are some 10,000 kilometres (6,200 miles) of gravel and dry-weather roads throughout Ethiopia, and some 3,600 kilometres (2,232 miles) of asphalt roads. A good bus network operates to and from the countryside from its terminal in Addis Ababa's Mercato.

Taxi services

Taxis are immediately available at Bole International Airport. They can also be found outside most hotels in Addis Ababa and at the country's major centres. There are two types: privately owned blue-and-white vehicles or, in Addis Ababa, Mercedes Benz taxis operated by the National Tour Operation (NTO). The larger blue-and-white taxis have standard routes and pick up and let off passengers along these routes, operating like little buses. There are no meters; there are low standardized prices for the fixed routes, and all prices for special hire should

be negotiated in advance to avoid later misunderstandings. NTO taxis can be booked at any of the major hotels. Trips are paid for in advance according to destination; again, the taxis are not metered. These taxis are about ten times more expensive, on average, than the little blue taxis hailed on the street.

Car rental

Several firms operate car hire services in Addis Ababa. Vehicles may be hired with or without driver. For trips outside the city it is possible to hire insured cars appropriate for the trip (a four-wheel-drive vehicle with driver/translator is recommended).

Driving

Drivers require a valid International Driving Licence, which can be obtained by exchanging your local licence at the Transport and Communications office on Asmara Road in Addis Ababa.

Visitors can recover their original licences a day or so prior to departure. Vehicle owners will require the necessary permit from the Ministry of Transport and Communications. Driving is on the right.

Rail services

The 778-kilometre (482-mile) Franco-Ethiopian Railway runs from Addis Ababa to Djibouti by way of Nazaret, Awash Station, and Dire Dawa. There are both night and day trains between the capital and Dire Dawa, and the trip takes approximately ten hours. There are first, second, and third classes. The Ethiopian Tourism Commission (ETC) or a travel agent can assist you with schedules and making reservations, or you can go directly to the station, which is located near the junction of Churchill and Ras Makonnen avenues.

Climate

Despite its proximity to the equator, Ethiopia's high altitude, averaging some 2,400 metres (7,800 feet), ensures a temperate, moderate, even cool climate — certainly not tropical. The highest daytime temperatures rarely exceed 21 or 22°C (70 or 71°F) and for much of the year seldom rise above 16 or 18°C (61 or 64°F). Temperatures at night frequently drop to a chilly 10°C (50°F) or less. There are two rainy seasons: the irregular short rains from late January to early March, and the long rains that stretch from June until mid-September. May is the warmest month and is usually a time of bright sunny days. Daytime temperatures in January run just as high, but the nights are chillier. June, July, and August are grey, wet, and cool.

Currency

The local currency is the Ethiopian birr, made up of 100 cents. Notes are issued in denominations of 1, 5, 10, 50, and 100 birr. There are five different coins: 1, 5, 10, 25, and 50 cents. In June 1994, five birr were equivalent to one US dollar.

Currency regulations

There is no limit to the amount of foreign currency imported to Ethiopia, but it must be declared on the currency declaration form obtained on arrival. Up to Ethiopian 10 birr may be legally imported. Foreign currency may be changed only at authorized banks and hotels. The currency declaration form must be retained as this will be required by Customs on departure.

Visitors may change back any excess Ethiopian birr to foreign currency at the airport before departure. If you do have birr to cash in at the airport, you must, in addition to the currency declaration form, bring with you all receipts for exchange transactions.

Banks

Banks have two sets of hours: cash and business. Cash hours are from 08.00 to 11.00 and 13.00 to 16.00 Monday through Thursday, and from 08.00 to 11.30 and 13.30 to 16.00 on Friday.

Business hours are from 08.00 to 12.00 and 13.00 to 17.00 Monday through Thursday and 08.00 to 10.00 and 13.00 to 17.00 on Friday. All the major banks offer currency exchange.

Credit cards

Some credit cards are accepted in the major hotels and some of the larger restaurants. American Express is the most widely accepted. The Hilton also accepts Visa, MasterCard, Diners Club, Access, and Eurocard.

Government

Ethiopia, a member of the United Nations and the Organization of African Unity, is an independent republic, operating under the Transitional Government of Ethiopia. The president is the head of state, while the prime minister heads the main administrative office for the government. There is a Council of Ministers and Council of Representatives, with permanent secretaries in each ministry.

Local government consists of sixty-five National/Regional Transitional Self-Governments, each comprising a national/regional executive committee, a judicial organ, a public prosecution office, an audit and control office, a police and security office, and a services and development committee. All local officials are elected by the people within each region. Each National/Regional Transitional Self-Government is accountable to the Central Transitional Government.

Language

Amharic is the official language of Ethiopia, although English, Italian, French, and Arabic are widely spoken. In areas outside of the larger cities and towns, indigenous languages are likely to be spoken — of which there are eighty-three, with some 200 dialects. The most common of these are Orominya and Tigrinya.

Religion

Nearly half of the population of Ethiopia (forty-five per cent) subscribes to Christianity in the form of the Ethiopian Orthodox Church, while a large thirty-five per cent are Sunni Muslims. Eleven per cent of Ethiopians, however, still adhere to traditional beliefs. The remainder subscribe to a variety of other faiths, including Judaism. Although most of the Falashas, or Ethiopian Jews, were airlifted out of the country at the time of the civil war, it is believed there is still a small remnant population.

Time

Ethiopia is three hours ahead of Greenwich mean time. Time remains constant throughout the year. The Ethiopian day is calculated in a manner similar to that in many equatorial countries, where day and night are always the same length: counting starts at Western 6.00 a.m. and 6.00 p.m. Western 7.00 a.m. is therefore one o'clock, noon is six, 6.00 p.m. is twelve o'clock, and so on.

Daylight

Being relatively close to the equator, there is an almost constant twelve hours of daylight. In Addis Ababa, the sunrise and sunset start at around 06.30 and 18.45 respectively.

Calendar

Ethiopia follows the Julian calendar, which consists of twelve months of thirty days each and a thirteenth month of five days (six days on leap year). The calendar is seven years and eight months behind the Western (Gregorian) calendar.

Business hours

Government offices remain open from 08.30 to 12.00 and 13.30 to 17.30 Monday through Thursday, and from 08.30 to 11.30 and 13.30 to 17.30 on Friday. Government offices are closed on public holidays, Saturdays, and Sundays. Most shops are open from 09.00 to 18.00 or 20.00 from Monday through Saturday with a lunch break from 13.00 to 15.00. Some shops or businesses close on Saturdays at 13.00. A few small all-purpose shops off Arat Kilo are open on Sunday mornings.

Security

The same rules apply for Addis Ababa as for almost any city anywhere. Be careful and take the usual precautions to safeguard yourself and your belongings. Street crime exists, but it is generally non-violent pickpocketing or the snatching of handbags or gold neck chains and earrings.

Be aware of this petty thievery risk if you walk the streets during the day and avoid walking the streets at night — take a cab.

Common sense rules apply, such as not wearing gold jewellery on the street and not carrying large sums of cash or valuables on your person. Don't leave valuables in your hotel room; make use of the hotel safe-deposit box. Items of any great value should be deposited with a bank.

Communications

Telephone, telex, fax, and airmail services connect Addis Ababa to all parts of the world. Services are available at the General Post Office and its many branches, as well as in the main hotels. International direct dialling is available from all the major centres in the country, which are served by microwave.

Media

There are several foreign-language newspapers published in Ethiopia, including the English daily *Ethiopian Herald*; the English *Addis Tribune* and *Monitor*, both weekly; and the Arabic weekly newspaper *Al-Alem*. The government daily, published in Amharic, is the *Addis Zeman*, while the weekly is *Yezareytu Ethiopia*. There are several private daily and weekly Amharic newspapers and monthly magazines.

The national news agency is the Ethiopian News Agency, and there are several foreign bureaux operating in Addis Ababa, including the British Broadcasting Corporation (BBC), Voice of America (VoA), and Reuters.

ETV, Ethiopian Television, broadcasts every evening from about 18.30, beginning with one hour in Tigrinya, followed by two hours in Amharic, one hour in Orominya, and finishing with English from 22.30 until the end of the broadcast day, which varies.

Radio service is provided by the Voice of Ethiopia. Its external service, which broadcasts daily from late afternoon until 23.00 or 24.00, features daily programmes in English, Arabic, French, and Amharic. An internal service broadcasts for a longer period of time, with programmes in many local languages.

Energy

Ethiopia uses 220 volts and 50 Hz. It is best to bring your own round, two-prong adapter. American visitors should bring a small step-down voltage converter.

Medical services

Medical facilities are limited and of generally poor standard. Existing facilities are sorely overtaxed. Tourists and non-citizen residents should go to private hospitals and clinics. Even there, the facilities are inadequate to cope with the needs. Contact your embassy for referral to a recommended doctor. If you fall seriously ill or are gravely hurt, you may want to consider evacuation to nearby Nairobi or to Europe. Air rescue services are available, and you might want to make arrangements with one before your trip.

Medical insurance

Medical insurance should be purchased before you leave and preferably include emergency air evacuation coverage.

Chemists/pharmacies

Medical supplies are limited in Ethiopia. Visitors should carry an adequate supply of all medicines they may need with them. Those wearing glasses should carry an extra pair — just in case — or, failing that, a prescription. Most chemists and pharmacies maintain regular business hours. Most are open all day on Saturday and there is a system of 'on-duty' pharmacists open to 22.30 or 23.00 and Sundays.

Liquor

Ethiopia's several brands of commercially brewed beers are very tasty and inexpensive, as are the very palatable local wines. Imported spirits, on the other hand, are expensive. Local drinks such as *tej*, a type of mead or honey wine, or *tella*, a local home-brewed beer, are cheaper — but some can be quite potent.

Tipping

Tips up to ten per cent are an accepted practice and appreciated. At night, tipping the guard who is watching your car outside a restaurant, usually with one birr, is common practice. During the day, street parking boys will want a tip for watching your car while you shop. You are not required to tip them for their unsolicited services, but you may, if you wish to do so. You are not expected to tip a taxi driver on a standard route, just as you would not tip a bus driver. But you can tip the driver of a negotiated trip if the service has been good. In this case, a tip of ten per cent is considered generous.

Clubs

Clubs are a prominent feature of Ethiopian social life, particularly for expatriates. Most are organized around sport, some are philanthropic. Many have excellent facilities and welcome visitors, especially members of international clubs and societies with reciprocal arrangements. Some charge a temporary membership fee.

Sport club activities include angling, badminton, basketball, ten-pin bowling, cricket, golf, horse-riding, handball, polo, rugby, soccer, softball, squash, swimming, Tae Kwon Do, and tennis.

ENGLISH–AMHARIC

Simple pronunciation guide:
a as the a in father
e as the e in set
i as the i in ship
o as the o in go
u as the oo in boot
gn as the gn in compagne (French)

Amharic spellings that follow are phonetical as per the above guide to aid in pronunciation.

Meeting and Greeting

Hello	Halo
Good morning	Endemn adderu
Good afternoon	Endemn walu
Good evening	Endemn ameshu
Goodbye	Dehna hunu
How are you?	Tenayistillign
I am well	Dehna negn
Thank you (very much)	(Betam) ameseghinallehu
You're welcome (don't mention it)	Minim aydel
Please come in	Yigbu
Please sit down	Yikemetu
What is your name?	Simewo man no
My name is . . .	Sime . . . no
Where do you come from?	Hagerish yet no?
I come from . . .	Ke . . . metahu
My country is . . .	Hagere . . . no
Can you speak Amharic?	Amaregna yechelalu?
Only a little	Tinish
I want to learn more	Yebeletememar ifeligalehu
How do you find Ethiopia?	Itiyopiya endet agegnuat?
I like it here	Itiyopiya yisimamagnal

Useful words

Today	Zare
Tomorrow	Nege
Yesterday	Tilant
Now	Ahun
Quickly	Tolo
Slowly	Kes
Mr	Ato
Mrs	Weyzero
Miss	Weyzerit
I	Ene
You	Ersewo
He, She	Essu, Essoa
We	Egna
They	Egna
They	Ennessu
What?	Min?
Who?	Man?

When?	Metche?
How?	Endet?
Why?	Lemin?
Which?	Yetignaw?
Yes (all right)	Eshi
No	Aydelem
Excuse me	Yikirta
I am sorry	Aznallehu
Good	Tiru
Bad	Metfo

Directions/Emergencies

Where? (Place)	Yet?
Where is it?	Yet no?
Where? (Direction)	Wodet?
Street / road	Menged
Airport	Awiroplan marefeya
Where is the hotel?	Hotelu yet no?
Where are you going?	Yet iyehedk no?
I am going to . . .	Wede . . . iyehedku no
Turn right	Wede kegn yitatefu
Turn left	Wede gra yitatefu
Go straight	Ketita yihidu
Please stop here	Ezih Yikumu
Come	Na
Go	Hid
Stop	Kum
Help	Irdugn
Hospital	Hospital / Hakem bet
Police	Polis

Restaurants/Shops/Hotels

Hotel	Hotel
Room	Kifil
Bed	Alga
To sleep	Metegnat
To bathe	Galan metateb
Where is the toilet?	Shint betu yet no?
Where may I get something to drink?	Yemiteta neger yet agengalehu?
Coffee	Buna
One (cup of) coffee	And (sini) buna
Beer	Birra
Cold	Kezkaza
Hot	Muk
Tea	Shay
Food	Migib
Meat	Siga
Fish	Assa
Bread	Dabo
Butter	Kebe
Sugar	Sikuar
Salt	Cho
Pepper	Berbere
Shop	Suk
To buy	Megzat
To sell	Meshet
Money	Genzeb
Cent	Centime
How much does this cost?	Wagaw sint no?
That is quite expensive	Betam wood no

In Brief

Ethiopia national parks

The national parks of Ethiopia have been set aside by the government as wildlife and botanical sanctuaries that enjoy a high degree of protection and management. The 20,756 square kilometres (8,014 square miles) of national park land serves a conservational, educational, and recreational purpose for Ethiopians and overseas visitors and, together with the country's famed Historic Route, form the mainstay of the country's tourist industry.

Strict Conservation Areas

Ethiopia's Strict Conservation Areas comprise **National Parks**, **Wetlands Reserves**, and **Strict Nature Reserves**. These are the basic and most important instruments designed exclusively for nature conservancy in the country. They can be established or altered only by proclamation enacted by the highest body of government, which thus affords in them the greatest security and permanency attainable.

All human activities are excluded as far as is possible from Strict Conservation Areas, except for managerial, recreational, cultural, educational, or scientific purposes, and official activity and other activities specifically approved by the Minister of Agriculture, Environmental Protection, and Development in furtherance of the requirements of the Wildlife Conservation Proclamation.

However, Strict Conservation Areas may be zoned to allow for long-term traditional forms of land use to continue within them, which may in some cases enhance the wildlife conservation objectives of the area.

A **National Park** is an area retained in as near natural a state as possible in order to conserve representative ecosystems and their wild species of plants and animals. The requirements of the natural ecosystems and their wild plant and animal species in a National Park are considered to be paramount in management considerations of the areas so defined.

A **Wetlands Reserve** is similar in all respects to a National Park except that its purpose is exclusively for the protection of aquatic ecosystems — mainly lakes, swamps, and marsh habitats — on which numerous wild fauna and flora are dependent, and in particular those aquatic ecosystems which are important to bird migrations in and through Ethiopia.

A **Strict Nature Reserve** is identical to a National Park in its conservation objectives except that it is managed in such a manner as to promote the free, undisturbed interaction of natural ecological factors without any interference whatsoever, excepting that deemed indispensable by the Minister of Agriculture, Environmental Protection, and Development for the safeguard of its natural quality and its continued existence for posterity.

Wildlife Conservation Reserves

Wildlife Conservation Reserves are areas considered to be of significance for the maintenance of the wildlife resources of Ethiopia, but here the requirements of wildlife conservation are considered on equal terms with those of other forms of land use. Comprising **Wildlife Reserves** and **Controlled Hunting Areas**, Wildlife Conservation Reserves are used wherever possible to form buffer zones around Strict Conservation Areas. They are established by order published in the *Negarit Gazetta* by the Minister of Agriculture, Environmental Protection, and Development.

Wildlife Reserves serve as reservoirs of fauna for Controlled Hunting Areas and Strict Conservation Areas.

Controlled Hunting Areas are designated for the balanced and controlled utilization of wildlife through sport hunting and capture (which, as of mid-1994, has been temporarily banned).

Ethiopian Wildlife Conservation Organization

All matters concerning wildlife in Ethiopia fall under the responsibility of the Ethiopian Wildlife Conservation Organization. This is a government department, found within the Ministry of Agriculture, Environmental Protection, and Development. It falls under a vice-minister, directly within the Environmental Protection and Development main department, together with Forestry, Fisheries, Land Use Planning, Soil and Water Conservation, and other environmental concerns.

EWCO has a staff of more than seventy people at the headquarters in Addis Ababa, and almost 300 people in the field, at thirteen locations.

Ethiopian Tourist Commission

Tourist aspects relevant to wildlife in Ethiopia fall under the responsibility of the Ethiopian Tourist Commission, within the Ministry of Finance and Planning. This Commission is responsible for the Ethiopian Hotels Corporation, the Ethiopian Tourist and Trading Corporation, and the National Tour Operation, until recently the only travel and tourist agency in the country. There are now, however, numerous travel agencies making good use of the opportunities offered by the removal of government monopoly of the tourist trade.

National Park regulations

1. No person shall enter the park without a valid entry permit.
2. Such a permit shall not in any way be deemed to make the Ethiopian Wildlife Conservation Organization liable for any injury or damage done while in the park to the person or persons, vehicles, or any other possessions of such person or persons to whom the permit has been issued.
3. No person may camp, except in the areas marked as campsites, unless permission is acquired.
4. No person may cut, destroy, or remove any vegetation within the park, other than the removal of dead timber for use as firewood in park campsites.
5. No person may hunt, kill capture, or chase any animal within the park.
6. No person within the park may leave the park roads or tracks, unless accompanied by a park official.
7. No person may enter or move within the boundaries of the park between the hours of 19.00 and 06.30, without the permission of the warden.
8. Save with the permission of the warden, no two-wheeled vehicle is allowed in the park; no person shall drive a vehicle at a speed greater

than 40 kph within the park; no motor horn shall be used within the park; no vehicle shall obstruct any road; all drivers shall obey the signals given by park officials; no person shall use any road or track closed by park officials.

9. No person may take any photograph or film within the park for publication, distribution, or any form of commercial or professional use save with a photographic permit.
10. No person shall bring any arms or ammunition into the park without the warden's permission.
11. No person shall light any fire in the park, except in recognized campsites.
12. No person shall bring any dog, sheep, goat, cow, cat, or any other animal or bird into the park, without the prior written permission of the warden.
13. No personal shall leave any litter within the park boundaries.
14. No person shall introduce, or allow to be introduced, any pesticides, poisons, or other noxious substances to the park.
15. No wirelesses, tape-recorders, or other musical instruments may be played in the park.
16. Any person infringing any of the above conditions may be required to leave the park, and shall be liable to prosecution.

Addresses

Ethiopian Wildlife Conservation Organization
PO Box 386
Addis Ababa

Ethiopian Tourism Commission
PO Box 2183
Addis Ababa

National Parks

Abijatta-Shalla Lakes National Park
Size: 887 sq km
Region: Shewa
Geographical location: Rift Valley, 200 km south of Addis Ababa
Altitude: 1,540–2,075 m
Physical features: 482 sq km of the park is water, comprising the fluctuating shallow pan of Lake Abijatta and the deep, steep-sided Lake Shalla, both of which are saline. Several hot springs bubble up by the shore and flow into Lake Shalla. Mount Fike, 2,075 metres high, is situated between the two lakes. Temperatures can be high, reaching 45°C at maximum and 5°C at minimum. Rain falls between March and April, and June and September, averaging 500 mm.
Vegetation: Savannah and acacia woodland. Many areas are adversely affected by people practising

charcoal production and livestock grazing, particularly near the roads.

Fauna: Thirty-one species of mammal, including greater kudu, Grant's gazelle, warthog, Anubis baboon, grivet and colobus monkeys, oribi, klipspringer, black-backed and common jackal.

Bird life: 299 species, including six endemics. Park created for the water birds, especially great white pelican, greater and lesser flamingo, cormorants.

Visitor facilities: Hotels (government and private) and camping on nearby Lake Langano, self-catering rest house at Gike.

Awash National Park

Size: 756 sq km

Region: Shewa / Arsi

Geographical location: Bordering the Awash River in the upper Rift Valley, 225 km west of Addis Ababa

Altitude: 750–2,007 m

Physical features: Nearby Lake Basaka is home to many water bird species. The park's southern boundary is, in part, the Awash River, one of the major rivers of Ethiopia. In the middle of the park is the dormant volcano of Fantale, reaching a height of 2,007 m on its rim. The park also includes the dramatic Awash Falls and the unbelievably clear blue — but hot — pools of the Filwoha hot springs. Temperatures can reach as high as 42°C. Nights are cooler, with temperatures between 10° and 22°C. Rain mainly falls between February and April, and June to August, and averages 619 mm.

Vegetation: Arid and semi-arid woodland and savannah, but also riverine forest. The plains are covered by grass species, with scattered small tree species. Areas of shallow soil over rock are covered in dense thickets of acacia species. The rocky valleys to the north of the park are heavily bushed. Along the river is a thin belt of dense riverine forest, including acacia, tamarind, and fig species.

Fauna: Forty-six species, including Beisa oryx, greater and lesser kudu, Soemmering's gazelle, Swayne's hartebeest, lion, hamadryas and Anubis baboon and their hybrids, Defassa waterbuck, Salt's dik-dik.

Bird life: There are five endemics among the 392 species to be found in the park. Resident species include green wood hoopoe, red-and-yellow barbet, emerald-spotted wood dove, carmine bee-eater, several bustard species, fish eagle, tawny eagle, lanner and pygmy falcon, black-shouldered kite, dark chanting goshawk, several varieties of kingfishers and rollers, ostrich, and lammergeyer.

Visitor facilities: Very basic caravan lodge on edge of Awash gorge, campsite beside river. Museum.

Bale Mountains National Park

Size: 2,470 sq km

Region: Bale

Geographical location: South-east Ethiopia, southern end of eastern edge of Rift Valley mountain chain, 400 km from Addis Ababa

Altitude: 1,500–4,377 m

Physical features: This extensive Afro-alpine area contains alpine lakes and the highest peak in southern Ethiopia, Tullu Deemtu. The area of the park is divided into two major parts by the Harenna Escarpment that runs from east to west. North of this escarpment is a high-altitude plateau area, which is dissected by many rivers and streams that have cut deep gorges into the edges over the centuries. In some places this has resulted in scenic waterfalls. The northern part of the park is riverine plains, bushland, and woodland; the centre is a high plateau of 4,000 metres, which is crossed by the highest all-weather road in Africa. The southern part of the park is forest. Temperatures range from -7°C to 26°C, depending on the season. Rainfall is high, averaging 1,150 mm, and usually falls between March and October, but also in other months.

Vegetation: In the north, there are grass riverine plains bordered by bands of bushes, particularly St. John's wort. Wild flowers form carpets of colour. Fringing the hills are stands of hagenia and juniper and above them are montane grasslands. Higher up the mountains heather appears. The high Sanetti Plateau is characterized by Afro-alpine plants, some coping with the extreme temperatures by becoming small and others by becoming large. The best example of the latter is the giant lobelia. The dominant wild flower in the park is the everlasting. The southern part of the park is heavily forested. The heather forest is particularly mature here, draped with many lichens.

Fauna: The park was originally established to protect two of Ethiopia's endemic species: the mountain nyala and the Simien fox (or jackal). There are sixty-four species of mammal in the park (eleven of them endemic), including Menelik's bushbuck, Bohor reedbuck, grey duiker, warthog, serval cat, colobus monkey, giant molerat, African wild dog, bushpig, giant forest hog, lion, and Anubis baboon.

Bird life: The 220 bird species of Bale include sixteen endemic species, many of which are easily seen. These include wattled ibis, black-winged lovebird, blue-winged goose, Rouget's rail, and thick-billed raven. Wattled cranes are often seen on the high plateau in the wet season, when they breed.

Visitor facilities: Self-catering lodge and campsite at park headquarters, camping allowed in park while trekking. Hotels in nearby Goba and Robe. Museum.

Gambella National Park

Size: 5,060 sq km

Region: Ilubabor

Geographical location: West Ethiopia, 850 km west of Addis Ababa

Altitude: 400–768 m

Physical features: Extensive swamps and wetlands of the Akobo river system. Rainfall is 1,500 mm a year, falling between April and October. Temperatures are high.

Vegetation: Semi-arid open woodland, savannah, swamp.

Fauna: The park contains forty-one species, many representative of neighbouring Sudan and not found elsewhere in Ethiopia, such as Nile lechwe and the white-eared kob, the latter migrating in large numbers. Roan antelope, topi, elephant, buffalo, lelwel hartebeest, lion, and giraffe are also present.
Bird life: The most important of the 154 bird species present here is the whale-headed stork, an unusual large-billed, tall bird seen standing in the swamps.
Visitor facilities: No development yet.

Mago National Park

Size: 2,162 sq km
Region: Gamo Gofa
Geographical location: 770 km south-west of Addis Ababa, touching east bank of Omo River
Altitude: 450–2,528 m
Physical features: The highest point is Mount Mago situated in the north of the park. Temperatures here swing between 14° and 41°C and rainfall — which falls from March to May and October to December — is low, being 480 mm on average.
Vegetation: Mainly grass savannah, with some forested areas around the rivers. Very dense bush makes for difficult game viewing.
Fauna: The park was set up to conserve the large numbers of plains animals in the area, particularly buffalo, giraffe, and elephant. Also among the fifty-six species of mammal seen here are topi and lelwel hartebeest, as well as lion, cheetah, leopard, Burchell's zebra, gerenuk, oryx, and greater and lesser kudu.
Bird life: The birds are typical of the dry grassland habitat, featuring bustards, hornbills, weavers, and starlings. Kingfishers and herons can be seen around the Neri River, which provides an alternative habitat. There are 153 species, three of them endemic.
Visitor facilities: Campsite by Neri River.

Nechisar National Park

Size: 514 sq km
Region: Gamo Gofa
Geographical location: 500 km south-west of Addis Ababa, near Arba Minch.
Altitude: 1,108–1,650 m
Physical features: The park is an impressive swathe of white grass plains set against the backdrop of clearly defined, deeply cut hills and mountains. Seventy-eight square kilometres of the park is water — parts of lakes Chamo and Abaya. There are hot springs at the far eastern sector of the park. Temperatures range between 11° and 26°C. Rainfall averages 880 mm and mainly falls from March to May and September to November.
Vegetation: Savannah, dry bush, groundwater forest.
Fauna: Thirty-seven species, including bushbuck, bushpig, Anubis baboon, vervet monkey, colobus monkey, Swayne's hartebeest, Burchell's zebra, African wild dog, greater kudu, genet cat, Grant's gazelle, Guenther's dik-dik, black-backed jackal, crocodile, and hippopotamus.

Bird life: The 188 bird species — including two endemics — of the area are quite varied, reflecting the different habitats within the park. Both the red-billed and the grey hornbill are common here, and the Abyssinian ground hornbill is also seen. Also common are fish eagle, kingfishers, and rollers. Various bustard species are found in the park, including the large and impressive kori.
Visitor facilities: Campsite in forest near Kulfo River. Hotels in nearby town of Arba Minch.

Omo National Park

Size: 4,068 sq km
Region: Kaffa
Geographical location: 870 km south-west of Addis Ababa, on west bank of Omo River
Altitude: 440–1,183 m
Physical features: Belts of forest along the Omo and Mui rivers, hot springs, extensive wilderness. The grass plains are relieved by bands of hills to the north and south of the centrally located park headquarters. Temperatures are high, ranging from 14° to 41°C, and the rainfall averages 500 mm a year, falling between March and April, and September and October.
Vegetation: Savannah, riverine forest, deciduous woodland, acacia bush.
Fauna: The park's wildlife includes large herds of eland and buffalo, elephant, giraffe, cheetah, lion, leopard, and Burchell's zebra. Lesser kudu, lelwel hartebeest, topi, and oryx are all found here, in addition to deBrazza's and colobus monkeys and Anubis baboon. A total of fifty-seven species of mammal can be found in the park.
Bird life: 306 species, one endemic.
Visitor facilities: Campsite on Mui River, museum.

Simien Mountains National Park

Size: 179 sq km
Region: Gondar
Geographical location: 760 km north of Addis Ababa, via Bahar Dar, Gondar
Altitude: 1,900–4,430 m
Physical features: Spectacular scenery; gorges and escarpments. Just outside the park is Ras Dashen, Ethiopia's highest peak at 4,543 metres. Temperatures can fall below freezing at night. The daytime temperatures are in the region of 11.5° to 18°C. The rainfall averages 1,550 mm a year.
Vegetation: Afro-alpine, montane savannah, heather. Much of the vegetation has been altered by humans over the years and few trees will be seen in the area except the introduced eucalyptus. But in inaccessible areas, such as the escarpment, natural habitats are preserved and plants such at St. John's wort and heather may be seen as small trees or bushes, and many smaller herbs form carpets of colour.
Fauna: Walia ibex, Simien fox, gelada baboon, grey duiker, and klipspringer are among the twenty-one

species (three endemics) to be found in the park.
Bird life: Lammergeyers and choughs are present among the sixty-three species of birds here, which include seven endemics: thick-billed raven, black-headed siskin, white-collared pigeon, wattled ibis, white-billed starling, spot-breasted plover, and white-backed black tit.
Visitor facilities: Camping at various sites.

Yangudi-Rassa National Park

Size: 4,730 sq km
Region: Harerge
Geographical location: 500 km north-east of Addis Ababa, on Awash–Assab road
Altitude: 400–1,459 m
Physical features: Temperatures are high, as in Awash National Park. Very little rain falls as the area is semi-desert.
Vegetation: Semi-desert trees and scrub, savannah, open woodland.
Fauna: Thirty-six species of mammal, including wild ass, Grevy's zebra, gerenuk, Beisa oryx, hamadryas baboon, Soemmering's gazelle, and Salt's dik-dik.
Bird life: The 136 species of birds include two endemics.
Visitor facilities: Not yet developed. Hotel in Gewane.

Sanctuaries

Babille Elephant Sanctuary

Size: 6,982 sq km
Region: Harerge
Geographical location: South-east Ethiopia, 570 km west of Addis Ababa, south-east of Harar
Altitude: 1,000–1,788 m
Physical features: Volcanic and rocky; nearby is the Babille 'Valley of Marvels', filled with unusual volcanic formations where tall columns of black and red rock, withered and twisted by the elements, stand topped by loose, precariously balanced boulders.
Vegetation: Semi-arid open woodland.
Fauna: Number unknown. The sanctuary was created for the protection of the endemic subspecies of elephant, *Loxodonta africana orleansi*, and also contains black-maned lion, kudu, and wild ass.
Bird life: No information.
Visitor facilities: None.

Kuni-Muktar Mountain Nyala Sanctuary

Size: Not yet known
Region: Harerge
Geographical location: 350 km east of Addis Ababa, on Dire Dawa road eighteen km west of Asbe Teferi
Altitude: 1,800–3,030 m
Physical features: Two small hills with forested peaks.

Vegetation: Montane evergreen forest, *Juniperus/ Podocarpus*, high-altitude grassland, heather.
Fauna: The sanctuary was established to provide another conservation area for the endemic mountain nyala. There are also nineteen other species of mammal here, including Menelik's bushbuck.
Bird life: The twenty-four species of birds found here include four endemics.
Visitor facilities: No development yet.

Senkele Swayne's Hartebeest Sanctuary

Size: 54 sq km
Region: Shewa
Geographical location: 320 km south of Addis Ababa, on Shashemene-Sodo road
Altitude: 2,020–2120 m
Physical features: Largely undeveloped savannah.
Vegetation: Savannah, wooded grassland.
Fauna: The sanctuary was established to protect its once large resident population of Swayne's hartebeest, one of Ethiopia's endemic subspecies, whose numbers were sadly depleted during the recent civil war. The twelve other species resident here include oribi, Bohor reedbuck, and greater kudu.
Bird life: Ninety-one species.
Visitor facilities: No development yet.

Yabello Sanctuary

Size: 2,496 sq km
Region: Sidamo
Geographical location: 550 km south of Addis Ababa, on road to Moyale on Kenya border.
Altitude: 1,430–1,800 m
Physical features: The sanctuary is a dry savannah/ acacia bush area with some low hills and an area of juniper woodland nearby. The area is noted for its red soil.
Vegetation: Savannah, acacia bush.
Fauna: Originally established for the protection of Swayne's hartebeest, the sanctuary is also home to twenty-four other species of mammal, including greater and lesser kudu, gerenuk, and Burchell's zebra.
Bird life: The 194 species include three endemics, two of which are Stresemann's bush crow and the white-tailed swallow.
Visitor facilities: No development yet. Hotels in nearby Yabello town.

Animal Checklist

An asterisk (*) denotes an endemic species.

Mammals

INSECTIVORES
(Insectivora)
Four-toed Hedgehog
Desert Hedgehog
Rufous Elephant Shrew

BUSHBABIES, BABOONS, & MONKEYS
(Primates)
Guereza
Senegal Bushbaby
Anubis Baboon
Gelada Baboon*
Hamadryas Baboon
Yellow Baboon
Black & White Colobus Monkey
Blue Monkey
DeBrazza's Monkey
Grivet Monkey
Patas Monkey
Syke's Monkey
Vervet Monkey

PANGOLINS
(Pholidota)
Ground Pangolin

HARES & RABBITS
(Lagomorpha)
Fagan's Hare
Starck's Hare*
Crawshay's Hare
Abyssinian Hare

RODENTS
(Rodentia)
Geoffroy's Ground Squirrel
Unstriped Ground Squirrel
Huet's Bush Squirrel
Gambian Sun Squirrel
Crested Rat
North African Crested Porcupine
Common Molerat
Naked Molerat
Giant Molerat*

CARNIVORES
(Carnivora)
Ruppell's Sandfox

Pale Sandfox
Simien Fox*
Side-striped Jackal
Golden Jackal
Black-backed Jackal
African Hunting Dog
Bat-Eared Fox
Striped Polecat (Zorilla)
Ratel (Honey Badger)
Spotted-necked Otter
Cape Clawless (Menelik's) Otter
Abyssinian Genet
Common Genet
Rusty-spotted Genet
African Civet
Egyptian Mongoose
Slender (Lion-tailed) Mongoose
Marsh Mongoose
Banded Mongoose
White-tailed Mongoose
Southern Dwarf Mongoose
Somali Dwarf Mongoose
Libyan Striped Weasel
Aardwolf
Striped Hyena
Spotted Hyena
Lion
Leopard
Cheetah
Caracal
Serval
African Wild Cat

AARDVARK
(Orycteropodidae)
Aardvark

ELEPHANT
(Proboscidea)
African Elephant

HYRAX (DASSIE)
(Hyracoidea)
Rock Hyrax
Yellow-spotted Hyrax

ODD-TOED UNGULATES
(Perissodactyla)
African Wild Ass
Grevy's Zebra
Burchell's Zebra
Black Rhinoceros

EVEN-TOED UNGULATES
(Artiodactyla)
Bush Pig
Giant Forest Hog

Warthog
Hippopotamus
Giraffe
Bush Duiker
Salt's Dik-Dik
Guenther's Dik-Dik
Oribi
Beira
Klipspringer
Abyssinian Bushbuck
Menelik's Bushbuck*
Mountain Nyala*
Sitatunga
Lesser Kudu
Greater Kudu
Eland
Beisa Oryx
Roan
Waterbuck
White-eared Kob
Nile Lechwe
Bohor Reedbuck
Mountain Reedbuck
Tiang
Lelwel Hartebeest
Swayne's Hartebeest*
Tora Hartebeest
Dorcas Gazelle
Grant's Gazelle
Red-fronted Gazelle
Soemmering's Gazelle
Speke's Gazelle
Thomson's Gazelle
Dibatag
Gerenuk
Nubian Ibex
Walia Ibex*
Cape Buffalo

Birds

OSTRICH
(Struthionidae)
Ostrich

GREBES
(Podicipidae)
Little Grebe
Black-necked Grebe
Great Crested Grebe

PELICANS
(Pelecanidae)
Great White Pelican
Pink-backed Pelican

CORMORANTS
(Phalacrocoracidae)
White-necked Cormorant
Long-tailed Cormorant
Socotran Cormorant

DARTERS
(Anhingidae)
African Darter

HERONS, EGRETS, & BITTERNS
(Ardeidae)
Night Heron
White-backed Night Heron
Squacco Heron
Green-backed Heron
Black Heron
Reef Heron
Grey Heron
Black-headed Heron
Goliath Heron
Purple Heron
Cattle Egret
Great White Egret
Yellow-billed Egret
Little Egret
Little Bittern
Dwarf Bittern

HAMMERKOP
(Scopidae)
Hammerkop

STORKS
(Ciconiidae)
Whale-headed Stork
European White Stork
European Black Stork
Abdim's Stork
Woolly-necked Stork
Saddlebill Stork
Open-bill Stork
Marabou Stork
Yellow-billed Stork

IBISES & SPOONBILLS
(Threskiornithidae)
Sacred Ibis
Wattled Ibis*
Hadada Ibis
Glossy Ibis
African Spoonbill
European Spoonbill
Waldrapp

FLAMINGOS
(Phoenicopteridae)
Greater Flamingo
Lesser Flamingo

DUCKS & GEESE
(Anatidae)
Fulvous Tree Duck
White-faced Tree Duck
Ruddy Shelduck
Knob-billed Goose
Black Duck
Yellow-billed Duck
Red-billed Duck
Tufted Duck
Maccoa Duck
White-backed Duck
Blue-winged Goose*
Egyptian Goose
Spur-winged Goose
Pygmy Goose
Gadwall
Cape Wigeon
European Wigeon
European Mallard
European Pintail
European Teal
Hottentot Teal
Garganey
European Shoveler
Cape Shoveler
African Pochard
European Pochard
White-eyed Pochard

SECRETARY BIRD
(Sagittariidae)
Secretary Bird

VULTURES
(Accipitridae)
Egyptian Vulture
Hooded Vulture
White-backed Vulture
Ruppell's Griffon Vulture
Griffon Vulture
Lappet-faced Vulture
White-headed Vulture
Lammergeyer

BIRDS OF PREY
(Accipitridae)
Honey Buzzard
Grasshopper Buzzard
Lizard Buzzard
Common Buzzard
African Mountain Buzzard
Long-legged Buzzard
African Red-tailed Buzzard
Augur Buzzard
African Fish Eagle
European Snake Eagle
Brown Snake Eagle
Smaller Banded Snake Eagle
Lesser Spotted Eagle
Greater Spotted Eagle

Tawny Eagle
Imperial Eagle
Wahlberg's Eagle
Verreaux's Eagle
African Hawk Eagle
Booted Eagle
Ayres' Hawk Eagle
Long-crested Eagle
Crowned Eagle
Martial Eagle
Bateleur
African Cuckoo-Falcon
Dark Chanting Goshawk
Pale Chanting Goshawk
Gabar Goshawk
African Goshawk
Bat Hawk
African Harrier Hawk
European Marsh Harrier
Pallid Harrier
Montagu's Harrier
Black-shouldered Kite
Swallow-tailed Kite
Black Kite
Shikra
Great Sparrowhawk
Ovampo Sparrowhawk
European Sparrowhawk
Rufous-breasted Sparrowhawk
African Little Sparrowhawk
Levant Sparrowhawk

OSPREY
(Pandionidae)
Osprey

FALCONS
(Falconidae)
Pygmy Falcon
Red-footed Falcon
Red-headed Falcon
Eleonora's Falcon
Sooty Falcon
Lanner Falcon
Saker Falcon
Taita Falcon
Peregrine Falcon
European Lesser Kestrel
Greater Kestrel
Fox Kestrel
Common Kestrel
Grey Kestrel
European Hobby
African Hobby

FRANCOLINS & QUAILS
(Phasianidae)
Coqui Francolin

Crested Francolin
Grey-wing Francolin
Archer's Grey-wing Francolin
Harwood's Francolin*
Clapperton's Francolin
Chestnut-naped Francolin
Erckel's Francolin
Scaly Francolin
European Quail
Harlequin Quail
Blue Quail
Yellow-necked Spurfowl
Arabian Chukor
Sand Partridge
Stone Partridge

GUINEAFOWL
(Numididae)
Helmeted (Tufted) Guineafowl
Vulturine
Guineafowl

BUTTONQUAILS
(Turnicidae)
Buttonquail
Quail Plover

CRANES
(Gruidae)
European (Common) Crane
Wattled Crane
Demoiselle Crane
Crowned Crane

**CRAKES, GALLINULES, &
RAILS**
(Rallidae)
Corn Crake
African Crake
Little Crake
Lesser Spotted Crake
Spotted Crake
Black Crake
White-winged Crake
Red-chested Crake
Buff-spotted Crake
Purple Gallinule
Allen's Gallinule
Kaffir Rail
Rouget's Rail*
Lesser Moorhen
Moorhen
European Coot
Red-knobbed Coot

FINFOOTS
(Heliornithidae)
African Finfoot

BUSTARDS
(Otididae)
Kori Bustard

Arabian Bustard
Denham's Bustard
Heuglin's Bustard
Buff-crested Bustard
White-bellied (Senegal) Bustard
Black-bellied Bustard
Little Brown Bustard

JACANAS
(Jacanidae)
African Jacana
Lesser Jacana

PAINTED SNIPES
(Rostratulidae)
Painted Snipe

LAPWINGS & PLOVERS
(Charadriidae)
Long-toed Lapwing
Crowned Lapwing
Spur-winged Plover
Blackhead Plover
Black-winged Plover
Wattled Plover
Spot-breasted Plover*
Sociable Plover
Golden Plover
Grey Plover
Ringed Plover
Little Ringed Plover
Kittlitz's Sand Plover
Three-banded Plover
Kentish Plover
Mongolian Sand Plover
Grand Sand Plover

SANDPIPERS & SNIPES
(Scolopacidae)
Marsh Sandpiper
Wood Sandpiper
Green Sandpiper
Common Sandpiper
Terek Sandpiper
Curlew Sandpiper
Great Snipe
European Common Snipe
African Snipe
Jack Snipe
Whimbrel
Curlew
Black-tailed Godwit
Bar-tailed Godwit
Greenshank
Redshank
Spotted Redshank
Turnstone
Dunlin
Long-toed Stint
Little Stint
Temminck's Stint

Sanderling
Ruff

AVOCETS & STILTS
(Recurvirostridae)
Avocet
Black-winged Stilt
European Oyster-Catcher

**STONE CURLEWS
(THICKNEES)**
(Burhinidae)
Stone Curlew
Senegal Thicknee
Spotted Thicknee

COURSERS & PRATINCOLES
(Glareolidae)
Cream-coloured Courser
Temminck's Courser
Two-banded Courser
Heuglin's Courser
Violet-tipped Courser
Pratincole
Madagascar Pratincole
Black-winged Pratincole
White-collared Pratincole
Egyptian Plover

GULLS & TERNS
(Laridae)
Black-headed Gull
Slender-billed Gull
Grey-headed Gull
Black-backed Gull
Herring Gull
Gull-billed Tern
Caspian Tern
Whiskered Tern
White-winged Black Tern
Black Tern

SKIMMERS
(Rynchopidae)
African Skimmer

SANDGROUSE
(Pteroclididae)
Spotted Sandgrouse
Chestnut-bellied Sandgrouse
Black-faced Sandgrouse
Yellow-throated Sandgrouse
Lichtenstein's Sandgrouse
Four-banded Sandgrouse

DOVES & PIGEONS
(Columbidae)
Turtle Dove
Pink-breasted Dove
Red-eyed Dove
Mourning Dove

Vinaceous Dove
Ring-necked Dove
Pink-headed Dove
White-winged Dove
Laughing Dove
Namaqua Dove
Tambourine Dove
Blue-spotted Wood Dove
Emerald-spotted Wood Dove
Black-billed Blue-spotted Wood
Dove
Lemon Dove
White-collared Pigeon*
Speckled Pigeon
Olive Pigeon
Green Pigeon
Bruce's Green Pigeon

LOVEBIRDS & PARROTS
(Psittacidae)
Black-winged Lovebird*
Red-headed Lovebird
Yellow-fronted Parrot*
Brown Parrot
Orange-bellied Parrot
Rose-ringed Parrakeet

TURACOS
(Musophagidae)
White-cheeked Turaco
Prince Ruspoli's
Turaco*
Bare-faced
Go-Away-Bird
White-bellied
Go-Away-Bird
Eastern Grey Plantain-Eater

CUCKOOS & COUCALS
(Cuculidae)
Great Spotted Cuckoo
Black-and-white Cuckoo
Levaillant's Cuckoo
Red-chested Cuckoo
Black Cuckoo
European Cuckoo
Klaas' Cuckoo
Didric Cuckoo
Emerald Cuckoo
Black Coucal
Blue-headed Coucal
Senegal Coucal
White-browed Coucal
Yellowbill

OWLS
(Tytonidae)
Cape Grass Owl
Barn Owl
Scops Owl
White-faced Scops

Owl
Cape Eagle Owl
Spotted Eagle Owl
Verreaux's Eagle Owl
Pel's Fishing Owl
Pearl-spotted Owlet
Little Owl
African Wood Owl
Long-eared Owl
Short-eared Owl
African Marsh Owl

NIGHTJARS
(Caprimulgidae)
Egyptian Nightjar
European Nightjar
Nubian Nightjar
Northern Dusky Nightjar
Donaldson-Smith's Nightjar
Abyssinian Nightjar
Plain Nightjar
Star-spotted Nightjar
Freckled Nightjar
Slender-tailed Nightjar
Long-tailed Nightjar
White-tailed Nightjar
Standard-winged Nightjar

SWIFTS
(Apodidae)
Alpine Swift
Mottled Swift
European Swift
Nyanza Swift
Scarce Swift
Horus Swift
White-rumped Swift
Little Swift
Palm Swift

MOUSEBIRDS
(Coliidae)
Speckled Mousebird
Blue-naped Mousebird

TROGONS
(Trogonidae)
Narina's Trogon

KINGFISHERS
(Alcedinidae)
Giant Kingfisher
Pied Kingfisher
Half-collared Kingfisher
Malachite Kingfisher
Pygmy Kingfisher
Woodland Kingfisher
Striped Kingfisher
White-collared Kingfisher
Grey-headed Kingfisher

BEE-EATERS
(Meropidae)
European Bee-eater
Blue-cheeked Bee-eater
Little Green Bee-eater
Carmine Bee-eater
White-throated
Bee-eater
Little Bee-eater
Blue-breasted Bee-eater
Somali Bee-eater
Red-throated Bee-eater
Swallow-tailed Bee-eater

ROLLERS
(Coraciidae)
European Roller
Abyssinian Roller
Lilac-breasted Roller
Rufous-crowned Roller
Broad-billed Roller

HOOPOES
(Upupidae)
African Hoopoe

**WOOD HOOPOES &
SCIMITARBILLS**
(Phoeniculidae)
Green Wood Hoopoe
Violet Wood Hoopoe
Black Wood Hoopoe
Abyssinian Scimitarbill

HORNBILLS
(Bucerotidae)
Grey Hornbill
Red-billed Hornbill
Von der Decken's Hornbill
Yellow-billed Hornbill
Hemprich's Hornbill
Crowned Hornbill
Silvery-cheeked Hornbill
Abyssinian Ground Hornbill

BARBETS
(Capitonidae)
Double-toothed Barbet
Black-billed Barbet
Vieillot's Barbet
Banded Barbet
Black-throated Barbet
Red-fronted Barbet
Yellow-breasted Barbet
D'Arnaud's Barbet
Red-and-Yellow Barbet
Yellow-fronted Tinkerbird
Red-fronted Tinkerbird

HONEYGUIDES
(Indicatoridae)
Scaly-throated Honeyguide

323

Black-throated Honeyguide
Lesser Honeyguide
Cassin's Honeyguide
Walberg's Honeyguide

WOODPECKERS
(Picidae)
Nubian Woodpecker
Little Spotted Woodpecker
Cardinal Woodpecker
Golden-backed Woodpecker*
Brown-backed Woodpecker
Grey Woodpecker
Bearded Woodpecker
European Wryneck
Red-breasted Wryneck

PITTAS
(Pittidae)
African Pitta

LARKS
(Alandidae)
Singing Bush Lark
Friedmann's Bush Lark
Rufous-naped Lark
Flappet Lark
Collared Lark
Fawn-coloured Lark
Gillett's Lark
Pink-breasted Lark
Degodi Lark*
Sidamo Long-clawed Lark*
Hoopoe Lark
Sand Lark
Short-toed Lark
Red-capped Lark
Rufous Short-toed Lark
Masked Lark
Short-tailed Lark
Calandra Lark
White-fronted Sparrow Lark
Chestnut-backed Sparrow Lark
Chestnut-headed Sparrow Lark
Crested Lark
Short-crested Lark

MARTINS & SWALLOWS
(Hirundinidae)
European Sand Martin
Banded Martin
African Sand Martin
European Crag Martin
African Rock Martin
House Martin
Rough-winged Swallow
White-headed Rough-winged
Swallow
European Swallow
Red-chested Swallow
Wire-tailed Swallow

Ethiopian Swallow
White-tailed Swallow*
Mosque Swallow
Red-rumped Swallow
Striped Swallow
Grey-rumped Swallow

WAGTAILS, PIPITS, &
LONGCLAWS
(Motacillidae)
Yellow Wagtail
Grey Wagtail
Mountain Wagtail
White Wagtail
African Pied Wagtail
Tawny Pipit
Richard's Pipit
Plain-backed Pipit
Long-billed Pipit
Little Tawny Pipit
Tree Pipit
Red-throated Pipit
Golden Pipit
Abyssinian Longclaw*

CUCKOO SHRIKES
(Campephagidae)
White-breasted Cuckoo Shrike
Red-shouldered Cuckoo Shrike
Grey Cuckoo Shrike
Black Cuckoo Shrike

BULBULS
(Pycnonotidae)
White-vented Bulbul
Zanzibar Sombre Greenbul
Yellow-throated Leaflove
Northern Brownbul

HELMET SHRIKES
(Prionopidae)
White-crowned Shrike
Crested Helmet Shrike

SHRIKES
(Laniidae)
Rosy-patched Shrike
Red-naped Bush Shrike
Sulphur-breasted Bush Shrike
Grey-headed Bush Shrike
Red-backed Shrike
Lesser Grey Shrike
Great Grey Shrike
Puffback
Woodchat Shrike
Nubian Shrike
Fiscal Shrike
Grey-backed Fiscal
Taita Fiscal
Somali Fiscal
Pringle's Puffback

Northern Brubru
Blackcap Bush Shrike
Three-streaked Bush Shrike
Black-headed Bush Shrike
Tropical Boubou
Slate-coloured Boubou
Black-headed Gonolek

THRUSHES, WHEATEARS, &
CHATS
(Turdinae)
Rock Thrush
Blue Rock Thrush
Little Rock Thrush
Song Thrush
African Thrush
Olive Thrush
Bare-eyed Thrush
Ground-scraper Thrush
Abyssinian Ground Thrush
Common Wheatear
Somali Wheatear
Pied Wheatear
Black-eared Wheatear
Desert Wheatear
Red-rumped Wheatear
Isabelline Wheatear
White-rumped Wheatear
Abyssinian Black Wheatear
Red-breasted Wheatear
Whinchat
Stonechat
Black-tailed Rock Chat
Brown-tailed Rock Chat
Sombre Rock Chat
Red-tailed Chat
Hill Chat
Cliffchat
White-winged Cliffchat*
White-fronted Black Chat
Ruppell's Chat*
Red-capped Robin Chat
Ruppell's Robin Chat
White-browed Robin Chat
White-crowned Robin Chat
Snowy-headed Robin Chat
Black Redstart
European Redstart
Black Bush Robin
White-winged Scrub Robin
White-throated Robin
Rufous Warbler
Spotted Morning Warbler
Nightingale
Sprosser
Bluethroat

BABBLERS & CHATTERERS
(Timaliidae)
Abyssinian Hill Babbler
Brown Babbler

White-headed Babbler
Scaly Babbler
Dusky Babbler
White-rumped Babbler
Fulvous Chatterer
Rufous Chatterer
Scaly Chatterer
Abyssinian Catbird*

WARBLERS
(Sylviidae)
Little Rush Warbler
Cinnamon Bracken Warbler
Bamboo Warbler
Fan-tailed Warbler
Grasshopper Warbler
Savi's Warbler
River Warbler
Sedge Warbler
Marsh Warbler
Reed Warbler
Southern Great Reed Warbler
Great Reed Warbler
African Reed Warbler
Swamp Warbler
Yellow Flycatcher-Warbler
African Moustached Warbler
Icterine Warbler
Olive-tree Warbler
Upcher's Warbler
Olivaceous Warbler
Barred Warbler
Orphean Warbler
Garden Warbler
Desert Warbler
Ruppell's Warbler
Ménétriés's Warbler
Willow Warbler
Bonelli's Warbler
Brown Woodland Warbler
Red-wing Warbler
Cricket Warbler
Red-faced Warbler
Buff-bellied Warbler
Grey Wren Warbler
Blackcap
Whitethroat
Lesser Whitethroat
Chiffchaff
Red-faced Cisticola
Singing Cisticola
Rattling Cisticola
Winding Cisticola
Stout Cisticola
Croaking Cisticola
Ashy Cisticola
Tiny Cisticola
Red-pate Cisticola
Siffling Cisticola
Foxy Cisticola
Zitting Cisticola

Desert Cisticola
Black-backed Cisticola
Boran Cisticola
Striped-backed Prinia
Tawny-flanked Prinia
Pale Prinia
Black-breasted Apalis
Grey-backed Camaroptera
Yellow-bellied Eremomela
Yellow-vented Eremomela
Green-backed Eremomela
Crombec
Red-faced Crombec
Somali Long-billed Crombec
Short-billed Crombec
Banded Tit-Flycatcher
Brown Tit-Flycatcher

FLYCATCHERS
(Muscicapinae)
European Spotted Flycatcher
Gambaga Dusky Flycatcher
Dusky Flycatcher
Grey Tit-Flycatcher
Collared Flycatcher
Abyssinian Slaty Flycatcher
Black Flycatcher
Grey Flycatcher
Pale Flycatcher
Yellow-bellied Flycatcher
Grey-headed Puff-back
Flycatcher
Pygmy Puff-back Flycatcher
Black-headed Puff-back
Flycatcher
White-tailed Crested Flycatcher
Paradise Flycatcher
Wattle-eye Flycatcher
Silverbird

TITS
(Paridae)
Grey Tit
Black Tit
White-backed Black Tit*
Mouse-coloured Penduline Tit
Sennar Penduline Tit

SPOTTED CREEPER
(Salpornithidae)
Spotted Creeper

SUNBIRDS
(Nectariniidae)
Violet-backed Sunbird
Collared Sunbird
Pygmy Long-tailed Sunbird
Pygmy Sunbird
Olive Sunbird
Amethyst Sunbird
Scarlet-chested Sunbird

Hunter's Sunbird
Variable Sunbird
Olive-bellied Sunbird
Tsavo Purple-banded Sunbird
Mariqua Sunbird
Shining Sunbird
Copper Sunbird
Tacazze Sunbird
Red-chested Sunbird
Beautiful Sunbird
Smaller Black-bellied Sunbird
Malachite Sunbird
Bronze Sunbird

WHITE-EYES
(Zosteropidae)
White-breasted White-eye
Yellow White-eye
Green White-eye

BUNTINGS
(Emberizidae)
Cinerous Bunting
European Ortoland Bunting
Cretzschman's Bunting
Somali Golden-breasted Bunting
Brown-rumped Bunting
Cinnamon-breasted Bunting
House Bunting

CANARIES & SEED-EATERS
(Fringillidae)
Yellow-fronted Canary
White-bellied Canary
Grosbeak Canary
Yellow-crowned Canary
Yellow-rumped Seed-eater
White-rumped Seed-eater
Yellow-throated Seed-eater*
Streaky Seed-eater
Brown-rumped Seed-eater
Streaky-headed Seed-eater
Ankober Seed-eater*
Salvadori's Seed-eater*
White-throated
Seed-eater
African Citril
Black-headed Siskin*

WAXBILLS
(Estrildidae)
Yellow-bellied Waxbill
Fawn-breasted Waxbill
Crimson-rumped Waxbill
Black-rumped Waxbill
Common Waxbill
Black-cheeked Waxbill
Zebra Waxbill
Green-backed Twinspot
Abyssinian Crimsonwing
Cut-throat

Green-winged Pytilia
Orange-winged Pytilia
Red-winged Pytilia
Purple Grenadier
Red-cheeked Cordon-bleu
Blue-capped Cordon-bleu
Black-faced Firefinch
Bar-breasted Firefinch
Red-billed Firefinch
Jameson's Firefinch
African Firefinch
Quailfinch
Silverbill
Grey-headed Silverbill
Magpie Mannikin
Black-and-White Mannikin
Bronze Mannikin

WHYDAHS, WEAVERS, &
SPARROWS
(Ploceidae)
Pin-tailed Whydah
Fischer's Whydah
Steel-blue Whydah
Paradise Whydah
Broad-tailed Paradise Whydah
Indigo-Bird
Grosbeak Weaver
Baglafecht Weaver
Little Weaver
Golden Palm Weaver
Ruppell's Weaver
Northern Masked Weaver
Masked Weaver
Vitelline Masked Weaver
Speke's Weaver
Black-headed Weaver
Jubaland Weaver
Yellow-backed Weaver
Chestnut Weaver
Compact Weaver
Spectacled Weaver
Black-necked Weaver

Red-headed Weaver
Parasitic Weaver
White-billed Buffalo Weaver
Red-billed Buffalo Weaver
White-headed Buffalo Weaver
Stripe-breasted Sparrow Weaver
Chestnut-crowned Sparrow
Weaver
Donaldson-Smith's Sparrow
Weaver
Grey-headed Social Weaver
Black-capped Social Weaver
Speckle-fronted Weaver
Rufous Sparrow
Somali Sparrow
Grey-headed Sparrow
Swainson's Sparrow
Parrot-billed Sparrow
Sudan Golden Sparrow
Chestnut Sparrow
Pale Rock Sparrow
Cardinal Quelea
Red-headed Quelea
Red-billed Quelea
Yellow-crowned Bishop
Yellow Bishop
Black Bishop
Black-winged Red Bishop
Red Bishop
White-winged Widowbird
Red-collared Widowbird
Fan-tailed Widowbird
Yellow-shouldered Widowbird
Yellow-spotted Petronia
Bush Petronia

STARLINGS
(Sturnidae)
Stuhlmann's Starling
Red-wing Starling
Somali Chestnut-wing Starling
Slender-billed Chestnut-wing
Starling
White-billed Starling*

Bristle-crowned Starling
Splendid Glossy Starling
Lesser Blue-eared Starling
Blue-eared Glossy Starling
Ruppell's Long-tailed Glossy
Starling
Violet-backed Starling
Sharpe's Starling
Magpie Starling
Fischer's Starling
White-crowned Starling
Chestnut-bellied Starling
Shelley's Starling
Superb Starling
Golden-breasted Starling
Wattled Starling
European Starling

OXPECKERS
(Buphagidae)
Yellow-billed Oxpecker
Red-billed Oxpecker

ORIOLES
(Oriolidae)
Golden Oriole
African Golden Oriole
Black-headed Oriole
Black-headed Forest Oriole*

DRONGOS
(Dicruridae)
Drongo

CROWS
(Corvidae)
Stresemann's Bush Crow*
Pied Crow
Brown-necked Raven
Fan-tailed Raven
Thick-billed Raven*
Cape Rook
Piapiac
Chough

Wildlife Profile

(Amharic name, if any, is indicated in parentheses after the species' Latin name.)

Giant molerat, *Tachyoryctes macrocephalus* (Filfal): Confined only to the high meadows and sub-alpine moorland of the Bale Mountains, but numbers are high. Only seen when it emerges to gather food from around its hole when the temperatures rise. Favoured food for the Simien fox and many birds of prey. Bale Mountains National Park.

Porcupine, *Hystrix Cristata* (Jart): Widely distributed in many habitats, including open and wooded grassland and forests. Nocturnal. Abijatta-Shalla, Awash, Bale, Gambella, Mago, Nechisar, Omo, Simien, and Yangudi-Rassa national parks; Yabello and Babille sanctuaries.

Grivet monkey, *Cercopithecus aethiops* (Tota): Wooded grassland, at the edges of forest and in forest, even small patches along rivers. It does not live in trees as much as other monkeys and sometimes can be found feeding in grassland a short distance from trees. Also found near villages and cultivated areas. Abijatta-Shalla, Awash, Gambella, Simien, and Yangudi-Rassa national parks. Nearly indistinguishable from the grivet is the **vervet monkey**, which is widespread throughout the south of Ethiopia and commonly found in Bale, Nechisar, Mago, and Omo national parks; Yabello Sanctuary.

Gelada baboon, *Theropithecus gelada* (Chilada): Endemic. Confined to the rocky highlands and alpine grasslands to the north, west, and east of the Rift Valley, usually at elevation of 2,500 m and over. Simien Mountains National Park, also often seen near the road to the Debre Libanos monastery.

Anubis baboon, *Papio anubis* (Zinjero): Most common species of baboon in Ethiopia, found in good numbers in many areas of forest, open grassland, and wooded grassland. It can forage far from trees, but prefers some for safety from enemies. Often seen in hilly areas with steep rocks where a troop can sleep safely at night. Not found in very dry areas. Abijatta-Shalla, Awash, Bale, Gambella, Mago, Nechisar, Omo, and Simien national parks; Yabello Sanctuary.

Hamadryas baboon, *Papio hamadryas* (Neche zinjero): Found only in drier areas at comparatively low altitudes, where it generally roosts on rocky cliff ledges. Awash, Simien, and Yangudi-Rassa national parks; Babille and Senkele sanctuaries. In Awash National Park, Anubis and hamadryas baboons hybridize.

Colobus monkey, *Colobus abyssinicus* (Gureza): Fairly widely distributed — although endangered by hunting for its skin — in forest areas, wooded grassland with big trees, small patches of forest along river valleys. Also known to be found on the tops of hills far from large forest areas. Abijatta-Shalla, Awash, Bale, Gambella, Mago, Nechisar, Omo, and Simien national parks.

Zorilla, *Ictonyx striatus* (Faro): Widespread, occurring in habitats from open grassland to high mountains. Abijatta-Shalla, Awash, Bale, Mago, and Omo national parks.

Ratel, *Mellivora capensis* (Kefo-defi): Seldom seen but widely distributed throughout most types of habitat. Awash, Bale, Gambella, Mago, Omo, and Simien national parks; Yabello Sanctuary.

Clawless otter, *Aonyx capensis* (Akusta): Also known as Menelik's otter. Found in large, slow rivers in grassland areas or quiet lakes, also may be seen some distance from the water. Originally recorded from Lake Tana but not known in any conservation area.

Spotted-necked otter, *Lutra maculicollis* (Akusta): Also known as river otter. Prefers large streams or rivers and lakes, or even mountain streams. Will not move far from the water. Awash National Park.

African hunting dog, *Lycaon pictus* (Tekula): Frequents open areas, such as open and wooded grassland, also seen in thick forest such as is found in the Bale Mountains. Not often seen because there are few packs and each covers a large area. Awash, Bale, Gambella, Mago, and Omo national parks.

Bat-eared fox, *Otocyon megalotis* (Joro sefi kebero): Open and dry places, such as semi-desert, dry short grassland, and wooded grassland. Chiefly nocturnal. Abijatta-Shalla, Awash, Mago, Nechisar, Omo, and Yangudi-Rassa national parks; Yabello Sanctuary.

Simien fox, *Canis simiensis* (Key kebero): Also known as the Simien jackal, Abyssinian wolf, or red jackal. Endemic. Confined to mountain plateaux between 3,000 and 4,500 m with dense tree heather and thickets, intermixed with bogs and swamps with sedge grass and giant lobelias. Fairly common in the Bale Mountains, becoming increasingly rare in Simien. Also found in other small areas between the two parks where there are not too many people. Bale Mountains and Simien Mountains national park.

Side-striped jackal, *Canis adustus* (Kebero): Inhabits savannahs and plains, prefers regions with plentiful cover of bush or open woodland. In hills up to 2,000 m. Mainly nocturnal. Babille Elephant Sanctuary.

Black-backed jackal, *Canis mesomelas* (Kebero): Savannah, bush, light woodland with good cover preferred to open plains and semi-desert. Up to 2,000 m. Mainly nocturnal, although can be seen by day. Abijatta-Shalla, Awash, Mago, Nechisar, Omo, and Yangudi-Rassa national parks; Yabello Sanctuary.

Common jackal, *Canis aureus* (Kebero): Also known as golden jackal, Asiatic jackal, or oriental jackal. Widely distributed in open country with good cover in form of trees, bushes, thickets, copses, high grass, rocks, ravines, vineyards, gardens, fields. Follows human settlements. In mountains up to 2,000 m or more. Mainly nocturnal, although can be seen by day. Abijatta-Shalla, Awash, Bale, Mago, Nechisar, Omo, Simien, and Yangudi-Rassa national parks; Senkele Sanctuary.

Civet, *Viverra civetta* (Tirigne): Living in patches of thick bush of grass, often near water, civet is found in all habitats, from quite dry and open grasslands to thick forest and high moorland. Abijatta-Shalla, Awash, Bale, Gambella, Mago, Nechisar, Omo, and Yangudi-Rassa national parks; Yabello Sanctuary.

Abyssinian genet, *Genetta abyssinica* (Shelemlem shelemetimat): Widely distributed in the highlands, open dry country with good ground cover, in plains and mountains; also near villages. Nocturnal. Awash National Park.

Common genet, *Genetta genetta* (Shelemlem shelemetimat): Also known as small-spotted genet. Favours open districts, from dry savannah to semi-desert, with sufficient ground cover. In mountains up to 2,500 m. Nocturnal. Mago, Nechisar, Omo, and Yangudi-Rassa national parks.

Rusty-spotted genet, *Genetta rubiginosa* (Shelemlem shelemetimat): Also known as large-spotted genet. Prefers forest edges, forest clearings, moist savannahs, bush country, agricultural regions, reed thickets, long grass. Favours water and swampy areas. Nocturnal. Bale Mountains National Park.

Marsh mongoose, *Atilax paludinosus mitis* (Shelemetimat): Chiefly nocturnal. Inhabits swamps, marshes, and other wet areas in savannah and forest, up to 2,000 m. Uses hiding places in holes in banks, hollow trees, thickets of tall grass, reeds, and rushes. Awash, Bale, and Gambella national parks.

Somali dwarf mongoose, *Helogale hirtula* (Shelemetimat); and **southern dwarf mongoose,** *Helogale parvula* (Shelemetimat): Prefers savannah and bush country with termite and ant hills, burrows, fallen trees, stone heaps, rock piles, and other hiding places as living quarters. Awash, Abijatta-Shalla, Gambella, Mago, Nechisar, and Omo national parks; Yabello Sanctuary.

Lion-tailed mongoose, *Herpestes sanguineus* (Shelemetimat): Also known as slender mongoose. Widespread over all types of country from deserts to mountains to about 3,000 m. Dense cover and proximity to water preferred. Sometimes follows settlements and may occur in villages and near towns. Abijatta-Shalla, Awash, Bale, Gambella, Mago, Nechisar, and Omo national parks; Yabello Sanctuary.

Egyptian mongoose, *Herpestes ichneunon* (Shelemetimat): Habitat varies but includes semi-desert, moist and dry savannah, steppes, and mountains up to 2,000 m. Prefers vicinity of water and does not avoid vicinity of villages. Awash, Bale, and Nechisar national parks.

Banded mongoose, *Mungos mungo* (Shelemetimat): Common in dry and moist savannahs, prefers vicinity of water, avoids closed forests. Babille Sanctuary.

White-tailed mongoose, *Ichneumia albicauda* (Faro): Inhabits dry and moist savannahs, dense bush, forest edges, and other areas rich in cover — often near water and sometimes near villages. Mainly nocturnal. Abijatta-Shalla, Awash, Bale, Mago, Nechisar, Omo, and Yangudi-Rassa national parks.

Aardwolf, *Proteles cristatus* (Kemer-jib): Nocturnal. Found in dry areas of grassland and bushland, not in mountains or forest. Common in Awash, also Gambella, Mago, Omo, and Yangudi-Rassa national parks; Yabello Sanctuary.

Striped hyena, *Hyaena hyaena* (Shilemlem jib): Rarer and less widely distributed than the spotted hyena. Mainly nocturnal. Favours dry, semi-desert areas, usually open or wooded grassland. Awash, Mago, Omo, Yangudi-Rassa national parks; Yabello Sanctuary.

Spotted hyena, *Crocuta crocuta* (Tera jib): Very widespread. Prefers semi-desert to moist savannah, not in closed forest or very wet areas. Often found around towns and villages. Predominantly nocturnal. Abijatta-Shalla, Awash, Bale, Gambella, Mago, Nechisar, Omo, Simien, and Yangudi-Rassa national parks; Senkele and Yabello sanctuaries.

Cheetah, *Acinonyx jubatus* (Aboshemane): Usually prefers open grassland but also can be found where there are a few trees or some patches of bush. Can live in very dry areas without water and roam over large areas. Awash, Mago, Omo, and Yangudi-Rassa national parks; Senkele Sanctuary.

Serval, *Felis serval* (Aner): Found in all types of habitat, from open and wooded grassland to gallery forest and alpine moorland up to 3,000 m. Although widely distributed, it is seldom seen as it prefers thick vegetation and is mainly nocturnal in habit. Proximity to water is also a necessity. Abijatta-Shalla, Awash, Bale, Gambella, Mago, Omo, Simien, and Yangudi-Rassa national parks; Yabello Sanctuary.

Caracal, *Felis caracal* (Dalganbesa): Mainly nocturnal, but also hunts by day. Widely distributed. Can climb trees, but usually found on the ground in wooded and open grassland areas. Likes thick bush, rocks, or hills in which to hide by day. Not found in thick forest. Abijatta-Shalla, Awash, Bale, Gambella, Mago, Nechisar, Omo, Simien, and Yangudi-Rassa national parks.

Leopard, *Panthera pardus* (Nebir): Active mainly by night, but also in the early morning and evening. Adept at climbing trees, it lives in a wide range of habitats from dense forest to arid desert, as long as there are places for it to hide by day. In Ethiopia the species has been practically exterminated because of continued hunting, but it has been seen in Abijatta-Shalla, Awash, Bale, Gambella, Mago, Nechisar, Omo, Simien, and Yangudi-Rassa national parks; Senkele Sanctuary.

Lion, *Panthera leo* (Anbessa): Found in all habitats in Ethiopia, from alpine moorland to very dry areas. Although numbers and range have been greatly reduced owing to indiscriminate hunting, it has been seen in Awash, Bale, Gambella, Mago, Nechisar, Omo, and Yangudi-Rassa national parks and Senkele Sanctuary. Most common in Harerge and the south-western regions near the Kenya and Sudan borders.

.

Hippopotamus, *Hippopotamus amphibius* (Gumare): Usually seen in the water, lying on river banks, or on sandbanks in the river by day. Inhabits small to large waters with flat banks and sand banks, bordering rich grass plains. Dense high reed beds and forested banks are avoided, and mothers with young also avoid strong currents and rocky shores. Needs water temperatures of 18°–35°C. Awash, Gambella, Mago, Nechisar, Omo, and Yangudi-Rassa national parks.

Giant forest hog, *Hylochoerus meinertzhageni* (Yedur assama): Does not live in burrows. Mainly nocturnal. Usually found in forests with plenty of thick bush near the ground or on open grassland bordering the forest edge. Fond of bathing and sleeping in muddy or sandy wet, cool places, like small stream beds. Bale and Gambella national parks.

Bushpig, *Potamochoerus porcus* (Assama): Lives in thick forest and bush areas, as well as in bush and forest along river banks. May move some distance from bush or forest at night when feeding. Mainly nocturnal. Access to water preferred. Bale, Gambella, Mago, Nechisar, Omo, and Simien national parks.

Warthog, *Phacochoerus aethiopicus* (Kerkero): Widespread and common in forest, wooded grassland, and open grassland. Prefers treeless open plains and light savannahs, avoiding dense cover or steep slopes. Up to 2,500 m in mountains. Likes water for drinking and bathing but can do without if necessary. Usually favours short grass for feeding, so is less common where grasses grow very tall. Abijatta-Shalla, Awash, Bale, Gambella, Mago, Nechisar, Omo, Yangudi-Rassa national parks; Senkele and Yabello sanctuaries.

Giraffe, *Giraffa camelopardalis* (Kechine): Frequents more open areas, usually bush and tree savannahs — especially thorn acacias — up to 2,000 m from sparsely wooded grasslands to thickly overgrown savannah. Nubian variety found in Gambella National Park; reticulated variety in Mago and Omo national parks.

Lelwel hartebeest, *Alcelaphus buselaphus lelwel* (Key korke): Inhabits open plains and savannah woodland. Gambella, Mago, and Omo national parks.

Swayne's hartebeest, *Alcelaphus buselaphus swaynei* (Korke): Endemic and rare. Favours fairly dry open plains and savannah woodland. Found only in Awash and Nechisar national parks; Senkele and Yabello sanctuaries.

Tora hartebeest, *Alcelaphus buselaphus tora* (Korke): Found in open, bushed, and wooded grassland, also at the edge of swamp areas, but never in forest. Common in north-west Ethiopia from the Blue Nile northwards to Eritrea, but not found in any conservation areas.

Tiang, *Damaliscus korrigum* (Tikur korke): Found in open grassland, also in bushed, wooded, and swamp grassland. Gambella, Mago, and Omo national parks.

Common or **grey duiker,** *Sylvicapra grimmia* (Midako): Also known as bush duiker. Found in all habitats, from forest to alpine moorland, as well as the more usual bushed grassland and forest. Largely nocturnal; though widely distributed, is not very often seen during the day unless disturbed. Abijatta-Shalla, Awash, Bale, Gambella, Mago, Nechisar, Omo, Simien, and Yangudi-Rassa national parks; Yabello Sanctuary.

Klipspringer, *Oreotragus oreotragus* (Ses): Widely distributed. Lives only in rocky areas on hills, mountains, and escarpments, with little vegetation apart from tufts of grass and small bushes and trees growing between the rocks. Abijatta-Shalla, Awash, Bale, Mago, Nechisar, Omo, Simien, and Yangudi-Rassa national parks.

Oribi, *Ourebia ourebi* (Feko): Inhabits grassland and wooded grassland, usually not far from water. Abijatta-Shalla, Gambella, Mago, and Omo national parks; Senkele Sanctuary.

Salt's dik-dik, *Madoqua saltiana* (Enshu): Inhabits often very dry bush and bushed grassland areas. Awash and Yangudi-Rassa national parks.

Guenther's dik-dik, *Madoque guentheri* (Enshu): Prefers bush and bushed grassland areas, often very dry. Needs low, thick undergrowth in which to hide and feed. Abijatta-Shalla, Mago, Nechisar, and Omo national parks; Yabello Sanctuary.

Phillips's dik-dik, *Madoqua phillipsi* (Enshu): Widely distributed in the low-lying arid country of eastern Ethiopia. Typically inhabits dry thorn scrub.

.

White-eared kob, *Kobus kob leucotis* (Nech joro korke): Found only in open and wooded grassland and riverine flood plains in a small area of Ethiopia, on the western border. Gambella National Park.

Nile lechwe, *Kobus megaceros*: Habitat consists of swampy areas bordering the Baro and Akobo rivers in western Ethiopia. Feeds on lush grass of the flood plains bordering the swamps. Gambella National Park.

Defassa waterbuck, *Kobus defassa* (Defarsa): Common and widespread; lives in a variety of habitats ranging from swamps and riverine forests to fairly open savannah woodland. Seldom occurs far from water. Awash, Gambella, Mago, Nechisar, Omo, and Yangudi-Rassa national parks.

Common waterbuck, *Kobus ellipsiprymnus* (Defarsa): Less common than the Defassa. Inhabits grass savannahs with bushveld or gallery forests or woodland patches as night refuge, with nearby standing water for daily drinking. Known to occur only in the region of the Wabi Shebele River and in neighbouring areas of south-eastern Ethiopia.

Bohor reedbuck, *Redunca redunca* (Bihor): Generally frequents areas of grassland and open savannah woodland within easy reach of water. Abijatta-Shalla, Bale, and Gambella national parks; Senkele Sanctuary.

Mountain reedbuck, *Redunca fulvurofula* (Yedega bihor): Usually found on rocky mountain tops where there are areas of short grass. Comparatively rare. Abijatta-Shalla, Awash, Mago, Nechisar, and Omo national parks.

Dibatag, *Ammodorcas clarkei*: Rare. Typical habitat consists of very dry, hot areas of low thorn bushes or open grassland, usually far from water. Occurs in the Ogaden in the region of the Ethiopia-Somalia border and there have been unconfirmed reports of its presence between the northern end of Lake Turkana and Chew Bahir near the Ethiopia–Kenya border. Found in no conservation areas.

Soemmering's gazelle, *Gazella soemmeringi* (Yemeda-fiyel): Normally favours dry, open grassland areas, which may have bushes or acacia scrub. Sometimes found among rocky hills and areas of scattered trees or thorn scrub. Very common in Awash and Yangudi-Rassa national parks.

Grant's gazelle, *Gazella granti* (Rejim kend yemeda-fiyel): Typically found in open and bushed grassland and plains. Abijatta-Shalla Lakes National Park is the northern limit of the Grant's gazelle in Africa. Also found in Mago, Nechisar, and Omo national parks and Yabello Sanctuary.

Gerenuk, *Litocranius walleri* (Angete-rejime): Inhabits very dry, thorn-bush areas or desert. Water not essential. Mago and Yangudi-Rassa national parks; Yabello Sanctuary.

Roan, *Hippotragus equinus* (Chile-balegame): Favours open, wooded, and sometimes bushed grassland. Nearby water necessary. Known to occur only in the regions of Ilubabor and Welega. Gambella National Park.

Beisa oryx, *Oryx beisa* (Salla): Typically found in open plains country, dry steppes, and semi-desert, as well as bush and tree savannahs in dry season. Awash, Mago, Omo, and Yangudi-Rassa national parks; Yabello Sanctuary.

Lesser kudu, *Tragelaphus imberbis* (Ambaraile): Inhabits dry thorn-bush country with dense thickets in plains and hills up to 1,300 m. Sometimes also found in savannah river gallery forests. Abijatta-Shalla, Awash, Mago, Omo, and Yangudi-Rassa national parks; Yabello Sanctuary.

Greater kudu, *Tragelaphus strepciceros* (Yekola agazen): Widely distributed in very dry bushed and wooded grassland areas, usually in rocky, hilly places. Abijatta-Shalla, Awash, Mago, Nechisar, Omo, and Yangudi-Rassa national parks; Senkele and Yabello sanctuaries.

Mountain nyala, *Tragelaphus buxtoni* (Yedega agazen): Endemic. Found at altitudes above 3,000 m east of the Rift Valley. Favours areas of giant heather and alchemilla bog on the high moorlands but may also sometimes be found in the forest at lower altitudes. Range is confined to the mountains of Arsi and Bale regions and to the Chercher Mountains in Harerge region. Bale Mountains National Park, Kuni-Muktar Sanctuary.

Abyssinian bushbuck, *Tragelaphus scriptus* (Dekula): Most common of the many races of bushbuck in Ethiopia. Widely distributed but seldom seen because of its nocturnal habits, it is found in forest, savannah, woodland, thicket, and on scrub-covered hillsides — almost anywhere other than in open country. Abijatta-Shalla, Gambella, Mago, Nechisar, Omo, and Yangudi-Rassa national parks.

Menelik's bushbuck, *Tragelaphus scriptus meneliki* (Dekula): Endemic. Prefers forest and bush at high altitudes to about 4,000 m. Much darker than other races of bushbuck; nearly black. Bale and Simien national parks.

Common eland, *Taurotragus oryx* (Wendebi): Found in plains and open savannah woodland, moving long distances in its search for food. Can go for long periods without water. Omo National Park.

Walia ibex, *Capra walie* (Walia): Endemic; the rarest animal in Ethiopia. Found only on very steep cliff areas on high mountains. Simien Mountains National Park.

Buffalo, *Syncerus caffer* (Gosh): The Cape or black buffalo is equally at home in forest, swamp, open grassland, and bush country. Most common in the Gambella area. A smaller race, the red buffalo, can be found in the dense forest areas of south-west

Ethiopia. Gambella, Mago, and Omo national parks. Recently extinct in Nechisar National Park.

Wild ass, *Equus africanus* (Yedur ahiya): Lives in open desert country, which may be mountainous and rocky. Yangudi-Rassa National Park.

Grevy's zebra, *Equus grevyi* (Yemeda ahiya): Inhabits dry savannah to semi-desert areas; also open acacia woodland. Yangudi-Rassa National Park and near Yabello Sanctuary.

Burchell's zebra, *Equus burchelli* (Yemeda ahiya): Favours open grass plains and savannah woodland. Mago, Nechisar, and Omo national parks; Yabello Sanctuary.

Black rhinoceros, *Diceros bicornis* (Awuraris): Usually inhabits dry, thickly bushed country with scattered trees or copses, but can be found in grassland with little cover. In other parts of Africa it also lives in forest and mountain forest. Once widely distributed in most of the lower lying country, the rhino has been heavily poached for its horn, which is in great demand as knife handles or medicine, and is now one of Ethiopia's rarest species. Found only in certain areas of the south-west, but in serious danger of extinction. Possibly Omo and Mago national parks.

African elephant, *Loxodonta africana* (Zihon): Found in all habitats — mountain forest, forest, wooded grassland, grassland, and swamps. Once widely distributed, it has been decimated by ivory hunters and its range is now restricted to certain areas in the west and south of the country. Gambella, Mago, and Omo national parks. An endemic subspecies (*Loxodonta africana orleansi*) is found in Babille Sanctuary.

Rock hyrax, *procavia capensis* (Shikoko): Found in rocky areas in a wide range of habitats, from dry grassland to high woodlands. Not found in thick forest. Abijatta-Shalla, Awash, Bale, Gambella, Mago, Nechisar, Omo, Simien, and Yangudi-Rassa national parks; Yabello Sanctuary.

Abyssinian hare, *Lepus habessinicus*; **Fagan's hare,** *Lepus fagani*; **Crawshay's hare,** *Lepus crawshayi* (Tinchel): Widely distributed, mainly nocturnal. All species prefer open country, deserts, semi-deserts, dry bush, hills, and mountains to 2,500 m. Abijatta-Shalla, Awash, Gambella, Mago, Nechisar, Omo, Simien, and Yangudi-Rassa national parks; Senkele and Yabello sanctuaries.

Starck's hare, *Lepus starcki* (Tinchel): Endemic. Found in open country of all types. Mainly nocturnal. Bale Mountains National Park.

Aardvark, *Orycteropus afer* (Awch): Inhabits all regions where there are sufficient termites, from dry savannah to rain forest. Avoids hard soils unsuited for digging its burrows. Sleeps in burrow by day. Common but seldom seen, as it is nocturnal. Abijatta-Shalla, Awash, Bale, Gambella, Mago, Nechisar, Omo, and Yangudi-Rassa national parks.

Bird Life Profile

With more than 800 species of resident and migrant birds, more than twenty of those endemic, Ethiopia has an abundant avifauna that attracts many ornithologists. Habitats range from arid semi-desert and lowlands to wetlands and highland massifs, each with its own characteristic bird communities.

Ostrich, *Struthio camelus*: This largest of birds is commonly found in grasslands and lightly wooded areas. The North African race can be seen in western and north-eastern Ethiopia, while the Somali race is more common in the south-eastern and southern parts of the country.

Grebes: The **great crested grebe**, *Podiceps cristatus*, can be frequently seen on both fresh and alkaline inland waters; sometimes on relatively small dams. The **little grebe**, *Podiceps ruficollis*, occurs on fresh and brackish lakes, dams, ponds, and slow-flowing rivers. Abundant on the Rift Valley lakes. More uncommon is the **black-necked grebe**, *Podiceps nigricollis*.

Pelicans: Vast numbers of **great white pelican**, *Pelecanus onocrotalus*, breed at Ethiopia's Lake Shalla. They also occur elsewhere on the larger lakes. The **pink-backed pelican**, *Pelecanus rufescens*, is also frequently seen in the same habitat.

Cormorants: Commonly seen on the larger fresh and alkaline lakes are the **white-necked cormorant**, *Phalacrocorax carbo*, and the **long-tailed cormorant**, *Phalacrocorax africanus*, the latter also frequenting highland streams and marshes. The **African darter**, *Anhinga rufa*, is also abundant in these habitats.

Herons: Ten species of heron have been recorded in Ethiopia. Most common is the **black-headed heron**, *Ardea melanocephaia*, which frequents pasture land in addition to inland waters. Also seen with some frequency are the **Goliath heron**, *Ardea goliath*, the largest African heron; **the grey heron**, *Ardea cinerea*; the **purple heron**, *Ardea purpurea*; the **black heron**, *Egretta ardesiaca*; the **green-backed heron**, *Butorides striatus atricapillus*; the **night heron**, *Nycticorax nycticorax*; and the **squacco heron**, *Ardeola ralloides*.

Bitterns: The **African dwarf bittern**, *Ardeirallus sturmii*, is resident but uncommon in Ethiopia. It prefers reeds and papyrus beds fringing fresh-water lakes. It is partly nocturnal. Migrants include the little bittern, *Ixobrychus minutus*.

Egrets: Four species of egret are resident in Ethiopia, the most abundant of which is the cattle egret, *Ardeola ibis*, occurring in almost any habitat where cattle are present. Also common are the great white egret, *Egretta alba*; the yellow-billed egret, *Egretta intermedia*; and the little egret, *Egretta garzetta*.

Storks: The unusual whale-headed stork, *Balaeniceps rex*, occurs in the swampy Gambella area of western Ethiopia, while the hammerkop, *Scopus umbretta*, is common to abundant near most inland waters. Eight other stork species are present, the most commonly seen being the yellow-billed stork, *Ibis ibis*; the ubiquitous marabou stork, *Leptoptilos crumeniferus*; Abdim's stork, *Ciconia abdimii*; and the European white stork, *Ciconia ciconia*.

Ibises: The sacred ibis, *Threskiornis aethiopicus*, is common throughout Ethiopia and frequents marshes, swamps, river banks, pasture and ploughed land, and flood plains. The hadada ibis, *Hagedashia hegedash*, frequents much the same area, while the closely related endemic wattled ibis, *Bostrychia carunculata*, occurs throughout the Ethiopian plateau from about 1,500 m to the highest moorlands. It is most common along highland river courses with rocky, cliff-like edges but is also found in open country, forests, and occasionally in eucalyptus stands. Also abundant throughout Ethiopia's Rift Valley lakes is the African spoonbill, *Platalea alba*.

Flamingos: Both the greater flamingo, *Phoenicopterus ruber*, and the lesser flamingo, *Phoenicopterus minor*, can be seen in Ethiopia, mainly at Lake Abijatta, with transient visitors often spotted at Lake Basaka near Awash National Park.

Geese and ducks: There are twenty-six ducks and geese recorded in Ethiopia, including the endemic blue-winged goose, *Cyanochen cyanopterus*, which inhabits plateau marshes, streams, and damp grasslands from about 1,800 m upward. Others commonly seen are the Egyptian goose, *Alopochen aegyptiaca*; the spur-winged goose, *Plectropterus gambensis*; and the knob-billed goose, *Sarkidiornis melanota*. Ducks include the fulvous tree duck, *Dendrocygna bicolor*; the white-faced tree duck, *Dendrocygna viduata*; the yellow-billed duck, *Anas undulata rupellii* (seen on mountain tarns as well as other inland waters); and the Cape wigeon, *Anas capensis*. Among the commonly seen migrants are the European wigeon, *Anas penelope*; the common teal, *Anas crecca*; the European pintail, *Anas acuta*; the garganey teal, *Anas querquedula*; the European shoveler, *Anas clypeata*; and the African pochard, *Netta erythrophthalma*.

Secretary bird: The secretary bird, *Sagittarius serpentarius*, can be seen foraging for insects, small rodents, and reptiles — including snakes — in grasslands and lightly wooded areas.

Vultures: Widely distributed throughout the region is the hooded vulture, *Necrosyrtes monachus*, found on both open plains and in 'big game' country; also in forested areas and cultivation. Less rare than in other parts of Africa, the lammergeyer, *Gypaetus barbatus*, can often be observed in the mountainous highlands of Ethiopia. The Egyptian vulture, *Neophron percnopterus*; lappet-faced vulture, *Torgos tracheliotus*; and Ruppell's vulture, *Gyps ruppellii*, can all be seen throughout the country's grasslands, the latter particularly abundant at carrion.

Kites and buzzards: Abundant near towns, villages, and cultivated areas — as well as the grasslands and lowland forests — is the black kite, *Milvus migrans*. Savannah woodlands and open grasslands are home to the black-shouldered kite, *Elanus caeruleus*, while the less common swallow-tailed kite, *Chelictinia riocourii*, shares some of the same habitats in southern Ethiopia and the Rift Valley. Probably the most frequently seen bird of prey is the augur buzzard, *Buteo rufofuscus*, often perching on telegraph poles and other high vantage points in many habitats, while the grasshopper buzzard, *Butastur rufipennis*, favours acacia country.

Eagles: The plaintive cry of the African fish eagle, *Haliaetus vocifer*, is heard around lakes and rivers throughout the country, while the distinctive bateleur, *Terathopius ecaudatus*, and long-crested eagle, *Lophoaetus occipitalis*, can be seen in riverine forest and savannah grasslands. The greater spotted eagle, *Aquila clanga*, and the tawny eagle, *Aquila rapax*, favour highland grasslands and, in the case of the latter, acacia country. Fourteen other eagles have been recorded in Ethiopia.

Hawks: Often-seen residents of the dry bush and acacia country are the pale chanting goshawk, *Melierax canorus* (in southern Ethiopia), and the dark chanting goshawk, *Melierax metabates*, in the west and through the Rift Valley. A forest species seen throughout the country is the African goshawk, *Accipiter tachiro*. Eight other hawk species have been recorded.

Harriers: The harriers, long-legged raptors with large wings and owl-like faces, are represented by four species, of which the migrant European marsh harrier, *Circus aeruginosus*, is the most common, occurring throughout the country's inland waters. The harrier hawk or gymnogene, *Polyboroides typus*, can also be seen in the lowland forests and tall grass savannahs.

Falcons: Most common among the sixteen species of falcon recorded in Ethiopia are the migrant **common kestrel**, *Falco tinnunculus*, and the **European lesser kestrel**, *Falco naumanni*, both abundant and frequently seen in open country grasslands and savannah, even arid semi-desert and desert. The most common residents are the **pygmy falcon**, *Polihierax semitorquatus*, which favours dry bush and savannah country, and the **lanner falcon**, *Falco biarmicus*, found almost anywhere—mountains, forests, grasslands, savannah, deserts, cliffs, and gorges.

Guineafowl: Ethiopia has two types of guineafowl. The **helmeted guineafowl**, *Numida meleagris*, occurs in three races throughout much of the country, usually in grasslands and savannah but also in lowland forests and occasionally desert areas. The **vulturine guineafowl**, *Acryllium vulturinum*, is a local resident of dry thornbush country and semi-desert areas.

Francolins: Although rarely seen, the endemic **Harwood's francolin**, *Francolinus harwoodi*, has been reported along about 160 km of valleys and gorges within the upper Blue Nile system extending to the east and north of the Addis Ababa–Debre Markos–Dejen road. Other more commonly seen members of this genus include the **crested francolin**, *Francolinus sephaena*, frequenting dry acacia bush country in many parts of the country; **Clapperton's francolin**, *Francolinus clappertoni*, often seen in the western highlands and north-eastern Ethiopia; and the **chestnut-naped francolin**, *Francolinus castaneicollis*, which favours mountainous areas with plenty of cover.

Quails: The resident **harlequin quail**, *Coturnix delegorguei*, is commonly seen throughout the country in all types of grassland and savannah, from highlands to semi-desert. A winter visitor occurring in large numbers is the **European quail**, *Coturnix coturnix*, which frequents highland grasslands as well as dry bush country.

Cranes: Favouring large fresh-water lakes and rivers and mainly seen along the Rift Valley, four types of crane have been recorded in Ethiopia. The two residents are the unmistakable **crowned crane**, *Balearica pavonina*, and the **wattled crane**, *Grus carunculatus*, which is more often seen in mountain moorland and highland grassland, marshes, and streams. Migrants to the area are the **European crane**, *Grus grus*, and the less frequent **demoiselle crane**, *Anthropoides virgo*.

Rails: A characteristic bird of the moorlands of Ethiopia is the endemic **Rouget's rail**, *Rallus rougetii*, common on the western and south-eastern highlands at higher elevations up to 4,100 m. Other members of this family seen with any frequency in

the country include the **black crake**, *Limnocorax flavirostra*, and the **red-knobbed coot**, *Fulica cristata*, both favouring the Rift Valley lakes and highland streams and marshes.

Bustards: Eight species of bustard occur in Ethiopia, the most common of which is the **buff-crested bustard**, *Eupodotis ruficrista*, inhabiting dry bush country and open woodlands throughout the country. The large **kori bustard**, *Otis kori*, is often seen in many parts of the country, favouring open plains country, open dry bush and semi-desert areas. The **white-bellied bustard**, *Eupodotis senegalensis canicollis*, is also fairly common in similar habitats.

Jacanas: The **African jacana**, *Actophilomis africanus*, sometimes called the 'lily trotter', is frequently seen on most fresh-water lakes and rivers. More rare in the same habitat is the skulking **lesser jacana**, *Microparra capensis*.

Plovers: The widely distributed but locally common **spot-breasted plover**, *Vanellus melanocephalus*, is an endemic usually found above 3,000 m in marshy grasslands and moorlands in both the western and the south-eastern highlands. Also frequently seen throughout the country is the **spur-winged plover**, *Vanellus spinosus*, favouring the country's lakes and streams; the **crowned lapwing**, *Vanellus coronatus*, occurring in dry bush country as well as near water; **Kittlitz's sand plover**, *Charadrius pecuarius*, particularly common along the Rift Valley lakes; and the migrant **Caspian plover**, *Charadrius asiaticus*, which favours different types of grassland and savannah in addition to grassy flats by the lakes.

Snipes: Although many members of this family occur in Ethiopia, most are migrants. The only resident is the **African snipe**, *Gallinago nigripennis*, occurring in the western and south-eastern highlands. It is most often seen along highland streams and marshes. The most commonly seen migrants are the **ruff**, *Philomachus pugnax*; the **little stint**, *Calidris minuta*; the **curlew sandpiper**, *Calidris ferruginea*; the **great snipe**, *Gallinago media*; the **common sandpiper**, *Tringa hypoleucos*; the **wood sandpiper**, *Tringa glareola*; and the **whimbrel**, *Numenius phaeopus*.

Coursers: A bird of the arid, semi-desert country, the **cream-coloured courser**, *Cursorius cursor*, can be seen in north-eastern Ethiopia, while the **Egyptian plover**, *Pluvianus aegyptius*, is more often seen around the Rift Valley lakes. The migrant **pratincole**, *Glareola pratincola*, is relatively common around the country's alkaline lakes, acacia savannah, and semi-desert areas, and the rarer **black-winged pratincole**, *Glareola nordmanni*—also a migrant—is reported to be locally abundant around fresh-water lakes and rivers in western Ethiopia.

Gulls: Some gulls and terns are seen on Ethiopian bodies of water. The most commonly seen are the resident **grey-headed gull**, *Larus cirrhocephalus*, and the three migrants: the **lesser black-headed gull**, *Larus fuscus*; the **gull-billed tern**, *Sterna nilotica*; and the **white-winged black tern**, *Sterna leucoptera*.

Sandgrouse: Six species of sandgrouse occur in Ethiopia. The most prevalent are the **spotted sandgrouse**, *Pterocles senegallus*, and the **chestnut-bellied sandgrouse**, *Pterocles exustus*. Both favour dry semi-desert and desert areas.

Pigeons and doves: The endemic **white-collared pigeon**, *Columba albitorques*, is the dominant pigeon on the plateau above 2,400 m. It mainly inhabits rugged areas of the western and south-eastern highlands, especially cliffs and escarpments, but it is also a common feature of many villages and towns. It is one of twenty species of pigeons and doves occurring in Ethiopia. The more commonly seen of the others include the **speckled pigeon**, *Columba guinea*; the **laughing dove**, *Streptopelia senegalensis*; and the **Namaqua dove**, *Oena capensis* — all favouring the country's grasslands. Abundant in the forests is the **red-eyed dove**, *Streptopelia semitorquata*.

Parrots: Mainly seen in the western and south-eastern highlands, the Rift Valley, and the western lowlands in forests and woodlands, the endemic **yellow-fronted parrot**, *Poicephalus flavifrons*, is one of six species of parrot occurring in the country. Another endemic inhabiting the same region is the **black-winged lovebird**, *Agapornis taranta*, widely distributed in forests and woodlands and commonly seen in gardens. The **rose-ringed parrakeet**, *Psittacula krameri*, is one of the more commonly seen, favouring open savannah woodland and acacia stands.

Turacos: Five species of turaco occur in Ethiopia, including the handsome endemic **Prince Ruspoli's turaco**, *Tauraco ruspolii*. Although once considered a rare and endangered species, recent sightings in juniper forests and especially in dry water courses in the southern part of the country suggest that the species may be more common than thought. Other often-seen members of this family include the **white-bellied go-away-bird**, *Corythaixoides leucogaster*, and the **eastern grey plantain-eater**, *Crinifer zonurus* — both favouring riverine forests and acacia woodland. Although not endemic, the **white-cheeked turaco**, *Tauraco leucotis*, is distributed mainly in Ethiopia, also preferring woodland and forested country.

Cuckoos: Of the fourteen species of cuckoo and coucal reported in the country, the most common are **Klaas' cuckoo**, *Chrysococcyx klaas*, and **Didric**

cuckoo, *Chrysococcyx caprius*. Both inhabit thornbush and acacia woodlands, although Klaas' cuckoo also favours a variety of forest habitats. Commonly seen in grassy bush country and in riverine forests is the **white-browed coucal**, *Centropus superciliosus*.

Owls: The tiny **pearl-spotted owlet**, *Glaucidium perlatum*, and the **African scops owl**, *Otus scops senegalensis*, are two of the thirteen species of owl occurring in Ethiopia. They are common in dry bush country, savannah woodlands, acacia stands, and riverine vegetation. The country's forests are home to the **African wood owl**, *Ciccaba woodfordii*.

Nightjars: Although difficult to identify, twelve species of this nocturnal insectivorous bird have been recorded in the country. The most common and widespread are the **Mozambique** or **slender-tailed nightjar**, *Caprimulgus clarus*; the **freckled nightjar**, *Caprimulgus tristigma*; and the **dusky nightjar**, *Caprimulgus fraenatus* — all grassland/savannah birds, with the latter preferring the highlands. Also common in the western and south-eastern highlands and the Rift Valley is the **Abyssinian nightjar**, *Caprimulgus poliocephalus*, favouring forest edges. **Donaldson-Smith's nightjar**, *Caprimulgus donaldsoni*, is often seen in the dry thornbush country in the south and south-eastern parts of the country.

Swifts: Of the country's nine swift species, the **European swift**, *Apus apus*, is a common Palaearctic migrant. The **palm swift**, *Cypsiurus parvus*, which glues its nest to the underside of palm fronds, is a prevalent resident. The **mottled swift**, *Apus aequatorialis*, is confined to cliffs for breeding but may occur anywhere, though it tends to favour the lowlands.

Mousebirds: The **speckled mousebird**, *Colius striatus*, is a resident across much of the country in forests and grassland/savannah areas. Less widespread but nevertheless common is the **blue-naped mousebird**, *Colius macrourus*, usually found in dry bush country.

Trogons: The beautiful **Narina's trogon**, *Apaloderma narina*, is mainly found in forested areas throughout the country. In south-west Ethiopia this species is found in rather arid woodland and thornbush along tributaries of the Omo River.

Kingfishers: Nine species of kingfisher occur in Ethiopia. The **pied kingfisher**, *Ceryle rudis*, is common to all waters, while the **giant kingfisher**, *Ceryle maxima*, the largest kingfisher in the world, also favours perennial water. The **grey-headed kingfisher**, *Helcyon leucocephala*, is more often seen in riverine forests and acacia savannah, and the tiny but beautifully coloured **malachite kingfisher**, *Alcedo cristata*, is a resident fishing species.

Bee-eaters: One of Africa's most spectacular bee-eaters, the **carmine bee-eater**, *Merops nubicus*, is among the ten species of this bird to be recorded in the country. Frequenting savannah, arid bush country, lakes, and rivers, this bee-eater has an interesting habit of using the backs of kori bustards as a perch from which to hunt its prey. The **European bee-eater**, *Merops apiaster*, a Palaearctic migrant, is also common throughout Ethiopia in a wide variety of habitats, while the beautiful **little bee-eater**, *Merops pusillus*, is resident in many parts of the country in grassland and savannah areas.

Rollers: One of the most common rollers is predictably the **Abyssinian roller**, *Coracias abyssinica*, occurring in riverine forest as well as open country, savannah woodland, and bush. The **broad-billed roller**, *Eurystomus glaucurus*, is also common in riverine forests, while the **European roller**, *Coracias garrulus*, is a frequent visitor to the country's woodland, savannah, and cultivated areas.

Hoopoes and wood-hoopoes: The **African hoopoe**, *Upupa epops africana*, which closely resembles the European species, is found throughout Ethiopia. Both the **green wood-hoopoe**, *Phoeniculus purpureus*, and the **Abyssinian scimitarbill**, *Phoeniculus minor*, are widespread in various types of woodland and acacia bush country.

Hornbills: The **grey hornbill**, *Tockus nasutus*, and the **red-billed hornbill**, *Tockus erythrorhynchus*, are both common in grasslands and savannah throughout Ethiopia, although the latter only at altitudes below 2,100 m. The large and noisy **silvery-cheeked hornbill**, *Bycanistes brevis*, is frequently seen jumping about in the trees of the country's lowland and riverine forests, while the unique-looking **Abyssinian ground hornbill**, *Bucorvus abyssinicus*, is widespread in grasslands and savannah up to 3,000 m.

Barbets: Of the eleven barbet species occurring in Ethiopia, one is endemic — the little-known and rarely seen **banded barbet**, *Lybius undatus*. It is widely distributed throughout the country between 300 and 2,400 m and lives singly or in pairs in trees near water. A barbet commonly seen in the eastern part of Ethiopia is the **yellow-breasted barbet**, *Trachyphonus margaritatus*, which frequents dry bush country and semi-desert savannah.

Honeyguides: The **black-throated honeyguide**, *Indicator indicator*, is the most commonly seen of the five species of this family recorded in Ethiopia, inhabiting dry acacia bush country and semi-desert areas.

Woodpeckers: Ethiopia's most common and widespread woodpecker is the **cardinal woodpecker**, *Dendropicos fuscescens*. The **golden-backed woodpecker**, *Dendropicos abyssinicus*, is an uncommon endemic of the Ethiopia highlands, favouring forests, woodlands, and savannahs.

Passerines: This group is represented by a great variety of families and species, including **larks, swallows, chats, flycatchers, sunbirds, canaries, whydahs, finches, starlings,** and **weavers**. Endemics belonging to this order include the **white-tailed swallow**, *Hirundo megaensis*, common but restricted to a small area of southern Ethiopia; the **Abyssinian long-claw**, *Macronyx flavicollis*, a common grassland bird of the western and south-eastern highlands; and the **white-winged cliff-chat**, *Myrmecocichla semirufa*, locally frequent to common in the highlands where it lives in gorges, on cliffs, on scrubby mountain sides, and in rocky open country. The rarer endemic **Ruppell's chat**, *Myrmecocichla malaena*, inhabits edges and sides of cliffs and gorges in the western highlands, while the **Abyssinian catbird**, *Parophasma galinieri*, is common in forests and gardens between 1,800 and 3,500 m and is considered one of the finest singers of all the African birds. Other endemics are the **white-backed black tit**, *Parus leuconotus*, found in woodlands, thickets, and forests in the western and south-eastern highlands; the **yellow-throated seed-eater**, *Serinus flavigula*, known to inhabit a few isolated areas in acacia savannah in southern and south-eastern Ethiopia; and the **black-headed siskin**, *Serinus nigriceps*, a little-known finch that lives in moorlands, highland grasslands, and the open areas of montane forests. The endemic **white-billed starling**, *Onychognathus albirostris*, is widely distributed in the country, usually living in association with cliffs and gorges near waterfalls, while the beautiful **black-headed forest oriole**, *Oriolus monacha*, prefers the evergreen forests and juniper woods of the highlands.

Shrikes: Ethiopia has four cuckoo-shrikes, two helmet shrikes, six bush shrikes, and sixteen shrikes. The **black-headed bush shrike**, *Tchagra senegala*, is common throughout the country's lowland and riverine forests and dry bush country, while the **fiscal shrike**, *Lanius collaris*, is frequent to abundant in a variety of habitats across Ethiopia. The **tropical boubou**, *Laniarius aethiopicus*, is another commonly seen family member, preferring much the same habitat as the black-headed bush shrike.

Oxpeckers: Both the **red-billed oxpecker**, *Buphagus erythrorhynchus*, and the **yellow-billed oxpecker**, *Buphagus africanus*, occur in Ethiopia. Though sometimes seen together, the red-billed is the more far-reaching of the two species.

Crows: Of the eight species of crow found in Ethiopia, two are endemic. The **thick-billed raven**, *Corvus crassirostris*, is by far the more common of the two, occurring in the mountains, forests, and highland grasslands throughout much of the country. The other, **Stresemann's bush-crow**, *Zavattariornis stresemanni*, is frequent to common only in a restricted area of southern Ethiopia favouring dry acacia bush country.

Demographic Profile

Although no official census has been taken since 1984, the population of Ethiopia today is estimated to be 55 million. The annual birth rate is 4.5 per cent; life expectancy averages fifty-one years.

Population density averages 49 people to the square kilometre, with uneven distribution. The southern highlands in Bale region and the western Ilubabor region are the least populated, while the central Shewa region (including the capital of Addis Ababa) is by far the most densely populated. Twelve per cent of the population live in urban areas.

Language

Although Amharic is considered the official language of Ethiopia, there are an astonishing eighty-three languages spoken in the country, with 200 dialects. However, they can be broken into four main groups: Semitic, Cushitic, Omotic, and Nilo-Saharan.

The Semitic languages of Ethiopia are related to both Hebrew and Arabic and are spoken mainly in the north and centre of the country. The most important of them in the north is Tigrinya, which is used throughout the Tigray region and is spoken by some fourteen per cent of the population.

The principal Semitic language of the centre of the country is Amharic, which is the language of Gondar and Gojjam, as well as much of Wollo and Shewa. Moreover, Amharic is also the language of the modern state, the language of administration, and the language of almost all modern Ethiopian literature. Amharic is spoken by approximately thirty-one per cent of the population.

Two other Semitic languages are spoken to the south and east of Addis Ababa: Gurage, used in a cluster of areas to the south of the capital, and Adarinya, a tongue current only within the old walled city of Harar.

The Cushitic languages are found mainly, but not exclusively, in the south of the country. The most important tongue in this group is Afan Oromo. It is used in a wide stretch of country, including Welega and parts of Ilubabor in the west, Wollo in the north, Shewa and Arsi in the centre, Bale and Sidamo in the south, and Harerge in the east. The Oromo languages are spoken by twenty-seven per cent of the population.

Other Cushitic languages in the area comprise Somalinya, which is spoken in the Ogaden region to the east as well as in the neighbouring Somali Republic and part of Djibouti, and the Sidaminya language, used in part of the Sidamo region. Cushitic

languages are also used in the north of the country, such as Afarinya, spoken by the Afar of eastern Wollo; Saho, in parts of Tigray; and Agawinya, in small pockets in different parts of western Ethiopia.

The Omotic group of languages is spoken in the south-west of the country, mainly in the Gamo Gofa region. They have been given the name in recent years because they are spoken in the general areas of the Omo River.

The Nilo-Saharan languages, which are largely peripheral to Ethiopian civilization, are spoken in a wide arc of the country towards the Sudan frontier.

Population

1994 estimate: 55 million, or 49 persons per square kilometre.

(All figures below are from the last census taken in Ethiopia in 1984, and include Eritrea, which is now a separate nation.)

1984 population: 42,616,876, or 35 persons per square kilometre.

Population by ethnic groups (1984)

Oromo	12,387,664 (29%)
Amhara	12,055,250 (28%)
Tigrawai	4,149,697 (10%)
Other	14,024,265 (33%)

Population by sex and age (1984)

	0-14	15-34	35-54	55+	Total
Males	10,685,875	5,356,932	3,408,257	1,985,878	21,436,942
Females	9,861,623	6,116,846	3,373,663	1,827,802	21,179,934

Regional populations (1984)

Arsi	1,662,790
Bale	1,017,336
Gamo Gofa	1,269,477
Gondar	3,018,909
Gojjam	3,273,524
Harerge	4,192,898
Ilubabor	975,658
Kaffa	2,478,957
Sidamo	3,813,075
Shewa (includes Addis Ababa)	9,525,508
Tigray	2,415,871
Welega	2,478,425
Wollo	3,746,144

Population of major urban centres (1984)

Addis Ababa	1,423,182
Arba Minch	20,280
Asela	32,954
Awasa	36,367
Bahar Dar	54,773
Debre Birhan	25,637

Debre Markos	41,138
Debre Zeit	55,657
Dessie	71,565
Dire Dawa	99,980
Goba	23,052
Gondar	80,675
Harar	63,070
Jijiga	24,716
Jimma	60,218
Makale	62,668
Metu	12,920
Nazaret	77,256
Nekemte	28,703
Shashemene	31,884
Sodo	24,278

Religious affiliation

Ethiopian Orthodox	45%
Sunni Muslim	35%
Traditional beliefs	11%
Other	9%

Gazetteer

(Second paragraph indicates kilometre distance between major towns. Populations given are from the 1984 census, the most recent taken in Ethiopia. n/a: Information not available.)

ADDIS ABABA
Shewa region.
Arba Minch 510, Asela 175, Awasa 268, Axum 1,005, Bahar Dar 578, Debre Birhan 130, Debre Markos 305, Debre Zeit 47, Dessie 397, Dire Dawa 453, Gambella 753, Goba 430, Gondar 748, Harar 523, Jijiga 628, Jimma 335, Lalibela 642, Makale 777, Metu 550, Nazaret 99, Nekemte 331, Shashemene 249, Sodo 330.
Alt: 2,450 m (8,036 ft). Pop: 1,423,182. Airport. Post Office. Black Lion Hospital Tel: 156170. Police Tel: 91. Petrol: Day; some 24 hours. Hotels. Customs and immigration.

AMBO
Shewa region.
Addis Ababa 105, Arba Minch 615, Asela 280, Awasa 373, Axum 1,110, Bahar Dar 683, Debre Birhan 235, Debre Markos 410, Debre Zeit 152, Dessie 502, Dire Dawa 558, Gambella 648, Goba 535, Gondar 853, Harar 628, Jijiga 733, Jimma 440, Lalibela 747, Makale 882, Metu 445, Nazaret 204, Nekemte 226, Shashemene 354, Sodo 435.
Alt: n/a. Pop: 29,539 (1993 estimate). Airport. Post Office. Agerehio Hospital Tel: 99. Police Tel: 16. Petrol: Day hours. Hotel.

ARBA MINCH
Gamo Gofa region.
Addis Ababa 510, Asela 446, Awasa 270, Axum 1,515,

Bahar Dar 1,088, Debre Birhan 640, Debre Markos 805, Debre Zeit 463, Dessie 907, Dire Dawa 802, Gambella 874, Goba 456, Gondar 1,258, Harar 872, Jijiga 977, Jimma (via Hosaina and Welkite) 491, Lalibela 1,152, Makale 1,287, Metu (via Jimma) 703, Nazaret 448, Nekemte 733, Shashemene 252, Sodo 122.
Alt: 1,200 m (3,936 ft). Pop: 20,280. Airport. Post Office. Arba Minch Hospital Tel: 99. Police Tel: n/a. Petrol: Day hours. Hotel.

ASAITA
Wollo region.
Addis Ababa 665, Arba Minch 1,175, Asela 664, Awasa 876, Axum 890, Bahar Dar 928, Debre Birhan 535, Debre Markos 970, Debre Zeit 712, Dessie 318, Dire Dawa 742, Gambella 1,418, Goba 920, Gondar 1,001, Harar 812, Jijiga 917, Jimma 1,000, Lalibela 601, Makale 670, Metu 1,215, Nazaret 587, Nekemte 996, Shashemene 858, Sodo 988.
Alt: n/a. Pop: 10,385 (1993 estimate). Post Office. Hospital: none. Police Tel: 2005. Petrol: Day hours. Hotel: none.

ASELA
Arsi region.
Addis Ababa 175, Arba Minch 446, Awasa 212, Axum 1,180, Bahar Dar 753, Debre Birhan 305, Debre Markos 480, Debre Zeit 128, Dessie 572, Dire Dawa 430, Gambella (via Addis Ababa) 928, Goba 256, Gondar 923, Harar 500, Jijiga 605, Jimma (via Addis Ababa) 510, Lalibela 817, Makale 952, Metu 725, Nazaret 76, Nekemte 506, Shashemene 194, Sodo 324.
Alt: n/a. Pop: 32,954. Post Office. Asela Hospital Tel: 02-311005. Police Tel: 02-311010. Petrol: Day hours. Hotel.

ASOSA
Welega region.
Addis Ababa 678, Arba Minch 1,080, Asela 853, Awasa 985, Axum 1,683, Bahar Dar 755, Debre Birhan 808, Debre Markos 340, Debre Zeit 725, Dessie 1,075, Dire Dawa 1,131, Gambella 515, Goba 1,108, Gondar 938, Harar 1,201, Jijiga 1,306, Jimma 589, Lalibela 1,320, Makale 1,455, Metu 416, Nazaret 777, Nekemte 347, Shashemene 927, Sodo 958.
Alt: n/a. Pop: 7,406 (1993 estimate). Airport. Post Office. Hospital: none. Police Tel: n/a. Petrol: none. Hotel: none.

AWASA
Sidamo region.
Addis Ababa 268, Arba Minch 270, Asela 212, Axum 1,273, Bahar Dar 846, Debre Birhan 398, Debre Markos 573, Debre Zeit 221, Dessie 665, Dire Dawa 532, Gambella 819, Goba 186, Gondar 1,016, Harar 602, Jijiga 707, Jimma (via Hosaina and Welkite) 396, Lalibela 910, Makale 1,045, Metu (via Jimma) 648, Nazaret 169, Nekemte 638, Shashemene 18, Sodo 154.

Alt: 1,760 m (5,773 ft). Pop: 62,943 (1993 estimate). Post Office. Shashemene Hospital Tel: 06-100286. Police Tel: 06-200034. Petrol: Day hours. Hotels.

AWASH

Harerge region.
Addis Ababa 224, Arba Minch 573, Asela 201, Awasa 414, Axum 1,229, Bahar Dar 802, Debre Birhan 354, Debre Markos 529, Debre Zeit 177, Dessie 456, Dire Dawa 229, Gambella 977, Goba 458, Gondar 972, Harar 299, Jijiga 404, Jimma 559, Lalibela 739, Makale 808, Metu 774, Nazaret 125, Nekemte 555, Shashemene 276, Sodo 406.
Alt: n/a. Pop: 7,750 (1993 estimate). Post Office. Hospital: none. Police Tel: n/a. Petrol: Day hours. Hotels.

AXUM

Tigray region.
Addis Ababa 1,005, Arba Minch 1,515, Asela 1,180, Awasa 1,273, Bahar Dar 554, Debre Birhan 846, Debre Markos 833, Debre Zeit 1,052, Dessie 572, Dire Dawa (via Addis Ababa) 1,458, Gambella (via Addis Ababa) 1,758, Goba 1,435, Gondar 360, Harar 1,528, Jijiga 1,633, Jimma 1,340, Lalibela 529, Makale 220, Metu 1,555, Nazaret 1,104, Nekemte 1,336, Shashemene 1,254, Sodo 1,335.
Alt: 2,150 m (7,052 ft). Pop: 30,812 (1993 estimate). Airport. Axum Hospital Tel: 99. Police Tel: n/a. Petrol: Day hours. Hotel.

BAHAR DAR

Gojjam region.
Addis Ababa 578, Arba Minch 1,088, Asela 753, Awasa 846, Axum 554, Debre Birhan 708, Debre Markos 279, Debre Zeit 625, Dessie 610, Dire Dawa 1,031, Gambella 1,013, Goba 1,008, Gondar 183, Harar 1,101, Jijiga 1,206, Jimma 913, Lalibela 529, Makale 696, Metu 628, Nazaret 677, Nekemte (via Bure) 408, Shashemene 827, Sodo 908.
Alt: 1,802 m (5,910 ft). Pop: 54,773. Airport. Felege Hiot Hospital Tel: 08-200170. Police Tel: 08-200926. Petrol: Day hours. Hotel.

BATI

Wollo region.
Addis Ababa 413, Arba Minch 923, Asela 588, Awasa 681, Axum 638, Bahar Dar 676, Debre Birhan 283, Debre Markos 718, Debre Zeit 460, Dessie 66, Dire Dawa 660, Gambella 1,166, Goba 843, Gondar 748, Harar 730, Jijiga 835, Jimma 748, Lalibela 349, Makale 418, Metu 963, Nazaret 512, Nekemte 744, Shashemene 662, Sodo 743.
Alt: n/a. Pop: 14,689 (1993 estimate). Post Office. Hospital: none. Police Tel: n/a. Petrol: Day hours. Hotel.

DEBRE BIRHAN

Shewa region.
Addis Ababa 130, Arba Minch 640, Asela 305, Awasa 398, Axum 846, Bahar Dar 708, Debre

Markos 435, Debre Zeit 177, Dessie 267, Dire Dawa 583, Gambella 883, Goba 560, Gondar 878, Harar 653, Jijiga 758, Jimma 465, Lalibela 512, Makale 647, Metu 680, Nazaret 229, Nekemte 461, Shashemene 379, Sodo 460.
Alt: n/a. Pop: 25,637. Post Office. Debre Birhan Hospital Tel: 811678. Police Tel: 812296. Petrol: Day hours. Hotel: none.

DEBRE MARKOS

Gojjam region.
Addis Ababa 305, Arba Minch 805, Asela 480, Awasa 573, Axum 833, Bahar Dar 279, Debre Birhan 435, Debre Zeit 352, Dessie 702, Dire Dawa 758, Gambella 734, Goba 735, Gondar 462, Harar 828, Jijiga 933, Jimma 640, Lalibela 808, Makale 1,005, Metu 560, Nazaret 404, Nekemte 340, Shashemene 554, Sodo 635.
Alt: 2,509 m (8,230 ft). Pop: 41,138. Airport. Post Office. Debre Markos Hospital Tel: 08-712643. Police Tel: 08-112015. Petrol: Day hours. Hotel: none.

DEBRE ZEIT

Shewa region.
Addis Ababa 47, Arba Minch 463, Asela 128, Awasa 221, Axum 1,052, Bahar Dar 625, Debre Birhan 177, Debre Markos 352, Dessie 444, Dire Dawa 406, Gambella 800, Goba 383, Gondar 795, Harar 476, Jijiga 581, Jimma 382, Lalibela 689, Makale 824, Metu 597, Nazaret 52, Nekemte 378, Shashemene 202, Sodo 283.
Alt: 1,850 m (6,068 ft). Pop: 55,657. Debre Zeit Hospital Tel: 33. Police Tel: n/a. Petrol: Day hours. Hotels.

DEMBIDOLO

Welega region.
Addis Ababa 683, Arba Minch 1,193, Asela 858, Awasa 951, Axum 1,286, Bahar Dar 732, Debre Birhan 813, Debre Markos 664, Debre Zeit 730, Dessie 1,080, Dire Dawa 1,136, Gambella 70, Goba 1,113, Gondar 915, Harar 1,206, Jijiga 1,311, Jimma 493, Lalibela 1,261, Makale 1,458, Metu 241, Nazaret 782, Nekemte 324, Shashemene 932, Sodo 862.
Alt: n/a. Pop: 25,739 (1993 estimate). Airport. Post Office. Dembidolo Hospital Tel: 99. Police Tel: n/a. Petrol: Day hours. Hotel.

DESSIE

Wollo region.
Addis Ababa 397, Arba Minch 907, Asela 572, Awasa 665, Axum 572, Bahar Dar 610, Debre Birhan 267, Debre Markos 702, Debre Zeit 444, Dire Dawa 850, Gambella 1,150, Goba 827, Gondar 683, Harar 920, Jijiga 1,025, Jimma 732, Lalibela 283, Makale 352, Metu 947, Nazaret 444, Nekemte 728, Shashemene 646, Sodo 730.
Alt: 2,540 m (8,331 ft). Pop: 71,565. Airport. Post Office. Dessie Hospital Tel: 03-111026. Police Tel: 03-111028. Petrol: Day hours. Hotel.

DIRE DAWA
Harerge region.
Addis Ababa 453, Arba Minch 802, Asela 446, Awasa 532, Axum 1,458, Bahar Dar 848, Debre Birhan 583, Debre Markos 758, Debre Zeit 406, Dessie 850, Gambella 1,206, Goba 851, Gondar 1,031, Harar 70, Jijiga 175, Jimma 788, Lalibela 1,095, Makale 1,230, Metu 1,003, Nazaret 354, Nekemte 784, Shashemene 428, Sodo 564.
Alt: 1,160 m (3,805 ft). Pop: 99,980. Airport. Post Office. Dile Chora Hospital Tel: 05-113247. Police Tel: 05-113057. Petrol: Day hours. Hotels.

GAMBELLA
Ilubabor region.
Addis Ababa 753, Arba Minch 874, Asela 928, Awasa 819, Axum 1,758, Bahar Dar 1,013, Debre Birhan 883, Debre Markos 734, Debre Zeit 800, Dessie 1,150, Dire Dawa 1,206, Goba 1,183, Gondar 1,196, Harar 1,276, Jijiga 1,381, Jimma 423, Lalibela 1,395, Makale 1,530, Metu 171, Nazaret 852, Nekemte 391, Shashemene 801, Sodo 811.
Alt: n/a. Pop: 8,043 (1993 estimate). Airport. Post Office. Gambella Hospital Tel: 99. Police Tel: n/a. Petrol: Day hours. Hotel.

GISHEN
Wollo region.
Addis Ababa 457, Arba Minch 967, Asela 632, Awasa 725, Axum 512, Bahar Dar 550, Debre Birhan 327, Debre Markos 762, Debre Zeit 504, Dessie 60, Dire Dawa 910, Gambella 1,210, Goba 887, Gondar 623, Harar 980, Jijiga 1,085, Jimma 792, Lalibela 223, Makale 292, Metu 1,007, Nazaret 504, Nekemte 788, Shashemene 706, Sodo 787.
Alt: n/a. Pop: 1,089 (1993 estimate). Hospital: none. Police Tel: n/a. Petrol: none. Hotel.

GOBA
Bale region.
Addis Ababa 430, Arba Minch 456, Asela 256, Awasa 186, Axum 1,435, Bahar Dar 1,008, Debre Birhan 560, Debre Markos 735, Debre Zeit 383, Dessie 827, Dire Dawa 851, Gambella 1,183, Gondar 1,178, Harar 921, Jijiga 1,026, Jimma 582, Lalibela 1,072, Makale 1,207, Metu 834, Nazaret 331, Nekemte 824, Shashemene 168, Sodo 304.
Alt: 2,743 m (8,997 ft). Pop: 23,052. Airport. Hospital: none. Police Tel: 07-610227. Petrol: Day hours. Hotel.

GONDAR
Gondar region.
Addis Ababa 748, Arba Minch 1,258, Asela 923, Awasa 1,016, Axum 360, Bahar Dar 183, Debre Birhan 878, Debre Markos 462, Debre Zeit 795, Dessie 683, Dire Dawa 1,031, Gambella 1,196, Goba 1,178, Harar 1,101, Jijiga 1,206, Jimma 1,096, Lalibela 712, Makale 879, Metu 811, Nazaret 847, Nekemte 591, Shashemene 1,010, Sodo 1,091.
Alt: 2,000 m (6,560 ft). Pop: 80,675. Airport. Post Office. Gondar Hospital Tel: 08-110174. Police Tel: 08-110125. Petrol: Day hours. Hotels.

HARAR
Harerge region.
Addis Ababa 523, Arba Minch 872, Asela 500, Awasa 602, Axum 1,528, Bahar Dar 918, Debre Birhan 653, Debre Markos 828, Debre Zeit 476, Dessie 920, Dire Dawa 70, Gambella 1,276, Goba 921, Gondar 1,101, Jijiga 105, Jimma 858, Lalibela 1,065, Makale 1,300, Metu 1,073, Nazaret 424, Nekemte 854, Shashemene 575, Sodo 705.
Alt: 1,856 m (6,088 ft). Pop: 63,070. Airport (Dire Dawa). Post Office. Misrak Arbegnoch Hospital Tel: 05-660231. Police Tel: 05-660400. Petrol: Day hours. Hotel.

JIJIGA
Harerge region.
Addis Ababa 628, Arba Minch 628, Asela 605, Awasa 707, Axum 1,633, Bahar Dar 1,023, Debre Birhan 758, Debre Markos 933, Debre Zeit 581, Dessie 1,025, Dire Dawa 175, Gambella 1,381, Goba 1,026, Gondar 1,206, Harar 105, Jimma 963, Lalibela 1,270, Makale 1,405, Metu 1,178, Nazaret 529, Nekemte 959, Shashemene 680, Sodo 810.
Alt: n/a. Pop: 24,716. Jijiga Hospital Tel: 99. Police Tel: n/a. Petrol: Day hours. Hotel: none.

JIMMA
Kaffa region.
Addis Ababa 335, Arba Minch 491, Asela 510, Awasa 396, Axum 1,340, Bahar Dar 913, Debre Birhan 465, Debre Markos 640, Debre Zeit 382, Dessie 732, Dire Dawa 788, Gambella 423, Goba 582, Gondar 1,096, Harar 858, Jijiga 963, Lalibela 977, Makale 1,112, Metu 252, Nazaret 434, Nekemte 242, Shashemene 378, Sodo 369.
Alt: 1,740 m (5,707 ft). Pop: 60,218. Airport. Post Office. Jimma Hospital Tel: 07-110867. Police Tel: 07-110458. Petrol: Day hours. Hotels.

JINKA
Gamo Gofa region.
Addis Ababa 738, Arba Minch 228, Asela 674, Awasa 498, Axum 1,743, Bahar Dar 1,316, Debre Birhan 868, Debre Markos 1,033, Debre Zeit 691, Dessie 1,135, Dire Dawa 1,030, Gambella 1,102, Goba 684, Gondar 976, Harar 1,100, Jijiga 1,205, Jimma 719, Lalibela 1,380, Makale 1,515, Metu 931, Nazaret 676, Nekemte 961, Shashemene 480, Sodo 350.
Alt: n/a. Pop: 9,520 (1993 estimate). Airport. Post Office. Hospital: none. Police Tel: n/a. Petrol: Day hours. Hotel.

KOMBOLCHA
Wollo region.
Addis Ababa 372, Arba Minch 882, Asela 547, Awasa 640, Axum 597, Bahar Dar 635, Debre Birhan 242, Debre Markos 677, Debre Zeit 419, Dessie 25, Dire Dawa 825, Gambella 1,175, Goba 802, Gondar 708, Harar 895, Jijiga 1,000, Jimma 707, Lalibela 308, Makale 377, Metu 922, Nazaret 419, Nekemte 703, Shashemene 621, Sodo 702.

Alt: n/a. Pop: 27,823 (1993 estimate). Airport (in nearby Dessie). Post Office. Hospital: none. Police Tel: n/a. Petrol: Day hours. Hotel.

LALIBELA
Wollo region.
Addis Ababa 642, Arba Minch 1,152, Asela 817, Awasa 910, Axum 529, Bahar Dar 529, Debre Birhan 512, Debre Markos 808, Debre Zeit 689, Dessie 283, Dire Dawa 1,095, Gambella 1,395, Goba 1,072, Gondar 712, Harar 1,165, Jijiga 1,270, Jimma 977, Makale 309, Metu 1,157, Nazaret 741, Nekemte 937, Shashemene 891, Sodo 972.
Alt: 2,630 m (8,626 ft). Pop: 7,591 (1993 estimate). Airport. Hospital: none. Police Tel: n/a. Petrol: none. Hotels.

LANGANO (BULBULA)
Shewa region.
Addis Ababa 210, Arba Minch 312, Asela 134, Awasa 78, Axum 1,194, Bahar Dar 767, Debre Birhan 319, Debre Markos 494, Debre Zeit 142, Dessie 586, Dire Dawa 454, Gambella 753, Goba 228, Gondar 937, Harar 524, Jijiga 629, Jimma 357, Lalibela 831, Makale 966, Metu 609, Nazaret 136, Nekemte 599, Shashemene 60, Sodo 190.
Alt: n/a. Pop: 5,340 (1993 estimate). Post Office. Hospital: none. Police Tel: n/a. Petrol: in nearby Bulbula, day hours. Hotels.

MAKALE
Tigray region.
Addis Ababa 777, Arba Minch 1,287, Asela 952, Awasa 1,045, Axum 220, Bahar Dar 696, Debre Birhan 647, Debre Markos 1,005, Debre Zeit 824, Dessie 352, Dire Dawa 1,230, Gambella 1,530, Goba 1,207, Gondar 879, Harar 1,300, Jijiga 1,405, Jimma 1,112, Lalibela 309, Metu 1,327, Nazaret 876, Nekemte 841, Shashemene 1,026, Sodo 1,107.
Alt: 2,130 m (6,986 ft). Pop: 62,668. Airport. Post Office. Makale Hospital Tel: 03-400127. Police Tel: 03-400193. Petrol: Day hours. Hotels.

METU
Shewa region.
Addis Ababa 550, Arba Minch 703, Asela 725, Awasa 648, Axum 1,555, Bahar Dar 628, Debre Birhan 680, Debre Markos 560, Debre Zeit 597, Dessie 647, Dire Dawa 1,003, Gambella 171, Goba 834, Gondar 811, Harar 1,073, Jijiga 1,178, Jimma 252, Lalibela 1,157, Makale 1,327, Nazaret 649, Nekemte 220, Shashemene 630, Sodo 621.
Alt: 1,940 m (6,363 ft). Pop: 12,920. Airport (Gore). Metu Hospital Tel: 99. Police Tel: n/a. Petrol: Day hours. Hotel: none.

MOYALE
Sidamo region.
Addis Ababa 967, Arba Minch 457, Asela 903, Awasa 727, Axum 1,972, Bahar Dar 1,545, Debre Birhan 1,097, Debre Markos 1,262, Debre Zeit 920, Dessie 1,364, Dire Dawa 1,259, Gambella

1,331, Goba 913, Gondar 1,715, Harar 1,329, Jijiga 1,434, Jimma 948, Lalibela 1,609, Makale 1,744, Metu 1,160, Nazaret 905, Nekemte 1,190, Shashemene 709, Sodo 579.
Alt: n/a. Pop: 5,933 (1993 estimate). Post Office. Hospital: none. Police Tel: n/a. Petrol: none. Hotel. Customs and immigration.

NAZARET
Shewa region.
Addis Ababa 99, Arba Minch 448, Asela 76, Awasa 169, Axum 1,104, Bahar Dar 677, Debre Birhan 229, Debre Markos 404, Debre Zeit 52, Dessie 444, Dire Dawa 354, Gambella 852, Goba 331, Gondar 847, Harar 424, Jijiga 529, Jimma 434, Lalibela 741, Makale 876, Metu 649, Nekemte 430, Shashemene 271, Sodo 401.
Alt: 1,622 m (5,320 ft). Pop: 77,256. Post Office. Haile Mariam Mamo Hospital Tel: 02-112424. Police Tel: 02-111485. Petrol: Day hours. Hotels.

NEKEMTE
Welega region.
Addis Ababa 331, Arba Minch 733, Asela 506, Awasa 638, Axum 555, Bahar Dar 408, Debre Birhan 461, Debre Markos 340, Debre Zeit 378, Dessie 728, Dire Dawa 784, Gambella 391, Goba 824, Gondar 591, Harar 854, Jijiga 959, Jimma 242, Lalibela 937, Makale 841, Metu 220, Nazaret 430, Shashemene 620, Sodo 611.
Alt: 2,005 m (6,576 ft). Pop: 28,703. Airport. Nekemte Hospital Tel: 07-611361. Police Tel: 07-611007. Petrol: Day hours. Hotel: none.

ROBE
Bale region.
Addis Ababa 416, Arba Minch 442, Asela 242, Awasa 172, Axum 1,421, Bahar Dar 994, Debre Birhan 546, Debre Markos 721, Debre Zeit 369, Dessie 813, Dire Dawa 837, Gambella 1,169, Goba 14, Gondar 1,164, Harar 907, Jijiga 1,012, Jimma 568, Lalibela 1,058, Makale 1,193, Metu 820, Nazaret 317, Nekemte 810, Shashemene 154, Sodo 290.
Alt: n/a. Pop: 21,138 (1993 estimate). Airport (in nearby Goba). Post Office. Hospital: none. Police Tel: n/a. Petrol: Day hours. Hotel.

SHASHEMENE
Shewa region.
Addis Ababa 249, Arba Minch 252, Asela 194, Awasa 18, Axum 1,254, Bahar Dar 827, Debre Birhan 379, Debre Markos 554, Debre Zeit 202, Dessie 646, Dire Dawa 428, Gambella 801, Goba 168, Gondar 1,010, Harar 575, Jijiga 680, Jimma 378, Lalibela 891, Makale 1,026, Metu 630, Nazaret 271, Nekemte 620, Sodo 130.
Alt: 1,580 m (5,182 ft). Pop: 31,884. Airport. Post Office. Shashemene Hospital Tel: 06-100286. Police Tel: 06-100043. Petrol: Day hours. Hotel.

SODERE
Arsi region.
Addis Ababa 125, Arba Minch 474, Asela 58, Awasa

195, Axum 1,130, Bahar Dar 703, Debre Birhan 255, Debre Markos 430, Debre Zeit 78, Dessie 470, Dire Dawa 255, Gambella 878, Goba 313, Gondar 873, Harar 325, Jijiga 430, Jimma 465, Lalibela 767, Makale 902, Metu 717, Nazaret 26, Nekemte 707, Shashemene 297, Sodo 427.
Alt: n/a. Pop: n/a. Post Office. Hospital: none. Police Tel: n/a. Petrol: Day hours. Hotel.

SODO
Sidamo region.
Addis Ababa 330, Arba Minch 122, Asela 324, Awasa 154, Axum 1,335, Bahar Dar 908, Debre Birhan 460, Debre Markos 635, Debre Zeit 283, Dessie 727, Dire Dawa 564, Gambella 811, Goba 304, Gondar 1,091, Harar 705, Jijiga 810, Jimma 369, Lalibela 972, Makale 1,107, Metu 621, Nazaret 401, Nekemte 611, Shashemene 130.
Alt: n/a. Pop: 24,278. Airport. Sodo Hospital Tel: 99. Police Tel: n/a. Petrol: Day hours. Hotel.

WELISO
Shewa region.
Addis Ababa 115, Arba Minch 347, Asela (via Addis Ababa) 290, Awasa 252, Axum 1,120, Bahar Dar 693, Debre Birhan 245, Debre Markos 420, Debre Zeit 162, Dessie 512, Dire Dawa 568, Gambella (via Jimma) 643, Goba 402, Gondar 863, Harar 638, Jijiga 743, Jimma 220, Lalibela 757, Makale 892, Metu 472, Nazaret 214, Nekemte 462, Shashemene 234, Sodo 225.
Alt: n/a. Pop: 28,430 (1993 estimate). Post Office. Hospital: none. Police Tel: n/a. Petrol: Day hours. Hotels.

ZIWAY
Shewa region.
Addis Ababa 163, Arba Minch 345, Asela 91, Awasa 111, Axum 1,168, Bahar Dar 741, Debre Birhan 293, Debre Markos 468, Debre Zeit 116, Dessie 560, Dire Dawa 469, Gambella 747, Goba 261, Gondar 911, Harar 539, Jijiga 644, Jimma 324, Lalibela 805, Makale 940, Metu 576, Nazaret 115, Nekemte 566, Shashemene 93, Sodo 223.
Alt: n/a. Pop: 9,399 (1993 estimate). Post Office. Hospital: none. Police Tel: n/a. Petrol: Day hours. Hotel.

Museums and Historical Sites

Addis Ababa Museum, Addis Ababa
Region: Shewa
Features: Formerly the home of Ras Biru Habtegebriel, Minister of War for Menelik II, the museum's focus is on the political, cultural, and architectural history of the capital.

Addis Alem Maryam Museum, Addis Alem
Region: Shewa
Features: The museum, within the Addis Alem Maryam church compound, contains the clothes and decorations of several former Ethiopian rulers.

Awash National Park Museum, Awash
Region: Shewa
Features: This small museum within the national park houses various stuffed birds, mammals, and reptiles, as well as some education and interpretive materials on the area's flora, fauna, geology, and peoples.

Axum Museum, Axum
Region: Tigray
Features: This small museum houses a remarkable collection of antiquities, including several stones bearing Sabaean and Ge'ez inscriptions and clay figurines that reveal the hair styles current in ancient Axum.

Church of Saint Mary, Addis Alem
Region: Shewa
Features: Intended by Emperor Menelik as the southern equivalent of the Church of Saint Mary of Zion at Axum, the church and sanctuary are decorated with an amazing variety of interesting paintings depicting wildlife, biblical scenes, and various Ethiopian rulers.

Church of Saint Mary of Zion, Axum
Region: Tigray
Features: There are two Saint Mary of Zion churches in Axum. The older was built in the early seventeenth century by Emperor Fasilidas. On the church compound is a small building (often referred to as a museum), which houses many treasures, including the crowns of many former emperors of Ethiopia. The church courtyard also contains many antiquities, including stone thrones on which the monarchs of the past were crowned. Although the church compound is closed to women, some of the treasures may be carried to the edge of the church precincts for viewing purposes.

Debre Damo Monastery, Debre Damo
Region: Tigray
Features: The monastery, which dates back to early Axumite times, is said to possess the oldest existing church in Ethiopia and has been in continuous use since the sixth century. Male visitors (women are not allowed) must ascend the mountain on which it is located with the help of a rope lowered by the friendly monks. Treasures within the church include an extensive collection of illuminated manuscripts.

Enda Kirkos, Wukro
Region: Tigray
Features: Built in 346 AD, Enda Kirkos is one of the

most easily accessible rock-hewn churches in Tigray. The fire-blackened walls, with damage attributed to Queen Yodit's raids in the tenth century, still retain vestiges of old murals and even older layers of decorations.

Entoto Museum, Entoto Mountain
Region: Shewa
Features: The museum, within the precincts of the church of Maryam on Entoto Mountain, contains religious manuscripts, crosses, and other church paraphernalia, as well as the vestments of several kings and political leaders of the past.

Ethnological Museum, Addis Ababa
Region: Shewa
Features: Part of the Institute of Ethiopian Studies, this exciting museum provides an interesting overview of Ethiopian crafts, culture, and art. The Ethnological Section includes displays of different types of clothing corresponding to the different regions of the country, as well as samples of jewellery and adornments, while the Art Section houses paintings reflecting the hunting and farming Ethiopia, folk legends, religion, and war. There are also fine illuminated manuscripts from Ethiopia's ancient Christian tradition. A separate section, located in a nineteenth-century house nearby, contains musical instruments.

Hadar Archaeological Site, Awash Valley
Region: Wollo
Features: Hadar is the most famous of many archaeological sites in the Awash Valley, as it is where the famous early hominid 'Lucy' (*Dinkenesh*) was discovered in 1974.

Harar
Region: Harerge
Features: The walls and gates of this centuries-old city are an attraction themselves, but other places of historical interest include the bizarre Rimbaud House, built in the late 1800s; the palace of Ras Makonnen, governor of the city in the 1890s; the tomb of Abu Said, an early Muslim ruler; and the sixteenth-century Grand Mosque. Harar is one of the most important centres of Islamic faith on the African continent.

Harar Community Museum, Harar
Region: Harerge
Features: Attached to the Culture Centre. Here visitors may see artefacts relating to the Hadari culture, including a typical house and clothing.

Harar Government Museum, Harar
Region: Harerge
Features: Houses a variety of antiquities from Harar and nearby areas, including memorabilia of the patriot Dejazmach Tefera.

Lake Tana monasteries
Region: Gondar / Gojjam
Features: Some twenty of the thirty-seven islands on Lake Tana shelter churches and monasteries of immense historical and cultural interest, dating from the mid-fourteenth century. They include the fifteenth-century Kebran Gabriel monastery, Birgida Maryam, Dega Estafanos, Dek, Narga, Tana Cherkos, Mitsele Fasilidas, and Debre Maryam. The peninsulas of Gorgora, Mandaba, and Zeghe also feature many ancient religious structures, such as the Ura Kidane Mehret, which also dates from the fifteenth century.

Lego Dooa, Dire Dawa
Region: Harerge
Features: A shelter with rock paintings dating from 2000 BC. Late Stone Age artefacts were discovered at the base of the shelter.

Makale Museum, Makale
Region: Tigray
Features: Formerly the palace of Emperor Yohannes, this interesting museum houses manuscripts, books, and furniture of the emperor's time, including a large and ornately carved wooden throne.

Melka Konture Archaeological Site, Awash River
Region: Shewa
Features: Melka Konture is the most extensive pre-historic archaeological site in Ethiopia. An abundance and great variety of stone artefacts have been discovered at the site, where geologists and archaeologists have had a compound since 1965.

Nagash, Tigray
Region: Tigray
Features: The town of Nagash is the site of a mosque and is reputedly the country's first Islamic settlement, established in the eighth century. The tower of the mosque affords a fine view of the surrounding countryside.

National Archaeological Museum, Addis Ababa
Region: Shewa
Features: The museum's collection, gathered largely from the northern provinces by French archaeologists, includes a replica of the early hominid 'Lucy' (*Dinkenesh*), as well as a valuable collection of historical artefacts, ancient coins, crowns, and costumes.

National Postal Museum, Addis Ababa
Region: Shewa
Features: This museum boasts a complete set of all the stamps ever printed in Ethiopia, as well as many of the original drawings, approved designs, examples of the printers' art, printers' proofs, and other items unique to Ethiopian philately. It also houses displays of stamps from other Universal Postal Union members, which are changed every six months.

Natural History Museum, Addis Ababa
Region: Shewa
Features: Collections of mammals, birds, reptiles, etc., found in Ethiopia. By appointment only.

Park of the Stelae, Axum
Region: Tigray
Features: In ancient times there were seven monoliths of granite standing together here, but the two largest fell. The third largest stele, which is slightly smaller, measuring twenty-three metres (75 feet), is, however, still standing with four others. All the stelae are made of single pieces of granite and resemble tall, slender multi-storeyed houses in the architectural style of the Axumite houses and palaces. Each was erected in the centre of a step platform of stone on a terrace of polished limestone. At the base of each standing stele is a stone altar.

Porc Epic Cave, Dire Dawa
Region: Harerge
Features: A *Homo sapiens* mandible was discovered here in 1933, but the site was not excavated until 1975, when a number of artefacts from the Middle Stone Age were discovered. Rock paintings are depicted on the cave walls.

Rock-hewn Churches of Lalibela
Region: Wollo
Features: Often called the 'Eighth Wonder of the World', the churches in this incredible cluster have been physically prised from the rock in which they stand. A complex and bewildering labyrinth of tunnels and narrow passageways with offset crypts, grottos, and galleries connects them all.
Six churches lie north of the 'Jordan River' within the town: Bet Golgotha, Bet Mika'el, Bet Maryam, Bet Meskel, Bet Danaghel, and Bet Medhane Alem. Bet Amanuel, Bet Merkorios, Bet Abba Libanos, and Bet Gabriel-Fufa'el are situated south of the river. All feature interesting carvings and architecture.

Saint George's Church Museum, Addis Ababa
Region: Shewa
Features: Crowns and relics relating to Haile Selassie's coronation.

Sanctuary Chapel, Axum
Region: Tigray
Features: The well-guarded sanctuary chapel is said to house the famed Ark of the Covenant. Visitors are not allowed.

Sof Omar Caves, Bale
Region: Bale
Features: These caves, now an important Islamic shrine named after the saintly Sheikh Sof Omar, who took refuge here many centuries ago, have a religious history that predates the arrival of Muslims in Bale — a history calibrated in thousands, not hundreds, of years.

Temple of the Moon, Yeha
Region: Tigray
Features: This is the oldest known sacred site in Ethiopia. Erected around the fifth century BC, the ruins of this large, pre-Christian temple consist of a single roofless oblong chamber, the walls of which are built of smoothly polished stones, some of them more than three metres (ten feet) long, carefully placed one atop the other without the use of mortar. There are some stelae in front of the temple.

Tiya Silte Megalithic Site, Shewa
Region: Shewa
Features: One of the best-known of hundreds of proto-historic megalithic sites in southern Ethiopia. Contains a number of standing stelae, believed to have been erected for commemorative purposes.

Other Historical Sites (with locations)

Abba Daniel (Korkor), near Dugum, Tigray (rock church, historical)
Abiy Addi Mikael, near Dugum, Tigray (rock church, historical)
Abraha and Atsbaha, near Wukro, Tigray (rock church, historical)
Abu Said Tomb, Harar (historical)
Abuna Tekle Haymanot, Hauzien, Tigray (rock church, historical)
Adadi Mariam Church, near Addis Ababa (rock church, historical)
Amba Mikael, near Haiki Meshal, Tigray (rock church, historical)
Ankober Palace ruins, Ankober (archaeological)
Arba Minch Museum, Arba Minch (ethnographical)
Arbatu Entzessa, Wollo (rock church, historical)
Arbatu Insisa, near Senkata, Tigray (rock church, historical)
Barka, near Atsbi, Tigray (rock church, historical)
Bilbila Giyorgis, Wollo (rock church, historical)
Birgida Maryam Church, Lake Tana (historical)
Church of Debre Tabor, Debre Tabor (historical)
Church of Heruy Giyorgis, Debre Tabor (historical)
Debre Genet Monastery, Makale (historical)
Debre Maar Giyorgis, near Dugum, Tigray (rock church, historical)
Debre Maryam (Korkor), near Dugum, Tigray (rock church, historical)
Debre Selam, near Atsbi, Tigray (rock church, historical)
Debre Sion, near Dugum, Tigray (rock church, historical)
Dega Estafanos Museum, Dega Estafanos Monastery, Lake Tana (historical)
Djima Museum, Djima (ethnographical)
Dugum Maryam Airefeda, near Dugum, Tigray (rock church, historical)

Dugum Selassie, near Dugum, Tigray (rock church, historical)
Enda Gabriel, near Senkata, Tigray (rock church, historical)
Enda Medhane Alem, near Senkata, Tigray (rock church, historical)
Enda Mika'el (Biet Maar), near Senkata, Tigray (rock church, historical)
Enda Mika'el (Melhai Zenghi), near Senkata, Tigray (rock church, historical)
Enda Yesus Fort, Makale (historical)
Gebre-Meskel Tomb, near Axum (archaeological)
Grand Mosque, Harar (historical)
Guh Korkor (Abba Yemata), near Dugum, Tigray (rock church, historical)
Gulubsha Maryam, near Dugum, Tigray (rock church, historical)
Gundefru, near Haiki Meshal, Tigray (rock church, historical)
Kebran Gabriel Monastery, Lake Tana (historical)
King Bazen Tomb, near Axum (archaeological)
Liche ruins, near Debre Birhan (archaeological)
Lioness of Gobedra rock carving, near Axum (archaeological)
Maitsebri Arbatu Insisa, near Dugum, Tigray (rock church, historical)
Maryam Church, Ankober (historical)
Maryam Church, Entoto (historical)
Maryam Barakeet, near Dugum, Tigray (rock church, historical)
Maryam Papaseiti, near Dugum, Tigray (rock church, historical)
Medhane Alem Church, Ankober (historical)
Menelik's residence, Addis Alem (historical)
Mika'el Aragawi, near Dugum, Tigray (rock church, historical)
Mika'el Menda, near Dugum, Tigray (rock church, historical)
Welega Museum, Nekemte (ethnographical)
Na'akuto La'ab, Wollo (rock church, historical)
Petros and Paulos, near Senkata, Tigray (rock church, historical)
Queen of Sheba's Grave, near Axum (archaeological)
Queen of Sheba's Palace ruins, near Axum (archaeological)
Raguel Church, Entoto (historical)
Ramha Tomb, Axum (archaeological)
Ras Makonnen Palace, Harar (historical)
Rimbaud House, Harar (historical)
Saint Michael's Church, near Addis Ababa (rock church, historical)
Sarsana Mika'el, Wollo (rock church, historical)
Tullu Gudo Monastery, Lake Ziway (historical)
Ura Kidane Mehret Monastery, Lake Tana (historical)
Wollo Museum, Dessie (ethnographical)
Yaed Kidane Mehret, near Dugum, Tigray (rock church, historical)
Yemrehanna Krestos, Wollo (rock church, historical)
Yohannes Meakuddi, near Dugum, Tigray (rock church, historical)

Public Holidays

7 January	Ethiopian Christmas (Genna)
19 January	Ethiopian Epiphany (Timkat)
2 March	Victory of Adwa Day
13 March *	Id Al Fater (Ramadan)
6 April	Patriots Victory Day
29 April *	Ethiopian Good Friday
1 May *	Ethiopian Easter
1 May	International Labour Day
28 May	Downfall of the Dergue
20 May *	Id Al Adha (Arefa)
29 August *	Birthday of the Prophet Mohammed (Moulid)
11 September	Ethiopian New Year
27 September	The Finding of the True Cross (Meskal)

* Dates change every year. Those given are for 1994.

The Ethiopian Calendar

Ethiopians follow the Julian calendar instead of the Gregorian one used by Europe and the Americas.

Ethiopian month:	(Gregorian calendar)
Meskerem (New Year)	11 September–10 October
Tikimt	11 October–9 November
Hidar	10 November–9 December
Tahsas	10 December–8 January
Tir	9 January– 7 February
Yakatit	8 February–9 March
Maggabit	10 March–8 April
Miyazya	9 April–8 May
Ginbot	9 May–7 June
Sene	8 June–7 July
Hamle	8 July–6 August
Nehasa	7 August–6 September
Pagume	6–10 September

LISTINGS

Airlines

Aeroflot
PO Box 7018
Addis Ababa
Tel: 510493

Air France
PO Box 2329
Addis Ababa
Tel: 519044

Alitalia Airlines
PO Box 3260
Addis Ababa
Tel: 514400/610606

CAAC China Airways
PO Box 5643
Addis Ababa
Tel: 650337
Telex: 21466

Ethiopian Airlines
PO Box 1755
Addis Ababa
Tel: 612222
Telex: 21012
Fax: 611474

Kenya Airways
PO Box 3381
Addis Ababa
Tel: 513018

Lufthansa
PO Box 3484
Addis Ababa
Tel: 515666
Telex: 21242
Fax: 512988

SAS Scandinavian
Airlines
PO Box 5603
Addis Ababa
Tel: 510437

Saudi Airways
PO Box 1189
Addis Ababa
Tel: 517746

Sudan Airways
PO Box 606
Addis Ababa
Tel: 513816/517746

Yemen Airways
PO Box 278
Addis Ababa
Tel: 515076/511809

Air Charter Companies

Ethiopian Airlines
PO Box 1755
Addis Ababa
Tel: 612222
Telex: 21012
Fax: 611474

Liftair International
PO Box 5609
Addis Ababa
Tel: 441380/515960
Telex: 21611
Fax: 613299

Airports

Bole Airport
PO Box 978
Addis Ababa
Tel: 187827/180359
Telex: 21162
Fax: 612533

Art Galleries

Menbere Joseph
PO Box 40757
Addis Ababa
Tel: 160443

Saint George Interior
Decorations & Art
Gallery
PO Box 7096
Addis Ababa
Tel: 510983
Telex: 21954 SAOMG ET

Banks

Commercial Bank of
Ethiopia
PO Box 255
Addis Ababa
Tel: 515004/515028
Telex: 21037A, 21037B
Fax: 514522/517866/
517822
Branch offices in major
towns.

Business Associations

Ethiopian Chamber of
Commerce and
Industry
PO Box 517
Addis Ababa
Tel: 518240/514005
Telex: 21213
CHAMBERCOM
ADDIS
Fax: 517699

Ethiopian Investment
Office
PO Box 2313
Addis Ababa
Tel: 512400/512403
Telex: 21572
Fax: 514396

Casinos

Ghion Hotel Casino
PO Box 2474
Addis Ababa
Tel: 513222

Cinemas

Addis Ketema Cinema
Addis Ababa
Tel: 130022

Ambassador
PO Box 3206
Addis Ababa
Tel: 519605/151046
Telex: 21080

Cinema Ethiopia
PO Box 22969
Addis Ababa
Tel: 129405/111268

Cinema Express
(Drive-In)
PO Box 90040
Addis Ababa
Tel: 181300/188822

Ethiopia Missions Abroad

Austria
Friedrich Schmidtplatz
3/3, A-1080
Vienna
Tel: 4028410-12
Fax: 4028413

Belgium
PO Box Clos
Henrivaes, 5
Brussels
Tel: 7348762/7339817
Telex: 62285 Ethbru
Fax: 7321851

Canada
Ottawa
Tel: 2356637
Fax: 2354638

China
No 3, xiu shui Nan jie,
Jian gue Men Wai
Beijing
Tel: 5321570/5321972
Telex: 22306 SEEBC CN
Fax: 5325591

Cote d'Ivoire
PO Box 3712
Abidjan
Tel: 213365
Telex: 23848 AMBETH
CI
Fax: 213709

Djibouti
PO Box 230
Djibouti
Tel: 350718/353711
Telex: 0979-5872
ETCON DJ
Fax: 354803

Egypt
Ibrahim Osman Street
Cairo
Tel: 3477805 / 3466902
Telex: 93234 ETHIOUN
Fax: 3479002

Eritrea
Asmara
Tel: 111172 / 116365

France
35, Avenue Charles
Floquet, 75007
Paris
Tel: 47838395
Telex: 205806EF
Fax: 43065214

Germany
PO Box 5300 Bonn 1
Bonn
Tel: 233041, 42, 43
Telex: 041-8869498
EEBND
Fax: 233045

Ghana
No 6 Adembra Road,
East Cantonment, 1646
Accra
Tel: 772978
Telex: 2110 ETEMB
Fax: 776807

Greece
253 Sigrou Avenue
Athens 17211
Tel: 9303483

India
7150-G, StayaMarg,
Chanakya pur, 110021
New Delhi
Tel: 604407 / 604411 /
688493
Telex: 317235 Eth
Fax: 6875731

Iran
PO Box 19575 / 544
Tehran
Tel: 283217 / 282312
Telex: 88-226621
Fax: 289441

Israel
69 Bugrashov Street,
63429
Tel Aviv
Tel: 5250406
Fax: 5250428

Italy
PO Box 16-1800161
Rome
Tel: 4402602 / 4403635
Fax: 4403676

Japan
2-16-12, Jamigaya,
Shibuya-ku
Tokyo 151
Tel: 3718-1003, 1005,
1018
Telex: 072 J28402
ETHIOEMB
Fax: 3718-0978

Kenya
PO Box 45198
Nairobi
Tel: 723035 / 723027
Telex: 0987-22864
Fax: 723401

Korea, North
PO Box 55
Pyongyang
Tel: 817269 / 817550-54
Telex: 0899-35034
Fax: 817618

Korea, South
Hannam Dong Yong,
Son Ku Seoul
Tel: 7908927 / 8
Telex: 22766 ETHMK
Fax: 7908929

Libya
Tripoli
Tel: 36662

Nigeria
PO Box 2488
Lagos
Tel: 613198
Telex: 0905-21694
ETHEMBNG
Fax: 615055

Russia
PO Box 129041
Moscow
Tel: 2801010 / 2801676
Telex: 413980
MPRTRSU
Fax: 2806608

Saudi Arabia
PO Box 94341
Riyadh
Tel: 4775285 / 4791425
Telex: 406633
ETHEMBSJ
Fax: 4768020

Saudi Arabia
PO Box 495
Jeddah
Tel: 6653444 / 6605034
Fax: 6653443

Senegal
PO Box 379
Dakar
Tel: 217573 / 223224
Telex: 51413 AMBETH
SG
Fax: 243732

Sudan
PO Box 844
Khartoum
Tel: 451156 / 442586
Telex: 24312 ETEKA
SD
Fax: 451141

Sweden
PO Box 26116
Stockholm
Tel: 6656030 / 6609166
Fax: 6608177

Switzerland
56 Rue de Millebeau,
1211 Geneva 19
Tel: 7330758 / 7330759 /
3628001
Telex: 414170 ETHIO
CH
Fax: 7401129

United Kingdom
17 Prince's Gate, SW1
1PZ
London
Tel: 5897212 / 5846984
Telex: 051-23681
ETHEMG
Fax: 5847054

**United States of
America**
866 United Nations
Plaza,
New York
Tel: 4211830-34
Telex: 023-234760
Fax: 7540360

**United States of
America**
2154 Kaloroma Road
NW
Washington DC 20008
Tel: 2342281 / 2342282-4

Telex: 023-440110
ETHIO
Fax: 3287950

Yemen
PO Box 234
Sanaa
Tel: 208833
Fax: 213780

Zimbabwe
PO Box 2743
Harare
Tel: 725822 / 23
Telex: 22745 ETHEMB
ZW
Fax: 720259

Ethiopia Tourist Offices

**Afar National
Tourism Bureau**
Asaita

Dire Dawa Tourism
PO Box 194
Dire Dawa
Tel: 05-113040

**Ethiopian Tourism
Commission (ETC)**
PO Box 2183
Addis Ababa
Tel: 517470
Fax: 251-1-513899
Telex: 21067, Cable
Ethiotourism

**Ethiopian Tourist
Trading Enterprise
(ETTC)**
PO Box 8640
Addis Ababa
Tel: 111878 / 512777
Telex: 21411
Fax: 610511

**National Tour
Operation (NTO)**
PO Box 5709
Addis Ababa
Tel: 512955
Telex: 21370 ETTC
Fax: 517688

Oromia Tourism
PO Box 8769,
Addis Ababa
Tel: 158261 / 157956

Region 1
Administration
Tourism Bureau
PO Box 124
Makale
Tel: 03-400769

Region 3
Administration
Tourism Bureau
PO Box 566
Bahar Dar
Tel: 08-200930

Region 5
Administration
Tourism Bureau
Gode

Region 6
Administration
Tourism Bureau
Asosa

Region 12
Administration
Tourism Bureau
Gambella

Region 13
Administration
Tourism Bureau
Harar
Tel: 05-661783/661772

Region 14
Administration
Tourism Bureau
PO Box 101513
Addis Ababa
Tel: 512700

Southern Ethiopian
People's Regional
Administration Bureau
Tourism
PO Box 135
Awasa
Tel: 06-200327

Ethiopia
Tourist
Offices
Abroad

see Ethiopian Missions
Abroad

Foreign
Diplomatic
Missions

Addis Ababa

Algeria
PO Box 5740
Tel: 711300/652300
Telex: 21302
Fax: 650187

Angola
PO Box 2962
Tel: 513456
Telex: 21141 EMBAN ET
Fax: 510085/515922

Austria
PO Box 1219
Tel: 712144
Telex: 21060
AUSTOAMB ET
Fax: 712140

Belgium
PO Box 1239
Tel: 611813/611643
Telex: 21157
Fax: 613646

Bulgaria
PO Box 987
Tel: 613370/613463
Telex: 21450

Burundi
PO Box 3641
Tel: 652878/651300
Telex: 21069 BRUNDI ET
Fax: 650299

Cameroon
PO Box 1026
Tel: 514844/514607
Telex: 21121
AMBACAN ADDIS

Canada
PO Box 1130
Tel: 713022/713033
Telex: 21053 DOMCAN
ET
Fax: 710333/713033

Chad
PO Box 5119
Tel: 611819
Telex: 21419
Fax: 612050

China
PO Box 5643
Tel: 711960
Telex: 21145
Fax: 711611

Congo
PO Box 5639
Tel: 514188/514331
Telex: 21046

Cote d'Ivoire
PO Box 3668
Tel: 711213
Telex: 21061
Fax: 712178

Cuba
PO Box 3668
Tel: 712525
Telex: 21306
Fax: 710355

Czechoslovakia
PO Box 3108
Tel: 516132/516382
Telex: 21021
Fax: 513471

Djibouti
PO Box 1022
Tel: 613006/613200
Telex: 21317
Fax: 612504

Egypt
PO Box 1611
Tel: 550021/553077
Telex: 21254
Fax: 552722

Equatorial Guinea
PO Box 246
Tel: 610034

Eritrea
PO Box 2571
Tel: 512940/514302
Telex: 21253
Fax: 514951

Finland
PO Box 1017
Tel: 513900
Telex: 21259 FINLA ET
Fax: 513854

France
PO Box 1464
Tel: 550066
Telex: 21040
Fax: 551180

Gabon
PO Box 1256
Tel: 611075
Telex: 21208
Fax: 613000

Germany
PO Box 660
Tel: 550433
Telex: 21015 AAADD ET
Fax: 551311

Ghana
PO Box 3173
Tel: 711402
Telex: 21249
GHANEMB ET
Fax: 712511

Greece
PO Box 1168
Tel: 654912
Telex: 21092 GREMB ET
Fax: 654883

Guinea
PO Box 1190
Tel: 651250/651308
Telex: 21757
AMBAGUI ET
Fax: 651250

Holy See Apostolic
Nunciature
PO Box 588
Tel: 712100
Telex: 21815
Fax: 711499

India
PO Box 528
Tel: 552394/552100
Telex: 21148
Fax: 552521

Indonesia
PO Box 1004
Tel: 712104
Telex: 21264
Fax: 710873

Iran
PO Box 1144
Tel: 710037
Telex: 21118
Fax: 712299

Ireland
PO Box 9585
Tel: 613361/612771

347

Israel
PO Box 1266
Tel: 610999/612456
Fax: 610608

Italy
PO Box 1105
Tel: 551565/553044
Telex: 21342 ITADI
Fax: 550218

Japan
PO Box 5650
Tel: 511088
Telex: 21108
Fax: 511350

Kenya
PO Box 3301
Tel: 610033/610303
Telex: 21103
Fax: 611433

Korea, Democratic
People's Republic of
PO Box 2378
Tel: 750069

Korea, Republic of
PO Box 2378
Tel: 710117/710125
Telex: 21189
Fax: 610861

Liberia
PO Box 3116
Tel: 513655/513791
Telex: 21083
Fax: 513655/513791

Libya
PO Box 5728
Tel: 511077/78
Telex: 21214
Fax: 511383

Madagascar
PO Box 60004
Tel: 612555
Telex: 21713 ARDM ET
Fax: 610127

Malawi
PO Box 2316
Tel: 712440
Telex: 21087
Fax: 710490

Mozambique
PO Box 5671
Tel: 719056
Telex: 21008
Fax: 710021

Namibia
PO Box 1443
Tel: 611966
Fax: 612677

Netherlands
PO Box 1241
Tel: 711100
Telex: 21049 HOLAND
ET
Fax: 711577

Niger
PO Box 5791
Tel: 651175/651305
Telex: 21284
Fax: 651296

Nigeria
PO Box 1019
Tel: 552308/552306
Telex: 21028
Fax: 552307

Norway
PO Box 8383
Tel: 710799
Telex: 21837
Fax: 711255

Palestine
PO Box 5800
Tel: 610811
Fax: 611199/610672

Romania
PO Box 2478
Tel: 610156/611191
Telex: 21168

Russia
PO Box 1500
Tel: 611828
Telex: 21534
Fax: 613795

Rwanda
PO Box 5618
Tel: 610300/610357
Telex: 21199
Fax: 610411

Saharawi
PO Box 30008
Tel: 150727
Telex: 21430 RASD ET

Saudi Arabia
PO Box 1104
Tel: 710303
Telex: 21194
Fax: 717799

Senegal
PO Box 2581
Tel: 611376
Telex: 21027
Fax: 610020

Sierra Leone
PO Box 5619
Tel: 710033
Telex: 21046
Fax: 711119

Spain
PO Box 2312
Tel: 550222
Telex: 21107 EMBESP
ET
Fax: 551131

Sudan
PO Box 1110
Tel: 516477
Telex: 21293
Fax: 518141

Sweden
PO Box 1029
Tel: 516699
Telex: 21039 SVENSK
ET
Fax: 515830

Switzerland
PO Box 1106
Tel: 710577/711107
Telex: 21123
Fax: 712177

Tanzania
PO Box 1077
Tel: 518155/511063
Telex: 21268
Fax: 517358

Tunisia
PO Box 100069
Tel: 653818
Telex: 21505 PMRTER
ET
Fax: 650233

Turkey
PO Box 1506
Tel: 612321
Telex: 21257
Fax: 611688

Uganda
PO Box 5644
Tel: 515285/513115
Telex: 21143 UGAEMB
ET
Fax: 514355

United Kingdom
PO Box 858
Tel: 612354
Telex: 21299
Fax: 610588

United States of
America
PO Box 1014
Tel: 551002/550666
Telex: 21282 AMEMB
Fax: 551166/552191

Yemen
PO Box 664
Tel: 710990/711811
Telex: 21346 MARBET
ET
Fax: 710991

Yugoslavia
PO Box 1341
Tel: 517804
Telex: 21233 YUEMBET
Fax: 516763

Zaire
PO Box 2723
Tel: 710111/710120
Telex: 21043
Fax: 711485

Zambia
PO Box 1909
Tel: 711302/711566
Telex: 21065
Fax: 711566

Zimbabwe
PO Box 5624
Tel: 613877/613476
Telex: 21351
Fax: 613476

Hospitals

Addis Ababa

ALERT Hospital
PO Box 165
Tel: 711256/711200

Amanuel Hospital
PO Box 1971
Tel: 134541

Armed Forces Hospital
PO Box 30151
Tel: 712020

Balcha Hospital
Tel: 446263

Black Lion Hospital
PO Box 5657
Tel: 156170

Ethio Swedish
Children's Hospital
PO Box 5657
Tel: 511211

Fistula Hospital
PO Box 3609
Tel: 200376

Ghandhi Hospital
PO Box 782
Tel: 515364

Menelik II Hospital
PO Box 433
Tel: 112950

Police Hospital
PO Box 199
Tel: 518470

Ras Desta Hospital
PO Box 1032
Tel: 553399

St Paul Hospital
PO Box 1271
Tel: 750125

St Peter Hospital
PO Box 30178
Tel: 100388

Tatek Sene 18 Hospital
Tel: 121865

Yekatit 12 Hospital
PO Box 257
Tel: 111753

Yemewodesh
Maternity Hospital
PO Box 7823
Tel: 125487/204741
Telex: 21392
Fax: 553609

Zewditu Memorial
Hospital
PO Box 316
Tel: 518085

Adea

Adea Hospital
Tel: 99

Adigrat

Adigrat Hospital
Tel: 99

Ambo

Agerehiot Hospital
Tel: 99

Arba Minch

Arba Minch Hospital
Tel: 99

Asbe Teferi

Asbe Teferi Hospital
Tel: 99

Asela

Asela Hospital
Tel: 02-311005

Asosa

Asosa Hospital
Tel: 99

Attat

Attat Hospital
Tel: 99

Axum

Axum Hospital
Tel: 99

Ayera

Ayera Hospital
Tel: 99

Bahar Dar

Felege Hilot Hospital
Tel: 08-200170

Bisidimo

Bisidimo Hospital
Tel: 99

Boba

Tahesas 11 Hospital
Tel: 99

Boru Meda

Boru Meda Hospital
Regional Office
Tel: 03-111717

Chencha

Chencha Hospital
Tel: 99

Debre Birhan

Debre Birhan Hospital
Tel: 811678

Debre Markos

Debre Markos Hospital
Tel: 08-712643

Debre Tabor

Debre Tabor Hospital
Tel: 99

Debre Zeit

Debre Zeit Hospital
Tel: 33

Deder

Deder Hospital
Tel: 99

Dembidolo

Dembidolo Hospital
Tel: 99

Dessie

Dessie Hospital
Tel: 03-111026

Dilla

Dilla Hospital
Tel: 99

Dire Dawa

Bile Chora Hospital
Tel: 05-113247

Nedir Babur Hospital
Tel: 05-113247

Dubity

Tendaho Hospital
Tel: 99

Fenote Selam

Fenote Selam Hospital
Tel: 99

Gambella

Gambella Hospital
Tel: 99

Gambu

Gambu Hospital
Tel: 99

Gendebret

Gendebret Hospital
Tel: 99

Gidole

Gidole Hospital
Tel: 99

Gimbi

Gimbi Hospital
Tel: 99

Gode

Gode Hospital
Tel: 99

Gondar

Gondar Hospital
Tel: 08-110174

Harar

Hiwot Fana Hospital
Tel: 05-660522

Nisrak   Arbegnoch
Hospital
Tel: 05-660231

TB Sanitorium Hospital
Tel: 05-660231

Hosaina

Hosaina Hospital
Tel: 99

Humera

Humera Hospital
Tel: 99

Jijiga

Jijiga Hospital
Tel: 99

Jimma

Jimma Hospital
Tel: 07-110867

Kebre Dehar

Kebre Dehar Hospital
Tel: 99

Makale

Makale Hospital
Tel: 03-400127

Maychew

Maychew Hospital
Tel: 99

Metehara

Metehara Hospital
Tel: 99

Metema

Metema Hospital
Tel: 99

Metu

Metu Hospital
Tel: 99

Mizan Tefere

Mizan Tefere Hospital
Tel: 99

Nazaret

Haile Mariam Mamo
Hospital
Tel: 02-112424

Negele

Negele Berena Hospital
Tel: 99

Nekemte

Nekemte Hospital
Tel: 07-611361

Pawie

Pawie Hospital
Tel: 99

Shakiso

Shakiso Hospital
Tel: 99

Shambu

Shambu Hospital
Tel: 99

Shashemene

Shashemene Hospital
Tel: 06-100286

Sodo

Sodo Hospital
Tel: 99

Weldiya

Weldiya Hospital
Tel: 99

Wonji

Wonji Hospital
Tel: 99

Yergalem

Yergalem Hospital
Tel: 99

Hotels

Addis Ababa

Abenet Hotel
PO Box 22248
Tel: 134285

Adda Hotel
Tel: 162648

Addis Ketema Hotel
PO Box 21461
Tel: 753888

Airport Motel
PO Box 100520
Tel: 610422/610577
Telex: 21700
Fax: 610577

Amba Ras Hotel
Tel: 157606

Aros Hotel
PO Box 23312
Tel: 116544

Assab Hotel
PO Box 732
Tel: 117616/118110

Axum Hotel
Asmara Road
PO Box 40318
Tel: 188832

Bekele Mola Hotels
PO Box 1349
Tel: 117404/514601
Telex: 21432 BMOL
Fax: 518223

Belete Hotel
Tel: 751541

Blue Nile Hotel
PO Box 1138
Tel: 511355

Carara Lounge
Tel: 124301

Central Venue Hotel
PLC
Behind OAU
PO Box 5695
Tel: 712255

Dama Hotel
Tel: 166358

Dessie Hotel
Tel: 136818

Ethiopia Hotel
PO Box 1131
Tel: 517400
Telex: 21072

Extreme Hotel
PO Box 6948
Tel: 118983/553777

Fairview Hotel
Tel: 200164/511265

Fasica Hotel
Tel: 110358

Filwoha Hotel
PO Box 2450
Tel: 511403/519316
Telex: 21459
Fax: 517533/151497

Gedera Hotel
Tel: 186177

Geshen Hotel
Tel: 160582

Ghion Hotel
PO Box 1643
Tel: 513222
Telex: 21112
Fax: 515381

Guenet Hotel
PO Box 397
Tel: 518125

Guenete Selam Pension
Tel: 157710

Hamle 19 Hotel
Tel: 121961

Harambee Hotel
PO Box 3340
Tel: 514000/514482

Harar Hotel
Tel: 130371

Harar Pension
Tel: 113900

Hawi Hotel
Debre Zeit Road
PO Box 32709
Tel: 544499/164713

Hilton International
PO Box 1164
Tel: 518400
Telex: 21204
Fax: 510064

Hotel D'Afrique
PO Box 1120
Tel: 517385/519614

Ibex Hotel
PO Box 21429
Tel: 654400/653736
Telex: 21790 IBEX ET
Fax: 653737

Kagnew Shaleka Hotel
PO Box 800
Tel: 134266

Korem Terara Hotel
Yeka
Tel: 612023/650662

Lem Hotel
Tel: 181302

Lido Hotel
PO Box 5383
Tel: 514488

Megenagna Hotel
Tel: 154098

Mekor Hotel
PO Box 2705
Tel: 162750

Meskel Flower
PO Box 3154
Tel: 651900

Mesrak Hotel
Nyalamoters
Tel: 181190

Mottera Hotel
PO Box 80086
Tel: 754633

National Hotel
PO Box 100052
Tel: 515166
Telex: 21112
Fax: 515381

Netsanet Goh Hotel
Tel: 130371
Park Hotel
PO Box 4246
Tel: 117138

Plaza Hotel
PO Box 4935/6615
Tel: 612200
Telex: 21742 PLAZA
ET
Fax: 613044

Ras Hotel
PO Box 1632
Tel: 517060/517063
Telex: 21485

Taitu Hotel
PO Box 7
Tel: 552643/553244

Tourist Hotel
Arat Kilo
PO Box 5518
Tel: 550122

Villa Verde
PO Box 939
Tel: 653299

Wabe Shebelle Hotel
PO Box 3154
Tel: 517187
Telex: 21416 WASO ET

West Hotel
PO Box 21649
Tel: 137085/756425

Woinhareg Hotel
Tel: 516260

Yemisrach Hotel
Tel: 135688

Yordanos Hotel
PO Box 1647
Tel: 515711/512470
Fax: 516655

Zuber Hotel
PO Box 50620
Tel: 511265/200164
Fax: 511800

Ambo

Ambo Hotel
PO Box 46
Tel 9 (via operator)
Telex: 21072

Arba Minch

Bekele Mola Hotel
Tel: (via operator) 46
Fax: 518223 (Addis
Ababa)

Asela

Asela Ras Hotel
PO Box 28
Tel: 02-311089
c/o Telex: 21485
(Addis Ababa)

Awasa

Awasa Hotel I
PO Box 61
Tel: 200004/00023/
200365
Telex: 21416 WASHO
ET

Awasa Hotel II
PO Box 61
Tel: 200415
Telex: 21416 WASHO
ET

Awash National Park

Kereyu Lodge
c/o PO Box 1632
Addis Ababa
Tel (by radio)
c/o Telex: 21485
(Addis Ababa)

Axum

Axum Hotel
PO Box 21
Tel: 5 (via operator)
Fax: 515381

Ezana Hotel
c/o Regional Tourism
Bureau
PO Box 124
Makale
Tel: 218 (Axum)

Kaleb Hotel
c/o Regional Tourism
Bureau
PO Box 124
Makale
Tel: 215 (Axum)

Yoha Hotel
c/o Regional Tourism
Bureau
PO Box 124
Makale
Tel: 377 (Axum)

Bahar Dar

Bahar Dar Ghion
PO Box 78
Tel: 200111
Fax: 515381

Tana Hotel
PO Box 78
Tel: 200554
Fax: 515381

Debre Zeit

Bekele Mola Hotel
Tel: 338005
Fax: 518223 (Addis
Ababa)

Hora Ras Hotel
PO Box 126
Tel: 338666
c/o Telex 21485 (Addis
Ababa)

Dessie

Ambassel Hotel
PO Box 32
Tel: 111115
Fax: 515381

Dire Dawa

Dire Dawa Ras Hotel
PO Box 85
Tel: 113255
c/o Telex: 21485 (Addis
Ababa)

Kara Mara Ras Hotel
PO Box 67
Tel: 113194
c/o Telex: 21485 (Addis
Ababa)

Gambella

Gambella Hotel
PO Box 44
Tel: 42 (via operator)
Telex: 21072

Gishen

Gishen Hotel
PO Box 32
Tel: 03-13
Fax: 515381

Goba

Bale Goba Ras Hotel
PO Box 77
Tel: 610024

Gondar

Goha Hotel
PO Box 182
Tel: 110634
Fax: 515381

Fogera Hotel
PO Box 182
Tel: 110405
Fax: 515381

Quarra Hotel
PO Box 182
Tel: 110040
Fax: 515381

Terara Hotel
PO Box 136
Tel: 110153
Fax: 515381

Harar

Harar Ras Hotel
PO Box 45
Tel: 660027
c/o Telex: 21485
(Addis Ababa)

Jimma

Gibe Hotel
PO Box 122
Tel: 110071
Telex: 21072

Jimma Ethiopia Hotel
PO Box 313
Tel: 110593

Lalibela

Roha Hotel
c/o PO Box 1643
Tel: (via radio)
Fax: 515381

Seven Olives Hotel
c/o PO Box 1643
Addis Ababa
Tel: (via radio)
Fax: 515381

Lake Langano

Bekele Mola Hotel
Tel: (via operator) 3
Fax: 251-518223 (Addis Ababa)

Langano Hotel
c/o P O Box 61
Awasa
Tel: (Bulbula 24) via operator
Telex: 21416 WASHO ET

Makale

Abraha Atsbaha Hotel
PO Box 108
Tel: 400288
Fax: 515381

Adulis Hotel
c/o Regional Tourism Bureau
PO Box 124
Tel: 03-400769

Ambassador Hotel
c/o Regional Tourism Bureau
PO Box 124
Tel: 242

Green Hotel
c/o Regional Tourism Bureau
PO Box 124
Tel: 03-400769

Harambee Hotel
c/o Regional Tourism Bureau
PO Box 124
Tel: 636

Meki

Bekele Mola Hotel
Tel: (via operator) 6
Fax: 518223 (Addis Ababa)

Moyale

Bekele Mola Hotel
Tel: (via operator) 30
Fax: 518223 (Addis Ababa)

Nazaret

Adama Ras Hotel
PO Box 133
Tel: 112188
c/o Telex 21485 (Addis Ababa)

Bekele Mola Hotel
Tel: 112312
Fax: 518223 (Addis Ababa)

Plaza Hotel
c/o PO Box 4953
Addis Ababa
Tel: 111088
Fax: 613044

Robe

Bekele Mola Hotel
Tel: (via operator) 65
Fax: 518223 (Addis Ababa)

Shashemene

Bekele Mola Hotel
Tel: 100599
Fax: 518223 (Addis Ababa)

Sodere

Sodere Resort Hotel
c/o PO Box 2450
Addis Ababa
Tel (via operator) or 113400
Telex: 21459

Sodo

Bekele Mola Hotel
Tel: (via operator) 52
Fax: 518223 (Addis Ababa)

Welega

Welega Hotel
PO Box 49
Tel: 611088
Telex: 21072

Weliso

Weliso Hotel
PO Box 3
Tel: 2(via operator)
Telex: 21072

Walga Hotel
PO Box 4
Tel 21 (via operator)
Telex: 21072

Wendo Guenet

Wendo Guenet Hotel
c/o PO Box 61
Awasa
Tel: 100330
Telex: 21416 WASHO ET

Ziway

Bekele Mola Hotel
Tel: (via operator) 21
Fax: 518223 (Addis Ababa)

Libraries

Academy of Ethiopian Languages
PO Box 1907
Addis Ababa
Tel: 152926

Alliance Ethio-Française Library
PO Box 1733
Addis Ababa
Tel: 550213/120812

British Council Library
PO Box 1043
Addis Ababa
Tel: 550022
Fax: 552544

Ethiopian Manuscript Microfilm
PO Box 30274
Addis Ababa
Tel: 510705

Ethiopian Press Library
PO Box 30232
Addis Ababa
Tel: 118382

Goethe Institute Library
PO Box 1193
Addis Ababa
Tel: 552888

Italian Book Centre
PO Box 476
Addis Ababa
Tel: 112453
Telex: 21350 ETCO ET

Italian Cultural Institute Library
PO Box 1635
Addis Ababa
Tel: 553427
Fax: 552670

Kennedy Library
Addis Ababa
University
PO Box 1176
Addis Ababa
Tel: 122875/117786

Municipality Library
Addis Ababa
Tel: 550111

National Public Library and National Archives
PO Box 1903
Addis Ababa
Tel: 512242

Russian Centre for Science and Culture
PO Box 1140
Addis Ababa
Tel: 551343/551004

Media

Addis Demts
(Amharic Weekly)
PO Box 2395
Tel: 118613/129524
Fax: 552110

Addis Tribune
(English Weekly)
PO Box 2395
Tel: 118613/129524
Fax: 552110

Addis Zemen
(Amharic Daily)
PO Box 30145
Tel: 114953/112041

Aemro
(Amharic Weekly/
Monthly)
PO Box 22455
Tel: 185196
Fax: 611747

Agence France Press
PO Box 3537
Tel: 511006/163562

Akutite - Meklit
(Amharic Weekly)
PO Box 101288
Tel: 712311

Al-Alem
(Arabic Weekly)
PO Box 30232
Tel: 121587

Almenar
(Amharic/Arabic
Weekly)
PO Box 5854
Tel: 750736
Telex: 21912

**ANSA Italian News
Agency**
Tel: 152077

Associated Press (AP)
Tel: 161726

BBC World Service
Tel: 613400

Berissa Newspaper
(Orominya Weekly)
PO Box 30232
Tel: 112417

Beza
(Amharic Weekly)
PO Box 34018
Tel: 124584

**British Broadcasting
Corporation (BBC)**
PO Box 30232
Tel: 552760/117817

Champion
(Amharic Weekly -
Sports)
PO Box 27412
Tel: 117803/118685

Dewol
(Amharic Weekly)
PO Box 455
Tel: 552657
Fax: 552633

**DPA German News
Agency**
PO Box 62580
Tel: 510687

Eritrean News Agency
Tel: 154666

Eshet
(Amharic Weekly)
Tel: 118685

**Ethiopian Government
Press**
PO Box 30232
Tel: 118500

Ethiopian Herald
(English Daily)
PO Box 30701
Tel: 112212/118247

Ethiopian News Agency
PO Box 530
Tel: 550011/114180

Ethiopian Review
(English Monthly)
Tel: 653680

Ethiopian Television
PO Box 4455
Tel: 116701/123974

Ethiopise
(Amharic Weekly)
PO Box 31244
Tel: 112829

Eyeta
(Amharic Weekly)
PO Box 3621
Tel: 518861

Feleg
(Amharic Weekly/
Monthly)
PO Box 21874
Tel: 127648

Football
(Amharic Weekly -
Sports)
PO Box 23085
Tel: 514256/516192

Interpress Service
Tel: 513330

Izvestia
Tel: 134533

Meklit
(Amharic Weekly)
PO Box 32522
Tel: 110873

Moged
(Amharic Weekly)
Tel: 127160

Oromiyaa
(Orominya Weekly)
PO Box 80006
Tel: 126479/ 128988

PANA
Tel: 513330

Press Trust of India (PTI)
Tel: 112669

**Radio France
International**
Tel: 514011

Reuters
PO Box 5691
Tel: 156505
Telex: 21407

Spanish News Agency
Tel: 162617

**Sudan News Agency
(SUNA)**
Tel: 516477/165646

The Monitor
(English twice weekly)
PO Box 22588
Tel: 183556

Tomar
(Amharic Weekly)
PO Box 80251
Tel: 512942

Voice of America
PO Box 1014
Tel: 550666

Voice of Ethiopia
PO Box 1020
Tel: 551011

Washington Post
PO Box 1169
Tel: 551340

Woine (Amharic
Weekly)
PO Box 80008
Tel: 126454

Xinhua News Agency
Tel: 151064/515676

Yekatit Magazine
PO Box 30232
Tel: 118037/112740

**Yezareyitu Ethiopia
Newspaper**
(Amharic Weekly)
PO Box 30727
Tel: 117463/118408

Zena Admass
(Amharic Weekly)
PO Box 24545
Tel: 128751

Museums

Addis Ababa

Addis Ababa Museum
Meskel Sq. Ras Biru
Bldg
Tel: 119113/153180
Fax: 159904

Entoto Mariam Church
Museum
Tel: 110276/125131

Ethiopian Postal
Museum
PO Box 1629
Tel: 515011

Ethiopian Studies and
Cultural Heritage
Tel: 157630

Ethiopian Tourism and
Hotel Commission
Permanent Exhibition
PO Box 2183
Tel: 517470/444575

Institute of Ethiopian
Studies
Ethnographic Museum
Ras Makonnen Hall,
Addis Ababa
University
Tel: 119469

Museum of National
History
Addis Ababa
University
Science Building
Tel: 553177

National Herbarium
Addis Ababa
University
PO Box 3434
Tel: 114323

National Museum and
Archaeological
Institute
PO Box 76
Tel: 117150

St George Church
Museum
PO Box 2208
Tel: 114689

Addis Alem

Addis Alem Maryam
Museum

Arba Minch

Arba Minch Museum

Axum

Axum Museum

Dessie

Wollo Museum

Djima

Djima Museum

354

Harar

Adari Museum
Harar Museum

Lake Tana

Dega Estephanos
Museum

Makale

Makale Museum
Yohannes IV Palace

Nekemte

Welega Museum

Night Clubs

**Azmari Betoch
(traditional music)**

Addis Ababa

Almaz Tito Azmari Bet
Casa Inchess

Banatu Azmari Bet
off Bole Road

Bitsat Azmari Bet
Kirkos

La Fonte Azmari Bet
Casa Inchess

Mariishet Azmari Bet

Martha Ashagari
Azmari Bet
off Asmara Road

Yashi Azmari Bet
Asmara Road

Modern Music

Addis Ababa

Black and White
Bole Road
Tel: 156805

Carara Lounge Night
Club
Gulele
Tel: 124301

Caribbean Club
PO Box 6991
Tel: 166981

Coffee House Club
Sidist Kilo
Tel: 612738

Dahlak Paradise
Near Harambee Hotel
Tel: 514000

Hilton/Harar Grill
Tel: 518400
Fax: 510064

Hotel D'Afrique Club
PO Box 1120
Tel: 517385

Ibex Night Club
off Bole Road
PO Box 2429
Tel: 654400

Karamara Folk Music
Club
Bole Road
Tel: 158053

L'Ombrele Club
(African music)
off Bole Road

Memo Restaurant and
Club
off Bole Road
Tel: 514193

Mimosa Night Club

Queen's Club
off Bole Road
Tel: 519887

Ras Night Club
Churchill Road
Tel: 517060

Shames Club
opp. Ethiopian Red
Cross
Tel: 153594

Star Club
Ras Desta Damtew
Road
PO Box 1421
Tel: 515673
Fax: 517774

Wabe Shebelle
Near Mexico Square
PO Box 3154
Tel: 517187
Telex: 21416

Public
Transport

Addis Ababa

Addis Ababa City Bus
Service
Tel: 188011

Addis Ababa Taxi
Association
PO Box 80322
Tel: 111925

Addis Ababa Taxi
Service
PO Box 5140
Tel: 127728

Africa Long Distance
Bus Pvt Enterprise
Tel 750445

Anabessa Public
Transport Enterprise
PO Box 5780
Tel: 514055/612000
Telex: 21371
Fax: 510720

Awraris Maxi and Mini
Bus Association
PO Box 26767
Tel: 135432

East & South Maxi and
Mini Bus Association
Tel: 652440

Ethio-Djibouti Railway
PO Box 1051
Tel: 517250
Telex: 21414

Fetan Long Distance
Bus Enterprise
PO Box 849
Tel: 516992

Gosh Maxi and Mini
Bus Association
PO Box 21636
Tel: 132522

National Tour
Operation
Head office:
PO Box 5709
Tel: 517688/512955

Bole Office:
Tel: 182177

Ghion Office:
Tel: 513222

Hilton Office:
Tel: 518400

Ras Hotel Office:
Tel: 152056

Northern Transport
Share Company
PO Box 40504
Tel 132314

Segon Maxi and Mini
Bus Association
Tel: 613745

Taxi Pool
Tel: 441948

Shashemene

Southern Maxi and
Mini Bus Association
Tel: 06/100274

Theatres

Abate Mekuria
Ethiopian
Theatrical Workshop
PO Box 90101
Addis Ababa
Tel: 115976

Children & Youth
Theatre
PO Box 335
Addis Ababa
Tel: 122558

City Hall Theatre
Addis Ababa
Tel: 112516
Telex: 21669

Hager Fikir Theatre
PO Box 1244
Addis Ababa
Tel: 119820/111268

National Theatre
Churchill Road
Addis Ababa
Tel: 516347

Ras Theatre
Tekle Haymanot
Square
Addis Ababa
Tel: 751643/130205

Travel, Tour, Safari Agents & Car Hire

Abera Habte Mariam
PO Box 702
Addis Ababa
Tel: 517226/110413

Adel PLC (APCO)
PO Box 90334
Addis Ababa
Tel: 515500
Fax: 511888

Aki Haddis
(Budget Rent-a-Car)
PO Box 5923
Addis Ababa
Tel: 516735

ALTAD Travel
PO Box 1223
Addis Ababa
Tel: 513755/513487
Telex: 21834
Fax: 712199

Belete Ayele
Addis Ababa
Tel: 164712

Bizane Tour Co.
Addis Ababa
Tel: 184917

Blue Nile Safari
PO Box 684
Addis Ababa
Tel: 517236/514133

Brana Tourist & Travel
Agency
(Rent a Car)
PO Box 1255
Addis Ababa
Tel: 550980/117787
Fax: 553660

Caravan Travel Agency
PO Box 3522
Addis Ababa
Tel: 516502/516501
Telex: 21506
Fax: 517454

Distance Travel Agency
Addis Ababa
Tel: 151715
Fax: 515951

Distant Travel
PO Box 1136
Addis Ababa
Tel: 511574/511233

Eastern Travel Agency
PO Box 1136
Addis Ababa
Tel: 511235/511378
Fax: 511468

Ethio-Adam Travel &
Tour
PO Box 3543
Addis Ababa
Tel: 183711/518003

Ethiopian Fauna Craft
Addis Ababa
Tel: 612273
Fax: 550298

Ethiopian Rift Valley
Safari
PO Box 41602/3658
Addis Ababa
Tel: 552140/551127
Fax: 550298

Experience Ethiopia
Travel (EET)
PO Box 9354
Addis Ababa
Tel: 152336/519291
Fax: 519982

Express Travel Group
PO Box 1688
Addis Ababa
Tel: 510999
Fax: 510655

Forship Travel Agency
PO Box 30754
Addis Ababa
Tel: 551493/552159
Telex: 21634

Galaxy Express
Services (AVIS)
PO Box 8309
Addis Ababa
Tel: 510355
Telex: 21949
Fax: 511236

Getachew Tefera
Addis Ababa
Tel: 128427/119086

Globe Travels
PO Box 5603
Addis Ababa
Tel: 510437/518951
Telex: 21305

Host Ethiopia Express
Travel
PO Box 5944
Addis Ababa
Tel: 151414

ITCO Travel Agency
PO Box 1048
Addis Ababa
Tel: 514334
Telex: 21131
Fax: 752903

Kaleb Travel Agency
PO Box 3541
Addis Ababa
Tel: 515661/515704
Fax: 515577

Khalid Travel
Agency
PO Box 23529
Addis Ababa
Tel: 183458/611866

Lalibela Travel
Agency
PO Box 2590
Addis Ababa
Tel: 158600/514403

Luxor Travel Agency
PO Box 30714
Addis Ababa
Tel: 515730
Fax: 517422

Mass Tourist & Travel
Agency
PO Box 100555
Addis Ababa
Tel: 181969
Telex: 21716
Fax: 613299

Mountain Travel -
Sobek
6420 Fairmount Ave.
El Centro
California,USA
Tel: 510 527 8100
Fax: 510 525 7710

National Tour
Operation (NTO)
PO Box 5709
Addis Ababa
Tel: 513383/512955
Telex: 21370
Fax: 517688

Nile Touring Co.
Ras Desta Damtew Road
PO Box 3228
Addis Ababa
Tel: 513553/518403
Telex: 21971 GBD
Fax: 513553

No. 9 Travel Agency
PO Box 26847
Addis Ababa
Tel: 112226
Fax: 551233

Orooro PLC
PO Box 31627
Addis Ababa
Tel: 112207
Telex: 21104
Fax: 551277

Packtra Pvt. Ltd. Co.
PO Box 5432
Addis Ababa
Tel: 519723
Telex: 21963
Fax: 513788

Peers Travel Agency
PO Box 3845
Addis Ababa
Tel: 515140/511779
Telex: 21939 AMZ-ET
Fax: 513177

Prime Tours
PO Box 8542
Addis Ababa
Tel: 515529
Fax: 515099

Remote River
Expeditions
PO Box 3055
Addis Ababa
Tel: 514712
Fax: 551277

Roky Valley Safari
PO Box 22867
Addis Ababa
Tel: 127436
Fax: 517454

Safeway Travel Tour
Agency
PO Box 8449
Addis Ababa
Tel: 511192/511600/
511137
Telex: 21950
SAFEWAY

Selam International
Travel and Tourist
Agency
PO Box 30208
Addis Ababa
Tel: 117444

Seyum Moges
Addis Ababa
Tel: 513789

Shalla Travel Service
S.C.
PO Box 3422
Addis Ababa
Tel: 513032/513033

Sheba International
Tour and Travel
Agency
PO Box 1255
Addis Ababa
Tel: 117787
Fax: 553660

Sibhat Safari
PO Box 2437
Addis Ababa
Tel: 516616
Fax: 517334

Skyline Travel &
Tours
PO Box 50145
Addis Ababa
Tel: 756656/754862

Solast Travel & Tour
Services
PO Box 5390
Addis Ababa
Tel: 513423
Fax: 515200

Sterling Travel & Tour
Agency
PO Box 41519
Addis Ababa
Tel: 511333/514666
Fax: 512944

Telul Foreign Trade
Auxiliary
PO Box 5576
Addis Ababa
Tel: 514342
Telex: 21345

Three G Safari
Addis Ababa
Tel: 210824

Transport Consult
International
(Travel Agency)
PO Box 1658
Addis Ababa
Tel: 519644/612189

Travel Ethiopia
PO Box 2865
Addis Ababa
Tel: 515216
Fax: 551276

UN Travel Services
Addis Ababa
Tel: 511831/43/48
Fax: 514091

Wildlife Safari Ethiopia
PO Box 2444
Addis Ababa
Tel: 553767
Fax: 551236

Yumo Tour Operation
PO Box 5698
Addis Ababa
Tel: 513783
Telex: 21313
Fax: 513451

Bibliography

Abijatta-Shalla Lakes National Park: Information Sheet (1990), published by the Ethiopian Wildlife Conservation Organization, Addis Ababa.

Addis Ababa (1987), published by the Ethiopian Tourism Commission, Addis Ababa and H & L Communications, London.

Around Ziqualla (1985), published by the Ethiopian Tourist Trading Corporation, Addis Ababa.

Awash National Park: Information Sheet (1990), published by the Ethiopian Wildlife Conservation Organization, Addis Ababa.

Bale Mountains National Park, Ethiopia (1985), by J.C. Hillman and S.M. Hillman, published in Swara (East African Wildlife Society) magazine, 8(5):25-27.

Bale Mountains National Park: Information Sheet (1990), published by the Ethiopian Wildlife Conservation Organisation, Addis Ababa.

Bale: Highland Wilderness (1988), by J.C. Hillman and S.M. Hillman, published by the Ethiopian Tourism and Trading Commission, Addis Ababa.

Beauty of Bale (1986), by J.C. Hillman and S.M. Hillman, published in Selamta (Ethiopian Airlines) magazine, 3(1):10-16.

Bird Watching in Ethiopia (undated), published by Ethiopian Airlines, Addis Ababa.

Birds of Britain and Europe, with North Africa and the Middle East (1979), by H. Heinzel, R. Fitter, and J. Parslow, published by Collins, London.

Birds of Eastern and North Eastern Africa, Vol.1 (1952), by C.W. Mackworth-Praed and C.H.B. Grant, published by Longmans Green & Co., London.

Birds of Eastern and North Eastern Africa, Vol.2 (1955), by C.W. Mackworth-Praed and C.H.B. Grant, published by Longmans Green & Co., London.

Birds of Prey of Southern Africa (1982), by P. Steyn and G. Arnott, published by David Philip, Cape Town, South Africa & Croom Helm, Beckenham, Kent, UK.

Birds of Wondo Genet (1979), by L. Sim, published by Orgut-Swedforest Consortium, Stockholm, Sweden.

Bringing Africa Together (1988), written and published by Ethiopian Airlines, Addis Ababa.

Caves of Sof Omar (1967), by C.S. Clapham and E. Robson, published by the Ethiopian Tourist Organization, Addis Ababa.

Checklist of the Birds of Ethiopia (1971), by E.K. Urban and L.H. Brown, published by Haile Selassie I Univ. Press, Addis Ababa.

Checklists of the Mammals and Birds of Ethiopia, and of Each National Park and Sanctuary, (1990), published by the Ethiopian Wildlife Conservation Organisation, Addis Ababa.

Discovering Ethiopia (undated), published by the Ethiopian Tourism Commission, Addis Ababa and H & L Communications, London.

Ethiopia's Endemic Birds (1987), by E.K. Urban and J. Poole, published by the Ethiopian Tourism Commission, Addis Ababa.

Ethiopia: A Cradle of History (1989), published by the Department of Press, Ministry of Information, Addis Ababa.

Ethiopia: Cradle of Mankind (undated), by J.D. Clark, T.D. White, and D.C. Johanson, published by the Ethiopian Tourism Commission, Addis Ababa.

Ethiopian Costumes (undated), by N. Donovan and J. Last, published by the Ethiopian Tourism Commission, Addis Ababa.

Ethiopian Cross (1988), by D. Hecht, published in Visitor's Manual, Addis Ababa, Institute of Ethiopian Studies, 103-107.

Ethiopian Processional Crosses (1971), by E. Moore, Addis Ababa.

Ethiopians and the Houses They Live In (undated), by J. Last, published by the Ethiopian Tourism Commission, Addis Ababa.

Field Guide to the Birds of East Africa (1980), by J. Williams and N. Arlott, published by Collins, London.

Field Guide to the Butterflies of Africa (1969), by J.G. Williams, published by Collins, London.

Field Guide to the Larger Mammals of Africa (1970), by J. Dorst and P. Dandelot, published by Collins, London.

Field Guide to the Mammals of Africa including Madagascar (1980), by T. Haltenorth and H. Diller, published by Collins, London.

Field Guide to the Snakes of Southern Africa (1980), by V.F.M. Fitzsimmons, published by Collins, London.

Field Guide to the Snakes and Other Reptiles of Southern Africa (1988), by W. Branch, published by New Holland Publishers, London.

Flora of Ethiopia, Vol.3, Pittosporaceae to Araliaceae (1989), by I. Hedberg and S. Edwards, published by the National Herbarium, Addis Ababa University.

Game Animals of Ethiopia (1953), by B. von Rosen, published by Swedish-Ethiopian Co., Addis Ababa.

Glossary of Ethiopian Plant Names, 4th edition (1987), by Michael Kelecha Wolde, published by Kelecha, Addis Ababa.

Hand Crosses of the IES Collection (1990), by D. Hecht, B. Benzing, and Girma Kidane, published by the Institute of Ethiopian Studies, Addis Ababa.

Handguide to the Butterflies of Africa (1981), by R.H. Carcasson, published by Collins, London.

La croix copte et son évolution (1973), by W. Korabiewicz, Warsaw.

Larger Endemic Mammals of Ethiopia (1990), by J. Last and J.C. Hillman, published by the Ethiopian Tourism Commission, Addis Ababa.

Nechisar National Park: Information Sheet (1990), published by the Ethiopian Wildlife Conservation Organization, Addis Ababa.

Other Side of Ethiopia, (1989), by S.M. Hillman and J.C. Hillman, published in Animal Kingdom magazine 92(4):34-45.

Poisonous Snakes of Eastern Africa, and the Treatment of Their Bites (1985), by A. Mackay and J. Mackay, published by Mackay, Nairobi.

Reptiles and Amphibians of East Africa (1983) by N.G. Hedges, published by the Kenya Literature Bureau, Nairobi.

Shell Guide to Ethiopian Birds (undated), by E.K. Urban and J. Poole, published by the Ethiopian Tourist Organization, Addis Ababa.

Shell Guide to the Wildlife of Ethiopia (1969), by J. Blower and J.F. von Wolff, published by Shell Ethiopia Ltd., Addis Ababa.

Simyen: the Roof of Africa (1986), by E. Drake, published by the Ethiopian Tourist Trading Corporation, Addis Ababa.

Some Wild Flowering Plants of Ethiopia (1976), by S. Edwards, published by Addis Ababa Univ. Press.

Trekking in Ethiopia (undated), published by Ethiopian Airlines, Addis Ababa.

Under Ethiopian Skies (1983), by G. Hancock, R. Pankhurst, and D. Willetts, published by H & L Communications, London.

Up, Up in Ethiopia (1989), by J.C. Hillman and S.M. Hillman, published in BBC Wildlife magazine, 7(11):724-728.

Upland Kenya Wild Flowers (1974), by A.D.Q. Agnew, published by Oxford Univ. Press, London.

White Plains and Blue Water (1988), by J.C. Hillman and S.M. Hillman, published in Selamta (Ethiopian Airlines) magazine, 5(3):12-14.

Wild Flowers of East Africa (1987), by M. Blundell, published by Collins, London.

Wildfowl of the World (1988), by E. Soothill and P. Whitehead, published by Blandford, London.

Year of the Jackal (1989), by D. Gottelli and C. Sillero-Zubiri, published in BBC Wildlife magazine 7(11):730-735

Index

(Illustrations are indicated in bold type.)